Commercial Due Diligence

Commercial Due Diligence

The Key to Understanding Value in an Acquisition

PETER HOWSON

GOWER

Published by
Gower Publishing Limited
Gower House
Croft Road
Aldershot
Hants GU11 3HR
England

Gower Publishing Company
Suite 420
101 Cherry Street
Burlington,
VT 05401-4405
USA

British Library Cataloguing in Publication Data
Howson, Peter, 1957–
Commercial due diligence: the key to understanding value
in an acquisition
1. Consolidation and merger of corporations – Management
2. Business intelligence
I. Title
658.1'62

ISBN 0 566 08651 4

Library of Congress Control Number: 2005934407

Typeset by Tradespools, Chippenham, Wiltshire
Printed in Great Britain by Antony Rowe Ltd, Chippenham, Wiltshire

Contents

List of Tables

List of Figures

Introduction

Many years ago, stock market guru Warren Buffet concluded that investing in superior businesses for the long term was better than buying poor, but cheap, businesses. Commercial due diligence (CDD) is about telling the difference between superior businesses and poor businesses, which is why this book is a mixture of business strategy, marketing analysis and market research. However, CDD is not about the bland application of analytical techniques. Cold rational analysis is a part but it is not the only part. CDD is about really understanding how businesses and markets work; it is about understanding what is really important for profits and growth. CDD is about magic. It is about unearthing the few magic ingredients that allow you to say with confidence whether or not a business is worth investing in. A 'tool box' of analytical techniques will only get you so far.

You need to develop an approach where you keep on asking the question 'why?' until finally a light goes on and you suddenly know you can say with confidence whether or not a business is worth investing in.

Experience helps, but this is true of due diligence in general. One of the reasons why due diligence is often seen as an expensive waste of time that only tells acquirers what they already know is that it is left to junior staff who, while they might be highly intelligent and well trained, do not really understand what they are supposed to achieve.

You must learn to tell what is important and what is not. Investigating companies, markets and competitive positions will throw up a wall of data, much of it contradictory and a great deal of it incomplete or only partially relevant. Being able to bring order to the mess and uncertainty inherent in the process is a special skill.

You must have confidence in your own judgement. So often the cry goes up 'we need more data', when in fact there is no more to be had. At some point you have to know when you have collected all you sensibly can and have the courage to dive in and make something of it all.

Oh, and by the way, you have approximately 3 weeks to pass judgement on the commercial prospects of a company that has been run by the founder for the last 20 years in a market you didn't know existed until yesterday ... You had better be good. It is the aim of this book to make you good by giving you a solid foundation on which to build experience and with which to develop judgement and confidence.

PART I The Basics

PART I Introduction

Commercial due diligence (CDD) is the poor relation of financial and legal due diligence and although now widely used, it is still misunderstood by many acquirers and professional advisers who frequently regard it as a bit of customer referencing combined with some market data gleaned from a published report. This first part of this book shows why CDD has to go much further than its financial and legal counterparts and discusses how to organize and structure a due diligence programme to get the maximum value from it.

CHAPTER

1 *What's It All About?*

CDD is all about understanding customers and markets. The idea that acquirers should investigate the customers and markets of the companies they were buying did not really take off until the early 1990s. Strange this when the value of any business is its future profits and profits depend on the strength of its market and its ability to sell to its customers.

Key to the development of CDD in the UK was the Ferranti story. Ferranti was a sizeable, publicly quoted, defence electronics company with sales of about £800 million. In 1987, it purchased a US defence electronics company called ISC. Not long after the deal was done, it became obvious that ISC had boosted its profits by creating $1 billion worth of fictitious contracts and transactions through offshore companies. Eventually Ferranti was dragged down by the weight of the $700 million it paid for a company that had little real sales, and had existed primarily on illegal arms dealings. The company declared bankruptcy in 1991 and sued ISC's CEO, James Guerin. Guerin claimed he had been working for the US government, but was disowned, and was eventually convicted and sentenced to 15 years for defrauding Ferranti of $1.1 billion, money laundering and illegal arms exports. Ferranti sued ISC's auditors for negligence. An out of court settlement of £40 million was reached, but that was scant comfort to shareholders who had owned a company with a market capitalization of £800 million before the ISC deal.

Although it is still scary how little some acquirers know about the businesses they are buying, CDD has evolved over the last decade and a half or so from the sort of customer referencing that Ferranti could have done with to more of a mini strategy review. As the market for companies tightened during the 1990s, so the need for CDD became increasingly recognized as an essential part of the deal-making process. Case Study 1 illustrates why. No longer were acquirers content to listen only to management's assessment of the target company's market prospects. With more and more of the deal value resting on growth and synergies they had to understand the target in depth.

CASE STUDY 1

USING CDD TO RUN RINGS AROUND THE INDUSTRY GIANTS

How did a small company manage to beat the giants of the software industry in an auction for a software provider? This was not a big deal as these things go, but nonetheless there was an impressive list of acquirers competing to acquire a small British payroll software company. Names included some of the biggest and most powerful in the industry, some of them household names, most of whom could have bought the target with their loose change. The winner was a tiny outfit. It outbid the others simply because it understood the target's market best. It took the trouble to work out the target's value proposition and how the

CASE STUDY 1 – *continued*

target's software fitted in. The target's customers were providing a payroll bureau service. Its software was vital to their service but its cost was only a fraction of their overall cost base (this is a theme examined in more detail in Chapter 8). The winning acquirer knew the target could increase prices without damaging the business first because price was not that important to its customers and second because they were locked into using the target's software. It factored this into its valuation and won the auction.

At the same time a new breed of acquirers, private equity houses, have become significant players in the market for companies. Private equity returns come from buying established businesses and selling them at a higher price three to five years later.[1] In order to sell at a higher price, investors must either buy well or improve the business while it is under their stewardship. The days of picking up a misunderstood subsidiary of a distressed plc at a bargain price are long gone. Nor does the modern-day private equity investor put too much faith in price/earnings (P/E) arbitrage – buying in unfashionable sectors at low multiples and selling on at higher P/Es when they come back in fashion. Figure 1.1 shows how private equity investors typically make companies worth more when they sell them than when they bought them. Something like 70 per cent comes from improvements in the trading position of their investments, of which half comes from operational improvements and half from market and sector improvements. The remaining 30 per cent comes from their deal-making abilities.

Typically, private equity houses want to make a minimum internal rate of return (IRR)[2] on their investments of 25 per cent. This is roughly equivalent to doubling their money over 3 years. To achieve this and to make sure they make full use of their limited equity resources, the capital structure in private equity deals must contain as much debt as is sensible. The reason for this is shown by the charts in Figure 1.2, which set out the mechanics of private

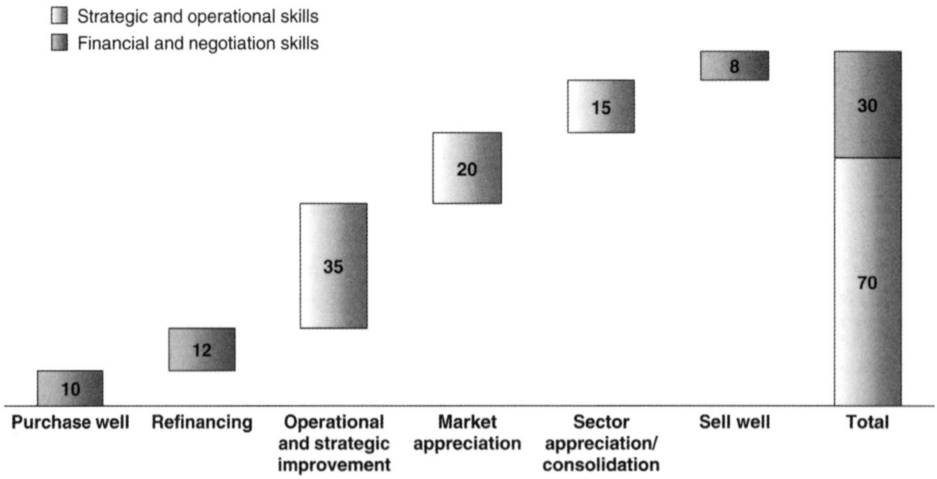

Figure 1.1 The sources of value added to portfolio companies in private equity transactions
Note: The numbers refer to the per cent of total value added

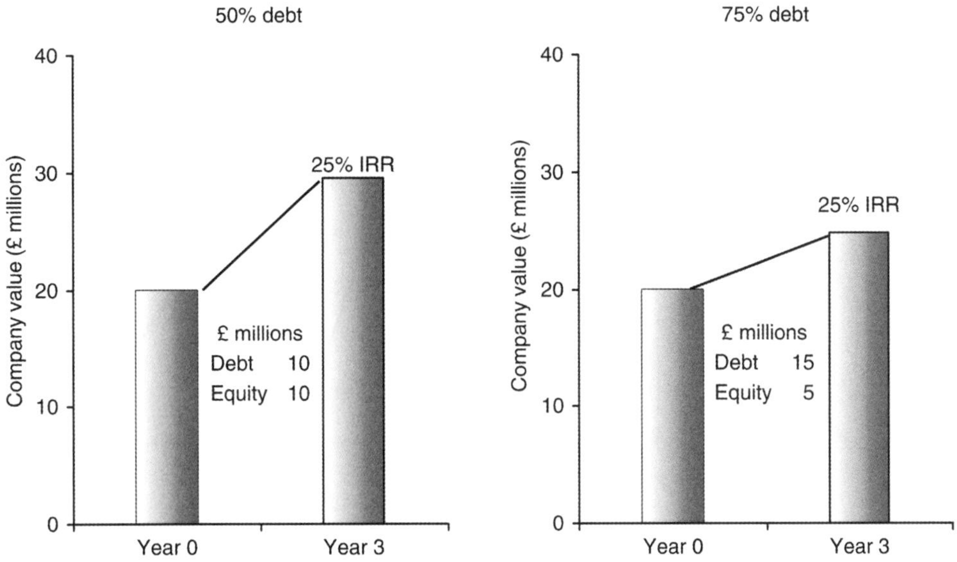

Figure 1.2 Achieving 25 per cent IRR with 50 per cent debt and 75 per cent debt

equity. Both charts show how much the value of a company bought for £20 million and held for 3 years must appreciate to give a compound return of 25 per cent per annum to shareholders.

If the deal is funded 50:50 debt:equity (the chart on the left-hand side), the business has to be worth £29.5 million at the end of year 3. The £10 million debt can be repaid leaving £19.5 million for the shareholders. If the deal is funded with 75 per cent debt the business only has to be worth £24.8 million at the end of year 3 for the investors to make their annual 25 per cent return. Once the £15 million debt is paid off, shareholders are left with £9.8 million, just under double their original £5 million stake.

What level of debt is 'sensible' depends on the size of the target's cash flows and their variability or, more crudely put, it depends on the chances that the target will not be able to meet its interest bill, because if it does not it will go bust. The more the variability of earnings, the higher the perceived risk. Figure 1.3 shows two companies with the same average, or expected, cash flows.

The cash flows for Company A are much less variable (and hence much more predictable) than they are for Company B. Moreover, if both have to meet interest payments of Z, there is no chance of Company A going broke, but there is a chance that Company B will. This variability in cash flows is called 'commercial risk'.

Looking at Figure 1.3, it does not take a financial genius to see that the higher the level of the annual interest bill (Z), the higher is the risk of failure too. Just where Z is depends on the level of debt (and the interest rate). This is called 'financial risk'. It is the amount of fixed obligations – that is, debt – in the capital structure.

So, going back to Figure 1.1 for the moment, investors can take on debt to improve their own returns, but they are also taking on more risk because they are adding financial risk (in the form of debt) to commercial risk (the variability in cash flow stemming from market and competitive forces). For a given level of risk, there are any number of combinations of financial and commercial risk.

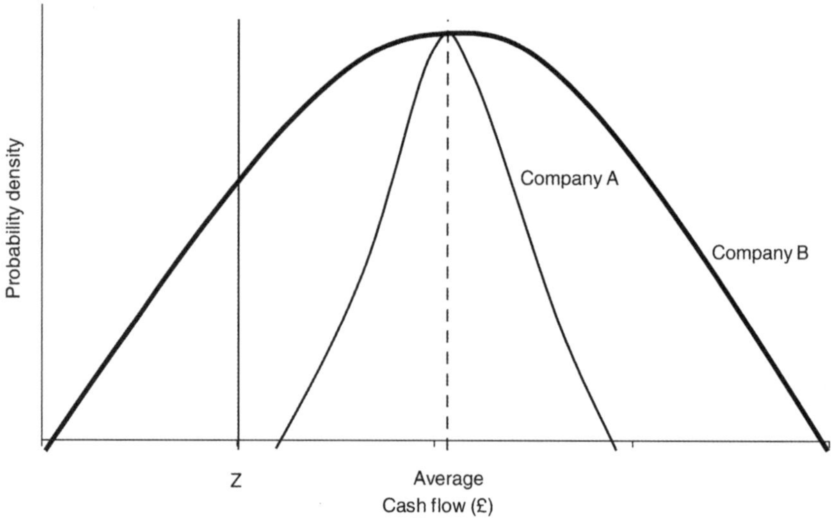

Figure 1.3 Two very different commercial risks

The lower the commercial risk, the higher the financial risk can be. For the private equity investor, this means the lower the commercial risk, the more debt can be taken on, less equity is needed and, if all goes to plan, a higher return. Private equity investors, therefore, need to understand commercial risk so that they can value the business and, as important, so that they can sell the desired financial structure to the lending banks. This is what makes CDD so important. It provides private equity investors with an independent assessment of a company's prospects, which helps them secure the debt funding they need to make their deals work.

If you thought banks only look at the books, you would be wrong. Lending banks look at any proposal brought to them in terms of risk and reward.

Ideally what they want is strong, stable cash flows and just like the private equity investor, they are well aware that financial risk magnifies the underlying commercial risk (and reward), as illustrated in Figure 1.4.

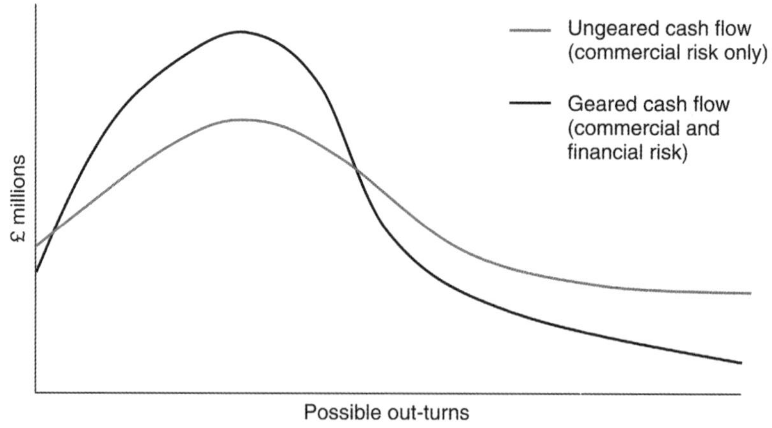

Figure 1.4 The variability of un-geared and geared cash flows
Note: Illustrative only

This means that the lending banks need to understand the commercial risk in detail in order to structure debt packages so that they receive an acceptable risk/reward profile across their portfolios. In turn, this means understanding how the future cash flows of the business will perform and repay the debt, reinforcing the importance of CDD. A well-established business with a good track record of profitability helps the 'story' immensely, but lending banks will focus as much on the commercial prospects of the business as they will on past financial performance because, just like the private equity investors, they need to understand the relative financial and business risks under different capital structures. Low commercial risk makes the banks more relaxed about high levels of debt funding, high commercial risk means funding must be more skewed towards equity.

What is CDD?

As already mentioned, CDD is all about understanding customers and markets. In its simplest form, it is customer referencing. What do customers think of the company you are thinking of buying? Are they all about to take their business elsewhere or are they about to double their orders because it does such a great job? Customer referencing is a proper and valuable part of CDD. The last thing an acquirer needs is a dissatisfied customer base just waiting for the first opportunity to take its business elsewhere – an acquisition will provide just such an opportunity. From a more positive perspective, poor post-acquisition integration is a major reason for failure. Knowing what the customers see as good and bad is not a bad start in working out that plan. As CDD has developed, its scope has extended far beyond the customer referencing that may have saved Ferranti; Case Study 2 demonstrates why.

CASE STUDY 2

WHY CUSTOMER REFERENCING IS NOT ENOUGH

Imagine you have been given the job of assessing the prospects of a manufacturer of replacement exhaust systems. Replacement exhausts are copies of the original equipment. They are typically fitted to cars that are more than 3 years old. Cars above 3 years tend to have been sold on by their original owners. The new owners are fairly price-conscious individuals who do not expect to keep the vehicle for more than a couple of years. Their primary purchase motivation is price, although convenience, such as having an exhaust fitted quickly and locally, is also a factor.

You quickly find out through desk research that the target company is the market leader in its market segment with a share of about 25 per cent. The next nearest competitor is H with a 20 per cent share and a US parent and sister companies throughout Europe. Next in importance is B with 17 per cent. B is a privately owned company with a number of plants across Europe. A small number of low-cost operators make up rest of this part of the market, which accounts for roughly 85 per cent of all exhausts sold in the UK every year. The remaining 15 per cent are sold through car makers' franchised dealers. This original equipment (OE) channel is distinct from the copies market. Market shares have been broadly stable. The market has seen 5 per cent per annum volume growth in each of the last five years, with growth especially strong in fitting stations. Fitting stations are a new form of retailer specializing in tyres, exhausts and other

CASE STUDY 2 – *continued*

fast-moving non-technical parts which, compared to the traditional independent garage, give the motorist the low prices and availability that they want. The target distributes its products through its own 'superdepots' and not through the wholesale distribution channel like the competition.

Management interviews give the impression of a superbly positioned, brilliantly run company. No surprises there, but it clearly does have first-class information technology (IT) and two highly flexible manufacturing plants. Management confirm the 5 per cent per annum market growth, which is in line with growth in the car population. The target has been growing a couple of percentage points above this on the back of the growth in fitting stations, which are taking share from the independent garages. Management also confirms market shares, although it says it is winning share from H, which sells through traditional wholesalers and is therefore stronger with local garages than it is with fitting stations. B they describe as a 'Belgian upstart'. B has the highest quality and widest range of all competitors.

You do your own due diligence by visiting the Enfield depot (30 000 sq ft just to the north of London). You are convinced that the superdepots work because:

- they give next day delivery on what are hard to stock products as far as customers are concerned;
- the target gets economies of scale through being able to move products around the country in bulk.

The Enfield manager takes you to visit some customers. The fitting stations like dealing direct and the security of having a 'local' depot, but above all they use the target because it gives next day delivery on the entire product range (some 3000 part numbers). This is important because one of the keys to its success is being able to give a 'while you wait' service to as many people as possible. Most have room to stock only around 500 part numbers. This is enough to satisfy around 60 per cent of demand but they do rely on speedy delivery on the other 40 per cent. Sometimes this has to be same-day delivery from the wholesalers, but often they can persuade the customer to wait until the next day in which case they can take delivery from the target at manufacturers' prices rather than wholesalers' prices.

Wholesalers are not so keen on the target. They do not like it dealing direct with 'their' retail customers and while they concede the target gives good prices and delivery on the range, they also report that it is not competitive on the Top 20 best-selling products, which are the bread and butter of the business.

Customers also confirm that B has a better range and better quality but is more than 10–15 per cent more expensive.

You are convinced that this is a good company in a leading position in the growth segment of a growing market and therefore recommend the purchase to your board. They are a conservative lot who, from bitter past experience and various executive conferences they have attended, know that acquisitions are risky and that possibly as many as two-thirds of them fail. They insist on CDD from a reputable supplier and draw up the following terms of reference:

Objective: To provide for the UK replacement exhaust systems market:

- An assessment of market trends
- An identification of retailers' key purchase criteria
- An evaluation of the perception of the target vis-à-vis competitors.

CASE STUDY 2 – *continued*

Key issues: The development of the market for replacement exhaust systems in the UK over the last 5 years on the following dimensions:

- Overall size of the market
- Drivers of the final demand
- Market segmentation
- Market shares
- Distribution channels used
- Overall price levels
- Market innovations
- Major future trends.

Methodology: Desk research and market interviews: By this time you are in a tearing hurry because your exclusivity runs out in 3 weeks' time and the investment bank selling the target is telling you in words of one syllable that the period of exclusivity will not be extended. You give the CDD providers 2 weeks to report back. The following is a summary of their findings:

- The Target is the UK market leader.
- Its only serious full-range competitors are H and B. B has a lot of credibility based on performance in the last 3 years.
- Other, much smaller, competitors tend to specialize in the 'fast moving' part numbers.
- The target put up its retail prices in January by an amount sufficient to cause disquiet among retailers. On the whole, UK prices are said to be some 30 per cent above those in the rest of Europe, despite lower quality products.
- Exhaust retailing is changing. Garages supplied through the traditional wholesaler 'motor factor' channel are being replaced by fitting stations.
- Kwik-Fit is the biggest fitting station chain. The tyre companies have also added exhausts to their retail units. There is also a large number of independents.
- The target is in No.1 position because it can offer fitting stations most of their requirements (stock and non-stock items) next day with 95 per cent availability, acceptable quality and at better prices than from wholesalers.
- Fitting stations offer immediate fitting but can stock only about 500 part numbers (maximum). This will cover 65 per cent of the car population. They will usually persuade customers to wait for 'exotic' items rather than buy them through wholesalers.
- H and B tend to be 'top-up' suppliers to fitting stations and major suppliers to wholesalers. The target is weak with wholesalers.
- Market size is around £125 million, and growing at 5 per cent per annum driven by more cars on the road.
- Market innovations are few, although there is widespread expectation that the UK will adopt the European 'aluminized' material specification in the next 2–3 years and that the UK will introduce catalytic converters some time soon.

On the basis of the above, the target was bought. The integration went well and the target performed as expected in years 1 and 2, but then began to lag market growth before sales turned down in year 3. Catalytic converters were fitted as standard to all Jaguar cars in the year the target was bought, but at the time it was not certain whether they would become standard on mass market models.

What went wrong? What went wrong was that the CDD, by concentrating on customer referencing, was picking up and reporting market gossip rather than focusing on the future profitability of the target. To be

CASE STUDY 2 – *continued*

fair to the CDD supplier, there was not enough time for them to do their work properly. As we will see in Chapter 2, two weeks is not enough to roll the numbers properly. The starting point should not have been the present market and the target's position, but what actually drives sales and what is likely to happen to the market.

A company's sales of replacement exhausts are determined by:

- the number of cars on the road over three years old;
- the average life of an exhaust system;
- the average number of pieces per system (there are usually three pieces to a system but it can be as few as one and as many as seven);
- the price per piece;
- market share.

The target's market share looked safe given that its ability to service fitting stations and the number of cars was increasing by 5 per cent per year. The average life of a system was less certain. The current life was 1.3 years, but introduction of the European specification could increase life anywhere between 10 per cent and 30 per cent. This would reduce market size by between 9 per cent and 23 per cent. The number of pieces per system was 2.1. The introduction of catalytic converters, which was just starting, would reduce this. Catalysts are so expensive that they have to be encased in something that will last the life of the car. This would mean either that the front pipe would never be replaced or that the two front pieces of the exhaust would last the life of car. This would reduce market size by anywhere between 15 per cent and 50 per cent. Given this data, it should be possible to model the market and produce scenarios for future volumes. The best case would be a 10 per cent market decline 3 years out. The worst case would be a fall of 65 per cent. Prices could only go one way too. The retail market would consolidate as the battle between Kwik-Fit and the tyre giants intensified. Powerful acquirers would emerge. While the target's ability to deliver the range would protect it to an extent, it would not be enough to prevent prices falling. In addition, the structure of the parts range was changing. Car makers were starting to design their cars around what they called common platforms. This means using a common structural base for a number of models and using body shape, engine types and interiors to make different models in the range different from each other. Car makers could now differentiate more finely. As exhaust systems were the last component to be designed, they had to be designed to fit around what was already there on the floorpan of a car. This led to an explosion in their complexity. For example, the number of part numbers needed to supply the Sierra range was 25 compared with nine for the Cortina range, which the Sierra had replaced. Whereas 3000 part numbers could satisfy 95 per cent of demand, soon 7000 would be needed to do the same thing and sales volume per part would fall dramatically. Even superdepots could not give an economic next-day delivery service on a parts range this fragmented. The target would have to supplement the ten superdepots with a large number of more local distributors on the 'superfactor', that is, super-wholesaler, model.

It was also doubtful that the target could continue to design and manufacture everything it sold because again volumes would be too small for the long tail of the product range. It would have to buy in a lot of the smaller running part numbers. These were those on medium-selling European models downwards. Suddenly it was at a manufacturing disadvantage against its two big competitors, who both had sister companies across Europe making and selling these medium movers in countries where they

CASE STUDY 2 – *continued*

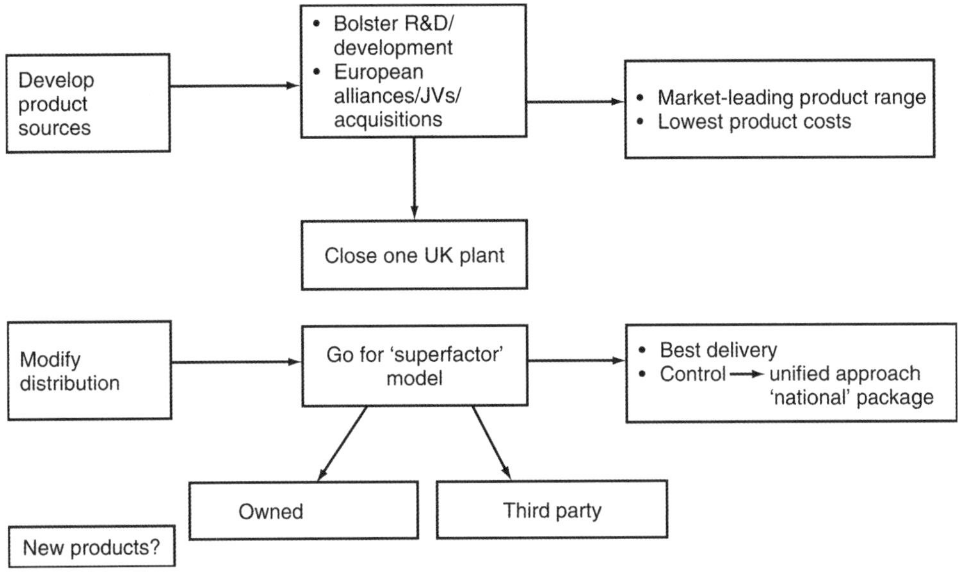

Figure 1.5 CDD is not just about finding risks, it is about the future

were fast movers. Figure 1.5 shows the changes that would be needed to keep the target competitive.

What looked like a great acquisition suddenly looks like a big risk. Just doing customer referencing is fine if you understand the market you are buying into. If not, you have no idea whether or not good marks from customers will translate into the reality of sales and profits. The market could be about to turn down, or competitors may be about to turn up the heat. Technology might be changing or there could be new regulations around the corner. You have to understand what is happening in the market as well as how well (or badly) your target company performs.

Market due diligence

CDD is sometimes seen as market due diligence. Looking at the market in addition to referencing customers is fine, but may not go far enough either. Just because the market is growing and margins are good is no guarantee that the target is going to do well in the future. Customer tastes have a nasty habit of changing and if the target cannot keep up with the changes or is not serving the growth segments, its prospects might not be that great. Nor do competitors stand still. Constant manoeuvring for advantage means market structures are dynamic and constantly changing. For it to be a relevant pointer to future performance, CDD has to look at the target's competitive position, current and prospective, and at management's ability to adapt to create advantage and adapt to change. Case Study 3, which is taken from CDD on a management buyout on the verge of bankruptcy, demonstrates why close examination of the target's competitive position as well as its market is so important.

CASE STUDY 3

ALWAYS EXAMINE COMPETITIVE POSITION

A leading UK company in a very mature industry was carrying out due diligence on one of its biggest competitors. The target had been the subject of a management buyout 2 years previously when CDD had been carried out for the private equity firm financing the deal. The CDD concentrated on the market. It contained some wonderfully creative charts detailing the trends in market size and share in each of the many end-user markets into which the target's products were sold. What it said was that although this was a mature industry, there was still plenty for the target to go at on a global basis. What it did not say, because it did not address competitive position, was that no company stood any chance of increasing market share in the USA because the US market leader had signed up all the best distributors (vital for sales in the USA). The best distributors flock to the best suppliers and the US competitor was not only market leader in this particular product range, but also in all the other products the distributors handled. The potential in Europe was even worse. The market was shared between five competitors all of roughly the same size, all competing with identical products and similar costs. As if this was not bad enough for prices, the German competitor had moved production to Hungary and was selling product in Western Europe at 20 per cent below everyone else. At the same time, customers had consolidated and introduced professional buying processes organized on a European basis, forcing prices down further. None of this came across in the CDD.

But in many cases, even customer referencing, plus a market study, plus an understanding of competitive position is not always enough. You can be buying into the best company in the best market in the world, but you will still be disappointed if you do not run the thing properly once it is yours. This means CDD must also look at management because there is no guarantee that a transaction will be successful unless the management is up to doing what is expected of it, as is shown by Case Study 4. Management ability is often overlooked. Its importance is confirmed by the fact that financial acquirers would rather back a good management in a mediocre market than a poor management in a good market. CDD should therefore be used to give an external perspective on management.

CASE STUDY 4

CAN MANAGEMENT DELIVER?

This was a case of poor management in a good market. The company is now no more, not because the market was not there and not because it did not have a strong position, but because there was a no one in overall control. It was a regionally based supplier of building services with a particular skill at the more difficult applications supported by a strong central design capability. The top end of the market was dominated by a handful of large players and the bottom end was the province of small, local, low-overhead players. The building industry was booming, the company was a strong player in mid-sized difficult applications. What went wrong? What went wrong was that the company had grown through the acquisition of regional branches, none of which had been properly integrated. Local manage-

CASE STUDY 4 – *continued*

ment was still inclined to do what it had always done and not play to the strengths of the company and there were no central controls to keep them in line. The north-east branch concentrated on the house building market, which meant competing against low-overhead operations for low-price, low-margin business. The east London branch was embroiled in a large fixed-price contract that it did not have the expertise to negotiate and could not get out of, and was making significant losses as a result. There was nothing wrong with the market, but there was a lot wrong with the management.

To recap on the story so far, CDD is about reducing the risk in an acquisition by filling the gaps in the acquirer's knowledge of the target. At the very minimum, it involves customer referencing. In its full form, it will also cover the market, the target's competitive position and the ability of its management. That is what CDD does, but there is another angle to think about: why are you doing it? To reduce the risk in the deal, right? Right, but the risk in an acquisition comes from a number of different sources, so CDD has to be geared up to deal with all of them. If this sounds blindingly obvious, it is. And of course no seasoned mergers and acquisitions (M&A) professional would be so negligent as not to cover all the angles, would they? Well, you only have to look at the failure rates of acquisitions to answer that question. Just about every study that has been carried out[3] concludes that at least 50 per cent of all acquisitions fail. The real failure rate is much higher, perhaps as high as 75 per cent. Let us explore where due diligence goes wrong and what its role should be in reducing the risk of failure.

Why due diligence is badly done

Due diligence is usually badly done. The reason is threefold:

- It is usually left to the last minute.
- The aims of due diligence are not well understood.
- Fear and greed get in the way of a properly executed process.

LEFT TO THE LAST MINUTE

Due diligence costs money. If a transaction does not go ahead, any money spent on due diligence will have been wasted. For these reasons, due diligence cannot begin until the deal is more or less guaranteed to happen. This cannot be helped, but that does not mean to say that acquirers cannot do a lot of the basic planning and thinking ahead of kicking-off due diligence.

THE AIMS OF DUE DILIGENCE ARE NOT WELL UNDERSTOOD

If due diligence only ever kicks-off when the deal is more or less guaranteed to happen, then all it can do is confirm that the transaction should take place, right? Wrong, wrong and thrice wrong. The reason why due diligence is misunderstood is that it is still the territory of lawyers and accountants. The guiding philosophy of both professions is the avoidance of risk. The lawyer is trained to see disaster round every corner and tries to get protection against everything that could go wrong, however remote. One of the fundamental principles of accounting is prudence, which teaches us that losses should be recognized as soon as there is a possibility that they will arise, but profit should not be booked until it is absolutely 100 per cent in the bag. There is a plenty of room for risk avoidance in acquisitions – you only have to look at the failure rate to see that – but that does not mean due diligence should be dominated by the transactional risks that the lawyers and accountants worry about. M&A is a strategic tool and a strategic tool is a long-term proposition. What happens after the deal is signed is much more important to a successful acquisition than what goes into getting the contract signed. Buying a poorly positioned company in a market that is about to bomb will cost you a lot more than a conservative stock obsolescence policy or a supply contract without a change of control clause.

FEAR AND GREED

At some point in the acquisition process, those two old bogies of human nature, fear and greed, propel acquirers into doing stupid things. A common mistake is getting so seduced by an opportunity that common sense and strategy go out of the window. Someone at the top falls in love and makes it plain that the deal is going to get done. If the numbers do not quite work, the assumptions are stretched until they do.

Using due diligence to reduce risk

There is no dictionary definition of due diligence. There is no standard legal definition either. A lawyer would probably define it roughly as follows:

> *a process of enquiry and investigation made by a prospective purchaser in order to confirm that it is buying what it thinks it is buying.*

Caveat emptor (buyer beware) is central to the whole acquisition process in Anglo-Saxon countries. Due diligence is the way the acquirer makes sure it understands exactly what it is buying.

A dealmaker might go further. A dealmaker, would say that due diligence is about reducing transactional risk. Translated this means reducing the risk of paying too much. The better the due diligence, the more an acquirer knows about a target and therefore the more it knows about the immediate risks it is taking on. As far as the dealmaker is concerned, therefore, due diligence allows an acquirer to:

- identify issues that feed into price negotiations, and hence reduce the risk of paying too much;
- de-risk the deal by identifying points against which legal protection should be sought.

This is fine, but it does not go far enough for the reasons mentioned above. What you do with the business after you buy it is critical to deal success and due diligence is your final chance to work out or confirm how the acquired business is going to recoup the premium you will pay for it.[4] Studies confirm that pre-deal synergy evaluation is one of the main keys to acquisition success.[5] This is defined as working out how extra value is going to be created and delivered post-acquisition. This is especially true today. The market for companies is pretty sophisticated and with advisers cooking up ever-more ingenious ways of extracting the maximum price, the days of the cheap deal are gone. Justifying an acquisition price relies more and more on the strategic and the synergistic.

It should now be obvious that due diligence should be made to give as good an insight as possible into post-deal implementation as to isolating pre-deal risks. Case Study 5 is not untypical of the kind of thing that goes on once the transaction is complete if implementation is not connected to market strategy.

CASE STUDY 5

DUE DILIGENCE SHOULD BE USED IN PLANNING POST MERGER INTEGRATION

Wells Fargo, a leading US bank, won a hostile bid for First Interstate, paying $11.6 billion to create the second-biggest bank in the West. What Wells was after was First Interstate's private banking division. Wells was relatively weak in private banking, whereas First Interstate had a strong presence in 13 American states and was especially strong in California where it was the strongest supplier to the Silicon Valley area. At the time, Silicon Valley was booming to the point of producing 13 dollar millionaires per day. You do not have to be a seasoned banking executive to figure out that private banking is all about customer service. It is ironic that, as soon it had won its bid, Wells Fargo announced plans to close 80 per cent of the Interstate retail banking operations in California and remove 50 per cent of the personal banking staff. Fourteen months after the bid, customer service at Wells Fargo was described as, 'as bumpy as a ride in one of its historic stage coaches'. One lady, for example, discovered she was thousands of dollars overdrawn because the bank had failed to record deposits she had made the previous week. She was told it would take 10 business days to investigate the matter and her request for a higher credit limit to make ends meet in the meantime was declined. Analysts were describing customer attrition as large and showing no sign of stabilizing. Wells tried just about everything to make up for its mistakes. It gave $25 each to about 22 000 former First Interstate customers in Arizona and Nevada because they were unable to use their ATM cards. The CEO apologized profusely in one of the bank's annual reports and called the combination with First Interstate Bancorp 'a sorry experience for far too many of our customers. We did not measure up to our own high standards for delivering service.' Competitors started aggressive marketing campaigns to gain disaffected Wells Fargo customers.

According to analysts at the time, Wells Fargo suffered meaningful harm from its merger execution errors. Above all, it misjudged the type of service and culture that many of its and First Interstate's customers wanted. The failure to integrate the IT systems prior to branch closure further reduced customer service. The approach integration was described as being like General Patton's – get in there and get it done quickly – which is not a bad dictum, but only if you can do it without alienating your customers.

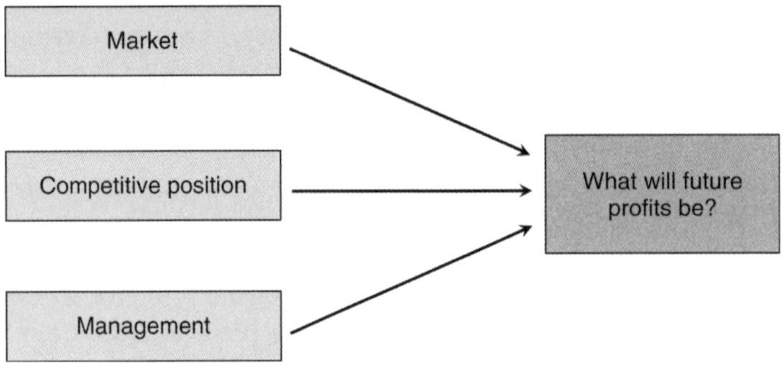

Figure 1.6 Areas to be covered by CDD

A definition of CDD

Acquirers should always move quickly post-acquisition. CDD should therefore be used as a means of verifying that the planned synergies are realistic, to point to the best way of realizing them, to check the new strategy is viable and to tell you what to do if it is not. In its full form, then, CDD is a mini-strategy review that is carried out by acquirers of companies to:

- confirm that the company they are buying has the commercial prospects they think it has;
- help plan integration; botched integration is one of the biggest reasons for the 50 per cent plus failure rate that acquirers continue to suffer;
- show how to position an acquisition or the combined entity for maximum value.

It is a mini strategy review only because of the limited time available. A CDD programme should be set up to:

- assess sales operations, channel structure, customer requirements;
- test volume, growth, price, mix, and margin assumptions against market realities;
- confirm the achievability and sensitivity of the business plan;
- identify the value drivers of the acquisition and confirm synergy assumptions;
- highlight risks and opportunities;
- provide an input to the implementation plan;
- give recommendations on long-term strategy;
- judge management ability against the industry.

CDD enquiries take place under three headings, as shown in Figure 1.6. The aim is to use all three to assess how the target will perform as both a standalone business and under new ownership (that is, after integration).

The risk and reward in an acquisition comes from the three boxes in Figure 1.6 – and is cumulative. The main questions to be covered under each heading are listed below.

MARKET

Under 'market' comes three sub-analyses:

- Market: what is its size, structure and growth potential?
- Customers: who are they and what do they want?
- Competitors: who are they and what are their strengths and weaknesses relative to delivering the benefits sought by consumers and relative to the target?

Market size, structure and growth

RISK

The market might not be as big as thought, or growing as quickly or may be structurally unsuited to making decent returns.

OBJECTIVE

To establish the current market size and to forecast the expected growth in the segments relevant to the target.

QUESTIONS

- How do the target's markets segment? The chances of calling the market are improved if the target's market is defined in terms of homogenous segments (see Chapter 3) and diminish if it is not.
- How large are the market segments which the target serves today?
- What are the drivers of growth?
- How fast are those segments growing?
- Are there threats from substitute products, new technologies or new entrants?
- Can suppliers, regulations or other external influences change the basis of profitability in the market?
- What does all this mean for pricing?
- In which segments does the target have the capabilities to compete in the future?

TYPICAL ACTIVITIES

- Carry out desk research.
- Interview management.
- Read industry reports.
- Interview experts.

OUTPUT

A robust market model defining the size of the relevant market segments that can serve as an important input to the revenue forecast in the valuation of the target.

Customer analysis

RISKS

- That the segments served by the target are shifting.
- That the benefits delivered by the product or service are or will be better delivered by something else and therefore that sales volumes will decline.
- That customer sophistication will push the product or service to price-based competition.

OBJECTIVE

To establish customers' key purchase criteria and their future buying intentions.

QUESTIONS

- Who are the target's major customers?
- What are their purchase criteria? What do they value?
- How does the target perform relative to those criteria? Competitive position improves if the target company's proposition is specifically targeted for each sub-market (see Chapters 3 and 5) and if the target focuses on understanding and delivering the benefits expected by customers in each sub-market both now and in the future.
- Are there unmet needs?
- Are there likely to be changes in buying behaviour?
- What are customers' switching costs?

TYPICAL ACTIVITIES

- Segment customers.
- Identify key decision makers.
- Interview a representative sample of customers.
- Interview non-customers and ex-customers.

Competitor analysis

RISK

That the target company does not have adequate resources and capabilities to survive the competition.

OBJECTIVES

To assess the competition's relative strengths and weaknesses.

QUESTIONS

- Who are the major competitors?
- What is the degree of competitive rivalry? The target's competitive position improves if it can avoid head-on competition.
- What are competitor strengths and weaknesses vis-à-vis:
  - Customer purchase criteria?
  - The target?

TYPICAL ACTIVITIES

- Carry out desk research into competitor activities.
- Review competitor literature.
- Interview competitors.
- Interview industry experts.

COMPETITIVE POSITION

RISK

That the target company is outperformed in open competition.

OBJECTIVES

To assess the target company's relative strengths and weaknesses.

QUESTIONS

- How is the target performing in the segments in which it competes?
- What does the target's market offering produce in customer value, satisfaction and loyalty?
- What are the target's strengths and weaknesses relative to the competition? The chances of success are best if the target plays to its strengths, minimizes its weaknesses and anticipates competitor moves.
- Does the target create sustainable value? To what degree has it chosen markets that give it a strong position based on differentiating capabilities that create a robust and sustainable value proposition to customers better than those of the competition?

TYPICAL ACTIVITIES

- Interview a representative sample of customers.
- Interview non-customers and ex-customers.
- Interview competitors.
- Interview industry experts.

MANAGEMENT

RISK

That management cannot deliver.

OBJECTIVES

To assess the strengths and weaknesses and any gaps in the capabilities of the management of the target company/combined entity.

QUESTIONS

- Can management drive the things that matter through the company to the marketplace?
- Can it deliver the strategy?

TYPICAL ACTIVITIES

- Carry out competency-based management interviews.
- Carry out market interviews.

Overlap with financial due diligence

A typical financial due diligence (FDD) exercise includes an analysis of the market and competitors and reviews profit forecasts. Figure 1.6 has the three boxes converging on 'what will future profits be?' In many assignments, that box actually reads 'sales' meaning that the border between financial and commercial is the sales line. CDD provides the assessment of likely future sales and financial does the rest, particularly since the detailed financial modelling will be the province of FDD.

As CDD is concerned with the 'environment', as the management textbooks call those events that take place outside of the company, and as a company is being bought for future profits not future sales, the border between CDD and FDD should not be fixed at sales. Gross margin should be as much the concern of CDD as it is of FDD because raw material suppliers are outside the company and can sometimes have a very big influence on sales, growth and profitability, as demonstrated in Case Study 6.

CASE STUDY 6

LOOKING AT GROSS MARGIN PROSPECTS

In December 1997, more than 160 nations met in Kyoto, Japan, to negotiate binding limitations on greenhouse gases for the developed nations. The outcome of the meeting was the Kyoto Protocol, in which the developed nations agreed to limit their greenhouse gas emissions, relative to the levels emitted in 1990. The USA agreed to reduce emissions from 1990 levels by 7 per cent during the period 2008 to 2012. Kyoto has had a knock-on effect in many industries, not least the market for insulating materials in houses. New building regulations in 2002 increased insulation requirements in new houses. The regulations were tightened further in 2006. The impact on the demand for thermal insulation materials, which incidentally took the industry by surprise, is shown in Figure 1.7.

Traditionally glass or mineral wool is used for thermal insulation. Where space is at a premium, builders have to use a material with higher insulation properties. The ideal solution is polyisocyanurate (PIR) foam, but it is a much more expensive solution. Glass fibre will cost about £2.20 per square metre, whereas PIR foam will be about £14 a metre. PIR foam is far more thermally efficient than other materials. For 60 mm of PIR foam you need 270 mm of glass wool. Because of the more stringent building regulations, PIR foam is the only way to achieve the necessary heat retention where space is at a premium, such as in loft conversions, where a house is built with a room in the roof and in high-density building where wall cavities are fairly thin. Recent UK building trends have meant huge increases in all of these. The market for PIR foam is therefore set for years to come ... providing manufacturers can source the raw materials.

PIR foam is the result of a reaction between two chemicals: MDI and polyol. As can be seen from Figure 1.8, global MDI capacity has decreased to the point where there is hardly enough to meet demand.

Furthermore, MDI is made from benzene. Look what has happened to the price of benzene (Figure 1.9).

Clearly there is going to be a step change in PIR prices. So far, they have hardly risen enough to cover increased raw material costs, let alone to reflect the supply situation. PIR suppliers will have to pay a lot more for their MDI – if indeed they can buy enough to meet demand for their product.

CASE STUDY 6 – *continued*

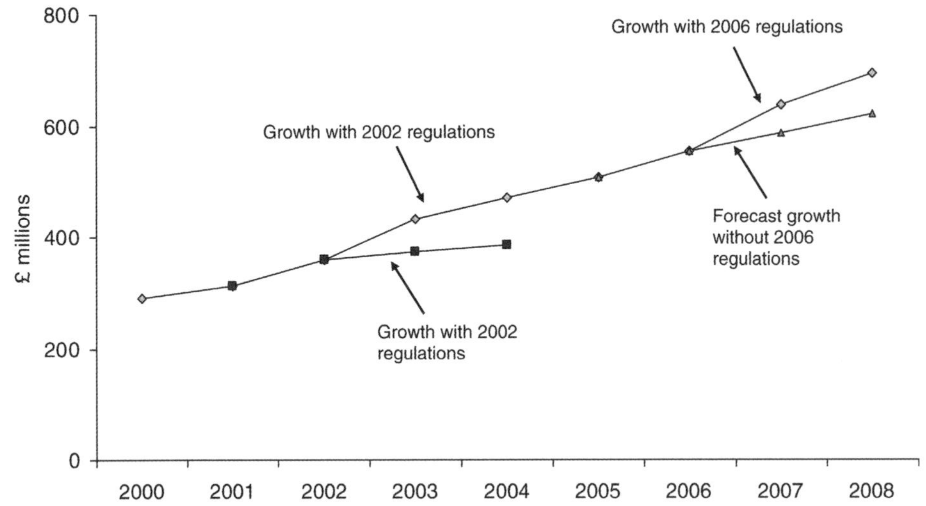

Figure 1.7 Impact of 2002 and 2006 building regulations on the insulation materials market
Source: AMR International

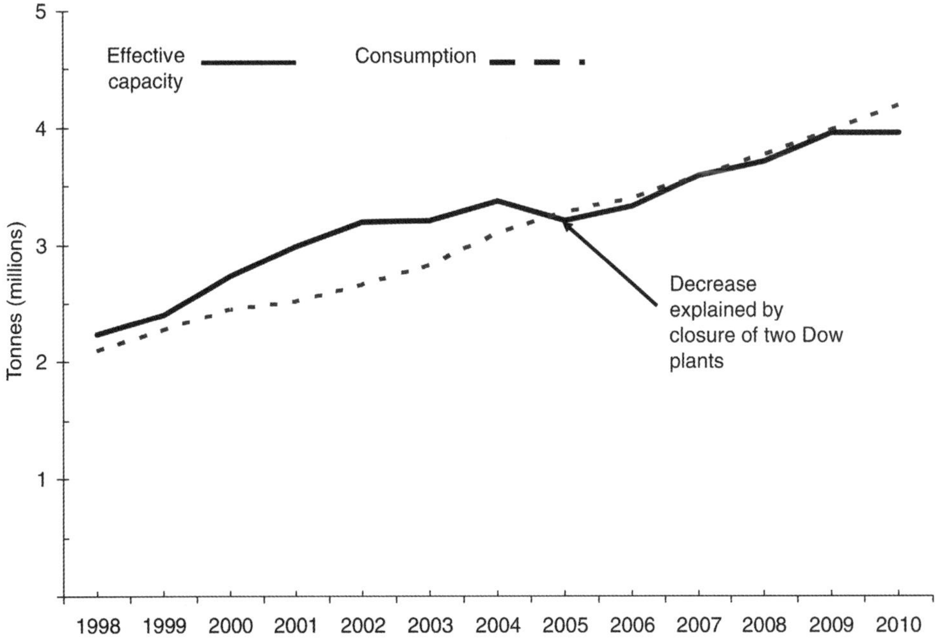

Figure 1.8 Global MDI supply and demand 1998–2010
Source: De Walque & Associates

CASE STUDY 6 – *continued*

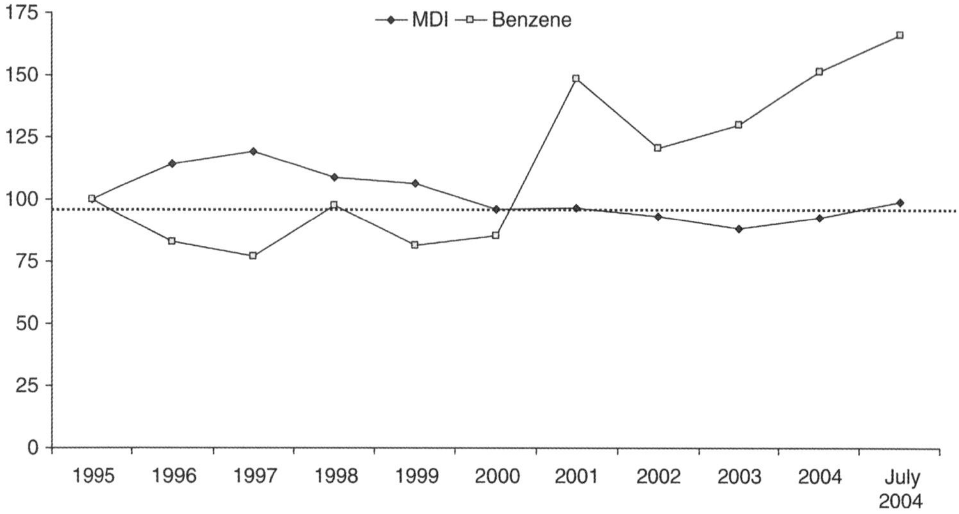

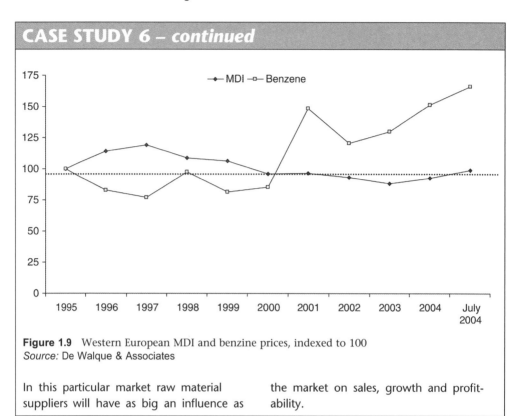

Figure 1.9 Western European MDI and benzine prices, indexed to 100
Source: De Walque & Associates

In this particular market raw material suppliers will have as big an influence as the market on sales, growth and profitability.

FDD AND CDD

While we are on the topic of where CDD starts and finishes, we should define the respective roles of CDD and FDD. We have already said that FDD will provide much of the information and analysis needed to form a view on commercial prospects, so why go to the trouble and expense of conducting detailed CDD? The first reason is that firms of chartered accountants will rarely go beyond commenting on the reasonableness of the assumptions behind a forecast and whether it has been added up properly. They are very reluctant to provide forecasts of their own and prefer to rely on the CDD provider if asked to do so. CDD can provide a market insight to forecasts and point to which sensitivities should be run as part of the financial modelling.

Where the business has fixed-term contracts, the quality of the due diligence will benefit greatly if the CDD and FDD teams can work together from the start with the CDD team providing an assessment of the chances of individual contracts being renewed (see also Case Study 7 below). In one assignment, when both CDD and FDD work had finished, the financial and commercial teams exchanged reports. The FDD report contained words such as 'CDD should investigate why the volume of work under this contract has fallen' and 'CDD should ascertain why this contract was not renewed'. Unfortunately the CDD team had selected the customers for interview at random and had therefore not spoken to some of those where FDD had thrown up important questions.

CASE STUDY 7

USING CDD TO ASSESS FORECASTS

A manufacturer of large and expensive sub-assemblies for big construction projects put together its own forecasts by listing the contracts bid for and multiplying a percentage probability of winning the project by its value. The resulting weighted average value is the forecast. The process is shown in Table 1.1.

The only way to validate these numbers was to speak to the contract awarders, confirm the amounts and get their views on the chances of the target's likely success.

Table 1.1 Contract analysis and sales forecasting

Contract	*Chance of winning (%)*	*Total value £ millions*	2007 (£ millions)	*Weighted value* 2008 (£ *millions*)	2009 (£ *millions*)
Singapore subway	60	210	20.0	70.0	36.0
Shanghai	40	115		10.0	36.0
Austrian tunnel	75	50	7.0	10.0	20.5
Trans-Australian railway	30	320			96.0

The second reason for conducting CDD is that FDD tends to be internally and historically focused. It collects its market and competitive information from management, it looks into customer churn from internal records and from those same records makes a judgement on the degree of risk from relying on a small number of customers or a small number of suppliers. What it does not do is go out and test that theoretical risk. Case Study 8 highlights the importance of this.

CASE STUDY 8

ASSESSING THE DEGREE OF RISK FROM A CONCENTRATED CUSTOMER BASE

Eighty-five per cent of the sales of a flat-pack furniture manufacturer came from two customers, both of whom were price-driven catalogue retailers. One of these customers accounted for over 50 per cent of sales. This was a management buyout and the deal was to be debt financed. In terms of theoretical risk, this is about as lethal a combination as can be imagined: dependence on two customers and high gearing.

The flat-pack furniture market accounts for roughly one-third of all furniture. All the indications were that market growth of 10 per cent over and above the overall furniture market was possible. As the furniture market was growing at around 4–5 per cent, there was no worry about the market dynamics as long as the UK economy continued to be healthy. Furniture is an impulse buy that relies on a strong economy. In mainland Europe, the average elasticity of the demand for furniture and disposable income is 1.5, which means that if the income increases by 1, the demand for furniture rises by 1.5, and vice versa. Furthermore, the flat-pack market in the UK was extremely underdeveloped. Penetration levels were below 10 per cent

CASE STUDY 8 – *continued*

compared with 34 per cent in Germany and 40 per cent in Scandinavia and Holland.

The worry was not the market, but the customer concentration and the type of customer. Every piece of logic and experience said that it was only a matter of time before these two large customers shifted their purchasing to low-cost economies. That is where the FDD would have stopped. CDD goes on to test the logic and what it found was the following:

- The target's largest client had only about 5 per cent of the flat pack market.
- It was launching a major campaign, backed by a new catalogue and an extended product range, to improve its position in furniture, which its own internal studies had revealed as one of three product ranges where its share was below what it should have been.
- As its stores tended to be small, without dramatic improvements in just-in-time supply, there would be no room to stock the extended ranges. Supply chain management was critical to the customer's success.
- The target had performed extremely well in the past on delivery and logistics. This was confirmed by the biggest customer. It had chosen the target to pilot a new project aimed at helping suppliers manage products from 'the factory floor to the back door'.
- Other suppliers to the same customer acknowledged that supply chain management was key and if you could demonstrate to the customer that you could meet its needs you could fight the threat of cheap imports.
- The customer's quest for just-in-time and its ability to get it from UK-based suppliers contrasted starkly with deliveries from European suppliers. They could manage monthly deliveries at best. Delivery from China would be even worse.
- Although the customer did import from China, this was for the high-volume, undifferentiated products such as book cases. Not the fast-changing, design-intensive, living-room furniture supplied by the target.

Once the real customer position was understood it was obvious that the loss of one of the two biggest customers was highly unlikely.

The third reason for conducting CDD is that relying on the target's management is not always the best way of coming at an assessment of future prospects. Companies are notoriously bad a looking outside and in any case management are almost bound to accentuate the positive. At the very least, if management say their products are the most highly rated by all the important customers in the marketplace, due diligence needs to check with those customers that this is, in fact, the case – and that it will continue to be the case. Case Study 9 is a real example where the need for an independent check on what was going on was critical.

CASE STUDY 9

WHAT IS REALLY GOING ON?

In one investigation of a tired UK brand, CDD very quickly discovered that all the major supermarkets wanted to stop stocking it. This was the 1990s and the product was very definitely a product of the 1970s. However, those supermarkets that did take it off their shelves quickly found themselves bombarded with telephone calls from disgruntled 'customers' demanding to know why they could no longer find their favourite product. Faced with such customer pressure, the supermarkets reinstated the range and the whole cycle of poor sales, de-listing and customer complaints would start again. What the supermarkets did not know was that those 'customers' were in fact out-of-work actors hired by the target to make a fuss and get the product back on the shelves.

The fourth reason for conducting CDD is that it does not need historical figures to come to a view about the future. This can be critical where there is no history or the future is going to be radically different from the past, as it is in Case Study 10.

CASE STUDY 10

CASE STUDY 9 REVISITED

Case Study 9, above, does have a happy ending. Figure 1.10 shows the target's sales against the UK market as a whole. As can be seen, it was going backwards while competing product sales were growing steadily.

This was a product very definitely in the doldrums. Included in the sales figures are those for its embryonic market in Germany, where it was only just starting out but where interviews on the ground confirmed a real customer need, pent up demand that the

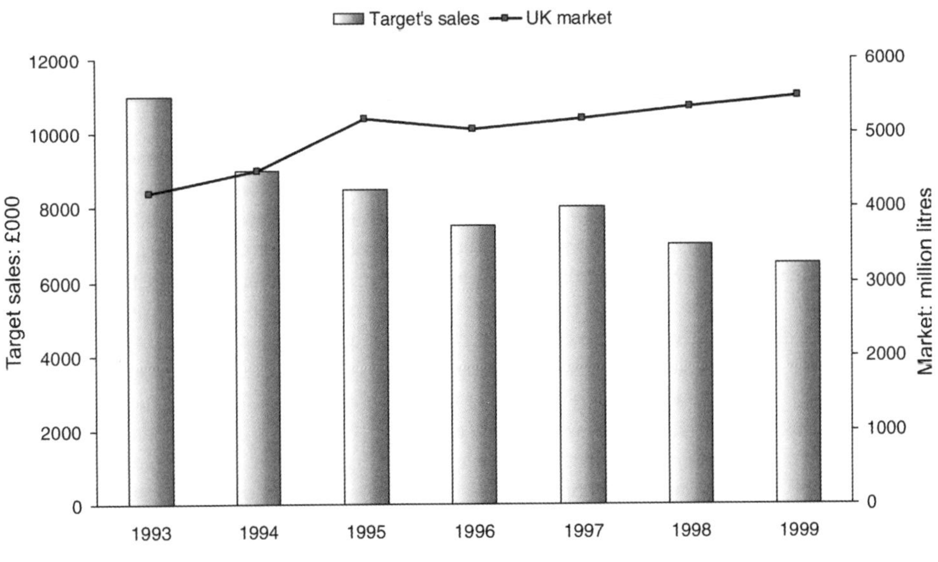

Figure 1.10 The target's sales vs. the UK market

CASE STUDY 10 – *continued*

company was unable to supply and where there was very little competition. With new distribution arrangements and a professional sales and marketing approach, there was a massive potential in Germany. This was confirmed by the fact that management bought the business for £3 million in March 1998 and sold it for £10.5 in November the same year.

The final reason why FDD cannot provide the same insights as CDD is that financials are backward looking. When you buy a company, you are buying its future and its future depends on the health of its market and how well it serves its customers. Quantitative financial analysis should not be the guiding force in due diligence. Acquirers who know what they are doing balance the quantitative with the qualitative as shown in Table 1.2.

It is only by understanding commercial forces that you can understand a company's future. Accounts are a summary of what has happened, not a guide to what will happen. Customers' buying habits have a tendency to change with time, so what has happened in the past cannot be a guide to the future. For example, personal computer distributors are now having to offer much more than the traditional supply and install. By getting most of its information from up-to-date sources outside the target, CDD comes to an independent view of the future. Figure 1.11, which shows the financial performance of Hypothetical Ltd,

Table 1.2 Why past financial performance is not a good guide to the future

Factor	*Description*
Product pipeline	In small and medium-sized companies, especially technically based ones, the influence of a small number of products can be substantial. As a result, the correlation between past and future performance is weak. Moreover, different stages of the product lifecycle make inter-firm comparisons problematic.
Customer pipeline	The same principle applies. If a company is about to win (or lose) a large customer, the future is going to be very different from the past.
Market changes	The rate of market and technical change can weaken the usefulness of past financial data.
Financial comparability	Even in the same jurisdiction, different companies apply the same rules in different ways making the comparability of past financial reports difficult. Moreover, different companies have different objectives. There is always a trade-off between current and future profits making direct profit comparison meaningless.
Portfolio comparability	Any market is divided into a myriad of product/market segments. Direct comparison is between companies that compete in different sub-sectors is limited.
Regulatory demands	The cost of complying with changing regulations and the impact they have on the market and competition make the past an unreliable guide to the future.
The importance of intangible assets	The tools and techniques of financial analysis were designed for a world in which tangible assets were central to success. If you are in any doubt about this, calculate return on assets for a people business, such as an advertising agency, and an engineering company. These days intellectual property, business systems, reputation and people are the critical success factors. People walk, reputations are easily lost and innovations easily copied, so how can historical numbers tell you much about the future?

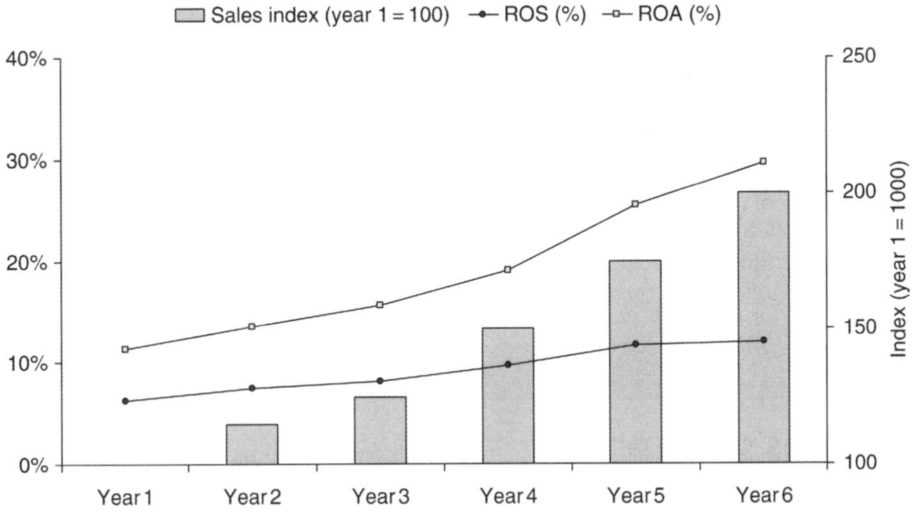

Figure 1.11 Hypothetical Ltd – financial performance

demonstrates why getting to the underlying commercial position is so important. Sales have doubled, margin has nearly doubled and return on assets has climbed from 11 per cent to 30 per cent. Not a bad performance at all ... until you look at Figure 1.12, which summarizes market performance.

Hypothetical's growth has lagged the market, market share has shrunk from 20 per cent to 14 per cent and customer retention has dropped from 88 per cent to 80 per cent. There is something very wrong and its causes are most likely the same as those that have contributed to the stunning financial performance – cuts in sales, marketing and research and development (R&D) expenditure that contribute to short-term financial gains but undermine the longer-term market position. FDD does not tell half the story. CDD and FDD

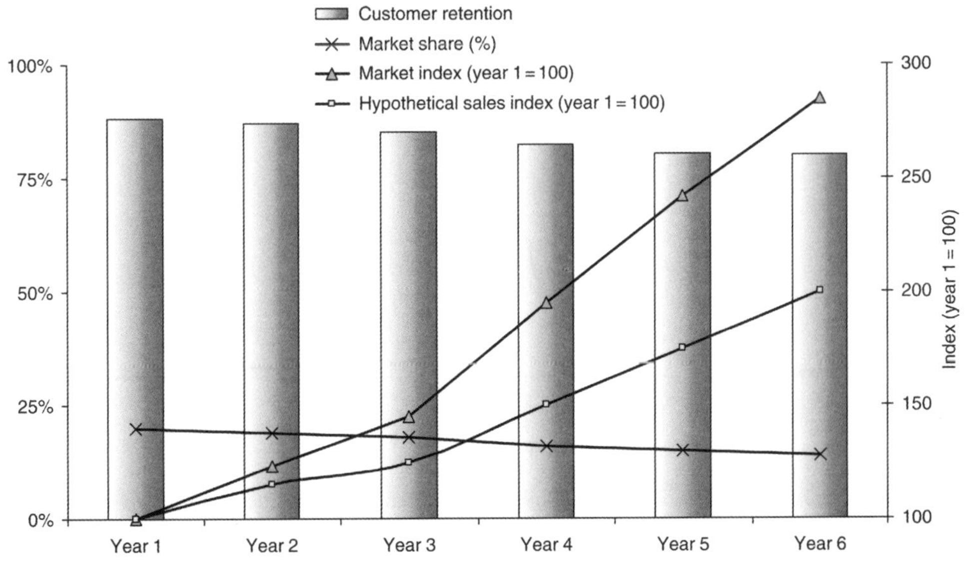

Figure 1.12 Hypothetical Ltd – market performance

should be seen as complementary. This complementarity should be recognized by ensuring the two teams work together. Both financial and CDD teams have access to sources and to information that can be valuable to the other. FDD will have access to debtors' lists for example. These will contain the identities of ex-customers. For obvious reasons, the CDD team will want to talk to ex-customers. In exchange, the CDD team can find and provide a wider range of estimates of market size and future growth rates that the valuation team can plug into their models and scenarios.

A final case study shows the power of understanding customers and markets.

CASE STUDY 11

INVESTORS SHOULD UNDERSTAND PRODUCTS, CUSTOMERS AND MARKETS

Baltimore Technology entered the FTSE 100 in March 2000 with revenues of less than £30 million, losses of £20 million and a market value of £4.25 billion. Its business was providing digital certificate technology, which guarantees that both sender and receiver in any transaction are genuine and encrypts any communications between them. Lack of security on the Internet was seen as one of the biggest hurdles to the widespread adoption of electronic commerce, and Internet banking in particular. Baltimore Technology's share price history is shown in Figure 1.13.

Even when Baltimore's share price began its steady fall, commentators were maintaining that there was still a lot of expectation built into the volatile share price. Had those same commentators had access to a piece of CDD on a similar company owned by another public company that was having cold feet about its subsidiary's real potential, they would have not been so optimistic. The

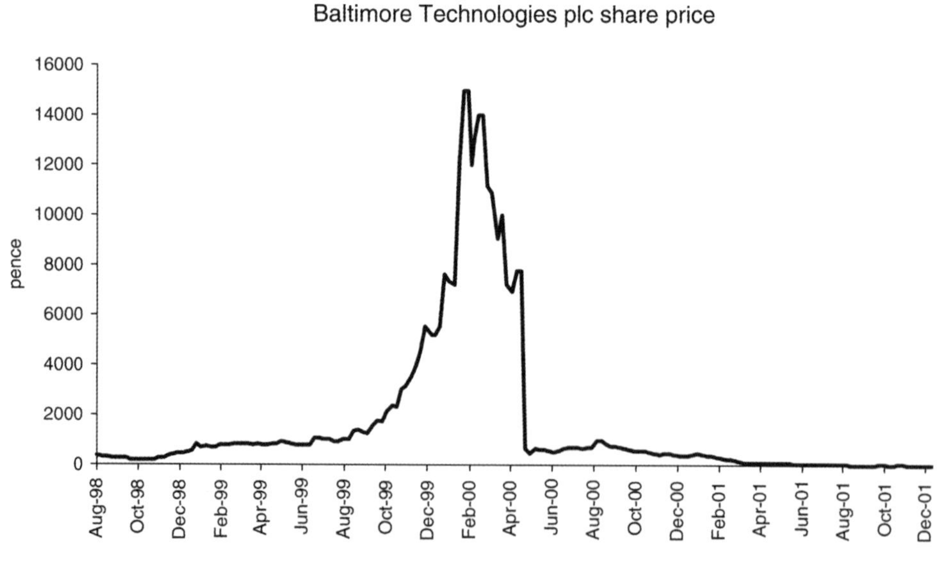

Figure 1.13 Baltimore Technologies demonstrates the need to understand a company's commercial position

Note: Weekly high not adjusted for dividends and splits: Stock split 10:1 in May-00 and 1:10 in Dec-01

Source: Dow Jones

CASE STUDY 11 – *continued*

CDD had shown that Public Key Infrastructure, to give the Baltimore product its proper name, was too complicated to implement. As there was no market for it, the share price was bound to bomb sooner or later. It is all very well having gross margins as high as 95 per cent, but if customers are not interested there will be no profit.

Applications of CDD

Most of this book talks about CDD in the context of acquisitions but of course its use is not confined to M&A. Chapter 9 discusses the use of CDD in joint ventures (JVs) and in recovery situations, but it can also be used in any business situation that calls for an understanding of market attractiveness, ability to compete and management's ability to deliver. Capital expenditure decisions, for example, are usually made from a purely financial perspective. Back in the 1980s, the decision to install a continuous caster in a steel mill could be made on the numbers alone. The cost saving was obvious, but what was not always obvious was what size of caster to install. Wrongly, this was an engineering decision. Continuous casters produce a continuous oblong of steel. The wider the cross-section of that oblong, the higher the quality of the finished product because the larger the cast section, the more the steel will have to be rolled to get it to the shape and size the customer wants to buy, and the more steel is rolled, the less brittle it becomes. However, rolling adds cost, so there is a trade-off between cast section and the cost of the finished steel. By understanding the different motivations of acquirers in the different steel markets and the trends and competitive pressures in those markets, CDD gives an insight on what size of caster to install.

Conclusion

Acquisitions are risky. More fail than succeed because they add to sales and profits, but do not build superior products or services, barriers to entry or long-term customer relationships. They build size not quality.

Due diligence is about much more than assessing the risks that need to be tackled in the deal negotiations. It should also assess the target's strategic fit and fundamental attractiveness and help ensure excellence in post-merger integration. CDD provides the most important insights on the future of the target and the merged entity. Broadly defined, it is a set of activities involved in evaluating a target company's market, customer relationships, competitive position and strategic direction. The knowledge gained from this evaluation becomes the critical input into determining the target's value to the acquirer.

Figure 1.6 defined CDD as examining the target's market, its competitive position and assessing its management and putting all three to together to map out how the target will perform both as a standalone business and under new ownership (that is, after integration). 'Market', 'competitive position' and 'management' are three very big topics that can and should be decomposed into their constituent parts to provide a more focused plan of enquiry.

We have also seen what CDD is not. It is not just customer referencing and it is not just an examination of the current market. Only by understanding market forces and the target's capabilities in some depth can CDD be of true service to an acquirer.

CDD is concerned with what is going on outside the target company and it is concerned with the future. It is therefore complementary to FDD, which tends to draw on historical information from inside the target.

Notes

1. Venture capital and private equity are slightly different things. Venture capital is all about venturing – backing start-up and early stage businesses and profiting from their eventual success. Private equity investors tend to invest in more established businesses. As the name suggests, it is the provision of equity from private sources as opposed to public stock exchanges.
2. The internal rate of return is that rate of discount in a discounted cash flow calculation that equates the present value of the stream of net receipts with the initial investment outlay.
3. See, for example, Rankine, D. (2001) *Why Acquisitions Fail, Practical Advice for Making Acquisitions Succeed*. London: Financial Times/Pearson Education.
4. For a fuller discussion on CDD and valuation see Chapter 11.
5. KPMG (1999) *Unlocking Shareholder Value: Keys To Success*. London: KPMG.

CHAPTER

2 *Getting Started*

Practitioners of CDD need to be briefed properly and in a timely manner. One of the most common mistakes in due diligence is for acquirers to instruct advisers in only general terms and then leave them get on with it. Every deal is different and so, therefore, is every due diligence exercise, but acquirers frequently forget that time spent planning and thinking carefully about what is needed pays enormous dividends when the programme gets going. Time will be short; it always is. Anticipating and dealing with obstacles is another useful task that acquirers need ensure they complete very early on. Practitioners of CDD need to recognize when acquirers have not set up the CDD exercise perfectly and deal with the shortcomings accordingly. However, even the perfectly planned CDD exercise will have its problems. This needs to be recognized from the beginning and to be factored in.

Is CDD needed?

There is no point in an acquirer spending money needlessly on CDD. Due diligence costs enough as it is. The first question that should be asked is:

- Is CDD needed at all?

This is three questions rolled into one:

- When should I carry out CDD?
- How much CDD should I do?
- What type of CDD is needed?

IS CDD NEEDED AT ALL?

Knowing how much due diligence to do and in which areas is a perennial problem to which there is no right answer. As a general rule, some kind of CDD is advisable, even if it is a limited customer referencing exercise. This is because surveys based on acquirers' past experience show the biggest areas of risk in a deal to be market related. In order of importance these are:

1 Market/Customers
2 Management
3 Financial
4 Competitors
5 The product
6 Technology questions

7 Legal issues
8 Environmental problems.

Deciding just how much CDD to do is not an exact science, but there are a number of pointers that give the acquirer a guide. These are:

- the particulars of the deal;
- existing knowledge;
- the perceived degree of risk.

The particulars of the deal

Chapter 1 summarizes what CDD is about and shows that ideally CDD should be a mini strategy review set up not just to detect the risks that need to be provided for in the deal negotiations, but also to give a blueprint for how the acquisition will help build a long-term competitive advantage. However, a CDD project does not have to cover everything. Like all topics in due diligence, what to cover is a matter of judgement that depends on the target business. An acquirer must decide early on what areas are likely to be the most important. In every transaction there are special areas of concern that stand out. To take an extreme example, if you were buying the remaining shares in a joint venture, you should already have an excellent insight into the market, into management and into the business's competitive position and should not need CDD – although you may well question why your partner is selling out. Case Study 12 is an example of how a US multinational structured a piece of CDD.

CASE STUDY 12

CONTROLS FOR CHILLER CABINETS

A very large US acquirer commissioned CDD on a small, entrepreneurial British company that supplies equipment to the major British supermarkets. The owner was a typical founder/entrepreneur. According to him, his was the perfect business worth at least twice what the Americans were offering, the customers loved it, and him, the product was a world beater, he was only selling out because he needed the money to develop an even more exciting business. CDD needed to check out all of these claims, but they were not the primary issues as far as the acquirer was concerned. The fact that the company was supplying UK retailers Marks & Spencer and Sainsbury's was enough to tell them that the product was good enough. What really worried them was:

- Whether the founder had 'borrowed' some intellectual property. If he had, it would hardly be worth the owner suing a small company, but if that company was owned by a big US multinational suddenly the owner of that intellectual property would have a worthwhile target.
- The integrity of one of the shareholders. The person concerned was based outside the UK, making him more difficult to check out, and was proposing a deal structure that treated him better than the other shareholders. As a large US corporation, it did not want to be caught up in any corrupt practices.

Existing knowledge

As with the joint-venture example above, deciding what to cover in due diligence is a function of how much an acquirer thinks it knows about a business and how much risk it attaches to areas where its knowledge is limited. Therefore the level of information already held on a business will be one of the factors determining the scale and focus of investigations. Figure 2.1 summarizes the thought process.

If you are in the same business and territory as the target company, you will feel more relaxed about the level and scope of CDD required than, say, when buying a business with a new product or that operates in different geographical markets. Still, if the risk is high, you might find CDD, or aspects of it, useful. Similarly, CDD is useful if you have little information on the key commercial aspects of the target business, even though the overall level of risk may be low.

The perceived degree of risk

Sources of risk vary from deal to deal. By 'risk' is meant the risk that the deal will not meet the aspirations of the acquirer. In some cases risk may stem from competitive reaction, in others it may be integration, in others it might be the validity of the strategy and in yet others it might be to do with intellectual property. Risk is therefore related to the reasons for doing the deal. Assuming an acquisition is being made for logical, well-thought-through, strategic reasons, as Joseph L. Bower[1] points out, there will be a link between the strategic intent behind a deal and the implications for integration that result. The same link can be made to due diligence. Bower lists five reasons for M&As, each of which, as shown in Table 2.1, is going to mean a different CDD focus.

Following Bower's logic, the CDD process will add the most value if it concentrates on those areas for which the deal is occurring. If market share is the aim, then CDD should be structured to give a thorough customer interview programme and a realistic assessment of post-deal competitive position. For example, despite a host of acquisitions, US companies have failed to capture as large a share of the UK greetings card market as perhaps they should. The reason for this is that apparently retailers prefer to multiple source their

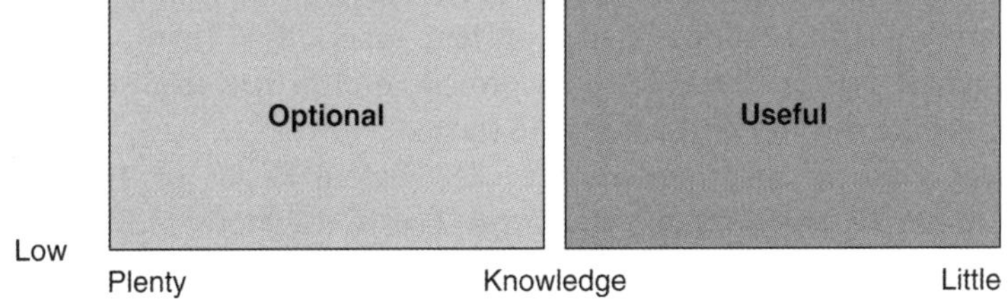

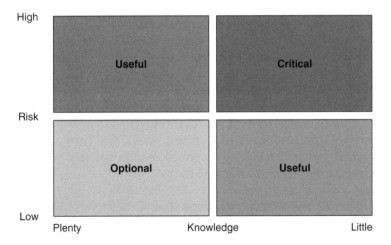

Figure 2.1 Whether to do CDD

Table 2.1 Different types of M&A and the implications for CDD

M&A Type	*Strategic objectives*	*CDD focus*
The over-capacity M&A	Eliminate over-capacity, gain market share/improve prices, achieve scale economies.	Validate the strategy. Market size and growth, relative market strength, projected market trends, strength of customer relations, relative strength of product lines, ability to rationalize without damaging sales.
The geographic roll-up M&A	A successful company expands geographically; operating units remain local.	Customer retention, strength of local management.
Product or market extension M&A	Acquisitions to extend a company's product line or its international coverage.	Relative robustness and strength of product/market positions. Cultural and systems integration.
The M&A as R&D	Acquisitions used instead of in-house R&D to build a market position quickly.	Technical assessment including scalability and substitutability. Assessment of ultimate market size, management strengths and weaknesses and retention of key people.
The Industry Convergence M&A	A company bets that a new industry is emerging and tries to establish a position by culling resources from existing industries whose boundaries are eroding.	Focus on market and customer benefits, ultimate market size and market growth rates, threats and weaknesses including threat of substitutes and new competitors, technical due diligence, retention of key staff.

greetings cards, so as one company is swallowed up by another, customers simply take their business elsewhere.

WHEN IS CDD CARRIED OUT?

CDD is normally carried out, like all due diligence, when the acquirer has a clear run at the target. This is usually after Heads of Terms has been signed, because that is the stage where acquirer and seller have signalled their commitment to the deal by drawing up an 'agreement to agree'. Heads heralds a period of exclusivity that gives some assurance that another party will not snatch the deal after a prospective acquirer has spent money on due diligence. As CDD is the least expensive type of investigation to commission from specialist consultants, it is a good idea if it is kicked off first, especially if there are doubts about the target's commercial future, because it can provide a clear pre-acquisition stop–go signal before the more expensive investigations are started.

Occasionally there is an argument for CDD before Heads of Terms. CDD can be conducted without the knowledge of the target. It can, therefore, provide an independent review of the business and does not raise the seller's expectations. It avoids embarrassment if the proposed acquisition opportunity is not progressed and helps with the pricing if there is competition for the target.

HOW MUCH CDD SHOULD BE DONE?

There is no right answer to the question, 'how do you know when you have done enough due diligence?' In structuring a programme, acquirers should always remember that due diligence is not about ticking boxes. It is not about collecting lots of information. It is done so that decisions can be made. Such decisions could include some or all of the following:

- to buy or not to buy;
- to negotiate a lower price;
- to draw up a proper post-acquisition implementation plan;
- to prioritize warranties and indemnities.

In the end it comes down to comfort. When an acquirer feels comfortable making a decision and has a list of post acquisition actions, the CDD team has done its work. CDD should be an iterative process in which acquirers and their advisers focus on issues as they arise, because you can guarantee that no one will know what all the issues are before the CDD gets started.

WHAT TYPE OF CDD IS NEEDED?

We saw in the Chapter 1 that there are three outputs from CDD:

- Confirmation that the company has the commercial prospects that the acquirer thinks it has (confirmatory CDD). This would also include confirmation that the acquirer's acquisition strategy is based on sound logic identifying where and how M&A can accelerate a company's growth and profits. Confirmatory CDD comes into its own when there is market uncertainty, where revenue projections appear aggressive compared to historic numbers or where a significant portion of the target's value is predicated on the success of new products, customers and/or markets.
- The information needed successfully to plan and execute integration of the acquired company. This would include identifying gaps in the capabilities of target/merged entity.
- A strategic analysis that shows how to position an acquisition or the combined entity should be positioned for maximum value (strategic CDD). CDD includes an analysis of the keys to success in an industry, how they will change over time and the resulting implications for the target/merged entity.

Acquirers and CDD practitioners are apt to forget, in the heat of the deal, where the CDD emphasis needs to be.

Where do we start?

The sensible starting point for any due diligence exercise is for the acquirer to do due diligence on itself. If an acquirer does not know what it wants from the exercise, it can be pretty sure that no one else will. Before diving into due diligence, acquirers should have asked themselves the following questions:

- What is the business strategy?
- How do acquisitions fit into the business strategy?
- How does the target fit the strategy?
- Have we carried out sufficient pre-acquisition planning?
- Are we sufficiently prepared for the due diligence exercise?
- Which areas are we going to investigate? Why?
- Do we know what we really need to know in each area of investigation?
- Do we have enough time to complete the process? If not, what are we going to do about it?
- Do we know where the synergies are going to come from? Have we tried to quantify them in detail? What further information is needed?
- Have we worked out an adequate implementation plan?
- Have we explored all the consequences of the deal, for example the effects on current operations, existing personnel, the industry and competitors?
- Have we set material limits for the due diligence investigation?
- Have we explained the process to the seller?
- Have we agreed access to people and documents with the seller?

CDD practitioners should make sure they run through the above questions with acquirers before they get started. Checklist 1 in Appendix A lists the questions in more detail.

Who should carry out the work?

There is a huge benefit to acquirers doing their own CDD because it gives them a first-hand insight into the business, which helps both in negotiations and in the aftermath of the deal. However, the chances are that outside consultants will be used. If they are, it is very important to select the right ones. To get the best out of them they must be managed. Like all project management, the key is to plan what needs to be done by when and by whom, co-ordinate the efforts of all involved and make sure everyone communicates.

Selecting CDD advisers

All acquirers get very nervous as the deal proceeds and a lot of their nervousness is dumped on advisers. Do not let this rattle you. With any luck, personal chemistry will have paid a big part in choosing a CDD provider, but do not take it for granted. It is highly likely that they have relied on industry experience as a basis for choosing a CDD supplier. There is far too much emphasis placed on sector experience. People, not companies, carry out CDD. Just because a company has sector experience does not mean that those with that experience will work on a particular CDD assignment. Besides, sectors are incredibly wide. Think of a relatively straightforward sounding sector like media. There is a world of difference between local radio and educational publishing. Would an adviser with experience in local radio be any more equipped than anyone else to work on an assignment in educational publishing? Probably not and anyway, if industry expertise is needed that much, it can be bought in if an industry experts' knowledge is more pertinent and detailed than that which can be developed by an industry outsider. Industry experts often lack essential specific process skills such as the ability to obtain and analyse information in the context of an acquisition. What counts is having the right people asking the right questions of the right sources.

After interpersonal factors, the main selection criterion should be the right mix of experience and skills. Experience required in order of importance is as follows:

1 Experience of carrying out CDD
2 Experience of the purchaser
3 Experience of the target company's sector.

What a good CDD team brings to the party are highly developed information gathering and analytical skills. Obtaining information from competitors is an excellent example. With a reasonable background knowledge of a business, CDD consultants can make a series of seemingly innocent enquiries that can lead to a detailed understanding of the strengths and weaknesses of a target company and its strategy.

BRIEFING ADVISERS

CDD advisers cannot be expected to turn in a half-decent job unless they know what is going on. The onus is on the acquirer to brief advisers properly and specify what information and analysis is needed. If the potential acquisition has been properly researched and the rationale for its purchase evaluated, a fairly logical set of due diligence issues should fall into place (see Table 2.1 above). It is surprising how often acquirers do not brief advisers properly. As a CDD practitioner, if you feel you have not been properly briefed, you must seize the initiative and go back to the acquirer with the questions you need answered. These are:

- Which other professionals will be working on the deal, what are they doing and where will the focus of their investigations be? As mentioned in Chapter 1, the CDD people should contact their financial due diligence colleagues as soon as is practicable to co-ordinate their plans of campaign. The two sides are not natural bedfellows and it is only the profit and loss down to gross margin that is of mutual interest, but the last thing the acquirer needs is the two reports not joining up.
- What due diligence does the purchaser intend to do itself?
- What are the reasons for doing the deal and the areas of greatest worry?
- Precisely what is wanted at the end of the exercise? One of the reasons why due diligence reports run to several hundred pages of often unrelated, but very detailed, facts is that the client has not specified (or not got across) what is wanted both in terms of the information needed and how it should be presented. This can work both ways. A private equity client once expressed disappointment with a piece of CDD saying that all it had wanted was output from the customer interviews instead of all the chart-based market analysis that it got. In its view, customer interviews told it far more about where the management could improve than charts on the market ever would. This is by no means the normal requirement of private equity investors.

Written terms of reference

CDD practitioners should work with written terms of reference. These should set out what is expected, by when and for how much. A written engagement letter should set out:

- the scope of the due diligence work to be carried out – incomplete scope is often a major obstacle to getting the best out of advisers; a full scope is set out in Checklist 2 in Appendix A, which would need to be adapted to the specific transaction;
- the CDD timetable and the deal timetable;
- whether an interim report or presentation is needed;
- fees;
- headings to be covered in the report (Checklist 2 in Appendix A suggests terms of reference for a CDD exercise);
- who will manage the assignment;
- confidentiality;
- the rights to the results;
- assignability of the results;
- liability insurance (if appropriate);
- what happens if the deal is abandoned and the work is terminated early.

There will always be pressure to deliver the maximum results in the minimum time. Over-promising is not a good idea, nor is putting the team through hell because there is not enough time or because the client's expectations have not been properly managed.

Planning the work

If establishing sensible terms of reference is the most important contribution to successful due diligence, probably the next most important is to plan how the work is going to be carried out. Figure 2.2 shows the stages in a typical CDD project.

Although CDD draws its conclusions from external data, the logical starting point is a meeting with the target company's management. Appropriate members of the CDD team

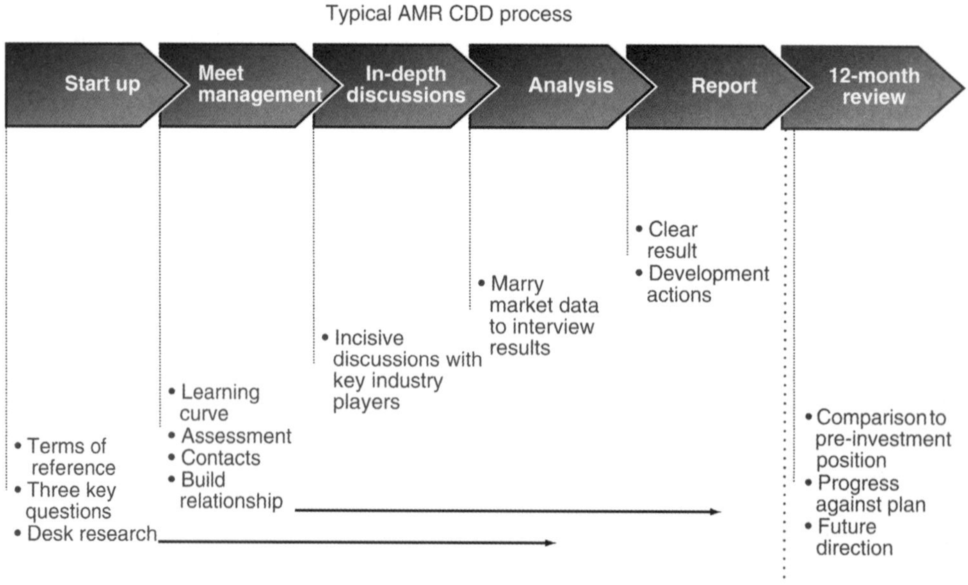

Figure 2.2 Stages in a typical CDD project

should meet the seller's top management independently of other due diligence providers. This meeting should:

- give the CDD providers an insider's briefing on the industry;
- prepare the ground for customer interviews;
- discuss other contacts and any sensitive issues;
- provide a starting point for the CDD team's assessment of management.

In order to ensure that time is not wasted and that the information and people are available, it is vital to plan the work in conjunction with the management of the target company. There is little point starting CDD if key people are not available or information is not immediately available.

The CDD team

CDD is not particularly difficult, but it does require a healthy slug of streetwise detective work and a lot of judgement. After that, specific skills matched to the peculiarities of the project are much more important than intellectual ability. In some assignments all that is needed are good customer referencers. In others you need an interviewer who can charm the innermost thoughts out of the target's biggest competitor. Some of the more experienced researchers have a knack of catching the competitor's sales director in the car during a 3-hour journey home on a Friday afternoon. This person is perfect for those projects where the industry is changing and you need depth of understanding. Team leaders need to lead from the front, they should be in touch with the work as it proceeds and should be able to talk sensibly about it as the project unfolds. People who carry out CDD are generally different, so do not expect CDD team members to be out of advisers' central casting. But however eccentric some of them may be, they are human beings. If you are in charge of a CDD investigation, it is up to you to look after team morale. Team members want to feel valuable; they want to know what is going on; they want something to aim at (so plot a steady course); they need to understand why they are doing what they are doing and understand its value. Treat them with respect. Never ask them to do something you would not do yourself and lead them to find the right answer, but never be tempted to impose your solution. Teams should be kept small. The more people working on an assignment, the more the information is dispersed between them. This is one of the problems with trying to compress timescales. Less time means more people to cover the ground, but more people also means less collective understanding.

Timetable

As Figure 2.3 shows, a typical piece of CDD takes about 3 weeks if everything is set up to start on day 1.

This can be shortened, but, if it is, there is a danger that quality will suffer. As already mentioned, putting more people onto a project does not guarantee that the analysis of findings will be carried out with enough thought or thoroughness. Analysis takes time and familiarity with all the findings. If you do not build in sufficient analysis time, CDD will not

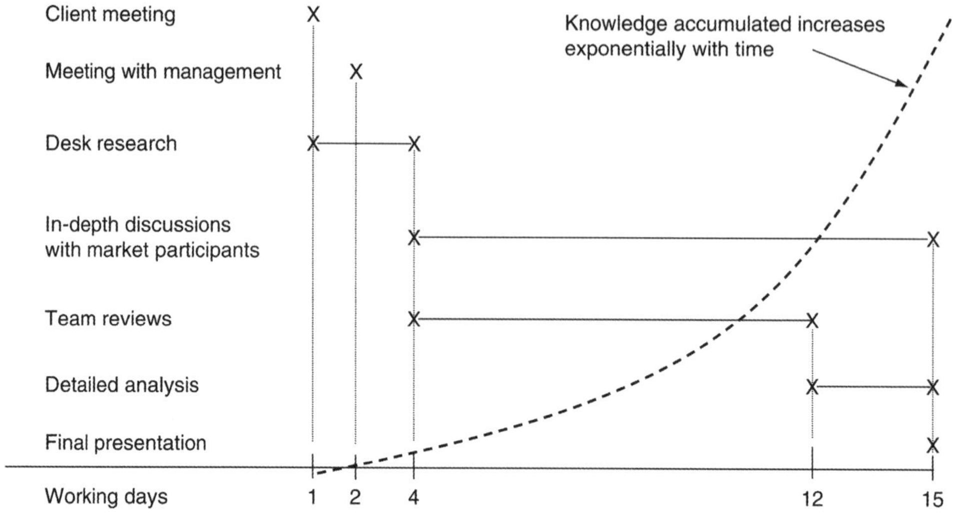

Figure 2.3 CDD takes 15 working days

be done properly. Acquirers should give advisers as much time as they can and involve them early. Even if the deal has not been finalized, it is still worth trying to get involved, then you can begin to plan the work, think about putting a team together and even start some of the background desk research. It should be in the acquirer's interests to involve advisers early as it allows them to pick your brains. Time spent in the early stages thinking through terms of reference will be time well spent.

Fees

In due diligence, you get what you pay for. Acquirers can have two of the following:

- A cheap report
- A good report
- A quick report.

Inevitably they will want all three. An important part of the initial specification phase is managing their expectations. It is normal for CDD to be carried out on the basis of a fixed fee. Contingent fees are becoming increasingly common. Here the exact fee charged depends on whether or not the deal completes. The usual arrangement is for there to be a discount on the fee if the deal does not go ahead and an uplift if it does. How much the fee varies around the 'normal' is really up to the adviser and the acquirer to negotiate. Contingent fee arrangements can vary from a small up/down right through to 100 per cent success fees (that is, nothing if the deal does not complete but a considerable uplift if it does).

Although contingent fees are a good way for acquirers to minimize costs, if a deal does not go ahead, they have to be aware of the obvious temptation they give for producing a positive report. No self-respecting adviser should ever let contingent fees influence the way the report is written, but to be sure it is best to calculate fees in a way that allows both sides to meet their objectives. The fairest mechanism is one that at least allows the advisers to eat if the deal does not go ahead, but gives them a reward if it does. As a rough rule of thumb, one-third of the price of CDD will be profit. On a contingent fee basis, this would mean knocking off one-third of the fee if the deal aborts and adding up to the same again onto the 'normal' price if it completes. On this basis, for a £60 000 exercise, the high/low fee would be £40 000 abort and up to £80 000 success.

Good CDD practice

SHARE INFORMATION

Acquirers sometimes struggle when deciding how much information to share at the outset of a CDD programme. Broadly, there are three approaches:

- Share nothing.
- Provide selected information.
- Share everything.

Share everything is best, but there may be occasions when you do not want to share because you have been asked to give independent verification. The advantages of sharing are:

- CDD consultants do not have time to 'reinvent the wheel' and acquirers should not want you too.
- Consultants' approach will be better, as it will be based on a clearer understanding of the issues. CDD is like peeling an onion: the more quickly the top skins are peeled, the more quickly investigations can focus on the important issues.

COMMUNICATE REGULARLY

There should be regular communication between the CDD advisers and the acquirer. Communication should not be a one-off event that takes place when the finished report is presented (or, more likely, when the executive summaries are circulated to management). This is not to say that there should be formal progress meetings on a weekly basis; the deal timetable is usually too short for that, but the acquirer will be looking for reasonably regular updates from external advisers as the enquiries proceed. If nothing else, this allows the acquirer to:

- communicate changes in their concerns;
- identify significant issues early on;
- make sure all advisers' efforts are co-ordinated.

The CDD should also hold regular meetings so that the commercial impact of what is being found out can be properly assessed, questions can be raised and fed back to the acquirer and other advisers and areas where further investigation is needed can be identified. CDD may unearth issues that kill the deal and the sooner these are uncovered, the better.

GIVE GOOD VALUE

Finally, a good piece of CDD should not be too heavily 'risk managed'. The result is a report that is rich in information but poor on advice. The acquirer is not paying advisers for information alone. What it really wants are clear, well-founded opinions and an assessment of opportunities as well as risks.

Conclusion

One of the secrets of due diligence is knowing what is required, from whom, and when. In other words, project management pure and simple. One of the realities of due diligence is that the project management skills of acquirers are often sadly lacking. They rarely think through what they want or give themselves enough time to plan properly. Nor do they ever admit after the event that CDD could have gone better if they had tried a bit harder. Do not let the acquirer's natural nervousness put you off your stride. You are a professional who knows how to conduct CDD properly, which is why you are going to fill any gaps in what the acquirer should have done. It is in your own interests to fill any planning gaps. Check that the acquirer is asking the right questions of CDD, that they have fully thought through the reasons for doing the deal, what they hope to achieve with it and make sure that you are properly briefed. Make sure you select the right team, get enough time to do the work and are rewarded properly for doing it. And finally, remember you are both in the same side so share information and communicate regularly.

Note

1. Bower, Joseph L. (2001) 'Not all M&As Are Alike and That Matters', *Harvard Business Review*, 79(3): 92–101.

PART II Analytical Techniques

PART II

Introduction

At some point in a CDD investigation you have to make sense of a sea of data you are going to collect, much of which will be incomplete and contradictory. You will soon discover a couple of real gems that will tell you everything, but in the meantime, to paraphrase an old saying, when you are up to your eyes in data, it is hard to remember that you set out to decide whether or not the target company is potentially a good acquisition. Above all, do not be tempted to fall into the 'holiday snaps trap'. This is the equivalent of visiting someone after their return from holiday, asking if they had a good time and being treated to a 2-hour slide show of their holiday snaps, most of which look the same and involve stories that only mean something if you were there at the time. All you wanted to know was whether the food was any good and if it rained. The CDD version goes something like, 'I have done 50 interviews and my goodness am I going to tell you about them!' All the would-be investor wants to know is: 'Is the target any good and should I do the deal?' It is for this reason that this part of the book precedes that on collecting the data. If you have a good idea about the data you need at the outset, collecting it will be much more efficient.

As mentioned in Chapter 1, a CDD exercise is 'confirmatory' – 'this acquisition target is a good buy' – and/or strategic – 'if you buy this company, this is what you should do with it'. Both call not for presenting data, but using it to come to a conclusion about the acquisition's prospects. To do this you need to be able to simplify the world so that you can see through that wall of data and pluck out the messages that really matter. CDD uses a number of fairly well-tried models to help with that simplification and that is what these next chapters are about. Many of the analytic techniques are frameworks that identify, classify and highlight the principal factors that have a bearing on the market and the target company's position within it.

Before we start, however, a word of warning. It is vital to recognize the limitations of strategic analysis. The techniques of strategy analysis do not by themselves tell you about the deal any more than does drawing up a set of accounts, calculating discounted cash flow or even carrying out market research. The strategic decisions in our personal lives are not amenable to sterile analysis and quantitative decision making techniques (Should I get married? Change my career from stock broking to plumbing? Buy a flat in London or a house in Scotland?) and the same is true in CDD. There are simply too many variables to reduce our analysis to programmed algorithms. Experience, understanding, creativity, intuition and imagination are just as important.

The first priority is to be clear about the market in which the target company competes. Getting this right will determine the quality of the rest of the work and it is not always easy as it sounds. This is the subject of Chapter 3. With that done, it is on to the models and simplification techniques mentioned above. This takes us into the realms of strategy analysis. The strategy literature these days goes two ways, as, interestingly, does the academic literature in most social sciences. The source of profitability is either structural or functional. The structuralists, Michael Porter et al., maintain that profitability depends on

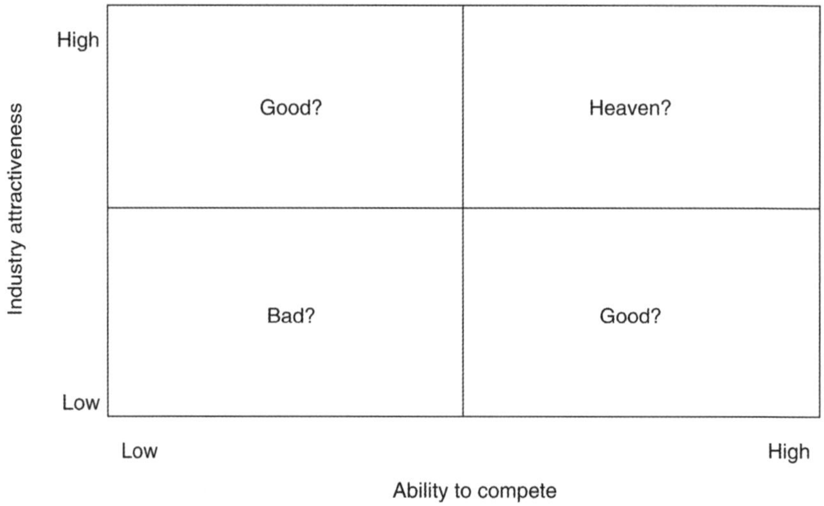

Figure II.1 Industry attractiveness and ability to compete

industry structure. The kinder the industry structure, the higher the profit potential. The more a company can shelter from structural forces that keep profits down, the higher the profit potential. The more a company succeeds with a strategy that modifies industry conditions and competitor behaviour, the higher also the profit potential. The functional school, on the other hand, says that profitability is all about a company's ability to compete. Ability to compete comes down to unique bundles of resources, capabilities, competences and market positioning. There is nothing new here. Ever since the 1950s, strategic analysis has been concerned with market attractiveness and ability to compete. What any acquirer really wants is a target company and/or the merged entity to be in the upper right quadrant in Figure II.1.

Chapter 3 looks at market definition, Chapter 4 at industry attractiveness, Chapter 5 at the target's ability to compete and Chapter 6 at market positioning. There do, however, seem to be some disturbing developments in modern markets. Innovations are quickly copied, customers are a cynical bunch and there is much more entrepreneurialism about. It could be that Chapters 4, 5 and 6 do not tell the whole story or they lull us into a false sense of security. Chapter 8 ('The New Reality') is there to remind us that understanding what is going on in the customer's head is just as important as the two-by-two matrices of modern strategy analysis.

CHAPTER

3 Which Market is the Target In?

Before we can even start to think about the target company's future performance, we must have a clear idea of what market it serves. Nothing makes sense without first defining the boundaries of the target's market by strategically segmenting it. This may sound like a fairly easy task and in many cases it is, but experience has taught me that it pays to make certain at the outset that the market you are investigating is properly defined and understood. The reason is that if you are going to analyse the attractiveness of the target's market and its ability to compete, you need to know where, on what terms and with whom the target is competing. If you do not draw boundaries, you cannot do that in any meaningful way. Not only that, there have been many occasions when an acquisition candidate has attempted to sell itself on market growth opportunity when it can only compete in a small part of that market. An acquirer should not pay for this upside.

It used to annoy me when academics would define, say, the market for cars as being part of the market for transportation. On this logic, BMW competes with Eurostar; it does not. In certain circumstances, it might be useful to define BMW's market this widely, but not usually in CDD. Nonetheless, it does show that with any definition of a market, there is a choice of where to draw the boundaries. The normally accepted definition of 'the market' is not always appropriate as a definition of where the target competes and the appropriate definition can narrow or widen, depending on the focus of the due diligence exercise. It is here where the problems usually come; not at the market level, but at the segment or sub-market level.

All business analysts are familiar with the concepts of market segmentation and differentiation but get terribly confused by them. In this chapter, we look first at differentiation. What is it and why is it not the same as that other basic concept of marketing strategy, focus? And why does it matter, anyway, whether a target company is differentiating or focusing? We then look at segmentation, which many analysts think of as a technique employed by advertising agencies and marketing managers to target their advertising. For the purposes of CDD, this is not what segmentation is about at all, as we shall see. Segmentation is a simple enough concept, but there is a huge amount of confusion out there on how best to operationalize it, which is a pity because it is fundamental to market analysis.

The basics

How companies address a market, that is, their market strategy, is based on how they define the market, which parts they serve, their value proposition and the key relationships they must establish and maintain to make their marketing strategies work. Customer

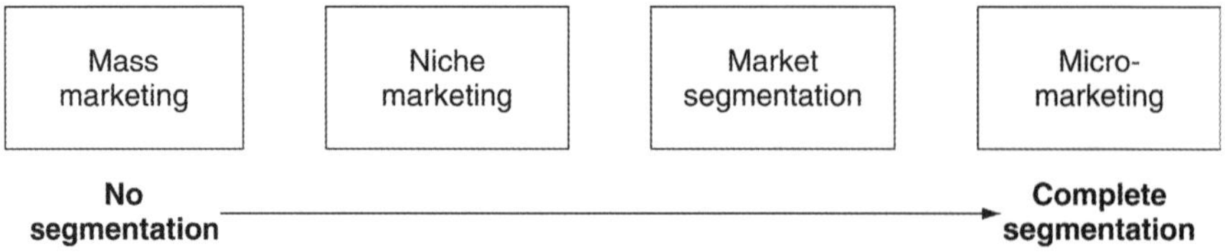

Figure 3.1 Levels of marketing segmentation

requirements underlie all of these, so when trying to work out what is going on in a market, always start with the customers. All segmentation starts with customer needs. Products are sources of satisfaction to consumers and this is the only way to think of them. Products and services should therefore be analysed in terms of the way they are perceived by customers in relation to:

- why they buy one product rather than another; and
- competitive offerings.

These define the appropriate segmentation.

There are four approaches any company can take to marketing a product or service. These are set out in Figure 3.1.

Recognizing which companies are following which approach is a good first step in defining market boundaries, but more on that in a moment.

Differentiation and segmentation are two totally different things ...

Differentiation involves:

- concentration on one or more key criteria which are valued by customers;
- adding costs selectively in the areas perceived to be important to acquirers and charging a premium price in excess the costs added.

The success of this strategy lies in finding opportunities for differentiation that cannot be matched by competitors while being clear about the costs involved and the amount of the price premium that can be charged. Differentiation means working out the product, service, and image characteristics that influence customer choice and positioning your production to appeal to a selection of them. Differentiation is not the same as segmentation, but differentiation is closely linked to choices over the segments in which a firm competes. Unique offerings may mean that a firm ends up targeting only certain market niches.

The term 'segmentation' appears to have been first coined by Wendel Smith[1] in the 1950s. He came at it from the perspective of a single product company that could either aim to secure a 'share of a broad and generalized market' through product differentiation or aim for 'depth of market position in the segments that are effectively defined and penetrated' through market segmentation. Philip Kotler[2] added a third, mass marketing. Mass marketing is where the seller produces 'one product for all buyers ... the traditional argument for [this] is that it will lead to the lowest costs and prices and create the largest potential market.'

So far so good, but from this point on things start to get terribly confused in the marketing literature, largely it seems because Kotler[3] at first misunderstood what Smith had said about product differentiation. Unfortunately Kotler's book went on to be the standard work. The result is that marketeers to this day see only two possibilities: mass marketing and segmentation. This oversimplifies and misunderstands what can be going on in a market.

To Smith there was a very real difference between product differentiation and market segmentation. As he said:

Strategies of segmentation and differentiation may be employed simultaneously, but more commonly they are applied in sequence in response to changing market conditions. In one sense, segmentation is a momentary or short-term phenomenon in that effective use of this strategy may lead to more formal recognition of the reality of market segments through redefinition of the segments as individual markets.

To appreciate what may seem like a small, irrelevant, almost academic difference between product differentiation and market segmentation, consider the case of waterproof matches:[4]

these may be bought for all sorts of reasons – for boating, for camping, or to light fires in the garden, or by smokers who don't own a raincoat and so on. The company pursuing a product differentiation strategy develops waterproof matches to obtain a minority share of the broad market for matches. The reason it is not the same as differentiation is because the only way in which the purchasers of this differentiated product are a group (or 'segment') is that they sometimes wish to use waterproof matches; presumably they continue to buy ordinary matches for household purposes as well.

As the above implies, the idea of segmentation is a fluid generalization that may not have a concrete foundation in the sense that you can see and kick any one particular segment; indeed, the work of Ehrenberg and Goodhart[5] demonstrates such fluidity. Their findings suggest that consumers do not choose the single brand that best delivers the benefits they want, but rather make different choices from amongst a set of possible products.

The reason for dwelling on differentiation versus focus is because the two are often confused. A company attacking a market through differentiated products such as waterproof matches is not necessarily pursuing a market segmentation strategy. The four approaches are set out in Figure 3.2.

Astute readers will, of course, see the link to Porter's three generic strategies.[6] For Porter, the generic strategies are approaches to outperforming competitors in an industry:

- Cost leadership requires aggressive construction of efficient-scale facilities and cost minimization in all areas of the business (including customer selection). Cost leadership often requires a high relative market share to give scale advantage.
- Differentiation is creating something that is perceived industry wide as being unique. There are many ways of creating a unique offering from product features (waterproof matches) design or brand image (Mercedes) to customer service (UK retailer Marks & Spencer's no-quibble returns policy). Differentiation usually involves lower market shares and higher costs.

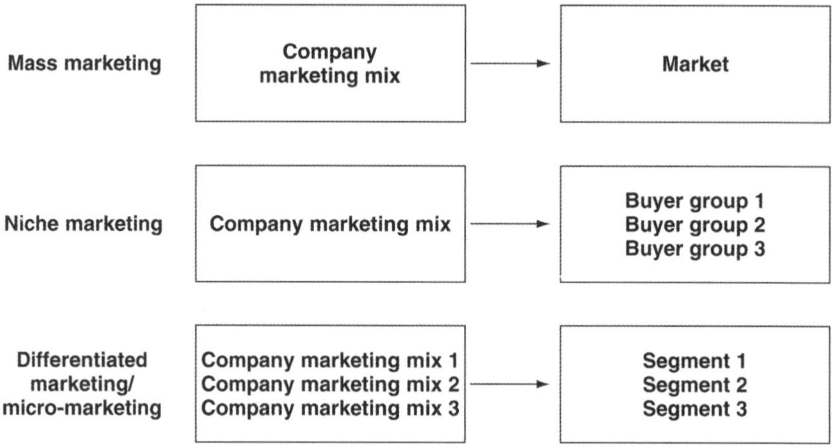

Figure 3.2 Four approaches to marketing

- Focus involves concentrating on particular buyer groups or segments. These are effectively sub-markets. How well the target serves these groups will determine its competitive position. This could be through lower costs in serving the segment or meeting its needs better (or, these days, both).

... And strategic and operational segmentation are not the same things either

Segmentation is the division of a market into distinct sub-units of homogenous buyers. These sub-units are bound together by the satisfaction of just one particular priority need, so for example in Figure 3.3, this is the need to work safely at height.

Figure 3.3 looks at two different means of working at height; access platforms and scaffolding. Which is used depends on the job. Access platforms are best for single jobs at height, such as changing the light bulbs on a motorway where anything else but a powered

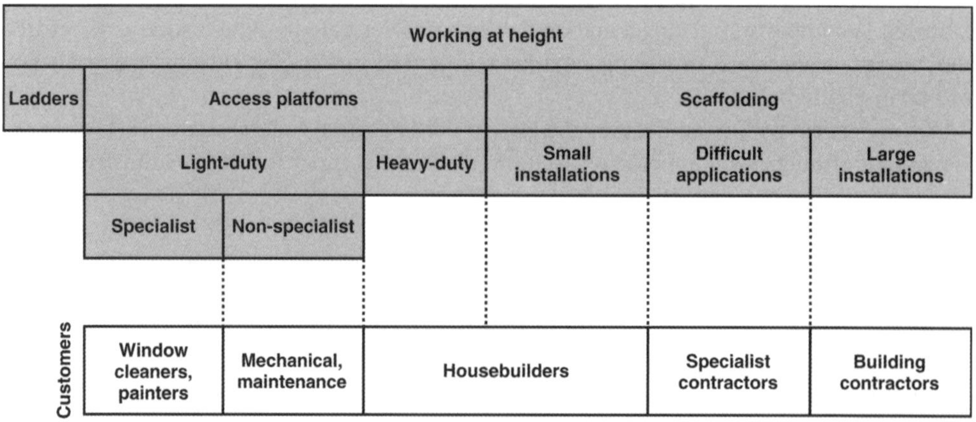

Figure 3.3 Strategic segmentation in action

access platform would not make sense. Scaffolding is used in building where it needs to take weight and can remain in place for some time. However, there are overlaps between these three sectors. Heavy-duty scissor lifts, for example, compete with scaffolding on some building sites. These are the 'heavy' access platform applications in Figure 3.3. Heavy-duty scissor lifts are a substitute for scaffolding in small installations, say building single houses, are used by the same customers and therefore belong in the same market.

Segmentation takes place at two levels: the strategic level and the operational level. CDD uses strategic segmentation to understand the market structure and market dynamics that apply to the target company and operational segmentation to compare the effectiveness of the target's product and marketing strategy.

The difference between strategic segmentation and operational segmentation is that:

- strategic segmentation defines markets by identifying unique bundles of customer needs that are satisfied by one product-market approach as opposed to another;
- operational segmentation is concerned with identifying distinctive groups of buyers within the markets defined by strategic segmentation.

Strategic segmentation 'combines buyer purchasing behaviour with the behaviour of costs, both production costs and the costs of serving different buyers ... it encompasses the entire value chain.'[7] Operational segmentation, on the other hand, identifies groups of buyers with common needs in order to formulate different product and market approaches. What strategic segmentation is not about is tactical issues such as where to advertise to get the best audience 'reach' for promotional messages; which types of distributive outlet have the optimum customer profile; and where the sales force can locate potential customers. The behavioural segmentation used in strategic segmentation differs from operational marketing segmentation because it is based on what consumers do rather than what they are or how they are organized. Strategic segmentation is about the circumstances in which customers find themselves. Operational marketing segmentation is about the customers themselves. Put another way, the critical unit of analysis for strategic segmentation is the circumstance not the customer.[8] Put simply, one is concerned with segmenting the market for strategic reasons and the other for marketing reasons. Often the differences are small, but nonetheless there is a huge difference in philosophy.

What strategic segmentation is going to tell us is why differences in products and buyers fundamentally affect the requirements for gaining competitive advantage. What operational segmentation tells us is that different groups of buyers should be approached in different ways in order to make a sale. For example, an airline might segment its customers into leisure, business and freight and offer a different package of benefits to each. Leisure passengers will be more price sensitive than business passengers, who buy more on comfort and convenience. Overlaying this is the product: long haul and short haul. For an airline, the combination of leisure passenger and short haul means a different way of doing business than leisure passenger/long haul. Short haul leisure services in Europe are characterized by severe price competition from 'no-frills' airlines. General carriers must either respond in kind by creating their own no-frills operations, as British Airways did with GO, or focus on the business passenger and sell surplus capacity at marginal cost to leisure travellers, as British Airways did once it had sold GO. Strategic segmentation tells us to identify product/buyer differences that give rise to differences in the basis of competition in the same market.

The trouble with most business text books is that they do precisely what I have just done. They take a perfectly obvious example with which everyone can identify to illustrate the point being made. The problem in CDD is that you are not dealing with clear-cut cases like the difference between Ryanair and British Airways, but with narrow, specialist markets where segmentation is a difficult and rarely tackled exercise. If, for example, you look further at Figure 3.3 above, you will soon discover that there are differences in the uses of both the access platform and scaffolding and the markets can be sub-segmented. There is a big difference between specialized access platforms (narrow and high, used for cleaning windows and light maintenance inside buildings) and non-specialized access platforms (motorized access platforms for light maintenance outside). The former are used by electricians, painters and window cleaners, the latter by mechanical maintenance companies. Similarly, with scaffolding. Large scaffolding installations, for example to refurbish a tower block and specialist applications, say inside Terminal 1 at Heathrow Airport, where the scaffolding has to be put up and taken down between 1:00 AM and 5:00 AM every night, satisfy different customer needs and require different operating styles. Arguably, therefore, they are different markets. A proper understanding of the customer needs satisfied by the target, coupled with some creative reasoning by an experienced team and a eureka moment the next day, will get you a sensible basis for strategic segmentation, but the point is that there is no escape from the fact that you will have to do the segmentation yourself and that this requires creativity.

There are no generally accepted and validated ways of segmenting markets and segmentation most certainly is not about rolling megabytes of customer data in the expectation that some magical understanding will pop out. Many managers have been trained to believe that precise information and immaculate information systems are the hallmarks of professionalism and that therefore a scientific approach is the only approach to business analysis. This is not the case in market segmentation. Segmentation is a process of critical thinking rather than the application of some predetermined set of criteria to the numbers. Meaningful strategic segments are not usually chunks of the market identifiable by concrete statistics such as sales by type of product or number of people with the same demographic and social class characteristics. The truth is more likely to be the exact opposite. Segmenting markets is a qualitative process. It must be, otherwise it would be impossible for successful entrepreneurs to define new ways of meeting customer needs. Market segmentation calls for creativity and tolerance of imprecise definitions as is demonstrated in Case Study 13.

CASE STUDY 13

SEVERE SERVICE VALVES

Valves are used in process industries to control the flow of liquids. By and large they are commodity products, although there is a premium for high performance valves that have to cope with extreme pressures, as in nuclear power stations, or extremely corrosive materials, for example in the manufacture of nitric acid.

In some process industries, there are a small number of valves which, if they go wrong, will cause the plant to under-perform. In extreme cases, failure of these same valves will cause massive damage. These are the valves that keep the production director awake. They are not necessarily the same as the high-performance valves. There is one company that specializes in supplying these

CASE STUDY 13 – *continued*

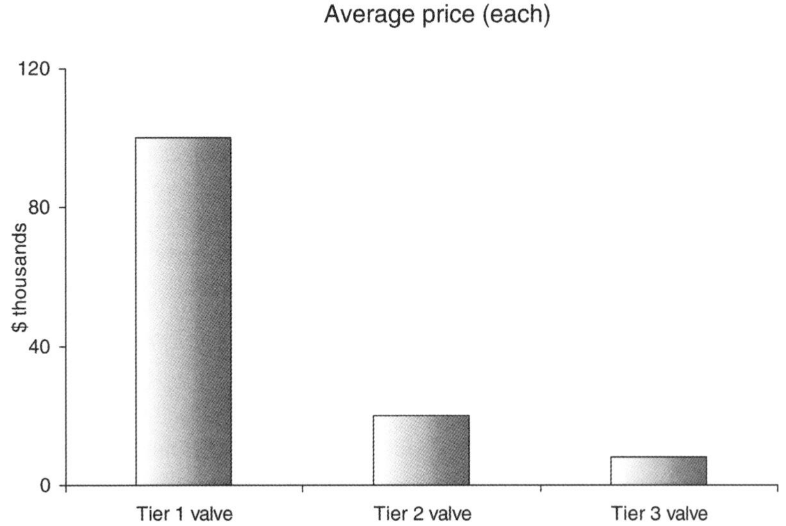

Figure 3.4 Relative price levels in the same 'commodity' market
Source: AMR International

critical valves or, more accurately, the engineering solutions that allow the production director to get a good night's rest, for they are a lot more than devices that control flow in critical areas. Figure 3.4 shows the price premium they attract.

The problem with segmenting the market for this company is that the borders between its 'severe service' valves and the rest of the market is a matter of degree. At the very top end of the market there are no substitutes, but the further you come from the top, the

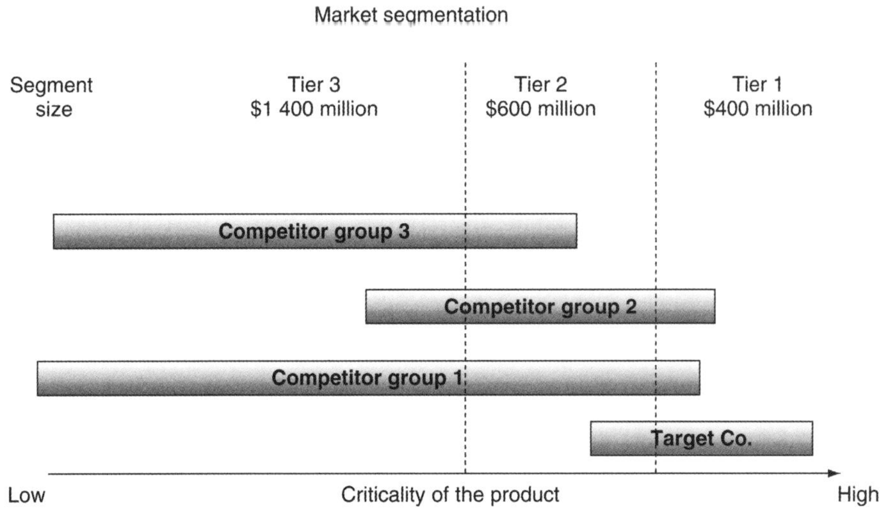

Figure 3.5 Segmentation of the 'commodity' industrial valve market
Source: AMR International

CASE STUDY 13 – *continued*

more substitutes there are. Beyond a certain point, whether or not a customer uses the company's solution or a substitute is partly a matter of budget and partly an attitude to risk. In identical plants there might be five of the company's valves in one and none in another. What, then, is the market potential for the product? Figure 3.5 sets out the possibilities.

The world market is somewhere between \$400 million and \$1,400 million, depending where you draw the line and the target either has an 80 per cent share or a 30 per cent share. Not much difference there then. The real truth is that although the theoretical market is \$1,400 million, the actual market will never be that big because of budget constraints. The potential is nearer \$600 million and the current market is a little above \$400 million.

The worry with such woolly thinking about boundaries is that markets will be drawn too narrow or too wide. Both are easily done. It is said, for example, that Jack Welsh at GE had his managers define their markets in such a way that GE had only a 1 per cent share. On the other hand, if I had a pound for every managing director who has told me his business has no competition, I would be a millionaire. It all comes back to thinking hard about customer wants. If you cannot satisfy those wants, you are not in the market. I suspect Mr Welsh's intention was to create a bit of entrepreneurial tension by making sure his managers had plenty to aim at. He wanted them to innovate and showing them that there was another 99 per cent of the market to go for was a sure way of doing it. At the other end of the spectrum, every organization has competitors – whether it accepts it or not. There may only be one Post Office in the UK, but there are hundreds of courier firms all taking a piece of the letter and small package delivery market and the explosive growth of email must be taking a large chunk of the Post Office's traditional letter market. Similarly, what market is the Police Force in and should it be worried by the rise in private security firms?[9]

Poor or non-existent market segmentation is surprising, since segmentation goes right to the heart of the marketing process. If market strategy is all about setting priorities on the basis of market attractiveness and market position, companies cannot hope to have a coherent market strategy if they do not first decide what segments they are serving and what customers in those segments want from them. The fact is, they cannot and do not. They tend to segment their markets instinctively and use a great deal of trial and error in so doing.

The real world of business is not quite the haven of scientific analysis the marketing text books would have us believe. However, as far as CDD is concerned, there is no excuse not to get strategic segmentation right because by definition there are structural reasons why markets segment as they do. The up side is that pinpointing the structural factors at work gets you half way to uncovering the magic mentioned at the beginning of this book.

Strategic segmentation

The starting point in segmentation is customer choice. The segmentation process means that in a multi-product company the market for each product range needs to be examined separately as in Figure 3.6. We return to this later in the chapter.

Customer groups \ Product varieties	Product variety 1	Product variety 2	Etc.
1. Customer group 1 (primary need 1 in common)			
2. Customer group 2 (primary need 2 in common)			
3. Customer group 3 (primary need 3 in common)			

Figure 3.6 A framework for defining strategic segmentation

As Mathur and Kenyon[10] point out, customers do not choose a product or a company; their unit of choice is the single offering. Competitive strategy is 'the triangular positioning of a single offering vis-à-vis a unique set of potential customers and competitors'. Thus, London's Dorchester Hotel comprises a number of separate offerings: luxury hotel accommodation, restaurant services, cocktail bar drinks, and various personal services and retail products. The customers for these may be much the same, but each will have a separate set of competitors and therefore its own unique market. One acquisition was halted when the acquirer examined the component parts of the target and found that while the target was growing overall, all the growth was coming from 'add-ons' and that the core business not growing all.

The result, then, is a much more micro view of the external environment and competitive strategy than that associated with the conventional industry analysis of Porter and others. These fail to take into account the specifics of competition at the level of individual offerings. In CDD, it is essential to understand the target's performance at this micro-level because the target's competitive position is the sum of the performance of individual offerings in relation to specific groups of customers and competitors.

ANALYSING MARKETS

As strategic segmentation is about different ways in which customer requirements are satisfied, the best way to start looking at markets is to start wide, by defining all the different approaches, and finish narrow by homing in on the specific segment(s) served. Start wide and focus down in steps until you reach a market boundary that best captures where the target competes. The segmentation process is set out in Figure 3.7.

Think of it as a series of photographs taken from the same spot, which start with a broad panorama showing the town and the fields beyond. One by one the vistas are cut out until the final photograph shows the particular feature or building of interest. The boundaries will always be blurred, but try to think in terms of the ease of substitution. If the customer need is for an orange and only an orange will do, the market we are looking at is the one for oranges. If an orange could be substituted by a grapefruit or a lemon, the market is for citrus fruit. If the customer is happy to swap an orange for a banana or an apple, the market is for fruit.

A market is not the same as an industry

The starting point in getting to a market definition is management's definition. What does it regard as the market? The drawback with this approach is that companies tend to define

Figure 3.7 Strategic segmentation and CDD

their market in terms of groups of companies that sell similar products and services, which is a definition of the 'industry' rather than the 'market'. There is an important distinction to be made between the two, which goes to the very heart of market analysis. Industries are groups of companies linked by technology or product similarities. Markets are groups of customers linked together by needs and wants. They may be the same, but often they are not.

BENEFITS-BASED BUYER SEGMENTATION

Customers are not interested in the 'industry', only in meeting their own needs. The buyer's decision process is set out in Figure 3.8.

Customer needs are therefore one of the two basic building blocks of market definition. (The other is the products and services that go into the market to meet these needs.) As already mentioned, as far as customer needs are concerned a market's boundaries are defined by substitutability. On the supply side, a market is defined by a group of firms competing to satisfy the same needs in a variety of different ways. Note, competing to satisfy the same needs, not supplying the same product.

Fortunately for us, we are in the business of defining markets and market segments from the inside. Our interest is in drawing boundaries. We are not in the highly creative business of coming up with new ways of segmenting markets, which is the focus of most of the academic literature on the topic. I say 'fortunately', because it means we are concerned for

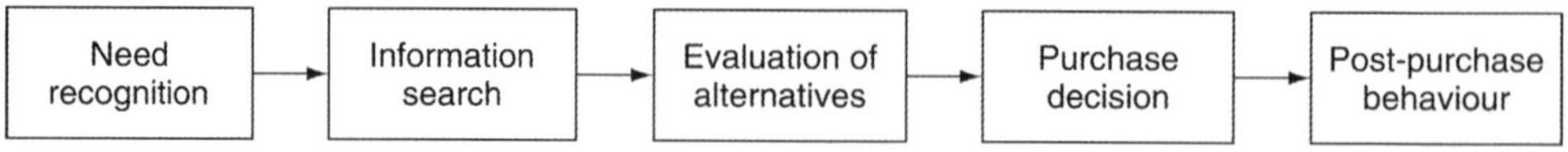

Figure 3.8 Acquirer decision process

the moment at any rate, with the status quo rather than what the market might be. This means that we can again start with questions to management to get from industry to markets and from there to segments within markets.

Sadly, such information usually has to be extracted. Although a fundamentally important concept for all businesses, segmentation is all too frequently neglected. Business plans do not normally talk about market segmentation in any meaningful sense, especially if they have been ghosted by the financial advisers on the deal. In fact, business plans written by financial advisers can be highly misleading, so handle them with great care. Management usually has a pretty good idea of how the market really works, as indeed you would hope and expect, but it usually takes a lengthy questioning session to get it out of them. The trouble is that companies' internal systems do not allow a view of the market that reflects the different groupings of customer needs – which is why meaningful segmentation does not reach the business plan – and in any case market segmentation is so obvious to management that it is taken for granted.

A useful way of extracting the analysis can simply be to go through the product range and list beside each the type of customer and why they buy, as shown earlier in Figure 3.6. But be warned, management will have difficulty doing this because to them each stock keeping unit (SKU) is a product. It is not. The important thing is to think like the customer. The customer thinks in terms of benefits, not in terms of specific products. This is page 1, paragraph 1 of any sales text book; companies sell benefits not features. This links back to strategy because for a target company, market attractiveness and competitive position are both about satisfying needs. If more people have more of the same need, then the market is growing and therefore attractive (but more on that later). If the target company can satisfy those needs better than the competition, it has a strong competitive position. Simple.

Therefore the key to strategic segmentation is to define the market from the customer's perspective. Focus on the fundamental customer benefits sought in different parts of the market, that is, the need or problem to be solved, whether from physical product differences or from non-product attributes. As with operational marketing segmentation and product segmentation, it is often necessary to use proxies to get at needs being satisfied in the various sub-markets. It is these that are now discussed.

PROXIES

Markets tend to structure themselves in certain ways for sound economic reasons to do with the different customer needs and how they are satisfied. There is a myriad of clues to look out for. The following sections list the most common.

Size of order

The size of the order, or average job size, can have a pervasive effect on the way an industry competes. For example, there are many companies capable of wiring up client/server computer systems. However, there are only three, maximum, in the whole of the UK capable of wiring up the gigantic computer installations used by the big financial institutions. Given the criticality of those systems, customers are extremely selective. Entry barriers are therefore high. The small system end of the market is a fragmented, near commodity type contracting business. The market at the large system end is a highly ordered duopoly where technical competence and creativity play a far greater part than price in the customer purchase decision.

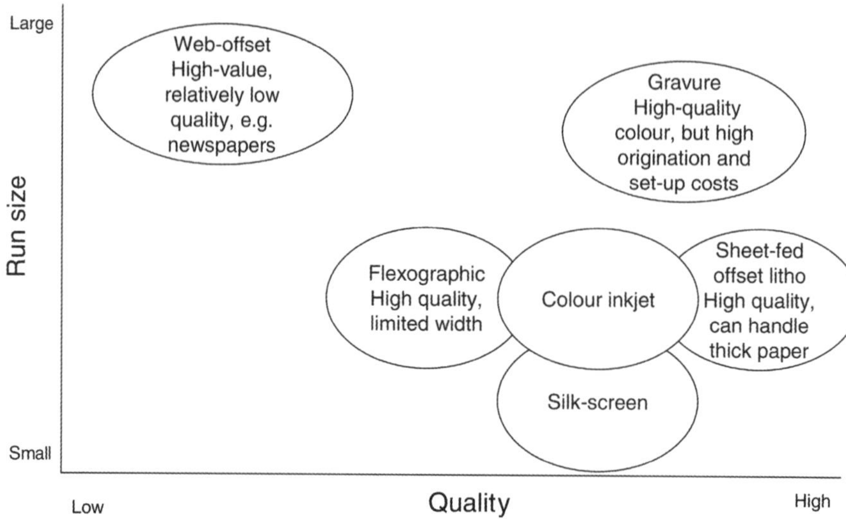

Figure 3.9 Segmentation of the printing industry by technology

Technology

Strategically segmenting markets by the different ways in which the same end result is achieved is the one of the most self-evident ways in which markets can be segmented. The printing industry, for example, can be segmented into a number of different markets as in Figure 3.9. Printing technology determines fixed and variable printing costs and print quality and therefore suitability for different types of job.

Believe it or not, there exist instruments for measuring the runniness of products such as toothpaste and mayonnaise. This is the science of rheometry. At one end of the market are highly sophisticated, flexible, machines costing £40 000 plus, bought and operated by specialists with PhDs in rheometry. At the other end of the market are scaled down instruments used by lab technicians to measure the viscosity of tarmac. These are two very different markets even though the machines do the same thing.

Customer technology

Customer technology often defines needs and therefore segmentation as Case Study 14 shows.

CASE STUDY 14

ENTERPRISE ELECTRICITY MANAGEMENT

Large industrial consumers of electricity have strategically placed electricity meters in large numbers in their factories. Such Enterprise Electricity Management (EEM) has been around for years. The potential purchaser of a successful Canadian manufacturer of electricity meters assumed that EEM would become more widespread as European electricity markets de-regulated allowing large industrial users of electricity to be more selective about tariffs and to trade any self-generated electricity. This would drive demand for meters. Here was a deal made in heaven. The Canadian company had years of experience in the already de-regulated North American market. The potential purchaser

CASE STUDY 14 – *continued*

had the sales infrastructure and contacts in Europe. Great, except that there is nothing special about EEM meters. They are commodity products supplied with specialist software by factory automation giants such as Siemens, usually as part of a much bigger package that the Canadian target company would not be able to supply and in which it had no expertise. What the client had not understood, although it should have, and the Canadian target had not bothered to make plain, but should have, is that the Canadians owed their success to supplying very specialist meters, loaded with software, which were used to improve the quality of electricity supply not to monitor electricity usage. Even a glance at its customer base showed that the bulk of purchases were by customers whose business relied on computers, such as banks and 'server farms', or other equipment with a low tolerance to spiky alternating current. The target's own website even included a case study on NASA's use of its meters because of its need for the 'clean' electricity supply.

Supplying NASA with hi-tech meters is a very different business to supplying paper manufacturers with EEM meters. Interviews with industrial customers in Europe confirmed the existence of a distinct hi-tech 'current cleaning' segment and it was no accident that the target's industrial customers in Europe were in southern Europe where electricity supply was not as reliable as in the north.

End market for the product

Sometimes where the end product is used is an important determinant of buyer characteristics and therefore central to strategic segmentation as in Case Study 15.

CASE STUDY 15

CYCLE COMPONENTS

Taking its name from the street in which its factory was located, the Raleigh Bicycle Company was formed in 1890. By 1951, Raleigh was producing over 1 million bikes and when it merged with TI (Tube Investments) Group in 1960, it became the world's largest producer of two-wheeled personal transport. Sturmey Archer had become part of Raleigh in the early 1900s. The Sturmey Archer three-speed gear hub, the world's first practical gearing system, was offered to the public in 1903. It was a great technological breakthrough that helped to change the face of cycling. By the early 1980s, Sturmey Archer was still best known for the three-speed hub gears that were common on 'utility' bicycles at the time and hub brakes, which were a standard piece of equipment on most European city bikes. Here it had a competitive advantage based on volume and brand name. Over the years, it had added other products to its portfolio on the back of its position as captive supplier to Raleigh. This was fine until Raleigh itself was forced into a painful period of restructuring, which exposed its competitive weakness in non-Commonwealth markets. One of the first actions of new management at the time was to critically examine the cost base, including the cost of components. Look at any bike and what you see is a tubular frame from which is hung a myriad of complex components. What the new management found, not surprisingly, was that it could buy most components more cheaply from specialist

CASE STUDY 15 – continued

manufacturers set up to supply them on a global basis than it could from Sturmey Archer. Raleigh soon started to source saddles from Italy, single-speed hubs from Austria and derailleur gears from Taiwan. Sturmey Archer management was devastated, but was left with no choice but to examine its own strengths and weaknesses. It soon defined itself as a manufacturer of gears – which it was with the three-speed hub – but what it did not do was to segment the market for gears quite enough. I can still remember the look of horror on the face of the young MBA who was told that five-speed gears were to be the saviour of the company and it was his job to put together a successful marketing plan. He soon realized that there were huge differences between five-speed derailleur gears for the mass market (at the time mainly 'racing' bikes for school kids), three-speed hub gears for utility bikes (mainly ladies and gents 'tourers') and 10-/15-speed derailleur sets for the enthusiast. While Sturmey Archer had a reasonable chance in the last two segments, where gears were bought on the basis of technical excellence and a recognized brand name, it had no chance in the first, where gears were bought on price from Far Eastern volume manufacturers such as Shimano.

Quality/performance requirements/desired features

Figure 3.10 shows segmentation in the truck hire market. Here, the market splits into three distinct groups determined by the sophistication of the truck in question and the amount of management required by the truck hirer as a result. At the top end are the customized vehicles required for specialist applications, for example baggage handling at airports. At the

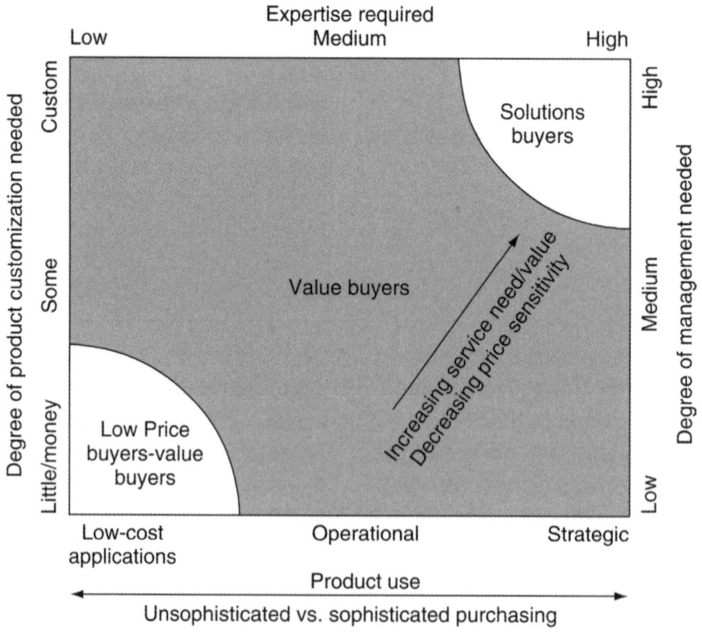

Figure 3.10 Customer needs segmentation model

bottom end are the standard trucks used in general freight applications where price is the most important competitive factor.

Company strategy

Different companies in the same market operate in different ways and these differences can form the basis for segmenting their suppliers. For example, 'A differentiated, high margin food processor is more concerned with ingredient quality and consistency than a private label food manufacturer that competes on cost.'[11] Steel makers have always been sniffy about steel stockholders, seeing them as parasites who steal business from UK mills by bringing in cheap imports. What they have never bothered to do is to look a bit more closely at those stockholders. Many do sell commodity products on price as machining feedstock, but many others provide a value-added service to customers who want to receive their material with basic pre-machining operations, such as cutting or drilling, already carried out so that they can concentrate on the proprietary manufacturing operations that add the most value. Which stockholders are in which group is largely a function of the strategy of their customers.

Strategic groups

Another way of homing in on the market is to understand the different ways in which customer needs are satisfied. Within most markets there will be different companies doing different things but, as with steel stockholders, it is usually possible to discern groups of companies that have adopted more or less similar approaches to competing within the industry that are quite different from those of other groups. The example given by Johnson and Scholes[12] demonstrates the concept admirably:

> *Ford and Morgan cars are in the same industry (automobiles) but are they competitors? The former is a publicly quoted multinational business, the latter is owned by a British family, produces about 500 cars a year and concentrates on a specialist market niche where customers want hand-built cars and are prepared to wait up to four years for one.*

Strategic group analysis uses the characteristics of firms as a proxy for strategic segmentation on the assumption that different groups serving the market in different ways must be serving different segments. A strategic group is a group of firms in a market following the same or a similar strategy. Similar approaches may include product market scope (product range and geographical breadth), choice of distribution channels, level of product quality, degree of vertical integration, choice of technology, and so on. The trick is to select the most important strategic dimensions and locate each firm in the industry along them:

1. Identify competitive characteristics that differentiate firms in a market from one another.
2. Plot firms on a two-variable map using pairs of these differentiating characteristics. Variables selected as axes should not be highly correlated and should be chosen to expose the big differences in how rivals compete. If more than two good competitive variables can be used, several maps can be drawn.
3. Assign firms that fall in about the same place on the map to the same strategic group.

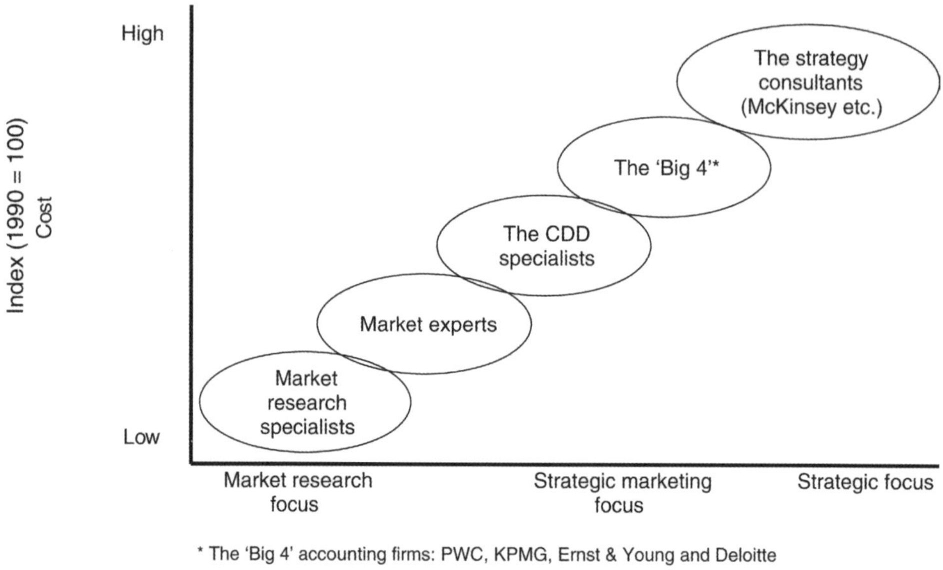

Figure 3.11 Strategic groups in CDD

4 Draw circles around each group, making circles proportionate to the size of the group's respective share of total industry sales. This allows the map to reflect the relative size of each strategic group.

Figure 3.11 shows an example of drawing strategic groups.

In addition to being a proxy for strategic segmentation, strategic group analysis can contribute substantially to the understanding of industry structure, firm strategy and industry evolution by helping to paint the broad picture mentioned earlier that includes the types of firms within in the industry, its viable strategies and how different firms are positioned in relation to one another. Figure 3.12, is a real-life example. The target claimed it was part of a fast-growing market and therefore had a great future. The prospective acquirer was not so sure. The acquirer was right for all sorts of reasons to do with end-use and technical specification and one of the most compelling pieces of evidence was the sales growth history of the target's product, which was completely different to that of the market as a whole, thus confirming that it belonged in a separate market segment.

GEOGRAPHIC BOUNDARIES

In most markets, both consumer and business-to-business, there will be clear geographic boundaries, defined by substitutability. In this case, substitutability is how far, geographically speaking, customers go to substitute supply. If a British supplier can be economically substituted by a German supplier but not a Chinese one, the relevant market is Europe. A good test of geographical boundaries is price. If there are no significant differences between the prices of the same product between different locations, these locations lie within a single market.

Sometimes geographic segmentation needs careful thought. Duropal, a German manufacturer, has around a third of the 'upmarket' sector of the UK laminate worktops

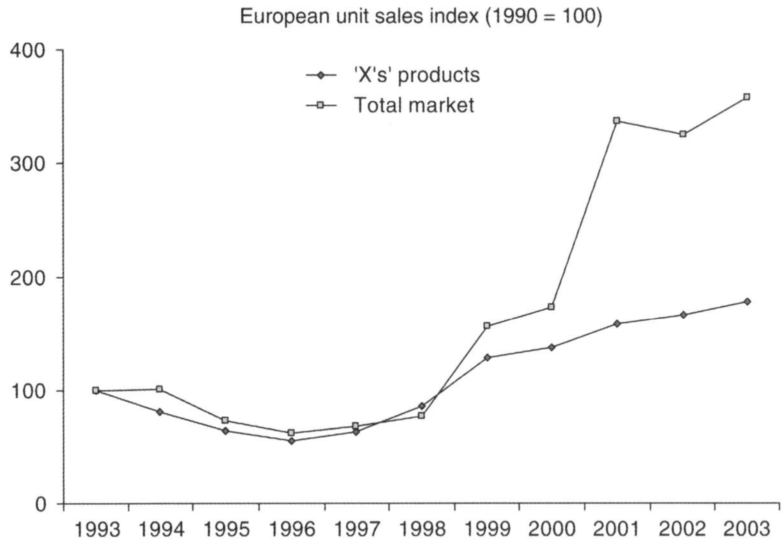

Figure 3.12 Sales of 'X's' products have followed a different pattern to the overall market

market. This does not mean that the relevant market is Europe. Laminate worktops are difficult to transport, raw materials are freely available and sales depend on access to distribution. Duropal has this access in the UK and can sell at a premium to recoup its cost disadvantage because of the brand reputation it was able to create in the early days of fitted kitchens, when to be a German supplier was a distinct advantage. Other German suppliers would find it difficult to replicate Duropal's success. The relevant boundary is the UK, where it just happens that there is a strong German supplier. The Duropal example notwithstanding, geographic boundaries will normally be confirmed by market shares. If German suppliers have a dominant share in Germany but not in Europe, the market is Germany.

Products and services that go into the market

By products we mean products and all variations. Products may be sold separately, they may be sold with a service or the service may be sold separately. Figure 3.13 is the classic definition of a product first set out by Theodore Levitt.[13]

The CDD technique is once again to start wide, by identifying everything, then slowly narrow the options until only realistic substitutes for the target's product or services are left. There is a long list of proxies that are used to uncover product differences that imply different ways of doing business. These are listed below:

- Size: different sized products may need different machines or need to be handled differently.
- Price levels: price can be a good indicator of design or physical features that sets one group of products apart from another. There is a huge price difference between machining steels and bearing steels. Although both are steel long products, they are sometimes made in different ways and have very different performance characteristics.

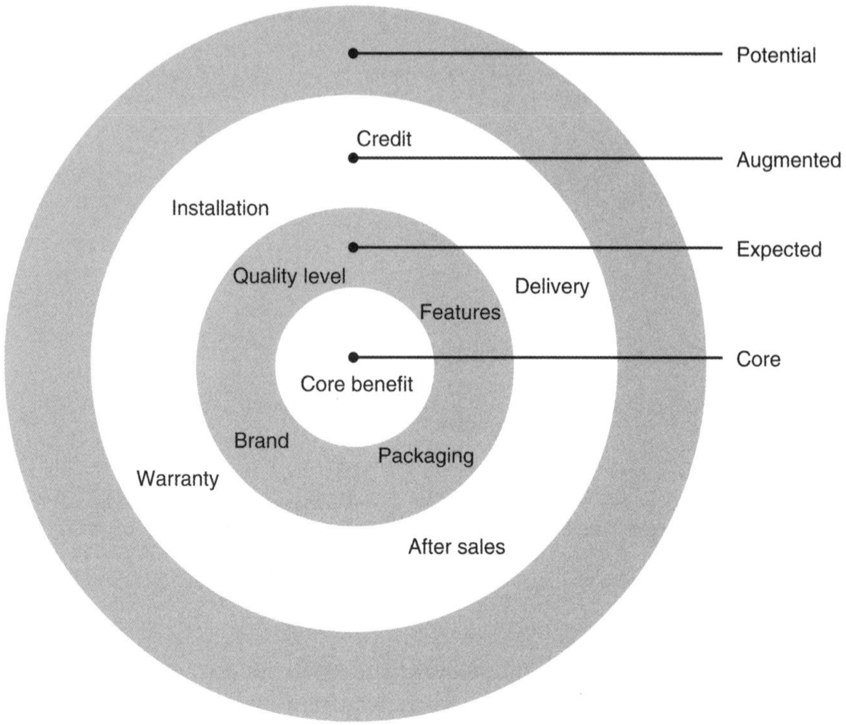

Figure 3.13 Four levels of product

- Features: features can point to strategic product differences such as differences in technological sophistication (see Case Study 14).
- Technology or design: for example, electrochemical sensors are very different from semiconductor sensors and serve different markets. Although ostensibly both technologies do the same job, there are big differences in what they can actually do. Electrochemical sensors work by generating an electrical signal in response to reversible physical or chemical changes brought about when they are exposed to gases. Semiconductor sensors are the closest rival to electrochemical technology, but have always been considered inferior in both their sensitivity and their reliability, and because they require a permanent power source, they cannot be used in many hazardous environments. Furthermore, the change in the silicon requires amplification equipment. This additional baggage limits the applications of the technology and makes them unsuitable for use in portable monitors, which is the biggest user of electrochemical sensors. Semiconductor sensors have therefore been traditionally limited to gas detection (that is, presence/absence of a gas) rather than monitoring and the major applications are for CO detection in homes, offices and car parks.
- Inputs: by and large, steel makers who use scrap as their raw material produce different products for different markets from those who use iron ore (Nucor in the USA is the famous exception).
- Volume/order size: there is a product-market difference between products used in bulk and those supplied singly. Figure 3.14 shows the UK stationery market. This segments by order size and frequency of order.

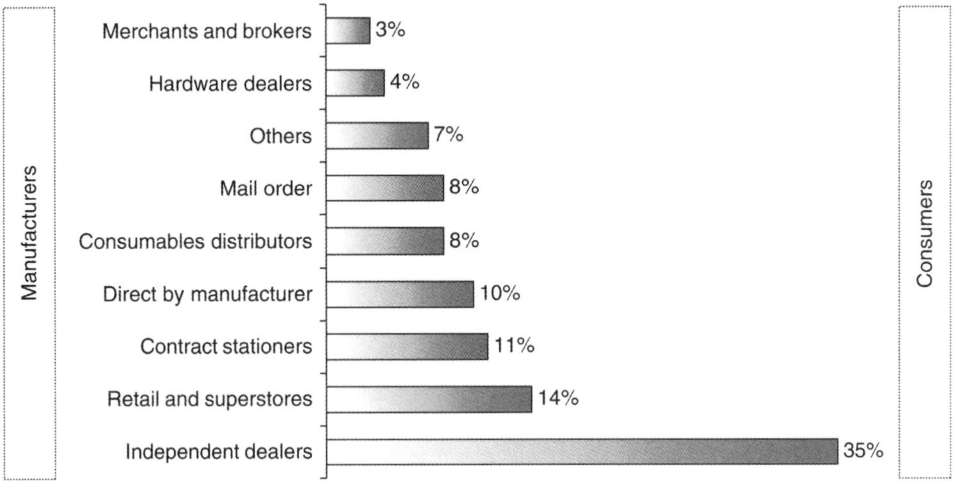

Figure 3.14 The supply of office products to the UK market

- Performance: for example, professional catering equipment is different from that which is found in domestic kitchens.
- New versus replacement: this can be a valid basis for strategic segmentation. In Germany, consumers want to replace the exhaust system, shock absorbers, brake pads and other wear items with an identical part from the original manufacturer. If you drive a BMW and you have to replace the windscreen wipers, you will only buy identical wipers to those originally fitted. It stands to reason that to be successful in the German replacement market you have to be a leading supplier to the car makers. The situation in the UK could not be more different. Apart from first-owned cars, which normally go back to the manufacturer's dealer for repair and servicing (and which are still under guarantee anyway), price is the dominant purchase criterion. As a result, there in exists in the UK a host of companies that supply non-genuine replacement car parts sold through a distinct replacement distribution channel.
- Bundled versus unbundled: facilities management is a loose term that covers everything from doing the cleaning and running the staff restaurant right through to the strategic management and servicing of global property portfolios. Its structure is outlined in Figure 3.15. The markets at the three different levels are very different from each other.

Market sizing

It is unlikely that there will be accurate data to size any specific product or niche market and the cost of making highly accurate estimates can be high. However, reasonable estimates can be made based on available data. You are trying to calculate the size of the 'relevant market', that is what the target company's sales would be if it were to capture 100 per cent of its specific niche of the market. This means taking a 'top-down' approach to sizing the market in which the market for any product can be viewed as a fraction of the overall target population. The trick is to define the target population(s) and make dependable estimations about the likelihood of individuals or groups within that population purchasing the product.

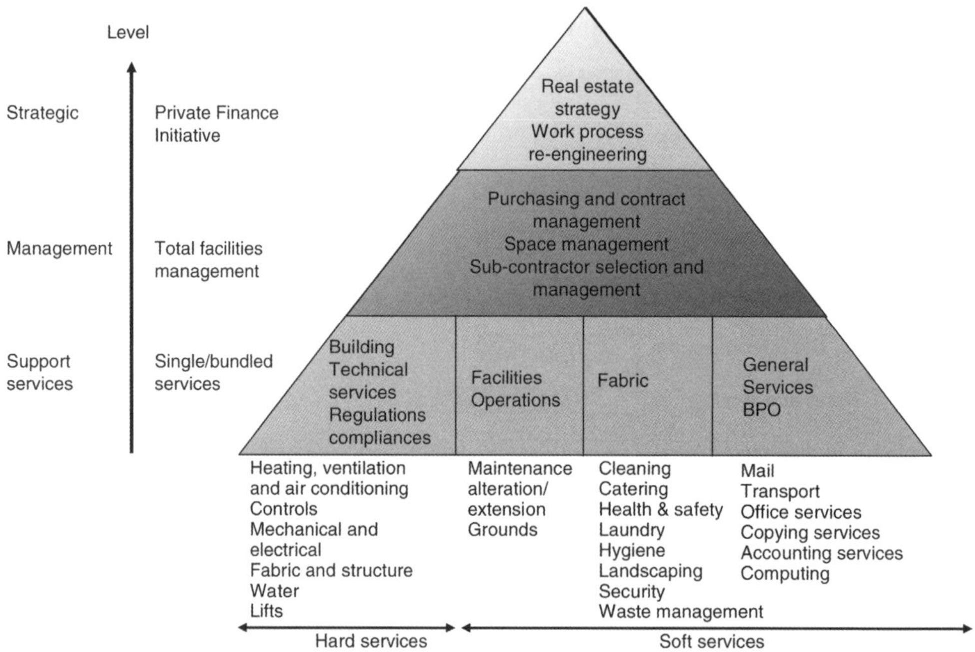

Figure 3.15 Facilities management covers a wide range of activities and takes place on three levels

DEFINE THE UNIVERSE

Begin by defining the universe: what is it you are trying to size, what it includes and what it does not include. Start with this generic market, remove pieces of it that are not relevant until the target population is established by having narrowed down larger populations, that is:

- Define the maximum possible population. This is the population that includes all groups of the potential end-users. For example, fast-food companies, women over 30, manufacturing companies. This represents the largest possible target market in the unlikely event that 100 per cent of the population buys the product.
- Define the sub-populations. Within the overall population, are there sub-populations of interest? For example, within the domain of manufacturing companies, maybe only those of 250 people or more are of interest, or within fast-food manufacturers, is it only certain operations that are of interest? This may be further refined to isolate specific sectors.

Figure 3.16 shows this logical approach applied to laser hair removal. In this case, population statistics to start the process going are easily obtained (17.8 million women aged between 16 and 74).

In other cases, it may be necessary to purchase data to start the process. Figure 3.17 shows the same approach to market sizing, starting wide and finishing narrow, but this time using bought data. Figure 3.17 sizes the potential market for an Internet-based chemist hoping to take advantage of a move to e-prescriptions.

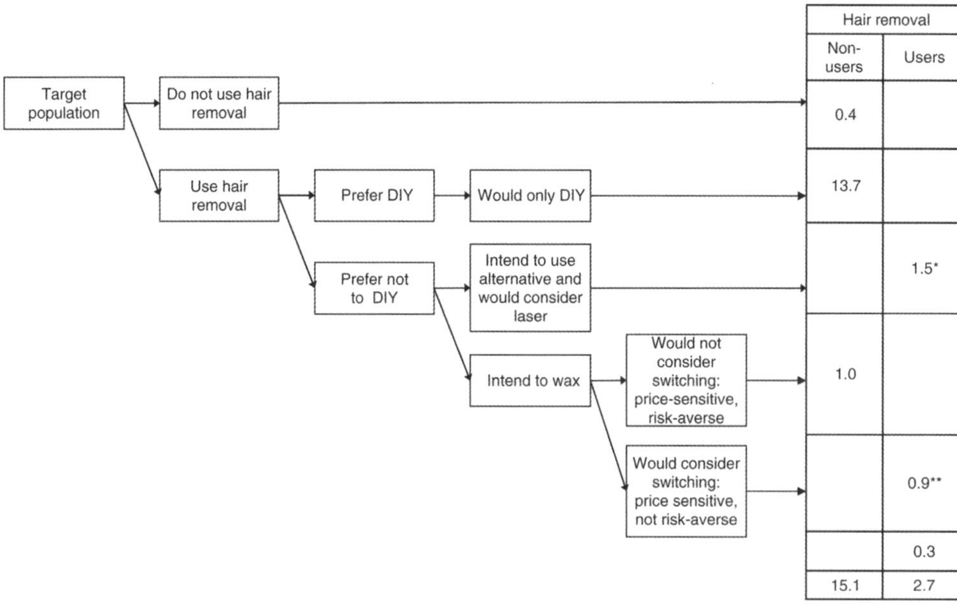

Figure 3.16 The potential population of female laser hair removal users (millions)
Notes: * Assumes 10% of the DIY market
** Survey data suggests roughly 50% of wax users would seek an alternative
DIY = do-it-yourself

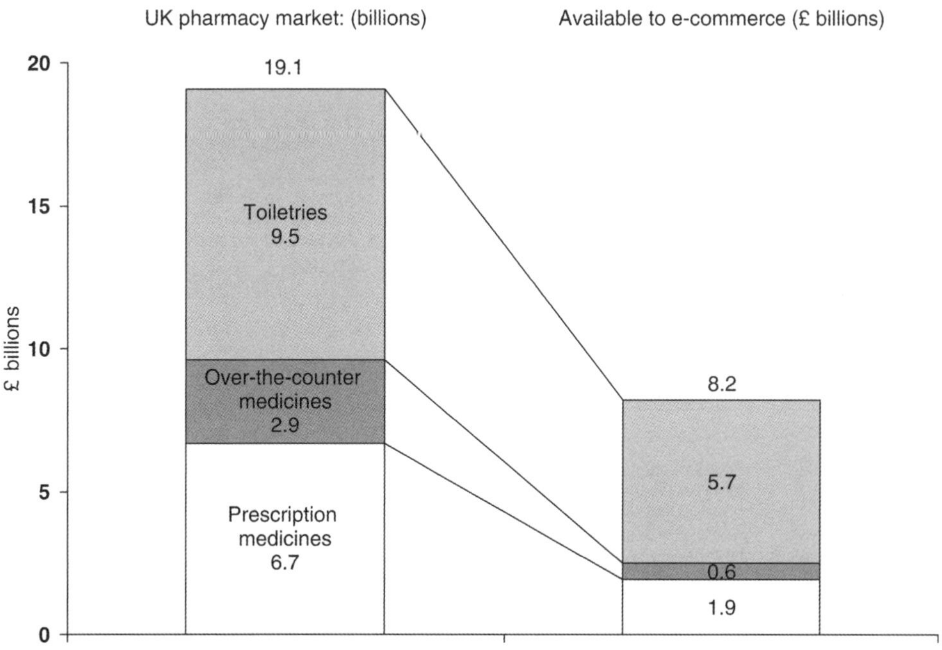

Figure 3.17 Potential market size for an online pharmacy

DO NOT BE AFRAID TO MAKE ASSUMPTIONS

For a typical market sizing exercise you may have six to 10 key assumptions. Keep them on a separate spreadsheet with notes alongside. You can then test these to death with all the sources you can find, particularly interviews.

Assumptions do not have to be wild guesses. The '10 per cent DIY would change' assumption in Figure 3.17 was an inspired guess based on asking around friends and acquaintances. Not terribly scientific, but good enough and it was tested for reasonableness quite rigourously later on. In another exercise, the market sizing had to come up with the number of modern houses built with a room in the roof. There are no national statistics on this but the chances are that the housing developments near you are not unrepresentative of the total, and once again it can be tested in interviews with builders and planning authorities.

KEEP THE PROCESS LOGICAL

Market sizing is all about using a logical process. If you can show your workings then other members of the team and the client can challenge your assumptions at every stage.

BUILD IN CROSS-CHECKS

If your target company has £25 million sales and thinks it has a 25 per cent share of the market (at manufacturer's selling prices), you can bet that the finance director will be cross-checking your market size figure against this. If you come up with a market at wholesale prices of £120–£150 million, you are probably OK; any difference and you'll have to answer in detail for your numbers. Tip: do the common sense cross-check before you finalize the numbers. Also do your market sizing from multiple angles. Figure 3.18 shows the process used to size the market for tool repairs. As can be seen there is a cross-check built in at every stage.

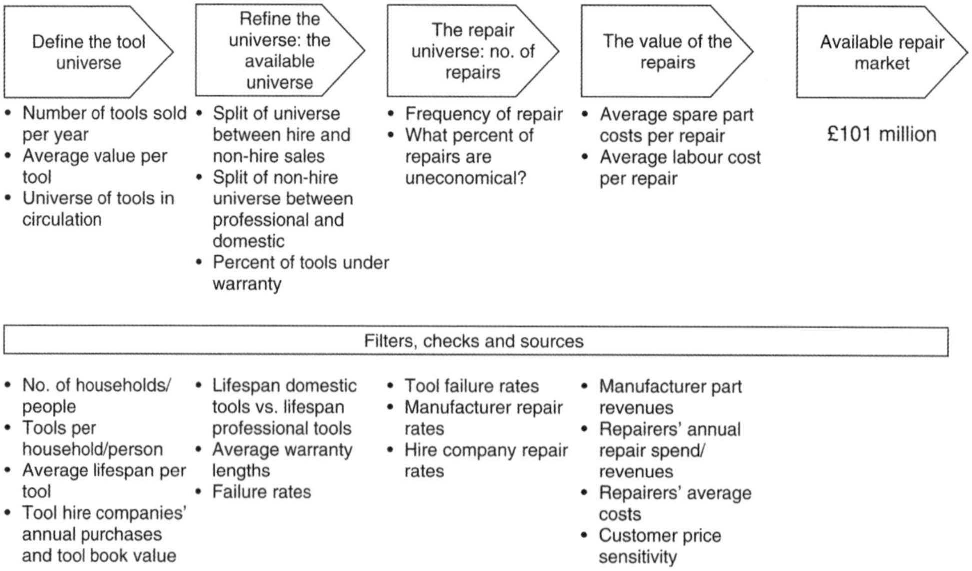

Figure 3.18 The key to market sizing is to follow a logical, deductive approach

USE TARGETED INTERVIEWS

Most market reports are rubbish, but inside most companies there will be people who spend a lot of time thinking about market sizes, shares, growth, and so on. Usually they love it if someone interested in the same subject calls them up. For example, some tool manufacturers (for example, Hilti) do all the repairs for their tools. Using their ratio of repairs to sales and applying market values to repair rates gives a good market benchmark. The research that went into Figure 3.18 included interviews with 25 manufactures to get their spares sales and repair revenue estimates. Using targeted interviews adds considerable value to market sizing.

CONSIDER ANALOGOUS MARKETS

If data is not available directly, are there any analogous markets? For example, if you are analysing machine tools, is there a relationship with the market for steel or usage of electricity? If you are estimating the market for water filters, is there a relationship to water consumption or maybe the sales of kettles? Are there any associations between the purchase of one product or another? For example, commercial vehicle production statistics may be related to the demand for truck tyres.

In developing markets, use case studies to look at what other markets have experienced when they have been through similar transformations, customer adoption rates in those markets, and so on.

MAKE SURE DEFINITIONS ARE CONSISTENT

Using units is the most certain way of estimating a market. You can always multiply by average price later. Some products do not have a single unit, in which case you have to convert everything to a standard. Make sure you do and that everyone understands what it is. Similarly with prices. Are you using retail price? Retail less discount? Wholesale price? It really does not matter which as long as you are consistent.

IDENTIFY UNCERTAINTIES

How confident are you in your assessments? Make sure assumptions, extrapolations and uncertainties are made clear.

YOU WILL NEVER BE 100 PER CENT RIGHT, SO DO NOT TRY TO BE

Obviously, market quantifications should be as accurate as possible. However, understanding trends and factors driving profitability within the market can be even more important than the market size itself. It is less relevant to know that a market is worth £90 million or £110 million than to know that in five years' time all the competitors will have had their margins halved due to intensifying competition.

Conclusion

This chapter started by pointing out the obvious. If you want to analyse the attractiveness of a target company's market, you first have to define what that market is. Defining the market(s) in which the company competes is fundamental to CDD. Its aim is to draw boundaries around the market. A market is not the same as an industry. Strategic market segmentation defines markets according to customer needs. Substitution defines the boundaries between one sub-market and the next. To define a market, you have to understand those customer needs and wants. A short-cut can be provided by observing the way in which the market defines itself and testing the resulting hypothesis. There are many variables that can used in strategic segmentation. The important point to keep in mind at all times is whether they lead to fundamental differences in industry structure. If so, they are meaningful variables in segmenting the market. The key test of the geographical boundaries of a market is price: if there are no significant differences between the prices of the same product between different locations, then these locations lie within a single market. Remember, though, that drawing boundaries around industries and markets is a matter of judgement and there will always be shades of grey around whatever borders are chosen. As long as we remain wary of external influences, we do not have to worry about absolute precision.

Having strategically defined the market, we then need to work out how big the market is. That is done first by using a strategic segment to define the universe population then applying a logical process involving hypothesis generation, testing and cross-checking until a market size figure is arrived at with the right feel.

Notes

1. Smith, W.R. (1956) 'Product Differentiation and Market Segmentation as Alternative Marketing Strategies', *Journal of Marketing*, 21(July): 3–8.
2. Kotler, P. (1991) *Marketing Management: Analysis, Planning, Implementation and Control* (7th edition). Englewood Cliffs, NJ: Prentice Hall.
3. Kotler, P. (1967) *Marketing Management: Analysis, Planning, Implementation and Control* (1st edition). Englewood Cliffs, NJ: Prentice Hall.
4. Wright, M. and Esslemont, D. (1994) 'The logical Limitations of Target Marketing', *Marketing Bulletin*, 5: 13–20.
5. Ehrenberg, A. and Goodhart, G. (1977) 'Essays on Understanding Buyer Behaviour'. New York: J. Walter Thompson and The Market Research Corporation of America.
6. Porter, M.E. (1980) *Competitive Strategy: Techniques for Analyzing Industries and Competitors*. New York: The Free Press.
7. Porter M. (1985) *Competitive Advantage: Creating and Sustaining Superior Performance*. New York: The Free Press.
8. Christensen C.M. and Raynor, M.E. (2003) *The Innovator's Solution*. Boston, MA: Harvard Business School Press.
9. Piercy N. (1997) *Market-led Strategic Change: Transforming the Process of Going to Market*. Oxford: Butterworth-Hieneman.
10. Mathur, S. and Kenyon, A. (1997) *Creating Value: Shaping Tomorrow's Business*. Oxford: Butterworth-Heineman.
11. Porter M. (1985) *Competitive Advantage. Creating and Sustaining Superior Performance*. New York: The Free Press.
12. Johnson G. and Scholes, K. (1988) *Exploring Corporate Strategy*. London: FT Prentice Hall.
13. Levitt, T. (1965) 'Marketing Myopia', *Harvard Business Review*, 38(September/October): 45–56.

CHAPTER 4 *Industry Attractiveness*

Whether or not an industry is attractive can be determined by some basic micro-economic analysis. This is applicable to any industry, from basic commodities such as cement right through to sophisticated services. Every industry can be analysed according to basic supply and demand analysis. In fact, the analysis is so basic that it is very often forgotten, which is why this chapter starts with a reminder not to forget the laws of economics before going to examine the conventional approach to assessing industry attractiveness.

Do not forget your basic economics

There are a number of basic economic laws that influence every business in every market. For an acquisition to be successful, the business should be capable of earning good post-acquisition profits. This occurs when these laws do not work perfectly. The great bulk of the strategy literature sets out to explain the conditions in which the laws of economics work imperfectly. Before reviewing the concepts and techniques of strategy analysis in more detail, it is as well to develop a firm grasp of the underlying economic thought behind them to give the strategic analysis the firm practical foundation it often lacks.

DEMAND

A market exists wherever there are buyers and sellers of a particular good. Buyers demand goods from the market. In economics, a demand curve models the quantity that consumers are willing and able to purchase at each and every price, all other things unchanged. This is illustrated in Figure 4.1.

The law of demand states that a higher quantity will be demanded at a lower price assuming all other factors remain constant. In Figure 4.1, movement from A to B shows the change in quantity demanded due to a change in price. This precisely what has happened with the budget airlines; they have expanded demand by lowering prices. The demand curve is downward sloping because of the law of diminishing marginal utility. Each extra unit of a product or service will give less satisfaction (utility) and therefore consumers will only buy more if they pay less.[1]

Price elasticity of demand

The amount the quantity demanded changes following a given change in price depends on the price elasticity of demand. Price elasticity of demand is a measure of the sensitivity of demand to a change in price. Graphically, the flatter the demand curve, the more elastic is demand, the steeper the demand curve, the more inelastic is demand, as shown in Figure 4.2.

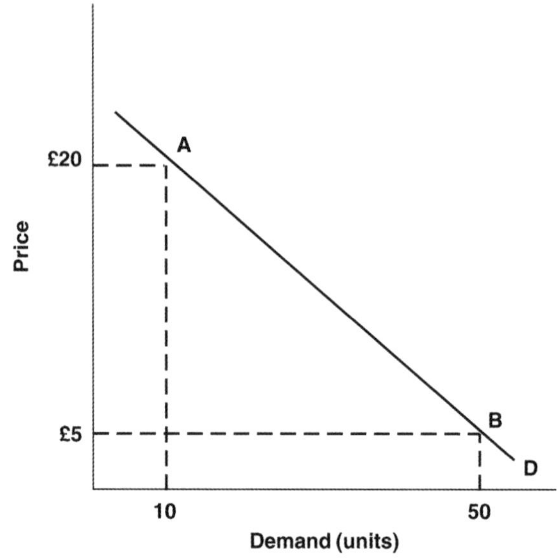

Figure 4.1 The demand curve

Price elasticity of demand depends on:

- The number and availability of substitutes and the ease with which consumers can switch.
- Time: in the short term it may not be easy to find alternatives and so demand is likely to be inelastic to start with (see Case Study 16 below).
- The importance of the good to the buyer: if the product is absolutely crucial to the buyer's product or process, demand will be inelastic.
- The amount spent on the good: subject to the last point, the bigger the proportion of buyers' expenditure the good accounts for, the more price sensitive buyers are likely to be.

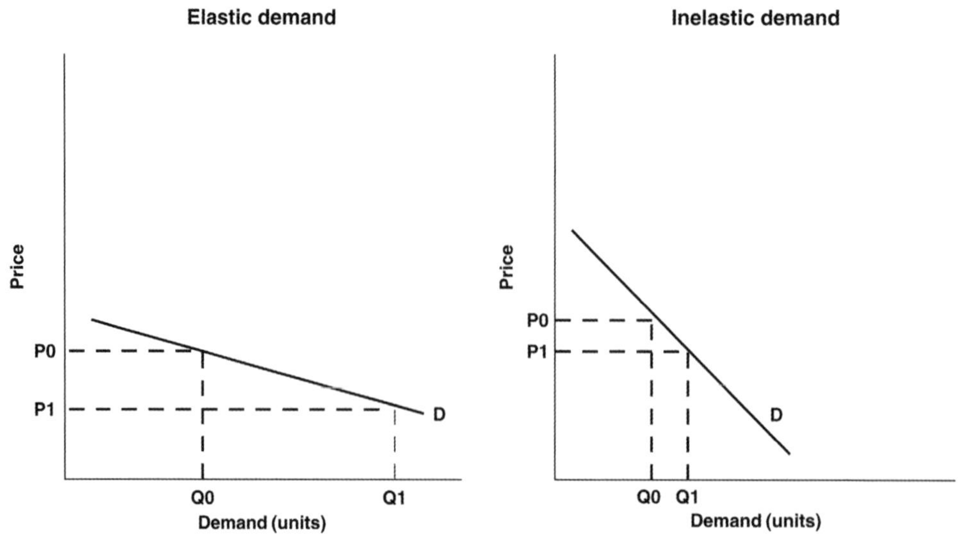

Figure 4.2 Elastic and inelastic demand

CASE STUDY 16

CHILDREN'S HOMES

Private children's homes is a market that has grown rapidly since the late 1990s in the UK, in response to the closure of local authority homes. They are expensive. Some cost as much as £1000 per night. For many of the children with extreme behaviour problems, there is nowhere else that social services departments can turn to house them. But there are no fixed boundaries between what constitutes extreme behaviour and what is just bad behaviour, therefore the product is not absolutely crucial in all cases, therefore demand is not inelastic. The amount spent on homes is potentially very large: £1000 per night for three years is £1 million. A typical social work manager has a budget of £800 000 per annum for a case load of 180 children. Although the money for residential care comes out of a different pot, under the circumstances, buyers are bound to be price sensitive especially when council provided residential care costs of £2500 per week. However, it takes time to make new arrangements, therefore demand will seemed inelastic at first. However, by 2005 it was clear that the market had started to change. Social services departments started to find ways of cutting down on costs. They found ways of avoiding expensive emergency placements, some joined buying consortia, some bolstered their fostering resources, all implemented measures to intervene early to cut down the number of children being taken into care.

- The type of good: some goods are bought out of habit and if they are a small part of a firm's expenditure, this can be without much concern about price.

Shifts in demand

If one or more of those 'other factors' changes, the demand curve shifts as in Figure 4.3.

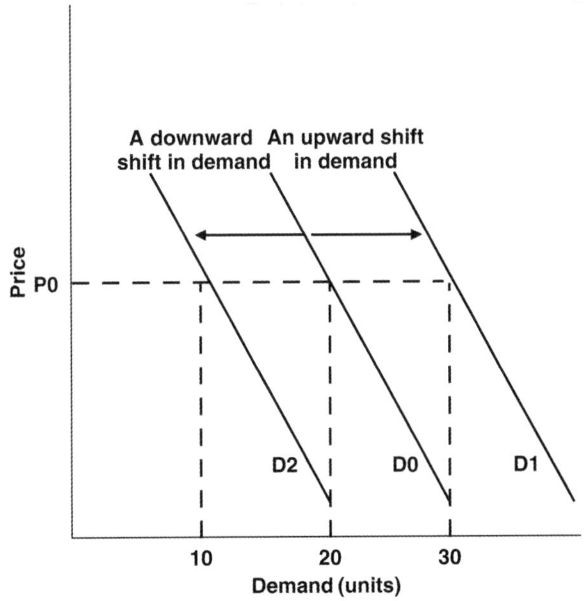

Figure 4.3 A shift in demand

For demand curves to shift to the left or right as shown in Figure 4.3, one or more of the following must have risen or fallen:

- Real incomes.
- The price of substitutes: if the supply of potatoes goes up, say because of adverse weather conditions, the demand for pasta will shift to the right.
- The price of complements, for example, cars and petrol or gin and tonic: if the price of gin goes down (we can but hope) more tonic will be demanded at the same price.
- The effectiveness with which the product has been promoted.
- The number of consumers.
- The availability of credit.
- Tastes have changed so that fewer, or more, people want the product.

SUPPLY

A supply curve, as in Figure 4.4, shows the quantity that producers are willing and able to supply at each and every price, all other things being equal.

The law of supply states that a higher quantity will be supplied at higher prices, providing nothing else changes. The supply curve slopes upwards because it assumes that firms are motivated by profit and will therefore produce more if prices increase and less if prices fall.

In Figure 4.4, movement from A to B shows the change in quantity supplied due to a change in price.

Price elasticity of supply

Just as with demand, the change in the quantity supplied following a given change in price depends on the price elasticity of supply. Price elasticity of supply is a measure of the

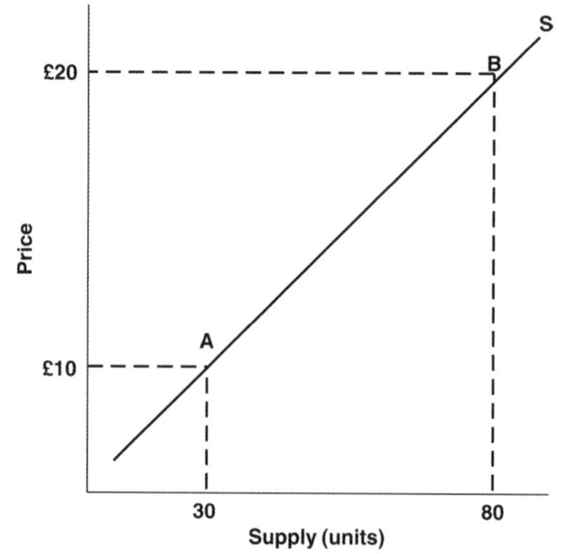

Figure 4.4 The supply curve

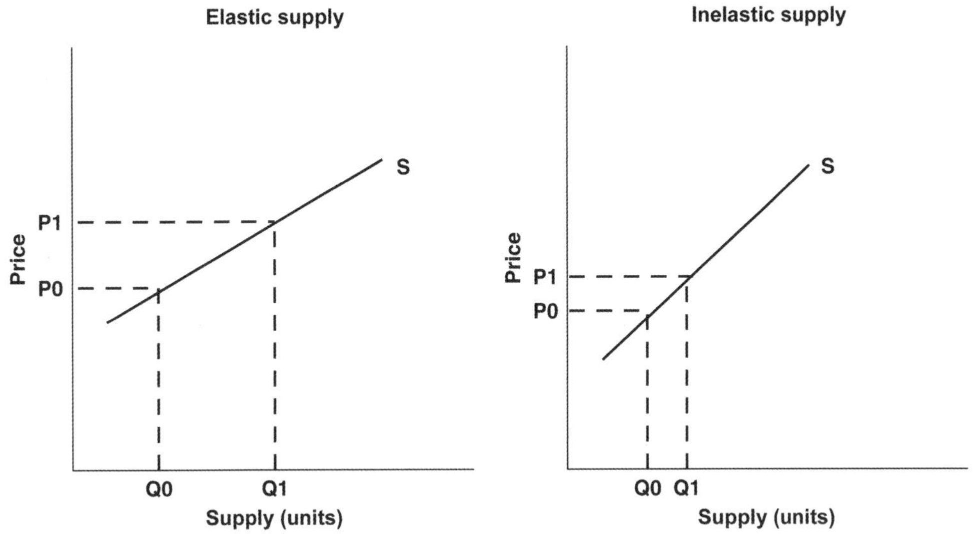

Figure 4.5 Elastic and inelastic supply

sensitivity of supply to a change in price. The flatter the supply curve, the more elastic is supply, the steeper the supply curve, the more inelastic is supply as in Figure 4.5.

Price elasticity of supply depends on:

- The number of producers: the more producers, the easier it should be for an industry to increase demand in response to increased prices hence the more elastic will be supply;
- Spare capacity: this also makes it easier to increase supply, hence making supply more elastic.
- Time: producing more may depend on installing new equipment and training in which case supply will be more elastic in the long term than it is in the short term. Similarly, if there is a long production period, it will take time to adjust production levels in response to price.

Shifts in supply

Supply curves can shift to the left or right just like demand curves, as in Figure 4.6.

For supply curves to shift, one or more of the following factors must be at work:

- The number of suppliers has increased.
- Technology has improved. Better levels of efficiency will encourage firms to produce more at the same price or the same amount at a lower price.
- A fall in production costs. If the price of raw materials falls, for example, more might be supplied at each price.
- Other factors affecting productivity, such as better weather leading to a better supply of agricultural products.
- A cut in taxes or an increase in subsidies.
- A change in price of related goods. If the price of A rises, producers may switch resources into A at the expense of B shifting the supply curve for B to the left.

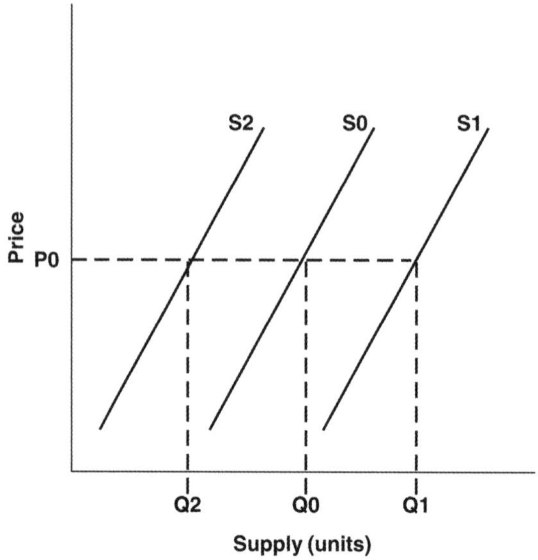

Figure 4.6 Shifts in supply

DEMAND AND SUPPLY

In free markets, price is the means by which resources are allocated. Remember this because it is going to come up later. Price will adjust until supply equals demand. Either:

- an increase in demand will lead to a price rise, encouraging suppliers to produce more or new entrants to come into the industry creating a new equilibrium; or
- an increase in supply will lead to lower prices, increasing the quantity demanded and reducing the amount supplied until a new equilibrium comes about.

Both are illustrated in Figure 4.7

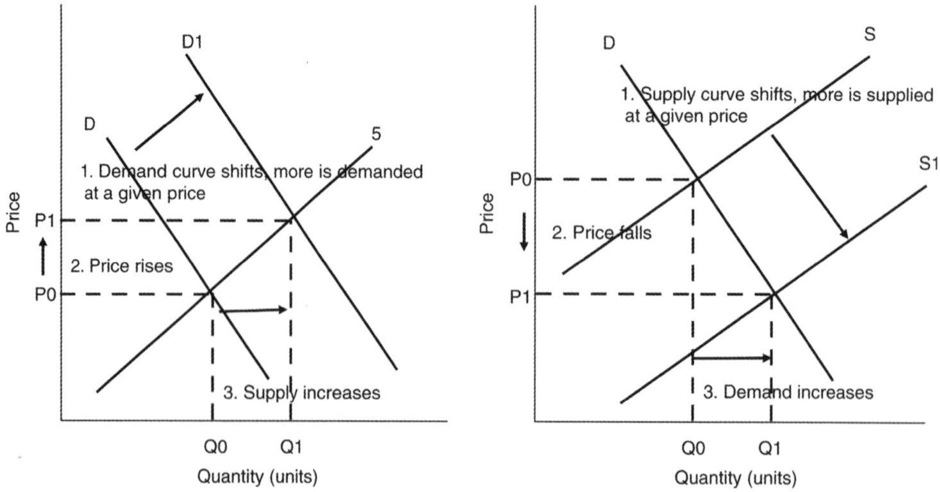

Figure 4.7 Supply and demand in action

PROFIT

Economics has several definitions of profit. 'Normal profit' is the amount of profit that is needed to keep resources in their present use in the long run. It is the reward to businesses that covers the risk of being in an industry. If firms are making a normal profit, there is no incentive for them to leave the industry or for others to join. Loosely translated this is the (risk-adjusted) amount you could earn in a savings account or, more technically put, it is the return that equals the cost of capital. Businesses in general, and acquirers in particular, are not interested in normal profits. They want abnormal profits. This is the profit in excess of normal profit in an industry. Fine, except that, other things being equal, and over the long term (which is not very long these days), all industries should tend to normal profit. If there are abnormal profits to be made, new firms will enter the industry driving down prices until abnormal profits have been eliminated. The theory behind this is as described below.

Firms will seek to maximize profit. The point at which profits are maximized is where the firm cannot make any extra profit by selling more. This is where the cost of producing the last unit equals the price at which that last unit can be sold (remembering that in economics, cost includes normal profit and price is assumed to differ at every level of supply as in Figure 4.5 above). This point is also where the cost of producing the last unit (the marginal cost) equals the average cost at that level of production. This is the equilibrium position under perfect competition and it is illustrated in Figure 4.8.

The equilibrium position in Figure 4.8 comes about because any abnormal profits will attract new firms into the market and shift the supply curve to the right until prices fall to the point where price equals marginal cost, as in Figure 4.9.

To make more than a normal profit, there must be something that prevents competition being perfect. It is identifying these market imperfections and assessing their longevity that

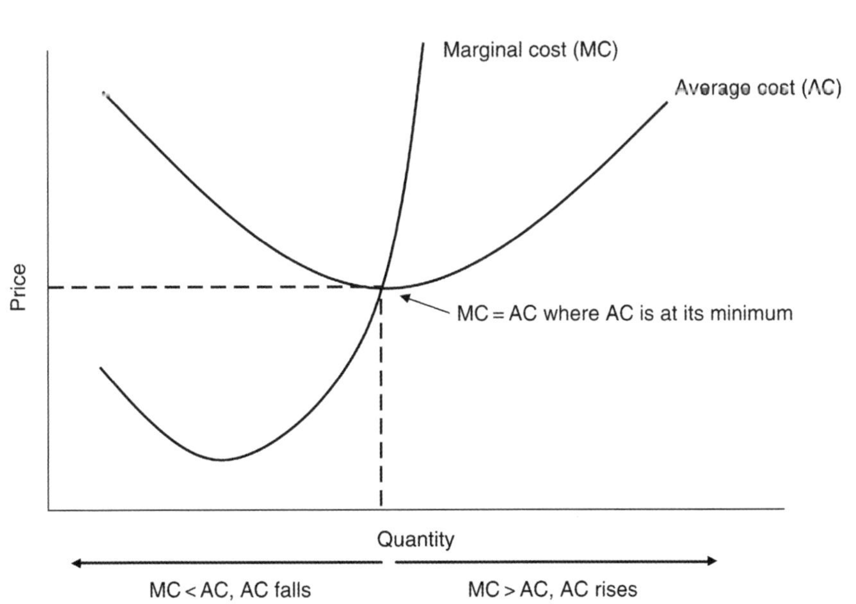

Figure 4.8 Output and price under perfect competition

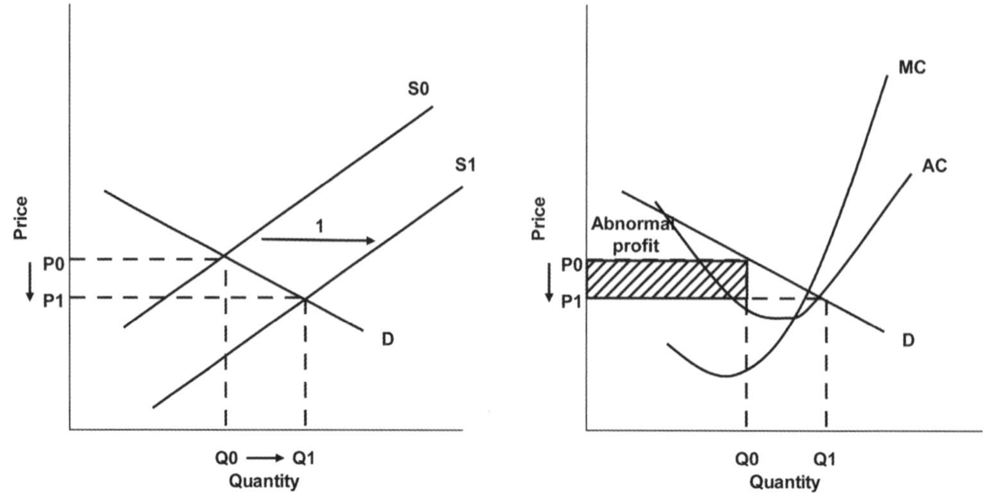

Figure 4.9 The short run and long run in perfect competition

really interests us in CDD. The assumptions of a perfectly competitive market are that:

- there are many buyers and sellers;
- there is prefect information, so buyers know what products are on offer at what price;
- there are no differences between the products;
- there are no barriers to entry, so that firms can easily enter (and leave) the industry;
- there are no technology or cost advantages to be had.

Looking back at Figure 4.9, there is a sixth factor and that is time. Even under perfect competition, it is possible to make excess profit in the short run until all those new entrants arrive. A good summary of the next section is that in order to earn abnormal profits, the market structure should have characteristics opposite to those in the above bullet points.

Analysing industry attractiveness

As we have just seen, where there are many firms supplying an identical product with no restrictions on entry or exit, the rate of profit falls to a level that just covers firms' costs of capital. The other end of the spectrum is a monopoly where a single firm is protected by barriers to the entry allowing it to make abnormal profits. In the real world, industries fall between these two extremes as is shown in Table 4.1.[2]

The key considerations in analysing an industry, which we look at in more detail below, are the economics of supply and demand.

SUPPLY ECONOMICS

There are nine elements to consider when analysing the economics of supply:

- The concentration of producers
- The level of import competition
- The diversity of producers

Table 4.1 The spectrum of industry structures

	Perfect competition	*Oligopoly*	*Duopoly*	*Monopoly*
Degree of buyer concentration		Many buyers		
Degree of industry concentration	Many firms	A few firms	Two firms	One firm
Information	Perfect information	Imperfect information		
Degree of differentiation	Homogenous product	Potential for differentiation		
Entry and exit barriers	No barriers	Significant barriers		High barriers
Technology or cost advantages	None	Few	Some	Significant

- The proportion producers' total cash costs represented by fixed costs
- Capacity utilization in the industry
- Technological opportunities within the industry
- The shape of the industry supply (cost) curve
- Barriers to industry entry
- Barriers to industry exit.

A widely used framework for classifying and analyzing these factors is Porter's Five Forces.[3] It says that the profitability of an industry is determined by the amount of pressure exerted by each of five sources of competitive pressure. These five forces of competition include three sources of 'horizontal' competition: competition from substitutes, competition from entrants, and competition from established rivals; and two sources of 'vertical' competition: the bargaining power of suppliers and buyers as set out in Figure 4.10. The strengths of each of these competitive forces is determined by a number of key structural variables listed in Checklist 4 in Appendix A and described below. Given the importance of changing regulations in many industries, there is an argument for including government as a separate sixth factor. Porter, however, maintains that the importance of government lies in an ability to affect the other five forces through changes in policy and new legislation.

DEMAND ECONOMICS

Understanding the demand economics in any industry requires analysis of four key elements:

- The availability of substitute products/services
- The differentiability of products/services
- The rate of demand growth within the industry
- The volatility and cyclicality within the industry.

The conclusion that prospective acquirers like best is that the industry has few substitute products, a strong basis for differentiation, strong demand growth, and little volatility or cyclicality of demand.

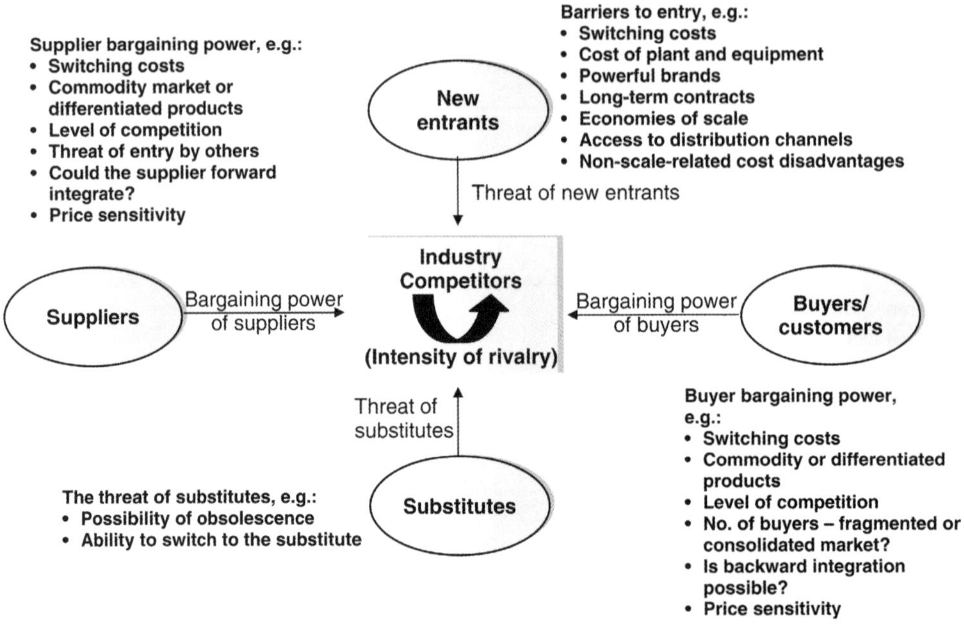

Figure 4.10 Porter's Five Forces

THE AVAILABILITY OF SUBSTITUTES

The price customers are willing to pay for a product depends, in part, on the availability of substitute products. An absence of substitutes makes demand inelastic (see Figure 4.2 above), whereas the existence of close substitutes means that customers will switch to substitutes if prices rise meaning that demand is price elastic – providing buyers are willing and able to switch. This in part depends on the relative price/performance characteristics of the product and its substitutes and the customer needs satisfied by the product or service. The closer the price/performance characteristics of substitutes, the less prices have to move before switching takes place. Substitutes matter when customers are attracted to the products of firms in other industries. An example would be the substitution of TV by the Internet. The more critical or complex the buyer needs satisfied by the product, the more difficult it is to substitute with something else. This is always an issue, for example, with businesses that sell information. Very often the data is collected from public sources; the question is therefore the ease with which clients can source it from elsewhere (including sourcing it themselves). The answer depends on what information businesses do with the data once they have collected it. The more it is customized to client needs, the more locked in those clients are.

THREAT OF ENTRY

If an industry earns a return on capital in excess of its cost of capital, it acts as a magnet to firms outside the industry. They will enter the industry, forcing profits to fall to normal levels. Even the threat of entry, rather than actual entry, may be sufficient to make established firms keep prices at competitive levels. European steel prices in the early 1990s give a good example of geographic boundaries, albeit from an odd perspective. European steel prices fell in the early 1990s after the Berlin wall came down. The reason was that the large integrated Russian steel works had lost their domestic markets and had begun talking to steel buyers in Europe. These buyers used their discussions as a lever to force down prices from their traditional suppliers. In this case the *threat* of substitution from Eastern Europe was enough to move prices. In fact, it was difficult to see how Russian substitution would work in practice, since in an era of just-in-time supply the steel in question had to be bought by the train load and it was not suitable for most western high-speed presses.

In an industry where there are no barriers to entry or exit, prices and profits can remain at fully competitive levels regardless of the number of firms in the industry if there are also no sunk costs. Sunk costs are the investment in industry-specific assets whose value cannot be recovered on exit. The reason that prices remain at fully competitive levels is because the absence of sunk costs makes the industry vulnerable to 'hit and run' entry whenever established firms raise their prices above the fully competitive level.[4]

In most industries, however, the new entrants cannot enter on equal terms with established firms. The size of the advantage that established firms have over new entrants measures the height of entry barriers. In turn, this determines the extent to which the industry can enjoy long run profits above the fully competitive/perfect competition level, although it must be remembered that the effectiveness of barriers to entry in deterring potential entrants depends on the resources of those potential entrants. For example, barriers that are effective for start-up companies may be ineffective for firms that are diversifying from other industries.

The principal sources of barriers to entry is as follows:

- Sizeable economies of scale
- Capital costs
- Cost advantages independent of size
- Inability to gain access to specialized technology
- Difficulties in gaining access to distribution channels
- The existence of strong learning curve or experience effects
- Strong brand preferences and customer loyalty
- Large capital requirements and/or other specialized resource requirements
- Regulatory policies, tariffs or trade restrictions
- Threat of retaliation.

Without barriers to entry, acquirers face the risk of returns to existing competitors in the industry being bid away in the future. For this reason, identifying and quantifying barriers to entry is a critical part of CDD. Each of the barriers to entry are dealt with in more detail in the sections that follow.

Sizeable economies of scale

Economies of scale exist wherever proportionate increases in the amounts of inputs employed in a production process result in lower unit costs. Economies of scale have been conventionally associated with manufacturing. Scale economies arise from three principal sources:

- Volume related economies: a 500 000-unit engine plant does not cost twice as much as one with half the output.

- Indivisibilities: many resources come only in big sizes and therefore need volume to make them viable. For example, a peak-time advertising slot only makes sense for big selling products and a blast furnace only makes sense if you are making volume steels.
- Specialization: expanding the number of inputs permits greater task specialization and therefore greater efficiency.

If existing players enjoy significant economies of scale, the theory is that new entrants are deterred from entry because of the losses they must suffer until they can build their own volume up to the point where they are no longer at a cost disadvantage, if indeed they ever can. This is a huge risk in theory but can be overdone. Because there are few industries where price and cost are everything, new entrants are by no means unknown in industries where economies of scale are important. Over the years, for example, Japanese manufacturers have taken significant shares of most car markets despite their relatively late entry.

The critical scale advantages of large companies are seldom in production. For example, consumer goods markets are dominated by a few giant companies because of scale economies in marketing. Advertising is a key indivisibility. The cost of producing and airing a TV commercial nationality is a fixed cost whether the product has a 5 per cent or 50 per cent market share.

Capital costs

Entry into industries that are capital or research or advertising intensive also requires a large-scale operation to give firms sufficient volumes over which to amortize the up-front costs. A feature of most software products is that the initial development costs are very high but, once developed, they can be copied and distributed at negligible cost and therefore late entry can be expensive.

The absolute capital costs of entry can be so large as to discourage entry. Sky TV's investment in satellite broadcasting seems to have been enough to discourage followers although Airbus's challenge of Boeing shows that capital costs are not always an absolute deterrent to entry.

Cost advantages independent of size

Apart from economies of scale, established firms may have a cost advantage over entrants simply because they entered earlier. Absolute cost advantages tend to be associated with the acquisition of low-cost raw materials, economies of learning, or unique access to resources or knowledge (see Case Study 17).

CASE STUDY 17

A LIBRARY OF TV ADVERTISEMENTS

If you are an advertising executive planning a TV campaign for, say, shampoo, there exists in London an agency that will supply you with every TV advertisement that has ever been made for shampoo (or any other product for that matter) in most countries in the world. They operate by having stringers around the world video taping new advertisements for them, then cataloguing and storing them for later retrieval and collation. This is an easy business to copy – but only for current advertisements. The disadvantage for all its competitors is that the agency has access to a library of early advertisements.

Inability to gain access to specialized technology

In knowledge-intensive industries, patents, copyrights and trade secrets can be major barriers to entry.

Difficulties in gaining access to distribution channels

Where distribution is important, gaining distribution can act as a barrier for the new company. Limited capacity in the distribution channels (for example, shelf space), distributors' aversion to the risk of carrying a new manufacturer's product or reluctance to make the investment in fixed and working capital involved in carrying an extra range of products can make life very difficult for new entrants.

The existence of strong learning curve or experience effects

The learning curve is dealt with in the next chapter. If there are strong learning curve effects, companies that have been in the industry the longest will have learnt more and will therefore have an advantage.

Strong brand preferences and customer loyalty

In theory, in an industry where products are differentiated, established firms possess the advantage of brand recognition and customer loyalty. If new entrants are going to take on incumbent suppliers head-on, they must spend disproportionately heavily on advertising and promotion to gain levels of brand awareness and brand goodwill similar to that of established companies. In practice, successful new entrants do not take on the incumbents head-on, but instead find new ways of competing. Dell, for example, did not take on IBM direct, but found a new way of selling PCs.

Regulatory policies, tariffs or trade restrictions

Regulation can be an important barrier to entry and shaper of the type and degree of industry competition. Maintenance of retail book prices has meant booksellers have had to compete on non-price terms while regulatory conditions imposed on children's homes in the UK has made it difficult for new entrants and for small players to remain in business.

Threat of retaliation

It is not just the threat of entry that counts, but also the reaction of existing firms to entry. We have already seen the reaction of the European steel industry to the threat of entry of low priced Russian steel in the early 1990s, for example. If industry management is not particularly dynamic, a new entrant will find progress much easier than if it comes up against managements that take no hostages. As Freddie Laker found to his cost and Richard Branson has shown, the airline industry is quick to retaliate against low-cost entrants. Expectations about the ferocity of retaliation by established firms is itself a barrier to entry. Retaliation against a new entrant may take the form of aggressive price cutting, increased advertising, sales promotion, or litigation.

INDUSTRY RIVALRY

For most industries, this is the most powerful of Porter's Five Forces with rivalry between existing players being the major determinant of the level of industry profitability. In some industries, firms compete to the point where no one makes very much money, in others price competition is limited with innovation, customer service or another non-price factor as the basis of competition. The following factors determine the degree of competition between established players:

- Seller concentration
- Diversity of competitors
- Import competition
- Product differentiation
- Market size
- Market growth
- Capacity utilization, excess capacity and exit barriers
- Cost conditions, scale economies and the ratio of fixed to variable costs
- The nature and pace of technological change.

Seller concentration

Seller concentration refers to the number and size of incumbent competitors. It is measured using the combined market share of the leading producers. For example, the four-firm concentration ratio (conventionally denoted 'CR4') is the market share of the four largest producers. Where a market is dominated by a small group of leading companies, price competition may be restrained, either by outright collusion or more commonly through 'parallelism' of pricing decisions. The theory has it that firms in an oligopoly have nothing to gain by under-cutting the others, so they compete using non-price weapons instead. As the number of firms increases, coordination of prices becomes more difficult and the likelihood that one firm will initiate price cutting increases. Industries with more than five or six competitors are said to have difficulty in consistently avoiding intense rivalry. This is the theory; unfortunately, research in this area has concluded that the relationship between seller concentration and profitability is statistically weak.

Diversity of competitors

The ability of firms in an industry to avoid price competition also depends to an extent on their similarities in terms of origins, objectives, costs and strategy. The more diverse the competition, the greater the chances of a loose cannon.

Import competition

Put simply, import competition reduces industry profitability by putting a cap on prices by making the industry supply curve perfectly elastic at the import price.

Product differentiation

The more similar the offerings among rival firms, the more willing and able are customers to substitute and the greater the incentive for firms to cut prices to increase sales – sometimes there is no other way. When the products of rival firms are virtually indistinguishable, the product is a commodity and price is the sole basis for competition. At the other end of the spectrum, in industries where products are highly differentiated, price competition tends to be weak, even though there may be many firms competing. Differentiation is dealt with in more detail in the Chapter 5, so suffice it to say here that often there is a gulf between the degree of differentiation claimed by target companies and what the market sees. There is a strong and misguided notion that product extension constitutes differentiation when all that it achieves is uniqueness, which is not the same thing at all. Fiddling with product features to achieve something 'new and improved' is not differentiation either. 'Differentiation' is only differentiation if it creates something that customers really care about that is different from what the competition is offering.

Market size

As far as investors are concerned, a large market is best because it means there is plenty to go for.

Market growth

Investors get unnecessarily excited about market growth. According to the empirical studies in this area,[5] market growth helps profitability only a little. The reason for this is that market growth attracts new entrants and hence exacerbates internal rivalry.

Capacity utilization, excess capacity and exit barriers

Profits fall during periods of recession because unused capacity encourages firms to offer price cuts to attract new business in order to spread fixed costs over a greater sales volume. Excess capacity may be cyclical, as in the semiconductor industry, for example, or demand and supply may be out of balance because of structural problem resulting, say, from over-investment and declining demand. When supply and demand is structurally out of balance, the key issue is whether excess capacity will leave the industry. Barriers to exit are costs associated with leaving an industry. Barriers are highest where:

- Assets are durable and specialized with no alternative use. Multiplex cinemas are a very good example. Over building in the USA led to there being too many screens relative to audiences. The result was an industry with persistently low profits, which is hardly surprising given the alternative uses for a building containing 10 small cinemas.
- The costs incurred in plant closure are high. Substantial cash costs may be incurred in redundancies, dismantling and demolition.
- Firms and/or governments are reluctant to close plants for emotional, moral or political reasons.

Cost conditions, scale economies and the ratio of fixed to variable costs

Where fixed costs are a relatively high proportion of cash costs, profits are very dependent on volume, as shown in Figure 4.11.

Companies are very sensitive around the break-even point. When industry capacity exceeds demand, firms will take on marginal business at any price that covers variable costs as a means of achieving volume.

Scale economies may also encourage companies to compete aggressively on price in order to gain the cost benefits of greater volume. Industry rivalry increases where fixed costs are high relative to variable costs.

As a general rule, competitors are more likely to avoid price competition when the industry supply curve is flat. When the industry supply curve is steep, it is less likely that the industry will indulge in collectively rational pricing decisions.

The nature and pace of technological change

Opportunities for technological advance have significant influence on producer conduct. Industries where there are significant opportunities for technological advance often

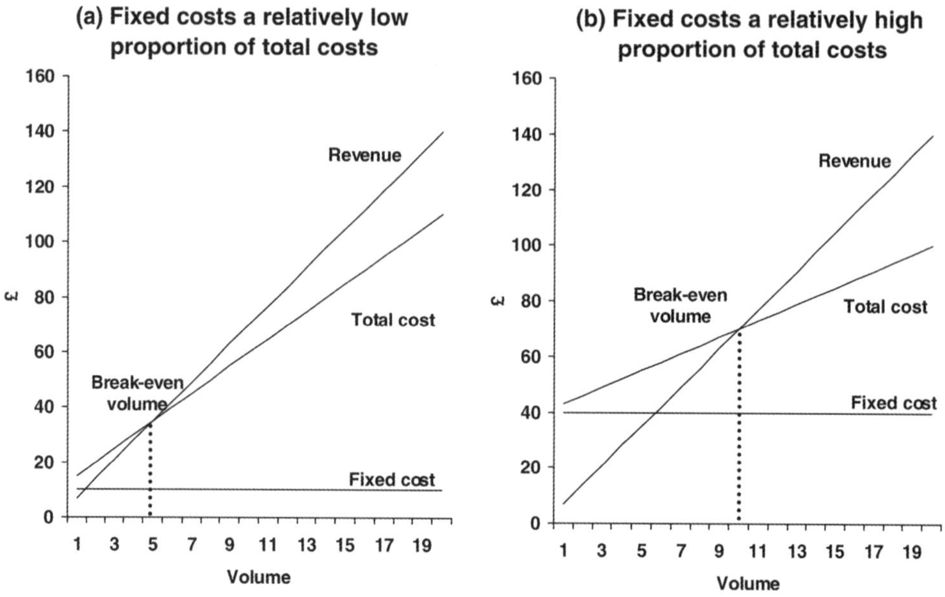

Figure 4.11 Low and high fixed costs

experience intense competition and when one of the players does make a breakthrough, the others are forced to spend heavily on catch up R&D.

Gauging industry rivalry

A big factor in determining the strength of rivalry is how aggressively rivals employ various tools of competition in seeking stronger market positions. The questions to ask yourself are:

- Is price competition vigorous?
- Are rivals continually:
  - Trying to improve quality?
  - Innovating?
  - Offering better performance features?
  - Improving their customer service?
- What is the intensity of advertising/sales promotion?
- Are there active efforts to build a stronger dealer network?
- Is there active jockeying for position among rivals, such as frequent discounting initiatives to gain sales and share?
- Are industry conditions such that some firms are tempted to go on the offensive to boost volume and share?
- Has one (or more) firms begun to make moves to strengthen its position?
- Are there many firms of roughly equal size and capability?
- Is there slow market growth?
- Do customers have low switching costs?
- Is the cost of exit higher than staying in the industry?
- Do firms have diverse strategies, corporate priorities, resources and countries of origin?

Finally, if you have constructed a map of strategic groups (see Chapter 3), the tendency is that the closer the strategic groups are on the map, the stronger the competitive rivalry among member firms tends to be.

Industry lifecycle

The concept of a product and industry life cycle has been around for a long time. It compromises four phases, as shown in Figure 4.12. The stage that the target's market has reached will play an important part in explaining the degree of rivalry between existing players and the viability of the target's strategy and the chances of decent post-acquisition profits. Figure 4.12 shows the normal representation of industry life cycle.

Before looking at each stage in more detail, we should understand the forces that are driving industry evolution because that will tell us a lot about the nature of competition and likely sales trends. Two factors are fundamental in shaping the curve shown in Figure 4.12, they are:

- Demand growth
- The creation and diffusion of knowledge.

DEMAND GROWTH

In the introduction stage, the industry's products are little known, customers are a few 'early adopters' and sales are low. The novelty of the product or service, its small scale and lack of experience among consumers means that costs, and prices, are high. The growth phase is characterized by accelerating market penetration as product technology becomes standardized and prices fall. Ownership spreads from higher-income, risk-tolerant customers to the mass market. Eventually growth leads to increasing market saturation. Sales of replacement products become more important than sales of new products, which causes the slowing growth of the maturity phase. Once there is saturation, demand is wholly replacement. Finally, when technologically superior substitute products come along, the industry reaches its decline phase.

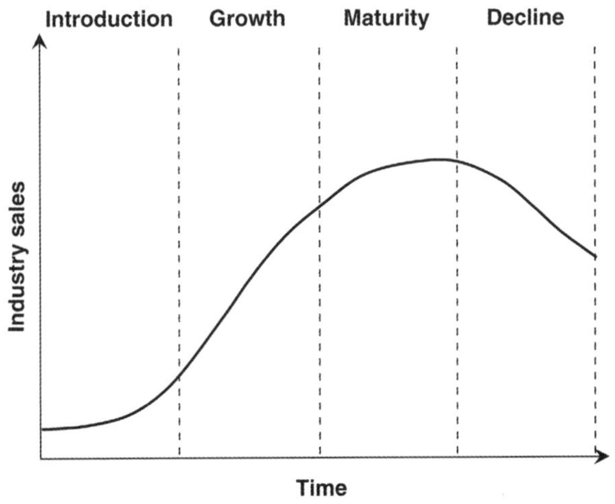

Figure 4.12 The industry life cycle

THE CREATION AND DIFFUSION OF KNOWLEDGE

New knowledge in the form of product innovation is responsible for an industry's birth. In the introduction stage, product technology advances rapidly. There is no dominant product technology, so competition is primarily between alternative technologies. Eventually there is convergence around a single technology. If at this point there is a shift from radical to incremental innovation, the industry growth phase can start. Standardization reduces risks to customers and encourages firms to invest in manufacturing. The result is a shift from product innovation to process innovation as firms seek to reduce costs and improve reliability. On the back of these comes increased market penetration. Knowledge diffusion is also important on the customer side. Over the course of the life cycle, customers become increasingly informed. As they become more knowledgeable about the performance attributes of rival manufacturers' products, so they are better able to judge value for money and become more price sensitive, a theme taken up in Chapter 8.

LIMITATIONS OF LIFECYCLE THEORY

Figure 4.12 is a conceptual representation of what theoretically goes on in all industries, but remember the product life cycle is a concept; it is not predictive. First, the duration of the life cycle and its various stages varies greatly from industry to industry. What can be said is that the general tendency has been for life cycles to shorten. At the same time, the development costs and times of the new products have increased, requiring companies to make early decisions on the commitment of development resource. For this reason, companies with a portfolio of products must think seriously about having different ones at different stages of the life cycle.

Second, The precise pattern of industry sales over time also differs with industry. Industries supplying basic necessities may never enter a decline phase because obsolescence is unlikely for such needs. Some industries may experience a rejuvenation of their life cycle. This is typically the result of resisting the forces of maturity through product innovations or developing new markets. Industries are likely to be at different stages of the life cycle in different countries.

THE LIFECYCLE AND INTERNAL RIVALRY

Market growth and technological change are major determinants of the structure of industries, although it is difficult to generalize. In most industries, the introduction phase is associated with a fragmented structure and diversity of products and technologies. Typically, new industries attract a flood of new entrants. The different origins of the entrants add to the diversity of technologies and business models. In the growth phase, fragmentation gives way to consolidation under pressure for lower costs through scale-efficient production. Large companies (with bigger R&D budgets) and those with successful products tend to grow, causing other firms to decline and exit. This trend accelerates in the transition to maturity, when the slowdown of market growth causes excess capacity and a 'shakeout' of weaker players. This shakeout period may mark the start of aggressive price competition.

The general trend, therefore, is for concentration to increase over time. The shakeout phase of intensive acquisition, merger, and exit occurs, on average, 29 years into the life cycle and results in the number of producers being halved. However, the evolutionary path in an industry is heavily dependent on the behaviour of barriers to entry. Where entry barriers rise through the growth phase due to increasing scale economics, capital requirements, product differentiation or access to distribution channels, seller concentration increases substantially over the life cycle. Where entry barriers fall because technology becomes more accessible or product differentiation declines, concentration declines.

Competition changes in two ways over the course of the industry life cycle. First, there is a shift from non-price to price competition. Second, the intensity of competition grows. During the introduction stage, competitors battle for technological leadership and competition focuses on technology and design. Gross margins may be high, but there are a lot of development costs. In the growth phase market demand can outstrip industry capacity, leading to high prices and good margins. Maturity increases the emphasis on price competition. How intense this is depends a great deal on the capacity/demand balance.

Classifying industries according to their stage of development can in itself be an insightful exercise:

- It acts as a shortcut in strategy analysis. Categorizing an industry according to its stage of development can alert us to the type of competition likely to emerge and the kinds of strategy likely to be effective.
- Classifying an industry encourages comparison with other industries. By highlighting similarities and differences with other industries, such comparisons can help us gain a deeper understanding of the strategic characteristics of an industry and also, if it is at an early stage, its likely development.
- It directs attention to the forces of change and direction of industry evolution, thereby helping us to anticipate change and therefore see the future.

BARGAINING POWER OF BUYERS

An exchange between two partners creates value for both parties to the transaction. How this value is shared between them in terms of profitability depends on their relative economic power. Dealing first with buyers, their power depends on two factors:

- Price sensitivity
- Relative bargaining power.

Price sensitivity

The extent to which buyers are sensitive to the prices charged by the firms in an industry depends on four main factors:

- The greater the importance of an item as a proportion of total cost, the more sensitive buyers will be about the price they pay.
- The less differentiated the product of the supplying industry, the more willing the buyers are to switch suppliers on the basis of price.
- The more intense the competition among buyers, the greater their eagerness for price reductions from their sellers.
- The greater the importance of the industry's product to the quality of the buyer's product or service, the less sensitive are buyers to the prices they are charged.

Relative bargaining power

Bargaining power rests, ultimately, on the refusal to deal with the other party. The balance of power between the two parties to a transaction depends on the relative ease with which they can do this. A buyer's relative power will be determined by:

- The size and concentration of buyers relative to suppliers. The smaller the number of buyers and the bigger their purchases, the greater the supplier's fear of losing one. Case Study 23 (Chapter 8) discusses the effect buyer concentration has had on the healthcare industry in the USA.
- Buyers' information. The better informed buyers are about suppliers and their prices and costs, the better they are able to bargain. Keeping customers ignorant of relative prices is an effective constraint on their buying power. Buyer information may be limited by high costs in comparing the product/service offerings of different suppliers because of high search costs, limited information availability or the sheer difficulty of comparing highly complex offerings. For example, the ability of buyers to bargain over the price of management consulting is limited by uncertainty over the precise attributes of the product they are buying.
- Ability to integrate vertically. In refusing to deal with the other party, the alternative to finding another supplier is to do it yourself. For example retailers have increasingly replaced suppliers' brands with their own brand products.

Empirical evidence suggests that buyer concentration depresses prices and profits in supplying industries as Case Study 23 (Chapter 8) shows.

BARGAINING POWER OF SUPPLIERS

The key issues with supplier power are the same as with buyer power:

- The ease with which the firms in the industry can switch between different suppliers
- The relative bargaining power of each party.

THE IMPORTANCE OF COMPLEMENTORS

Some commentators maintain that there should be a sixth force. Brandenburger and Nalebuff[6] introduce complementors as playing a key role in a firm's competitive environment. Complementors are the opposite of substitutes and have the opposite effect. They are enablers of profitability. The fact that mobile phone batteries are now the size of matchboxes and not the monstrously heavy objects that they were when cell phones first came out is a driver of industry value. The simplest way to cater for complementors is to add a sixth force to the Porter framework. Unlike the other Five Forces, complementors are not a competitive force; on the contrary, the more complementors there are and the closer their relationship to the products supplied by the industry, the greater the potential profit within the industry.

Other ways of classifying industries

Porter's Five Forces gives us a framework with which to build up a picture of industry attractiveness. By focusing our research on understanding each of the five (or six) components of industry profitability, we can satisfy ourselves that the business environment is sufficiently favourable for the acquisition to work. The Five Forces model allows us to deconstruct a complex situation into its component parts and by so doing make analysis of present and future profits a manageable proposition. There are other ways of doing this.

USING STRATEGIC ENVIRONMENTS

The Boston Consulting Group's (BCG) Strategic Environments Matrix says it is the nature of competitive advantage in an industry that determines which strategies are viable, which in turn determines the structure of the industry. The matrix uses two variables:

- The number of viable strategy approaches available. This depends on the complexity of the industry in terms of the diversity of sources of competitive advantage. Complex products (automobiles, restaurants) offer more scope for differentiation than do commodities. Among commodities, the potential for competitive advantage depends on whether there are opportunities for cost advantage.
- The size of potential competitive advantage. How big is the advantage available to the industry leader?

As shown in Figure 4.13, by understanding these two variables, you can place the target company in one of four industry types. The characteristics of these industry types will give a pretty good idea of present and future prospects from a industry structure point of view.

- Stalemate businesses are those where the sources of advantage are few and the size of potential advantage is small. The result is a highly competitive industry where firms compete with similar strategies, but none is able to obtain significant advantage. A business in a stalemate industry has to focus on operational efficiency, low administrative overheads, and a cost-conscious corporate culture for profitability and survival.
- Fragmented businesses are those where the sources of competitive advantage are many, but the size of advantage is small. They typically supply differentiated products where brand loyalty is low, technology is well diffused and scale economies are small.

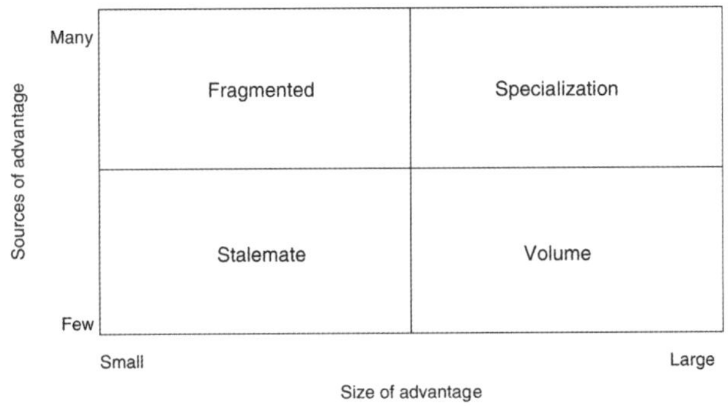

Figure 4.13 The strategic environments matrix

- Specialization businesses are those where the sources of advantage are many and the size of the potential advantage is substantial. Specialization businesses feature varied customer needs, first-mover advantages, brand loyalty, scale economics, and few economies of scope (so there are no major advantages to firms with a broad market or product scope).
- Volume businesses are those where the sources of advantage are few, but the size of advantage (typically resulting from scale economies) is considerable.

USING COMPETITIVE DYNAMICS

Some industries are comparatively stable right through their life cycles; others are in a sate of permanent revolution. Focusing on dynamic aspects of competition, such as the rate of new product introduction, duration of product life cycles, the rate of decline of unit costs, geographical scope, and the stability of supplier–customer relations, Jeffrey Williams identifies three industry types:[7]

- Local monopoly
- Traditional industrial
- Schumpeterian.

Local monopolies

Local monopolies meet the specific requirements of small groups of customers. They rely on close client contact, and exclusive products. Product differentiation is therefore high and customers are resistant to standardization. Not surprisingly, elasticity of demand is low, therefore prices tend to rise over time.

Traditional industrial markets

Traditional industrial markets are large, not heavily segmented, and feature modest rates of product innovation. Competition is all about size. Prices tend to be broadly stable or decline only slightly over time.

Schumpeterian markets

Schumpeterian markets are 'hypercompetitive'. Product innovation is the dominant from of competition, with established products continually displaced by new products. Imitation means that speed in exploiting new products is essential. Product innovation must be supported by the manufacturing and marketing capabilities required to move quickly down the experience curve. Semiconductors would be a good example. The so called 'killer apps' drive the industry. Demand for custom chips for PCs and mobile phones are the best examples. These drove demand to very high levels (and to over-supply and a price crash).

USING THE FIVE FORCES MODEL

Table 4.2 sums up the attractiveness of the competitive environment.

Understanding how the structural characteristics of an industry determine the intensity of competition and the level of profitability provides a basis for judging an acquisition target. For example, one implication of economies of scale is strong rivalry for market share. If the fixed cost of developing a new product can only be amortized over a huge sales base, firms will compete vigorously for market share. Another is that industry structure is just as

Table 4.2 The attractiveness of the competitive environment

Factor	*The industry is unattractive when*	*The industry is attractive when*
Rivalry	Strong	Moderate
Entry barriers	Low and entry is likely	High and entry is not likely
Competition from substitutes	Strong	No good substitutes
Suppliers and customers	Have considerable bargaining power	Are in a weak bargaining position

important in driving profitability in new industries as it is in old, as the collapse of new economy share prices in 2000 belatedly recognized. In fact, in many new industries, industry structure has even more importance than it does in traditional industries, as we shall see in Chapter 9.

Many industries are oligopolies, characterized by high barriers to entry and by high interdependence and uncertainty. Competitors are aware that any change in strategy by one of them will affect the other main rivals, but because they are uncertain of the reaction they behave cautiously. Generally competition will be non-price rather than price. The judgement there is how long this state of affairs can last.

In all cases, CDD must highlight which of the Five Forces is most significant. They can be different in different industries. First, identify the key structural features of an industry that are responsible for the levels of profitability, then consider the following:

- How well the target can exploit factors that improve profits and avoid those that have the opposite effect.
- Which of these structural features are amenable to change either by you, or despite you, post-acquisition.

Industries change because forces are driving industry participants to alter their actions. Understanding these driving forces is critical, since they are the major causes of changing industry and competitive conditions. Therefore CDD should identify those forces likely to exert the greatest influence over the next 1 to 3 years. Usually there are no more than three or four that qualify as real drivers of change. Common driving forces include:

- Internet/e-commerce
- Globalization
- Changes in industry growth rate
- Changes in who buys the product/how they use it
- Product/process innovation
- Technological change
- Marketing innovation
- Exit/entry of major firms
- Diffusion of technical knowledge
- Changes in cost and efficiency
- Market shift from differentiated to standardized (or, more rarely, the opposite)
- Regulatory policies/government legislation
- Changing societal concerns, attitudes and lifestyles.

Having analysed industry structure and come to a view on what this does for industry profitability, the job now is to forecast industry profitability. We are not going to be able to do this by projecting the present, but what we can do is predict changes in the underlying industry structure.

Forecasting industry profitability

Structural change in an industry is driven by:

- Changes in technology
- The strategies of the leading players
- Changes in infrastructure
- Changes in related industries
- Government policies.

If we understand the effect that current industry structure has on competition and profitability and we can project structural change, we can forecast future structure and with it the likely changes in competition and profitability. This is a two stage process:

1 Understand how past changes in industry structure have influenced competition and profitability.
2 Identify current structural trends and determine how these will affect the Five Forces of competition and resulting industry profitability.

However, competition is a dynamic force which continually transforms industry structure. So, not only does industry structure drive the intensity of competition, but competition transforms industry structure because firms change industry structure as they vie for advantage through acquisitions, new ventures, new technology, and novel approaches to distribution and segmentation. That said, empirical studies of changes in industry structure show that profit levels tend to persist over the long run. Similarly, structural change – notably concentration, entry, and the identity of leading firms – is slow. The only real forecasting difficulties come in the so called 'Schumpeterian industries'. These are industries that are subject to rapid innovation and steep experience curves. Using current trends in industry structure to forecast profitability several years ahead is unreliable here because:

- the relationship between competition and industry structure is unstable;
- changes in industry structure are rapid and difficult to predict.

SCENARIO ANALYSIS

In these circumstances, although we cannot predict the future, we can think about what might happen. And we can do so in a systematic way that builds on what we know about current trends and signals to future developments. This is what scenario analysis does. Scenario analysis is not a forecasting technique, but a process for thinking and communicating about the future. Scenarios are hypothetical sequences of events constructed for the purpose of focusing attention on casual process and decision points.

Table 4.3 Industry characteristics and their implications for future profits

Industry characteristics	*Implications*
Market size	Small markets do not tend to attract new firms; large markets attract firms looking to acquire rivals with established positions in attractive industries.
Market growth rates	Fast growth breeds new entry; slow growth spawns increased rivalry and the shake out of weak rivals.
Capacity surpluses/shortages	Surpluses push prices and profit margins down; shortages pull them up.
Industry profitability	High profit industries attract new entrants; depressed conditions lead to exit.
Entry/exit barriers	High barriers protect positions and profits of existing firms; low barriers make existing firms vulnerable to entry.
Product is big ticket item for buyers	Buyers will shop for lowest price.
Standard products	Buyers have more power because it is easier to switch from seller to seller.
Rapid technological change	Raises risk; investments in technology facilities/equipment may become obsolete before they wear out.
Capital requirements	Big requirements make investment decisions critical, timing becomes important, creates a barrier to entry and exit.
Vertical integration	Raises capital requirements, often creates competitive and cost differences among fully vs. partially vs. non-integrated firms.
Economies of scale	Increases volume and market share needed to be cost competitive.
Rapid product innovation	Shortens product life cycle, increases risk because of opportunities for leapfrogging.

As with most strategy techniques, the value of scenario analysis is not in the results, but in the process.

Conclusion

Analysing industry structure is an important part of CDD. The result will tell you about the environment in which the target operates and how this might change for the better or worse. Our interest is in the continuing imperfection of market forces that allow above normal profits to continue once the deal is done. Table 4.3 summarizes the industry characteristics and their implications for future profits.

Notes

1. There are exceptions, but this is the general rule.
2. Grant, Robert M. (1991), *Contemporary Strategy Analysis, Concepts, Techniques, Applications*. Oxford: Blackwell.
3. Porter, M.E. (1980) *Competitive Strategy: Techniques for Analysing Industries and Competitors*. New York: Free Press.
4. See Baumol, W.J., Panzar, J.C. and Willig, R.D. (1982) *Contestable Markets and the Theory of Industry Structure*. New York: Harcourt Brace Jovanovitch.
5. The PIMS (Profit Impact of Market Strategy) of the US Strategic Planning Institute, a large-scale study designed to measure the relationship between business actions and business results (www.pimsonline.com).
6. Brandenburger, A. and Nalebuff, B. (1996) *Co-operation*. New York: Doubleday.
7. Quoted in Grant, *Contemporary Strategy Analysis* (see note 2 above).

CHAPTER

5 Which Customers is the Target Serving?

In Chapter 3, we looked at strategic segmentation because, before we can even start to think about the target company's future performance, we must have a clear idea of what market it serves. Nothing else makes sense unless we first define the boundaries of the target's market. Having defined the market, a target company's market strategy is based on which parts of its market it serves, its value proposition and the key relationships it must establish and maintain to make its marketing strategies work. Operational segmentation is concerned with identifying distinctive groups of buyers within the market, as defined by strategic segmentation. CDD uses operational segmentation as a basis for comparing the effectiveness of the target's product and marketing strategy.

Operational marketing segmentation

Operational market segmentation is segmentation within a market. One of the most often quoted works on market segmentation in industrial markets by Shapiro and Bonoma[1] identifies five general segmentation criteria 'arranged as a nested hierarchy – like a set of boxes that fit one onto the other' (see Figure 5.1).

This neatly captures the process of segmenting a market. The segmentation criteria in the largest outermost nests are easily observable characteristics about a market. As you move inwards, the criteria become ever more subtle and hard to assess. Shapiro and Bonoma also note 'that it may not be necessary or even desirable for every industrial marketer to use every stage of the nested approach for every product'. But it is important to 'understand the approach before deciding on omissions and shortcuts'. They also remind us that factors in one nest affect those in other nests. For this reason, the nest should be seen as a framework rather than a blueprint for segmenting markets. It 'cannot be applied in a cook book fashion but requires, instead, careful, intelligent, judgment'.

The sections that follow look at the segmentation variables set out in Figure 5.1. These are grouped according to whether they are most appropriate in segmenting consumer markets or business-to-business markets, but there is no reason why those listed for one should not also apply to the other. Managers in business-to-business markets often look at the world in consumer marketing terms and segment by demographics or, more likely, by account size. The important thing is to find a meaningful basis for segmentation and not just go through the motions. The fact that 'big' customers act differently from 'small' customers is not usually the insight on which a winning market strategy has been built or can be sustained. The thing to remember is that marketing segmentation is not just looking for groups of buyers, but it is looking to understand the differences in buyer behaviour among different buyers of the same product or service. This is an iterative process, as the

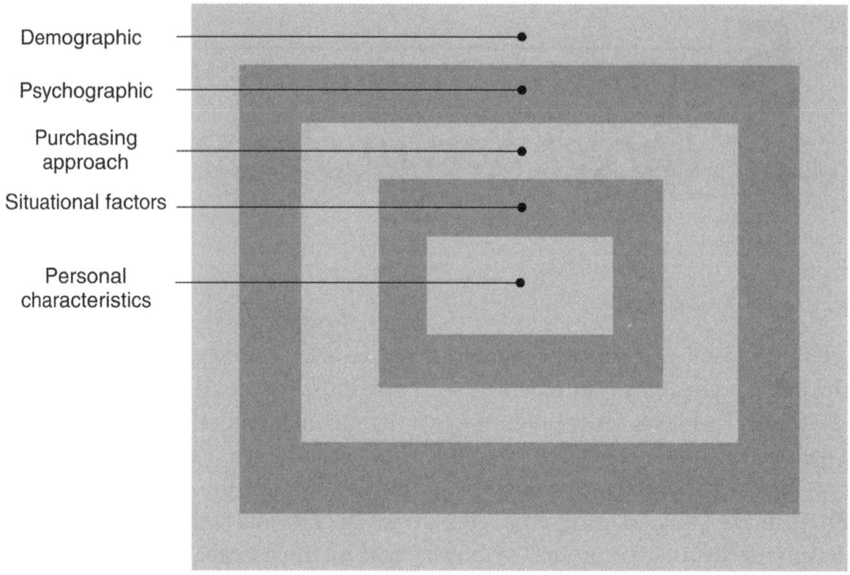

Figure 5.1 The nested approach to segmentation

groups are not always obvious and what works as a basis of segmentation in one market will not work in another. For example, over half of all male underwear is purchased by women, which means the female buyer segment represents and important buyer group for manufacturers and sellers of male underwear.

The five forms of market segmentation shown in Figure 5.1 have emerged as the most popular. They are used in CDD as proxies for differences in buyer behaviour that define different market segments. As mentioned above, some, or all, of the main approaches will be used but do not be surprised if what works as a basis of segmentation in one market does not work in another.

Demographic

Demographic variables include age, gender, stage of family life cycle, size and family type, income, educational level, race and nationality or combinations thereof. Clearly defined segments can be identified using demographic variables, but according to Beane and Ennis,[2] entire markets cannot usually be segmented by this method alone.

CONSUMER MARKETS

Age

Age is perhaps the most widespread basis of segmentation in consumer markets. Demand is often age related for a number of reasons. Tastes and needs change as we grow older as does our income and stage of family life cycle. One of the appeals of age as a basis of segmentation is that it provides an easy way of measuring segment sizes. Case Study 18 demonstrates the use of age as a basis of segmentation.

CASE STUDY 18

FITTED KITCHENS

Not that long ago (really) biscuits were sold from tins and there was a grocery store on every street corner. Now the supermarkets dominate food retailing just as the electrical 'sheds' sell the bulk of the TV sets we buy and out of town carpet stores sell us most of our carpets. Against this background, it is perfectly reasonable to wonder whether the same trend away from the high street and towards the mega store will not affect the kitchen market sooner rather than later. Figure 5.2 shows how the kitchen worktop market works.

Age, and with it, income, are the clues on the customer side. Young people are the natural customers for 'out of town' kitchen superstores. They fit them themselves or project manage the fitting. Fitting a kitchen is a major exercise involving at least three trades: carpenters, plumbers and electricians, and possibly four if the plumber is not qualified to fit gas appliances. The job is messy and has to be done quickly. As customers get older and more affluent, they want the kitchen fitted for them. As yet, home improvement superstores have not been able to offer a fitting service because of the difficulties inherent in managing and co-ordinating the (self-employed) tradesmen. One of the major chains tried and gave up. This forces the consumer back to the high street. One day, though, the home improvement superstores might crack the fitting problems, then what? Then we must think more carefully about segmenting the market. With a professional fitting service the home improvement superstores could take more of the market, but from whom? Kitchens are aspirational purchases. Kitchens available in the high street are more up-market than kitchens from DIY stores. The high street, then, is likely to keep the bulk of its customer base with the home improvement superstores picking up the less aspirational customers who require fitting. Right now, these are the customers of the third set of players in the market, the kitchen multiples.

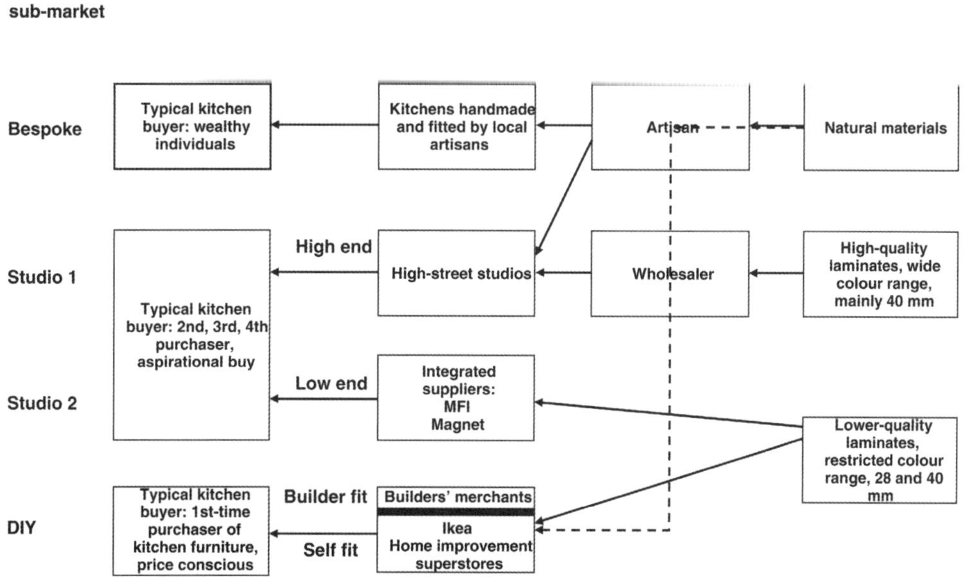

Figure 5.2 The market can be segmented into three distinct sub-markets

But age alone is not satisfactory as a basis of market segmentation because even within one age bracket there are a diversity of buying motivations. The consumption of whisky is age related, but there are massive differences in brand preference among whisky drinkers that are not just related to age. Also, biological age is not always the best measure of age because perceived age and biological age do not always go hand in hand. In fact, research in this area[3] suggests perceived age is much more important than actual age.

Gender

Gender is a very commonly used basis for segmenting markets, for obvious reasons. Not only does it often correspond to crucial differences in buying behaviour, it is also an easy one to measure. But gender as a biological construct does not tell the whole story – working women can be quite different from housewives.

Stage in the family life cycle

Figure 5.3 illustrates the family life cycle.

An individual's buying preferences are likely to change with each stage, as is their ability to fund those purchases. There are obviously different marketing opportunities associated with each stage. Dance music is going to have a much bigger appeal to group 2 than group 4 and vice-versa with baby products or nursery schools.

Of course, this is a stylized and to some extent hypothetical life cycle based on western experience. Single parent families, the rising divorce rate and later marriages are all playing their part to both muddy the segmentation waters and to create new opportunities for creative marketeers to re-segment markets.

Size and family type

Households are economic units whose behaviour varies according to their size and composition. Using household composition as a basis of segmentation therefore makes sense for a lot of products. Single person households have different needs from those of the traditional nuclear family. However, once again care is needed because the single person household that comprises a young professional bachelor will be quite different from the pensioner living alone.

Income

As most consumer marketers are aiming to increase their share of discretionary income, this is perhaps the best measure to use. Discretionary income is a measure of disposable income less expenditure on the necessities of life, such as mortgage payments. It can change suddenly if expenditure on items that make up a large proportion of expenditure, such as mortgages, suddenly go up or down.

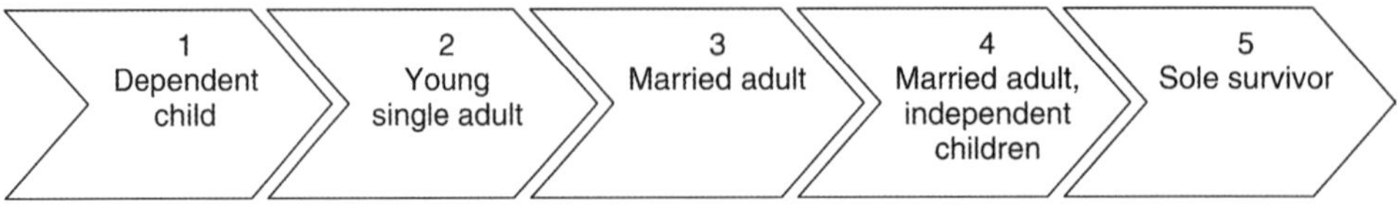

Figure 5.3 The family life cycle

Despite its neatness and apparent correlation with buyer behaviour for many products, segmentation on income has its problems. For a start many people lie about their income and behaviour can be quite different between individuals even in similar income segments.

Education

Education plays a huge part in our preferences. Educated households, for example, spend relatively more on books and fresh food.

Race/nationality

Ethnic groups, even after years of integration, still retain distinctive preferences and ethnicity can be a very important basis of segmentation for some industries. However, just like age and gender, strict segmentation along genetic lines can be a mistake. Within any one ethnic group there will be those at one end of the spectrum who identify strongly with their origins and at the other end, those who wish only to identify with the host country with, of course, every variation in between.

Geo-demographic

Geographical segmentation is a perfectly valid means of segmenting some markets. The underlying assumption of such geo-demographic segmentation is that where someone lives is closely linked to their lifestyles.[4] Apparently 'the long, dark and cold winter nights of northern England and Scotland have led the inhabitants of these regions to take proportionately more winter sun holidays than their counterparts in the south of England, despite the latter having higher average levels of disposable income.'[5] Segmentation can now be done at the postal code level linking geography to other social, demographic and economic data.

BUSINESS-TO-BUSINESS MARKETS

Customer industry

Industry says a lot about different customer types and their different needs in different purchase situations, how a product is used and therefore how it is bought, how important it is in the customer's value chain and so forth.

Company size

Large companies can differ from small companies in many ways. The volume/price trade-off is the obvious one in most industrial markets, but there are also many other behavioural differences. Case Study 19 gives an example of company size as a basis for segmentation.

CASE STUDY 19

RECRUITMENT PROCESS OUTSOURCING

Recruitment is a strategic resource and will not be outsourced. However, the recruitment process is a chore for many under-resourced human resources (HR) departments and it will be outsourced. Recruitment Process Outsourcing (RPO) is the outsourcing of all the tasks around recruitment from helping managers define the role that needs filling, placing advertisements, designing a recruitment website, maintaining a database

CASE STUDY 19 – *continued*

of candidates, writing rejection letters, arranging interviews, collecting interview feedback, making job offers and keeping the candidates 'warm' until they arrive. The 'win' of outsourcing is that specialist RPO companies have the volume and experience to be able to do it more cheaply than the firm that only recruits a dozen or so senior people per year and with an efficient process, recruiters can avoid the transactional approach, and all that means for getting the best candidates, of the traditional recruitment agencies as well as the 20 per cent plus of salary that they charge for successfully filling a vacancy. RPO appeals to mid-recruiters organized around a strong central HR department. Large companies already have volume and experience, small companies do not recruit enough to make RPO viable.

A similar process is at work with payroll outsourcing. There are two factors that make in-house payroll processing viable. The first is having enough work for at least two people. Because of illness and holidays, a staff of one is no good. The second is keeping abreast of the rules. Again this dictates a company of a certain size to make the cost involved worth it. Payroll is therefore outsourced as a matter of course by small companies and as a matter of persuasion by medium and large companies.

Psychographic

Psychographic market segmentation considers the effects of social class, lifestyle, attitudes, benefits sought and loyalty. This form of segmentation attempts to incorporate part of the inner person or their underlying motivations into the understanding of the market. These days, social class is not that widely used as a basis for segmentation because it is too value laden. Instead, more practical and more objective indicators of socio-economics are used.

CONSUMER MARKETS

Occupation

The ABC1 system set out in Table 5.1 will be familiar to most people.

Because of the modern-day work uncertainties and because so many people have joined the middle classes, this was revised in 1998 with the number of classifications increasing from six to 17. Even with this new, much more detailed classification, segmentation based on occupation remains crude compared with the geo-demographic methods discussed below.

Table 5.1 Occupation as the basis for socio-economic segmentation

Class category	*Occupation*
A	Higher managerial, administrative or professional
B	Intermediate managerial, administrative or professional
C1	Supervisory or clerical, and junior managerial, administrative or professional
C2	Skilled manual workers
D	Semi- and unskilled manual workers
E	State pensioners or widows (no other earners), casual or lower grade workers, or long-term unemployed

Lifestyle

It is very difficult to describe a lifestyle accurately, let alone measure the number of people following similar lifestyles. Nevertheless, as society splinters into ever smaller groups, marketeers have been more or less forced to match product and promotion to lifestyles with the development of many lifestyle definitions for specific sectors. Thus while lifestyle segments can be useful for defining a target market,[6] they are difficult to operationalize because of a paucity of data beyond that collected for specific sample surveys.

User status

To sell consulting to the chairman of a large public company demands a different approach to dealing with the managing director of a subsidiary or a line manager.

Attitudes

At least lifestyles are observable, while attitudes are often hidden and can be subject to change over time.

BUSINESS-TO-BUSINESS MARKETS

Industry sector

One of the most obvious ways of segmenting an industrial market is to look at industry sectors served. The IT and software industries have always been particularly focused on what they refer to as 'vertical markets'.

Size of firm

Some customers are big and will place big orders direct with manufacturers. For example, the big builders merchants buy insulation materials, such as mineral wool and polyisocyanurate (PIR) board, direct while the smaller ones buy from specialist insulation distributors.

Company capability

Technically weak customers in many chemicals and polymer businesses rely on compounders to put together the right packages of ingredients for the manufacture of their products. Some customers are always more sophisticated than others and will go for the no frills package rather than pay a premium for 'hand-holding'.

Original equipment manufacturers (OEMs) versus users

OEMs that incorporate a product into their own will require a different approach from users of the product.

Operating characteristics/service requirements

Different companies operate in different ways and therefore demand different approaches from their suppliers. For example, companies operating with tight materials inventories obviously look much more closely at a supplier's reliable delivery record.

Purchasing approach

Purchasing approach includes variables such as loyalty, purchase occasion, use occasion and frequency of purchase. Most will be common to both consumer and business-to-business markets, but those listed at the end of this section are unique to business-to-business.

LOYALTY

This is really another way of saying some brands in some markets have their followers, while others will see buyers switching quite readily for better prices or better benefits. There is, for example a marked difference between the approach of corporate buyers and financial buyers of CDD. Commercial acquirers tend to be incredibly loyal, whereas financial acquirers have a tendency to select their CDD advisers based on perceived suitability for the job on hand. They will go to a lot more trouble than corporate buyers to ascertain which CDD providers have experience in the same sector as the transaction being contemplated.

PURCHASE OCCASION

The same physical buyer may have different requirements, depending on the occasion, just like the purchasers of waterproof matches mentioned in Chapter 3. For example, car rental customers of Hertz are very different from the customers of EasyCar. The former tend to be business users, are relatively price insensitive but want a high level of service and convenience. Core EasyCar customers tend to be people who do not own a car but occasionally have need for one for personal use. They tend to be highly price sensitive, will put up with a rudimentary service, but could quite easily be, and in cities often are, the same people as those hiring from Hertz when on business.

USE OCCASION

A quick lunch is a very different proposition from a romantic dinner – even when taken in the same restaurant.

STAGE IN BUYING PROCESS

Complex products can be subject to a long buying process. The concerns at the beginning can be different form the concerns at the end, as indeed can the decision makers. Take software for example. If it does not satisfy the IT department at the beginning of the buying process that it will not cause the rest of the system to crash or will not require undue maintenance and training, the buying process will get no further. After the technical hurdle is crossed, the decision is with the user, whose basis of selection will be utility and user friendliness.

FREQUENCY OF PURCHASE AND/OR EXPERIENCE OF THE PRODUCT

Frequent buyers tend to know what they are doing and will therefore be much more sensitive to price and benefits than an infrequent buyers, whose main motivation will be reassurance. Price will be more important with frequent purchasers, whereas pre-sale technical support may be exactly what is needed for less frequent purchasers.

PURCHASING FUNCTION ORGANIZATION

The organization of purchasing can be a clue to segmentation. Purchasing in the UK National Health Service has changed radically in recent years. Professional purchasers are using the purchasing clout of an organization of size to drive down prices. Suppliers of products that not long ago had a healthy margin now have no choice but to compete on price. However, suppliers of those products that are 'close to the surgeon' can still make good returns because surgeons can overrule the purchasing function. For example surgeons will specify the make of rubber tube to be used to support breathing during an operation. Each is made in a slightly different way and they still specifically ask for the one with which they trained. On the other hand, PVC tubing is PVC tubing; therefore the PVC tubing used in heart by-pass operations is not specified and is much more price sensitive as a result.

COMPANY CULTURE

The culture of some companies is such that they will only buy from the market leader.

FORMALITY OF THE BUYING PROCESS

This, as a basis of segmentation, would look for differences in the number of people involved or the complexity of the process.

URGENCY

In all markets, except it sometimes seems to me in CDD, the more urgently you need something, the more you expect to pay. Everything is always urgent in CDD. In some markets, urgency can be a good proxy for a distinct market segment. The business of providing replacement parts for aircraft is very different to the original manufacture. Prices and stocks are higher and response times quicker than in original equipment manufacture.

One other thing to remember about segments is that it perfectly possible to go on segmenting to the customer level. For marketing practitioners this is becoming more of a necessity as we will see it Chapter 8 (customer satisfaction). However, for CDD it is as well to limit the number of individual segments examined to a sensibly small number. The following is the normal list of factors to take into account:

- Measurability, meaning the size, location and content of a segment, can be easily measured.
- Accessibility, meaning the segment can be reached and effectively served.
- Substantiality, meaning the segment is sufficiently large and profitable enough to merit attention.
- Actionability, meaning for our purposes that different marketing strategies are being implemented to serve the segments.
- Determinant, meaning that the buyers' decision factors can be clearly identified.
- Appropriate, meaning that the basis of segmentation is rational.
- Predictive, meaning that the segmentation basis links market behaviour to segment membership benefits sought.

Situational factors and personal characteristics

The data needed for a meaningful basis of segmentation in the innermost nests of Figure 5.1 is less visible, less permanent and requires an understanding of what is going on in the customers' heads . This is especially true when CDD is called on to judge the potential of new products and new markets (see Chapter 9). Collecting meaningful data is at the very heart of CDD interviewing, which is covered later in Chapter 13.

Conclusion

Segmentation helps map out the different types of customer market in which the target should have developed different market strategies and programmes if it is to be a serious player. To understand how well a target performs in its market, we must decide which segments it serves because its competitive position is the result of how well it meets the needs of the customers in those segments. If it meets them better than the competition, it has a strong competitive position. Definition of the market will help determine a target's competitive position because it will define who the competition is and where it is going to come from. Segmentation also helps take a view on the target's growth plans if these involve developing into new areas because there should be a link to its current business, its customer base and its capabilities.

For CDD, then, understanding a market and a target company's position within it starts with an understanding of the fundamental customer benefits sought in different parts of the market, whether these be from physical product differences or from non-product attributes. This should not come as any surprise, since any business's success is all about doing best what matters most to the customer and thus securing long-term competitive advantage through long-term customer satisfaction.

Understanding why the customer is buying the target's products, and what needs those products are satisfying, also helps us to see where the competition is coming from, and where it might come from in the future. It should also shed light on the likely success of any new, related, areas into which the target might be developing.

Segmentation is not a precise science. There are potentially as many segments as there are individual consumers because at the heart of market segmentation is what matters most to the customer and they are all individuals. The same product can have different benefits for different people. Cars can be a means of transport, a fashion statement, a status symbol and many other things besides. Each segment is likely to respond to the 4Ps[7] in a different way, but segments will blur and overlap. The trick is to find meaningful groupings of customer needs that are sufficiently different from other groups. It is an iterative process, rather like peeling an onion, and often relies on a number of proxies as short cuts to determining different preferences amongst different customer groups.

Having strategically segmented the market the next move is to define the groups of customers served by the target, because this is the first step to determining how well it performs relative to the competition. As with strategic segmentation, there are many proxies for operational market segmentation and much blurring of boundaries.

Notes

1. Shapiro, B.P. and Bonoma, T.V. (1984) 'How to Segment Industrial Markets', *Harvard Business Review*, 64(May/June): 104–70.
2. Beane, T.P. and Ennis, D.M. (1987) 'Market Segmentation: A Review', *European Journal of Marketing*, 21(5): 20–42.
3. Mayo, E.J. and Jarvis, L.P. (1981) *The Psychology of Leisure Travel*. Boston, MA: CBI Publishing.

4. See, for example, Experian's MOSAIC database, which draws on multiple sources of data to calssify UK households into 12 groups and 52 types. MOSAIC is a geodemographic segmentation system developed by Experian. The basic premise of geodemographic segmentation is that people tend to gravitate towards communities with other people of similar backgrounds, interests and means. For further details, see www.appliedgeographic.com.
5. Palmer, A. (2000) *Principles of Marketing*. Oxford: OUP.
6. Empty nesters, for example, older couples whose children have 'flown' and are often blessed with an affluence they have not seen before, especially if also 'SKIers', where 'SKI' stands for 'Spending The Kids' Inheritance'.
7. The so called 4Ps of marketing are product, place, price and promotion. Three more Ps are added for service industries – physical evidence, process and people.

CHAPTER

6 Ability to Compete

A favourable industry structure is all very well, but three factors spoil the party. First, competitive pressure has increased in most sectors to the point where few industries (or segments) offer cosy refuge from vigorous competition. Second, empirical research suggests that industry factors account for only a small proportion of the difference between the profitability of different firms.[1] Industry factors are certainly less important for the stars (and dogs) than they are for middle performers. Finally, you can segment the market beautifully and work out which are the most benign sectors, but if you do not have a competitive advantage in a segment, then it is not attractive. Hence, analysing the target's competitive advantage, or the acquirer's ability to create one by acquisition, is very important in CDD and more important than finding a way of avoiding vigorous competition. In the words of the Sage of Omaha, Warren Buffet, 'The key to investing is determining the competitive advantage of any given company and, above all, the durability of that advantage. The products or services that have wide, sustainable moats around them are the ones that deliver rewards to investors.'[2]

To understand a target's ability to compete we have to understand its capabilities, resources and competencies, where:

- resources are deployed in the activities of the business;
- capabilities are the skills that the business possesses (but not necessarily used);
- competences are the skills that underpin what it does, that is, the capabilities that are used.

What we are really interested in are unique resources and core competencies, as shown in Figure 6.1, because, if the customer is willing to pay for these, they are what allows the business to differentiate itself from the competition.

This chapter is therefore concerned with the identification, quantification and assessment of factors that can give rise to a competitive advantage and hence above-average profits.

The analysis of resources and capabilities

If resources, rather than positioning, are the key to superior profits, the most successful companies will be those that can exploit the differences between themselves and other companies in ways that better meet the needs of customers. This point is fundamental to CDD and our thinking about competitive advantage. Not only should we be looking for points of difference between the target company and its competition, but we should go on to understand how those differences relate to the target's resources and capabilities. If its resources and capabilities are unique, then it is impossible for other companies to replicate the basis of its success.

	Same as competitors or easy to imitate	Better than competitors and difficult to imitate
Resources	'Threshold' resources	Unique resources
Competencies	'Threshold' competencies	Core competencies

Figure 6.1 Plotting resources and competencies

RESOURCES

Tangible resources are the most easily identified and certainly worth thinking about as a source of competitive advantage. However, for most companies intangible resources contribute far more, as is demonstrated in Case Study 20.

CASE STUDY 20

BUNDY TUBING

Bundy is an American supplier of brake tubing (used to transport brake fluid under pressure to the brake drums on a car when the brake pedal is pressed) and refrigeration tubing (used to transport refrigerant from the condenser). There is nothing particularly special about Bundy tubing. It is made from low grade steel that is first coated in copper, then wound twice around a mandril (twice so that it can take pressure) and heated so that the copper melts and fills any gaps. The process was invented in the 1920s and has never been successfully replicated, despite the likes of General Motors trying hard to do so.

The intangible resources that are particularly important are:

- Reputation: company reputation is a valuable resource. Reputation is a long-lived asset unless undermined by misdeeds or ineptitude. As buyers become more sophisticated and judgemental (see Chapter 7), this is becoming an even more significant factor.
- Customer relationships are a resource because loyalty and trust gives a company the ability to defend market share and open up new markets.
- Channel power concerns dominance or weakness in distribution channels.
- Brand name: the value of a brand is the confidence it instils in customers. For them, a brand is a guarantee that reduces their uncertainty and search costs. The more difficult it is to discern quality on inspection and the greater the cost to the customer of purchasing

a defective product, the greater the value of a brand. This value is reflected in the price premium that a brand can command over an unbranded product and/or the extra market share a strong brand gives. Assessing brand strength is dealt with later in the chapter.

- Know how.
- Market information: this can be a critical marketing asset, in the sense that being able to understand the market or customer better and to respond faster and more effectively to customer demands creates competitive advantage.
- Human resources: identifying the stock of human resources within a firm is complex and difficult. However, it is not the resources that count, but the way their skills are harmonized and integrated, just like with a football team. One way in which harmonization takes place is through company culture, that unwritten set of rules and norms that govern how things are done. The culture of a business comes from the top. As Peters and Waterman put it, 'firms with superior financial performance typically are characterized by a strong set of core managerial values that define the ways they conduct business'.[3] Intuitively, to get the most out of people they need proper direction. Motivation is key and motivation depends on clear objectives. McGregor has argued that people need objectives to direct their efforts and that if objectives are not provided by the organization, they will create their own.[4] In a strong culture, this might not be as bad as it sounds, since, according to Porter et al.,[5] individual behaviour is affected by people's perceptions of what is expected of them. Cultural norms, therefore, are much more important than management direction.

ORGANIZATIONAL CAPABILITIES

The term 'organizational capabilities' refers to the target's ability to do what it does. What we are really interested in are 'distinctive competences' and 'core competences'.

- Core competencies[6] make a disproportionate contribution to ultimate costumer value, or to the efficiency with which that value is delivered. Core competencies are distinctive skills that yield competitive advantage and ideally are difficult for competitors to imitate.
- Distinctive competences can be defined as those things that a firm does particularly well relative to its competitors.

To identify a firm's capabilities, we need to have some basis for classifying and disaggregating its activities. The value chain analysis separates the activities of the firm into a sequential chain and distinguishes between primary activities (those involved with the transformation of inputs and interface with the customer) and support activities as shown in Figure 6.2.

Disaggregating activities takes place first at the top level (for example, inbound logistics, marketing) and subsequently at finer levels. Outbound logistics may be broken down into warehousing, inventory control, packing and distribution and these can be further broken down into more specialist capabilities performed by smaller teams of resources. This hierarchy of capabilities applies in every firm. More general, broadly defined capabilities are always formed from the integration of more specialized capabilities.

All activities can contribute towards competitive advantage. Certain areas may be more significant than others, although this may change over time.

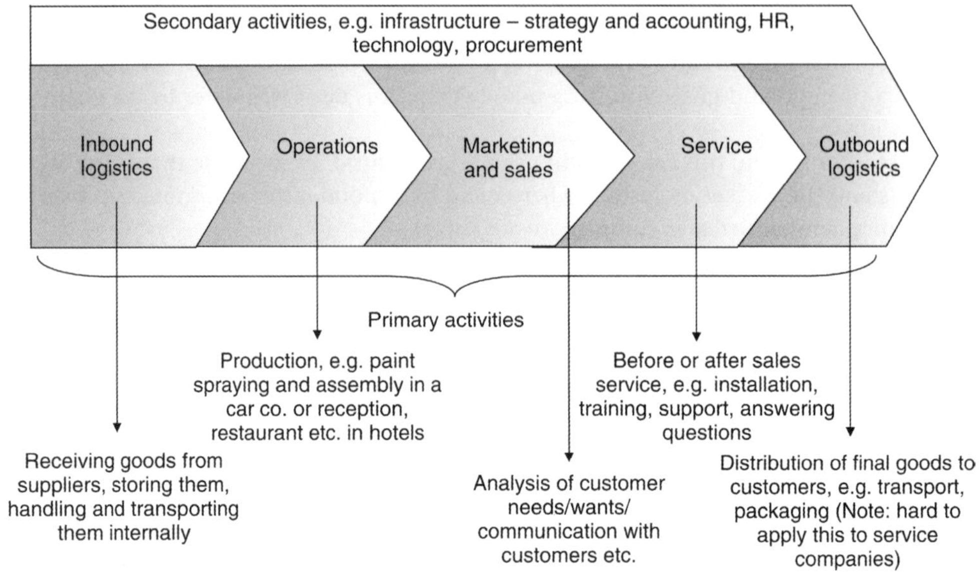

Figure 6.2 The value chain

The value chain describes the essential activities that add value to the product or service. In Figure 6.2, these primary activities are illustrated in a chain moving from left to right and, as already mentioned, they represent the activities of physically creating the product or services and transferring it to the buyer, together with any after sales service. They are linked to four support activities: procurement, technology development, HR management and the firm's infrastructure. Every one of the primary and support activities incurs costs and should add value to the product and service in excess of these costs. As far as the future of the acquisition is concerned, any cost reduction should not be at the expense of quality in areas that matter to customers. Equally, costs can be added justifiably if they add qualities that the consumer values and is willing to pay for. This is very important because, as Ohmae[7] reminds us, competitive advantage should be sought for one main purpose – serving customers' needs. It is not primarily to beat the competition, although the organization does need to be more effective than its rivals.

With multi-product companies servicing different market segments, each segment must be looked at separately. There will be linkages between the segments, for example a shared accounting resource or shared warehouse. The degree to which the linkages between the segments served are being exploited should not be overlooked. Do not forget that the competition will often have the same linkages.

Do not assume that the linkages will be automatic. Cultural differences between the business units can make it difficult to link value chains. An enforcement company (a firm of bailiffs that enforces non-payment of fines) was built in the UK from a London-based firm of bailiffs and a Birmingham-based trace firm specializing in tracking down missing non-payers. Given its trace background, the operations controlled from Birmingham had a different way of doing business from the London operations. It provided customers with a more effective service and one that was also more profitable. Bailiffs are only paid on success. A high proportion of debtors 'disappear' once enforcement proceedings are started. By using trace early on in the recovery process, it could find absconders and advise its customers on the best way of recovering the debt and at the same time determine whether or not it was worth making (expensive) enforcement visits to the debtor's last known address. The London operations, with their enforcement culture, would simply make the required visits to the last known address and, if the debtor was not there, would simply hand the debt back. The London operations had higher costs and a lower recovery rate (and more disgruntled customers).

Checklist 5 in Appendix A gives a list of the common types of resources and capabilities.

TURNING RESOURCES INTO CAPABILITIES

The key to turning resources into capabilities, according to Hamel and Prahalad,[8] is the firm's ability to leverage its resources. Resources can be leveraged by:

- concentrating them on a few clearly defined goals that have the biggest impact on customers' perceived value;
- accumulating them by learning from experience and borrowing from other firms through, for example, alliances and outsourcing arrangements;
- complementing them by linking them with complementary resources and capabilities, for example, by making sure design and marketing work together;
- using them to the fullest by applying them to different products, markets and product generations, and co-opting resources through collaborative arrangements with other companies;
- increasing the speed with which investment in resources generates cash returns, a key determinant of which is new product development cycle time.

TURNING RESOURCES INTO CAPABILITIES INTO PROFITS

As shown in Figure 6.3, earning profits from resources and capabilities depends on a firm's ability to:

- create a competitive advantage;
- sustain that advantage;
- appropriate the returns of that competitive advantage.

In deciding whether or not a resource or capability can create a competitive advantage for the target company, we have to determine whether two fairly self-evident conditions exist:

1. A resource or capability must be scarce. If it is widely available within the industry, having it may be an essential entry qualification, but it will not be a sufficient basis for winning.
2. The resource or capability must be relevant. Resources and capabilities are valuable only if they can be linked to one or more of the key success factors within an industry, that is, they must either help the target create value for its customers or help it survive competition.

If they do, the next test is the sustainability of the advantage created. For an advantage to be sustainable, resources and capabilities must have three characteristics. They must be durable and they must not be replicable or transferable:

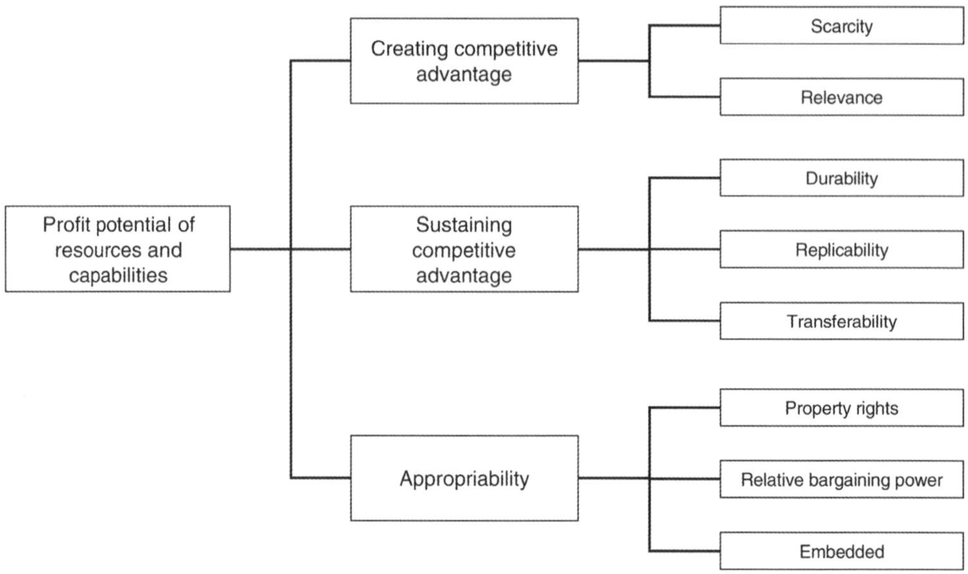

Figure 6.3 Factors affecting the profit potential of resources and capabilities

- Durability: some resources are more durable than others and therefore more secure as a basis for competitive advantage. The pace of technological change is increasingly shortening the useful life span of most resources.
- Replicability: if a firm cannot buy a resource or capability, it must build it. Some capabilities are just not worth the cost and effort. For example, if you are in the lobbying business, it is possible to subscribe to a database that gives you a suite of information that you need to do your job. The data is collected form sources such as Hansard, the daily verbatim record of what is said in the UK Houses of Parliament, press feeds and the daily papers. It would be very easy to replicate the data, but is it really worth it for something so specialist? Others appear simple, but prove difficult to replicate. Even where replication is possible, incumbent firms may benefit from the fact that resources and capabilities that have been accumulated over a long period are often less costly and more productive than the same assets that have been accumulated quickly by would-be imitators. OAG, publisher of the world famous ABC Guide to airline schedules, collects airline timetable information, which it gets free from the airlines, collates it and charges its customers for the resulting output. The business is easy to replicate because airlines will supply just about anyone with their timetable data. However, there are few direct competitors. First of all, travel agents only need one airline timetable – but it has to be right. The ABC guide has been around for many years and its accuracy has been proved. It has also developed its contacts and refined its systems over the years, such that in cost and speed it is far ahead of any would-be newcomers.
- Transferability: if competitors can imitate a successful company by acquiring the necessary resources, any competitive advantage will be short lived. The simplest means of acquiring those resources is to buy them, but this only works if they are mobile. Many are, especially in people-based businesses. Geography is one obvious barrier, but information is another. It is not always obvious to the outsider which people count, why and to what extent and therefore how much they are worth. Added to this is the risk

that the 'team' will not perform in the new outfit as they did in the old, because performance is either situation specific or dependent on complementary resources. In fact, there is a body of theory that maintains that success is based on capabilities that are the outcome of processes rather than individuals, assets or knowledge.[9]

Unique selling propositions (USPs) that can be easily copied are not a long-term sources of competitive advantage – and most things can be copied. A further word of warning: As we will see in Chapter 8, USPs eventually become expected and therefore not USPs any more. However, it is a part of CDD to judge how long 'eventually' is.

Having created a sustainable competitive advantage, the final question is the extent to which the profits created go to the firm. This problem manifests itself most in the acquisitions of people businesses and is the reason why professional services still tend to be partnerships. A partnership avoids many of the problems over company versus individual ownership of critical factors such as knowledge, reputation and customer relationships. If there is ambiguity about who 'owns' what, who gets what comes down to the bargaining power between individuals and the firm. The more the firm relies on the skill and experience of the individual as opposed to the accumulated skill and experience of the firm embedded in the way it does things, the greater the bargaining power of the individual. If winning the UK Premiership could be embedded in the tactics of Chelsea Football Club, there would be no need to pay the players tens of thousands of pounds a week. As the soccer transfer market demonstrates only too clearly, a player's weekly wage is determined by four factors:

- the degree to which a team's performance is identified with individuals;
- the more effective those individuals (or their agents) are at selling their wares;
- the more mobile players are;
- the ease with which they can play effectively elsewhere.

IDENTIFYING RESOURCES AND CAPABILITIES

To draw up a list of key resources and capabilities, look at both demand and the supply side. From the demand side, start wide by asking the target's management whether the target is as profitable as its competitors, why some firms are more successful than others and on what resources and capabilities their success is based. The starting point will be what it takes to be successful in this market and what resources and capabilities this implies. On the supply side, use the value chain as a framework for discussing the capabilities needed at each stage and the resources on which these capabilities are based.

Having established a working list, the importance of the various factors on it need assessing and their existence needs verifying. It is possible to do both through customer interviewing. Chapter 7 has a section on customer key purchase criteria and how these might translate into critical success factors and therefore which resources and capabilities are most important. We should not, however, concentrate solely on customer purchase criteria. What we must bear in mind is that our ultimate objective is not to attract customers, but to understand whether the target has a sustainable competitive advantage and can therefore make a superior profit. While customers will value many things about the target, many of these things will be necessary just to compete in the market. They will not be the 'scarce but relevant' resources shown in Figure 6.3. We have already seen the way to categorize resources and competencies in Figure 6.1.

IDENTIFYING RELATIVE STRENGTHS

In assessing their own competencies, organizations frequently fall victim to past glories, hopes for the future, and their own wishful thinking. The section on key purchase criteria in Chapter 8 shows one way of assessing relative strength, but it is not always about data. Highly successful companies are the ones that have recognized what they do well and have set their strategies accordingly. What you need is the insight and understanding to recognize what are distinctive capabilities and to recognize when these are being deployed most effectively. After all, a good strategy is one by which a company can gain significant ground on its competitors at an acceptable cost to itself. It can do this in four ways:

- Identify key success factors in an industry and concentrate resources in a particular area where the company sees an opportunity to gain the most significant advantage over its competitors.
- Exploit an area where a company enjoys relative superiority.
- Aggressively attempt to change the key success factors by changing the basis on which business is conducted.
- Innovate – open up new markets and develop new products.

These days, companies should not be doing anything that they are not really good at, because they can outsource the rest. Moreover, if companies do not specialize, they will not be as good as the competition where it matters

SWOT analysis

A SWOT analysis is one of the simplest ways of understanding the capabilities of a business. SWOT stands for: Strengths, Weaknesses, Opportunities and Threats. Distinguishing between external and the internal environment of the firm is common to most approaches to the design and evaluation of business strategies. A SWOT analysis does just that. As can be seen in Figure 6.4, it distinguishes between strengths and weaknesses – features of the internal environment – and opportunities and threats – features of the external environment.

Table 6.1 summarizes the pros and cons of SWOT analysis.

The SWOT framework is handicapped by difficulties in distinguishing strengths from weaknesses and opportunities from threats, but an arbitrary classification of external factors into opportunities and threats, and internal factors into strengths and weaknesses, is less important than a careful identification of these external and internal factors followed by an appraisal of their implications.

The problem with a SWOT analysis is that people normally enter the first thing that comes into their head without really thinking it through. It is too general and full of motherhood statements that tell you absolutely nothing. Come the presentation, of course, you have to justify the remarks made. With threats and opportunities, this tendency is even worse. Many a time someone has entered the CDD equivalent of 'and the sky may fall in' in the threats box simply because they could not think of anything else to write. Well, yes, the sky might well fall in, but how big a threat is there and if it does happen, how big will the

	Internal factors	External factors
Positive	Strengths • What is the target best at? • What specific skills/competitive advantages does it have?	Opportunities • What changes in the external environment can the target exploit? • What weakness in its competitors can it attack? • What new markets might be opening up?
Negative	Weaknesses • What is the target worst at? • What skills does it lack? • Where does it lag the competition?	Threats • What might the competition be able to do to hurt the target? • What new legislation might harm the target? • What social and / or economic changes might hurt the target – economic cycle for example?

Figure 6.4 SWOT analysis

impact on the target business? There really is no point adding items to a SWOT unless they have an important bearing on the business.

It is far better to take a more rigorous approach that forces you to tease out and prioritize strengths and weaknesses and opportunities and threats. This way you will also have plenty of ammunition for defending your conclusions. The best way to do this is to draw up a number of highly focused SWOTs as follows:

- Draw up one SWOT analysis for each component of the value chain, but include only those resources and capabilities that are recognized and valued by the customer.
- Score strengths and weaknesses relative to the competition.
- Rank strengths and weaknesses according to what is important in the target's customers' value chain.
- Construct one set of SWOTs per product market. You can always consolidate them later.

What we are doing here is forcing ourselves to identify the critical success factors in the target's business, its customers' needs, and hence factors influencing customer satisfaction. This helps us exclude the motherhood statements so often produced as a list of strengths such as 'old established', 'market leader' and 'well positioned'.

Table 6.1 The pros and cons of a SWOT analysis

Pros	*Cons*
Because it is qualitative, it is widely used as a discussion tool.	No use if strengths and weaknesses are not rated against the competition. Often they are simply listed.
A good first step before a more in-depth analysis or a good summary of detailed findings.	Can become too focused on the short term.
Helps isolate the key issues.	Analysts frequently overlook the fact that it is the management and use of resources that gives rise to strengths and weaknesses, not whether or not they exist.

The same discipline is required to view the opportunities and threats in the environment. Here the goal is to list those things in the relevant environments that make it attractive or unattractive to us. Opportunities and threats exist only in the outside world and they exist independently of our strategies, policies and actions – so no putting the target's plans down as opportunities.

The resulting matrices should be much more than the anodyne lists of traditional SWOT analysis. They should act as mirrors of the current position and testers of future strategies as described in the next three sections.

RELATIVE STRENGTHS AND WEAKNESSES

How does the target stand relative to the competition on what the customers regard as important. Where is it strong and where is it weak? How important, and how defensible, are its strengths? What will it cost, and how long will it take, to plug the weaknesses? Figure 6.5 shows the matrix that can now be completed.

Converting weakness into strength is likely to be a long-term task for most organizations and, in the short to medium term, a company is likely to be stuck with the resources and capabilities that it inherits from the previous period. Where a target company has strengths in certain activities within the value chain and weaknesses in others, the question to ask is whether it can specialize in those activities where it is strong and outsource the rest.

EXTENT OF MATCHING

Are the target's strengths matched to opportunities in the outside world? Strengths that do not match any known opportunity are of little value. Highly ranked opportunities for which the target has no matching strength are issues for the integration phase.

EASE OF CONVERSION

The goal with conversion strategies is to show the highly ranked weaknesses and threats that should be converted into strengths and opportunities. In some cases, this may be relatively straightforward. A weakness in sales coverage may mean adding to the sales force. In other cases, conversion might be more tricky, in which case these factors remain the limiting problems in this business and determine how attractive it is to us.

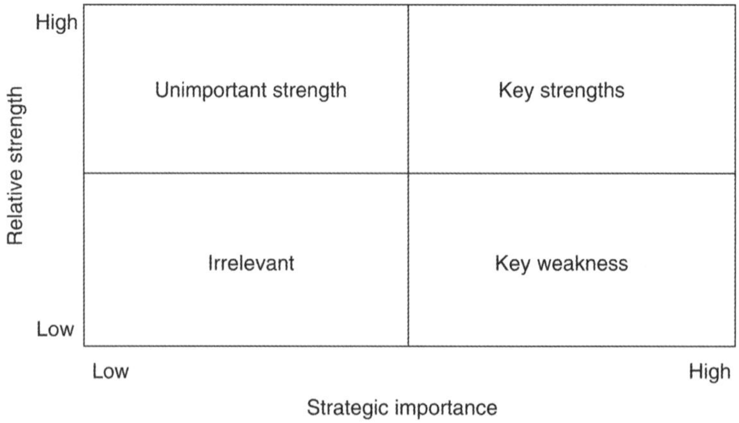

Figure 6.5 Appraising resources and capabilities

Table 6.2 The scored SWOT

	Opportunities			***Threats***	
Environmental issues	*Supply/demand balance*	*Policy changes*	*Expectation of industry consolidation*	*Labour shortages*	*etc*
Significance score	+5	+1	−4	−2	
Property acquisition	5				
Staff terms & conditions				2	
Staff training				3	
Cost base		–	–		
Pricing		5	5		
Total	10	6	1	3	

The scored SWOT

Table 6.2 sets out another approach to SWOT analysis, which introduces rigour into the process by scoring threats and opportunities.

First draw up a large grid. Along the top list all the environmental factors (see Checklist 6 in Appendix A) that may have a bearing on the business, along with a score that assesses their relative importance. Looking at the first column, the supply/demand balance is always important in any industry. If there is a big shortage of supply, the score will be positive. The bigger the shortfall, the bigger the score. The biggest scores (both positive and negative) are the most relevant issues.

The organization's resources are listed on the left-hand side. The target's relative strength or weakness in relation to the environmental issues is entered in the boxes. High scores imply an ability to deal with potential threats or capitalize on potential opportunities. Low scores imply a vulnerability to threats and only a limited ability to respond to opportunities.

Table 6.2 starts this process for a residential crisis care business for children in local authority care. Crisis care is the provision of emergency (that is, admitted on the same day as the enquiry), placements for children where existing care arrangements have broken down. The children concerned have severe emotional and behavioural difficulties (EBD) and pose a threat to either themselves or others and need intensive one-to-one or two-to-one care. They are often disturbed and traumatized, as they have often been the victims of abuse. Most have a history of failed placements in foster care or other children's homes.

Faced with a situation of having to find a suitable placement quickly, local authorities are not particularly price sensitive (although price is a factor). The most important purchase criteria are:

- The ability to accept and provide quality care for these most difficult children.
- 'Stickability' – the ability to keep the child in care for 6 months or more and not send the child back after a week or two. Having found a place for one of these children, the idea is to stabilize behaviour so that children can return to mainstream care. The last thing social services wants is instability caused by changing care arrangement before behaviour has settled down again.

This is a niche market. In the UK, there are between 750 and 1500 children at any one time who require intensive crisis-type care. There are around 600 suitable beds. Supply/demand balance is therefore very favourable. Hence the maximum positive score in the first box. However, this situation will not last. Emergency care providers are being bought up by venture capitalists who can see the growth opportunity. Our target was founded as a property company and still retains a formidable set of property development skills. If anyone can, the target can make the most of the capacity shortage by acquiring new properties quickly, hence the 5 against property acquisition. Emergency care is the preserve of the private sector, therefore despite government instructions that local authorities should use private childcare facilities, emergency care is largely unaffected by the closure of local authority children's homes, hence a score of plus 1. However, as the target tends to price more competitively than the competition, it is well placed to pick up whatever new business does flow out of the public sector.

A significant issue in this business is labour shortages, hence the minus 2 significance score. This is a very stressful job in difficult circumstances with strange hours and poor pay. At the same time, government regulations are dictating ever higher qualifications. Staff terms and conditions and staff training and development are clearly very important and our target is less than perfect on both counts, hence the scores of 2 and 3 respectively.

Drawing up the grid is a good way of focusing on the key issues while giving a summary of key opportunities and threats. The internal resources listed on the left-hand side of Table 6.2 are a good start in identifying strengths and weaknesses, although these should be assessed relative to the competition, rather than relative to opportunities and threats.

Another approach to the traditional SWOT analysis is suggested by Thompson.[10] He makes the point that success means managing the match between core competencies and key success factors (see Figure 6.6). The greater the congruence, the greater the likelihood that the organization is managing its resources effectively to match the key success factors dictated by the market.

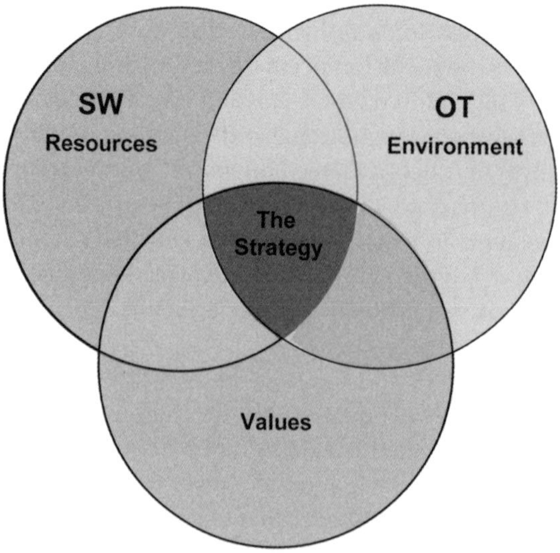

Figure 6.6 E-V-R congruence

Can competitive advantage be sustained?

A company is bought for its future earnings. The most important question in CDD is not whether a competitive advantage exists now, but whether and for how long that advantage can be sustained. The speed with which competitive advantage is undermined by competitors depends on the ability of competitors to challenge either by imitation, innovation or by positioning.

IMITATION

If a firm is to imitate the competitive advantage of another, it must understand the basis of its rival's success. In most industries, it is very difficult to isolate the resources and capabilities that generate a superior performance and the more a firm's competitive advantage is based on a number of different factors and the more each of those factors is based on complex bundles of organizational capabilities rather than individual resources, the more difficult it is for competitors to diagnose the determinants of success. Indeed, there is a body of thought that says that execution of a good strategy is the most important basis of competitive advantage and the most difficult to imitate.[11] What is certain is that USPs can only be long-term sources of competitive advantage if they cannot be easily copied and even then their longevity as a source of advantage may not be that great. Today's USP is tomorrow's expected attribute and therefore no longer a USP. Sadly, though, most things can be copied. Where sources of competitive advantage can be diagnosed, the imitator can mount a competitive challenge by assembling the necessary resources and capabilities. Competitive advantage lasts for the time it takes to do this.

For resources and capabilities to be bought, they must be mobile and transferable. The alternative to buying a resource or capability is to create it through internal investment. Where capabilities are based on organizational routines, accumulating the co-ordination and learning required for their efficient operation can take considerable time. Even in the case of 'turn-key' plants, developing the required operating capability can be a problem. Businesses that require the integration of a number of complex, team-based routines may take years to reach the standards set by industry leaders. Conversely, where a competitive advantage does not require the application of complex, firm-specific resources, imitation is likely to be easy and fast. In financial services, new products typically require resources and capabilities that all banks have. Hence, imitation of financial innovations is swift. However, do not despair. Anyone can copy, but not everyone can execute, and that is the key.

First-mover advantage

A firm's strategic advantage may be protected by first-mover advantage. The idea of first-mover advantage is that the initial occupant of a strategic position or niche gains access to resources and capabilities that a follower cannot match. The simplest form of first-mover advantage is a patent or copyright. By establishing a patent or copyright, the first mover possesses a technology, product or design from which a follower is legally excluded. First-mover advantage implies two things:

- being first;
- getting it right.

It sounds obvious, but, as many of the failed Internet ventures showed only too clearly, a surprising number of firms forget the second thing. Being first has a number of advantages:

- First movers get exclusive access to resources required for competitive success, which are scarce.
- Initial success can lead directly to longer lasting success in the form of profits that permit the firm to invest in extending and upgrading its resource base.
- The first mover in a market establishes a reputation with customers, distributors, and suppliers that cannot be initially matched by the follower. Displacing incumbents can be incredibly difficult unless the follower has something very special to offer.
- The first mover may have an advantage in setting the standard (for the importance of standards, see Chapter 9).
- Economies of learning suggest that the first mover can build a cost advantage over followers as a result of greater experience.

However, beware: do not fall for this without thinking it through and do not be spooked by the prospect of a target losing first-mover advantage. Sustainable advantage goes to the second or third entrant. These watch the early movers experimenting. They let them make the mistakes and refine their offering before wading in with the vision and necessary capital, just as the market starts to take off.

THE EXPERIENCE CURVE

The experience curve has its basis in the systematic reduction in the time taken to build airplanes and liberty ships during World War II. The concept of economies of learning was generalized by BCG to encompass not just direct labour hours, but the behaviour of all added costs with cumulative production. In a series of studies, ranging from bottle caps and refrigerators to long distance calls and insurance policies, BCG observed that a doubling of cumulative production typically reduced unit costs by 20 to 30 per cent.

The significance of the experience curve lies in its implications for the importance of market share. If costs decline systematically with increases in cumulative output, then a target's costs relative to competitors depend on its cumulative output relative to competitors. If a firm can expand its output at greater rate than its competitors, it is then able to move down the experience curve more rapidly than its rivals and can open up a widening cost differential. The implication drawn by BCG was that a firm's primary strategic goal should be market share.

The importance of market share

Market share is very important. Empirical studies suggest a positive relationship between market share and profitability. The Profit Impact of Market Strategy (PIMS) analysis was developed at General Electric in the 1960s and is now maintained by the Strategic Planning Institute. PIMS is a data pool containing the profiles of over 3000 strategic experiences. The most important factor to emerge from the PIMS data is a link between profitability and relative market share. PIMS found (and continues to find) that the higher a company's market share, the higher its return on investment. However, there are doubts about the wisdom of market share as a strategic goal:

- The most plausible explanation for the link between profitability and market share is that they are both consequences of some common underlying factor. For example, being more efficient or innovative would result in both high profits and a high market share.
- If the relationship between market share and profitability is known and accepted by all firms in the industry, all firms will compete for market share, thus eroding any superior profitability.
- Similarly, pursuing experience economies through pricing for market share may be successful for the individual firm but fatal when attempted by several competitors.

There is in fact a U-shaped relationship between market share and returns. Companies with a high share have high returns and companies with a small share tend to be profitable. However, the ones stuck in the middle tend to have middling returns. The high share companies are the powerful suppliers; the small ones are the nimble specialists or the tightly run, low-overhead, entrepreneurial outfits that feature in most industries. Those stuck in the middle are neither and get picked off from both ends. As the CEO of one FTSE 100 company put it: 'When you are only number three in a market and it turns down, then numbers one and two skin you alive.'[12]

INNOVATION

Innovation is doing new things. It not only creates competitive advantage, it provides a basis for overturning the competitive advantage of established firms. We typically think of innovation in its technical sense, that is, bringing new ideas and knowledge to new products and processes. However, we should also think of innovation as including new approaches to doing business. New ways of doing things are far more important than product innovation alone.[13] Even in mature industries, strategic innovation is the primary basis for competitive advantage and the principal driving force of industry change. One of the PIMS findings is that product innovation and differentiation lead to profitability, especially in mature markets. Central to such innovation is creating customer value by combining performance dimensions that were previously viewed as conflicting. If you think there is a trade-off between price, quality, range and service, have a look at UK supermarket Tesco. It is so successful because it leads in all four. Low price/high quality strategies have blown a number of other industries apart too. 'New game' strategies typically involve reconfiguration of the industry value chain so that a company can change the 'rules of the game' so as to capitalize on its distinctive competencies, catch competitors off guard, and erect barriers to protect the advantage created.

POSITIONING

A business can compete in a number of different ways, as set out in Figure 6.7.[14]

Starting at 1, as we go clockwise around the clock, we move from cost-based strategies to increasingly differentiated positioning. No frills and low price are both based on cost leadership. No frills (1) offerings serve specific segments, whereas low price (2) is a market wide position, usually in low margin commodities. Hybrid (3) is a combination of low price and differentiation, much like the strategies followed by some of the major supermarket groups. Differentiation (4) can be with or without a price premium. Some companies differentiate to gain share, others add enough perceived value to be able to charge more. Focused differentiation (5) is differentiating in specific market segments, selling a

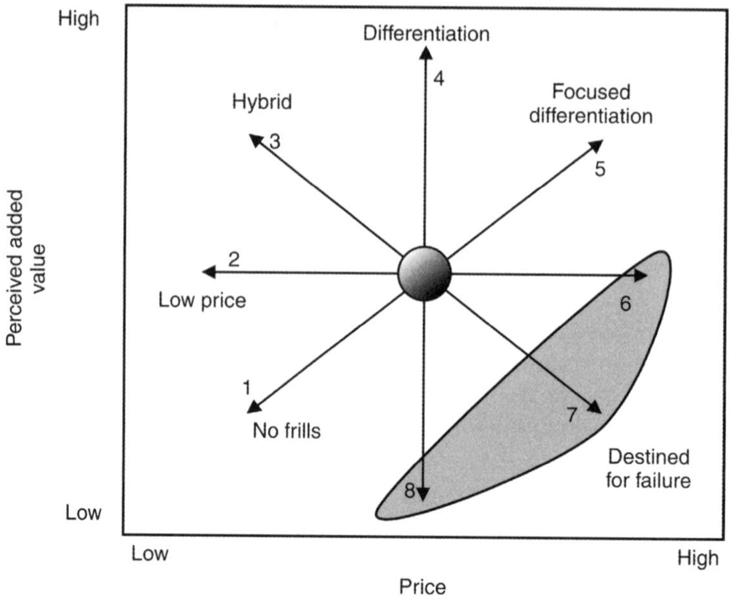

Figure 6.7 The strategy clock
Source: Johnson and Scholes (1997) *Exploring Corporate Strategies.* London: Prentice Hall.

differentiated product into selected customers. The sale of technically advanced electricity meters for customers who want a reliable electricity supply is an example. Position (6) is charging more for the same old thing. Position (7) is a charging more for something worse and position (8) is charging a standard price for something of low value. None of the last three are going to work unless the target has a monopoly.

Cost leadership

The strategy literature talks a lot about cost leadership as the primary basis for competitive advantage. In Chapter 4, it was noted that in free markets price is the means by which resources are allocated. The focus on cost advantage reflects economists' preoccupation with price as the principle medium of competition. Competing on price depends on cost efficiency. The preoccupation with cost also reflects the strategies of large manufacturing companies throughout the twentieth century, the main elements of which were a quest for economies of scale and scope through investment in mass production and mass distribution. A lot of the thinking on cost leadership is now out of date.

By definition, in any industry there can only be one cost leader, but the extent to which cost leadership is important is a moot point. In mature commodity industries it can be, but even here, where there are few opportunities for competing on much else other than cost, firms must decide on which customer requirements to focus and where to position their product or service in the market. A cost leadership strategy typically implies a narrow line, limited-feature, standardized offering. However, such a positioning does not imply that the product or service is an undifferentiated commodity. British Steel developed a strong position in the steel-framed building industry and was the prime innovator in tin cans. At the other end of the spectrum, even where competition focuses on product differentiation, intensifying competition has resulted in cost efficiency becoming a pre-requisite for profitability.

In most industries, cost leadership does not automatically mean market leadership. Market leaders tend to maximize customer appeal by reconciling effective differentiation with low cost. Cost leaders tend to be smaller companies that minimize overhead and operate with cheaply acquired assets. We will discuss the technique of value mapping, which links customer benefits with price, in Chapter 7.

Differentiation

A firm differentiates itself from its competitors 'when it provides something unique that is valuable to buyers beyond simply offering a low price'.[15] It can do this either by delivering more value to customers or by delivering comparable value at the same cost (or both). Successful differentiation must create enough value for customers to allow the firm to recoup the extra cost either in the form of premium prices or increased market share.

As a company strategy, differentiation tends to be a more secure basis for competitive advantage than is low cost. This is because cost advantage is vulnerable to unpredictable external forces, new technology and strategic innovation. As a result, companies that have been consistently successful over long periods tend to be those that have pursued differentiation rather than cost leadership.[16]

Differentiation is closely linked with what was discussed in Chapters 3 and 5. It is about understanding the target's customers and the needs its product is satisfying:

- Who are the customers?
- How does the product or service create value for them?
- Does it do it more efficiently and effectively than anyone else?

The potential for differentiating a product or service is partly determined by its physical characteristics, but differentiation extends beyond physical characteristics to encompass everything about the product or service that influences the value customers derive from it. This means that differentiation includes every aspect of the way in which a company does business.

Understanding differentiation begins with understanding why customers buy a product or service. What are the needs being satisfied? In getting this understanding, simple, direct discussions about the purpose of a product and its performance attributes are far more useful than market research data obtained from large samples of actual and potential customers. Figure 6.8 summarizes some key points of these discussions.

The process outlined in Figure 6.8 will match differentiation to segmentation. It will also show the degree of differentiation of the different market players. Some will be very focused, concentrating on the factors that segment a market and others will be more broadly based, offering the factors that all customers have in common. As a buyer will prefer a targeted product offering that matches their particular preferences, the challenge for broad-based differentiators is to stop focused differentiators displacing them. But focused differentiation also has its risks:

- Higher unit costs are incurred in supplying a narrow rather than a broad market.
- Market segments can change over time.
- The basis of segmentation may be wrong.

In analyzing differentiated positions, a distinction must be made between the tangible and the intangible.

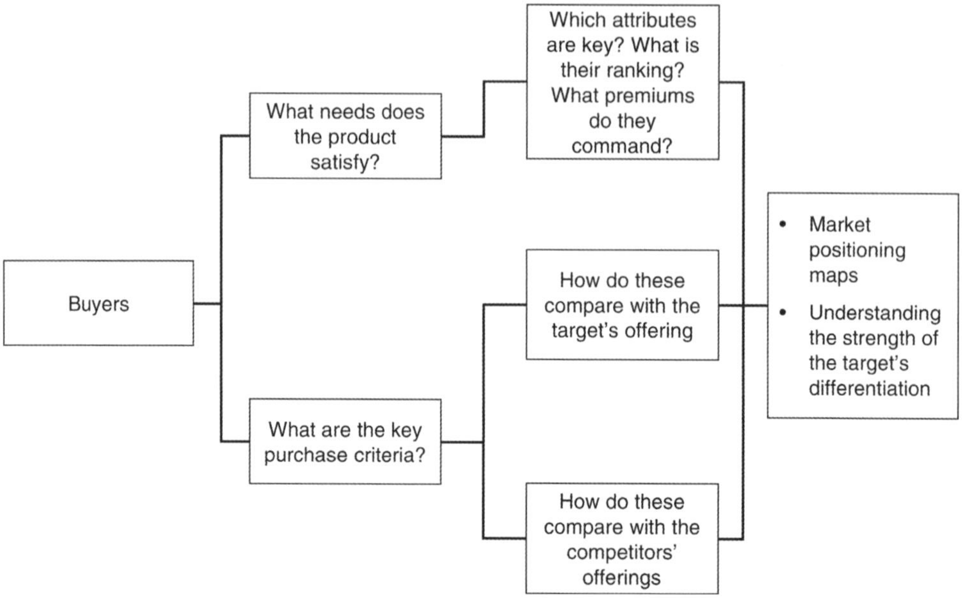

Figure 6.8 Identifying differentiation

TANGIBLE DIFFERENTIATION

Tangible differentiation is concerned with the observable characteristics of a product or a service that is relevant to the customer's buying decision such as size, colour, shape, weight, design, material and technology. Tangible differentiation also includes performance characteristics such as reliability, consistency, taste, speed, durability and safety. Complementary products and services are also important. These include pre- and after-sales services, accessories, availability, delivery, credit and the ability to upgrade the product in the future. Other drivers of differentiation include:

- Marketing activities (for example, rate of advertising spending)
- Technology embodied in design and manufacture
- The quality of purchased inputs
- Procedures influencing the conduct of each activities (for example, rigour or quality control, service procedures, frequency of sales visits to a customer)
- The skill and experience of employees
- Location
- The degree of vertical integration (which influences a firm's ability to control inputs and intermediate processes).

Tangible differentiation is more difficult with some products than with others, as shown in Table 6.3.

Remember, in assessing a target's differentiation it is important to look only at those activities that are the most essential as far as customers are concerned. Successful differentiation is being different from competitors in ways that matter to customers.

Table 6.3 Tangible differentiation possibilities

Differentiation more difficult	*Differentiation less difficult*
The product satisfies uncomplicated needs.	The product satisfies complicated needs.
The product is technically simple.	The product is complex.
The product must meet specific technical standards.	The product does not need to conform to stringent technical standards (wine, toys).

INTANGIBLE DIFFERENTIATION

Theodore Levitt's definition of the product (see Chapter 3, Figure 3.16) gives rise to opportunities for intangible differentiation. What buyers perceive in a product or service is not dependent exclusively on its tangible features or on its objective performance criteria. Indeed, customers cannot always be well informed about the goods they purchase. The economics literature distinguishes between search goods, whose qualities and characteristics can be ascertained by inspection, and experience goods, whose qualities and characteristics are only recognized after consumption. The benefits given by experience goods need to be signalled in some way, through advertising, warranties, brand name and so forth. The more difficult it is to test performance before purchase, the more important is such signalling. Perfume is promoted so lavishly because what is being sold is not a smell, but a means of augmenting the identity of the wearer and that cannot be proved at the shop counter. Brand names and the advertising that supports them are especially important as signals of quality and consistency because they are a guarantee by the producer to the consumer of the quality of the product. As far as the consumer is concerned, a brand name gives comfort that the producer is legally and morally accountable for its products and furthermore, as a brand represents a considerable investment on the part of the producer, there is an incentive to maintain quality and customer satisfaction.

POSITIONAL DIFFERENTIATION

Another way of thinking about differentiation is to see it as 'the process of perceiving new positions that woo customers from established positions or draw new customers into the market.'[17] These positions come from three distinct sources:

- Variety-based positioning – producing a specialized sub-set of an industry's products or services
- Needs-based positioning – targeting a particular group of customers
- Access-based positioning – where different customers are reached in different ways.

IDENTIFYING DIFFERENTIATION

The key to successful differentiation is matching the firm's capacity for creating differentiation to the attributes that the customers value most. For this purpose, the value chain provides a particularly useful framework (see Figure 6.2 above). Differentiation can come from any or all areas across the value chain.

PRIMARY ACTIVITIES

The following are examples of primary differentiation activities:

- Inbound logistics
- Operations: high quality, on time delivery
- Outbound logistics: rapid delivery when and where the customer needs the product
- Marketing and sales: knowledgeable and motivated sales force
- Service: rapid installation, speedy after sales service and repair.

SUPPORT ACTIVITIES

The following are examples of support differentiation activities:

- Procurement: high-quality materials, finished product stocks
- Technology development: development of unique features and new products and services, the use of IT to manage inbound and outbound logistics, sophisticated market analysis to enable segmentation, targeting and positioning for differentiation
- Human Resources management: high quality training and development, recruitment of the right people and appropriate rewards systems which help motivate people
- Firm's infrastructure: support from senior executives, customer relations, investment in the right things.

Using the value chain to identify differentiation advantage involves four principle stages:

1 Construct a value chain for the firm and the customer. Draw separate value chains for each of the main categories of customer. There is a lot to be said for subdividing the primary and support activities into their component parts when analysing costs and opportunities for differentiation. For example, what is 'good service'? Service is made up of a host of factors and these should be examined individually.
2 Identify the drivers of uniqueness in each activity, but confine the exercise to those activities that are the most essential as far as customers are concerned. Target company management has a habit of pointing to something that is different and assuring you that this constitutes differentiation. It only counts if it is something that matters to customers.
3 Locate linkages between the value chain of the firm and that of the acquirer. Differentiation gives the target an advantage. To do this it must create value for the customer. Creating value for the customer means either that the target lowers the customer's costs, or it helps the customer in its own product differentiation.
But, for a differentiation strategy to be effective, it needs to reflect what the target is best at doing – its core capabilities – not what the competition can do just as well.
4 Repeat the process for the competition.

Case Study 21 demonstrates how useful the value chain can be in CDD.

CASE STUDY 21

PORT OPERATIONS AND THE IMPORTANCE OF THE VALUE CHAIN

The value chain is a very powerful piece of analysis if done properly. Its power was brought home in the study of a port operator. This company had one customer, a Swedish newsprint manufacturer. The UK is an importer of newsprint, much of which comes from Sweden. The target operated

CASE STUDY 21 – *continued*

from a secondary British port in the south of England whereas all other Swedish newsprint destined for the printers of national newspapers in London was imported through Tilbury, to the east of London. Not surprisingly, a central question in the CDD was, 'will the Swedish customer switch to Tilbury?' This is a difficult question to answer. You could examine port economics, transport links with east London and so on, but the value chain gives the real answer. Newsprint is produced in big reels. The Swedish customer is next to a port in Sweden. Its paper reels for export to England come straight off the production line and straight into a ship. All the other mills are based inland (where the trees are) and so must containerize their paper for transport to the port. It makes sense for them, but not for our target's customer, to use a container ship to get their paper across the North Sea and therefore to use the Port of Tilbury which is billed as 'the UK's largest container port for timber and paper products'. As if that was not a compelling enough story, it gets better. Because the Swedish mill is further from the forests, it is economic, as well as politically expedient in a country renowned for its environmental concerns, for it to use waste paper in its production process. Sweden, with its small population does not have that much waste paper available for recycling but the UK, with its large, newspaper-reading population and only two newsprint mills of its own, does. So guess where the Swedes had set up their waster paper handling operations? Right next door to the target, which also helped them export the stuff by sorting it, bundling it into 1-ton bales and loading it onto the ships from which it had just unloaded newsprint.

Not only must we identify points of differentiation, but we need to think about the ease with which they can be sustained. Differentiation may only be temporary, especially if the target's only real strength is its differentiation. If it is not fully meeting the basic requirements of its customers, it is vulnerable to imitation. For example, there is a fish and chip shop in the centre of a town near me. It is central, close to the car parks and very popular. Its location is the basis of its differentiation from the others, which are in surrounding villages. However, everything is fried to order, which means if you want anything other than chips you have to wait 10 minutes or more. Moreover it closes at 10:00 pm. I expect fish and chip shops to be convenient. That means fast service and open after the pubs have closed. If someone did open up down the road, that is where I would be going.

On the other hand, the more differentiation is based on resources specific to the firms or skills that involve the complex coordination of a large number of individuals, the more difficult it is for a competitor to imitate. Equipping bailiffs with hand-held computers is an easily imitated source of differentiation. Achieving high recovery rates is a more sustainable source of differentiation.

DIFFERENTIATING CAPABILITIES

The above is the textbook way of defining the extent of differentiation. An alternative comes from a study by Treacy and Wiersema, who came up with some useful insights into the question of how leading companies differentiate to create value for the customer and build competitive advantage for themselves.[18] Their view is that market leaders dominate their chosen areas by achieving the highest value in the customer's eyes in a world where:

- different customers buy different types of value – few companies excel at everything, so the issue is one of choosing customers and narrowing the value focus, because market leaders excel in offering a specific dimension of value;
- as value standards rise, so do customer expectations, so you have to improve every year or be outpaced by competitors;
- producing an unmatched level of a particular value requires a superior operating model dedicated to that kind of value.

Treacy and Wiersema concluded that market leaders chose one of three 'value disciplines' and ruthlessly specialize in it:

- Operational excellence: here companies deliver a combination of quality, price and ease of purchase that no one in their market can match. They are not innovators or relationship-builders; their value proposition is guaranteed low price and/or hassle-free service.
- Product leadership: these are the companies that continually push products and services into the realm of the unknown, the untried or the highly desirable.
- Customer intimacy: where companies specialize in delivering the best total solution.

Differentiation is an important competitive weapon. As mentioned in Chapter 5, the important consideration from a CDD perspective is separating real, meaningful differentiation, which gives a competitive advantage, from product tinkering, which adds features but no customer benefits. It is important too not to be too seduced by the product differentiation story. There is a body of evidence that suggests that the companies that succeed are the ones that consistently satisfy basic customer needs better than the competition, not by continuously pitching them a USP.[19]

Speed and competitive advantage

To sustain any competitive advantage and grow, companies must innovate more quickly than their rivals. Speed is therefore important in terms of:

- Product development times
- Deliveries from suppliers
- Stock replenishment.

But more than improved efficiencies – it is about an attitude towards providing faster, better and customized service.

Quality and competitive advantage

Another PIMS finding is that competing on quality is better than many other options. According to PIMS, high relative product quality is related to high return on investment because quality is a key source of differentiation and competitive advantage. Figure 6.9 illustrates three very important things about quality:

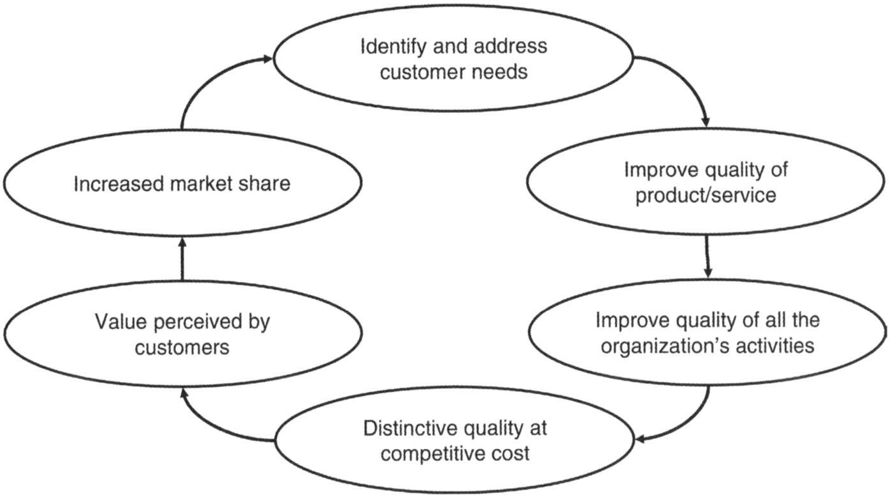

Figure 6.9 The virtuous quality circle

- Quality is in the eye of the customer. A constant theme of this part of the book is that differentiation only works if the target is doing something different and valuable in the eyes of the customer. Quality is a means of differentiation.
- Improving quality is a continuing process. For example, Tom Peters[20] suggests that opportunities to improve will never dry up and that organizations that seek to innovate and find new and better ways of doing things are more likely to create differentiation and reduce their costs.
- Quality involves the entire organization.

Brand strength

Brand can be a big issue even in business-to-business markets, but usually because target companies do not understand that a brand is a more than a name that customers recognize. A brand was originally what cowboys used to make a mark on cattle. Now it is used as a term to describe the personality surrounding a product or its core identity. Just as in the American Wild West, a brand should leave an indelible impression, but there is much more to it than that. The difference between a product and a brand is that while all brands are products, there is something extra in a brand. Products can be characterized by their functional features, whereas the branding process takes us into the realm of the psychological, where characterization becomes intangible, and abstract and emotion rather than rationality prevails. From the customer's perspective, brands allow them to shop with confidence. They are a short cut to their search so, for example, the customer does not have to become an expert in micro-electronics and software engineering to buy a computer, but can instead go with a name it trusts (apply the same logic to trainers and t-shirts and see what conclusions you reach!). So the real power of successful brands is that they meet the expectations of those that buy them or, put another way, they represent a promise kept. In economic terms, it would be argued that it is the simplification of the search process that gives rise to the premium prices brands can command. The name the consumer trusts the most amongst competing brands is the one with which it identifies the most, hence terms such as 'brand

Table 6.4 Aligning brand and consumer values

	Consumer values	*Brand values*
Central values	What kind of life do I want to lead?	Brand 'philosophy'
Expressive values	What kind of person do I want to be?	Brand personality, status, etc.; what the brand 'says' about the consumers who identify with it
Functional values	What kind of products/services do I want?	The functional benefits the brand provides to the consumer, e.g. cost, quality, appearance

personality'. When making a purchase decision, consumers look for a particular combination of product attributes that provide them with a specific set of functional values. However, consumers will prefer a product whose branding expresses their ideal self-image through its expressive and central values. 'Brands deliver a variety of benefits, which for ease can be classified as satisfying buyers' rational and emotional needs. Successful brands are those which have the correct balance in terms of their ability to satisfy these two needs.'[21]

A brand is nothing but a network of associations in the consumer's mind. If an association represents something that is personally and/or socially preferable to the consumer, it is called a value. Values come in three varieties, as shown in Table 6.4.

Consumers are predisposed to a brand when brand values and consumer values coincide.

In all this, be absolutely crystal clear about one thing, and that is that customers buy benefits not brands. They do not think about brands, they think about categories. A category is a set of competing choices, that, as seen by the buyer, share some key characteristics and provide broadly similar benefits.[22] This brings us full circle back to some of the issues discussed in Chapter 3. To understand the benefits sought, you have to be clear about the boundaries and to understand the boundaries, you have to be absolutely crystal clear about the benefits sought. And if a brand is effectively the guarantee to the consumer that benefits sought will be delivered, a brand must do the following:

- Have an ability to stay relevant. Strong brands connect with customers. They meet functional needs and also tap into and satisfy emotional needs and desires.
- Consistently deliver on its promise. Consumers must trust the brand and believe that it will deliver its promise. Strong brands give a 'continually rewarding experience', however sentimental that may sound.
- Represent superior products and services. Strong brands stand out from their competitors.
- Have distinctive positioning and customer experience. Unless a brand has a clear idea of the value it brings and to whom, it will have difficulty in ever making the brand stand for anything. Consumers should have some commitment to the brand.
- Guide the entire enterprise. Companies must have a rigorous process for designing a customer experience that consistently delivers the brand promise and the whole of the organization must play a part in that experience. Recruitment and training are both very important.
- Align the internal and external commitment to the brand.

Part of the problem with the thinking on brands is that people ignore many recent market developments of the last 5 years such as:

- Product parity in many categories has eliminated functional attributes, even quality, as differentiators.
- Price competition has marginalized the brand's equity and its role in driving consumer choice.
- Promotional tactics designed simply to take share from competitors have diminished the brand's capacity and motivation to grow the category.
- Trade dominance has undermined the brand's ability to achieve a bond with the consumer.

Many superficially robust brands in fact offer little more than passive reassurance. What values they once enjoyed in the consumer's mind have either eroded with time or are no longer relevant. Taking a position in the sense of showing leadership and vision in how your brand will meet its promise is increasingly important, not just because people are now more fussy, but also because of a blurring of boundaries.

TESTING THE BRAND'S STRENGTH

The only way to test the strength of a brand is to subject it to the disciplines of benchmarking – assessing it against the key success factors that determine brand competitiveness and then comparing its performance with known strong brands. The comparison will take place on two dimensions:

- Tangible:
  - What are the factors that reflect functional performance?
  - Are products differentiated and valuable to target customers?
- Intangible:
  - What degree of commitment does the brand enjoy from its customers?
  - To what extent are the perceived values of the brand consistent with those of the target market?
  - What is the proposition?
  - What does the brand offer?
  - How clear is the offer?
  - Is this valuable to target customers?
- People:
  - To what extent do people behave in a way that meets customer expectations and delivers the brand promise? People are one of the most important drivers of brand loyalty. Loyalty is gained above all out of customer contact and the experience customers have of a target company. The attraction of consumers to a brand is much more fundamental than a simple marketing exercise. The Carlson Marketing Group[23] conducted a survey in 2003 that quantifies the quality of the relationship between the consumer and the brand. Customer spend, retention and customers' willingness to recommend the brand to others were all influenced by the strength of the relationship. Those organizations in the lower quartile had retention levels of just 32 per cent

compared with 87 per cent for those brands with the strongest relationship scores. What is relationship strength?

- Processes:
  - Do processes create value for customers and deliver the brand promise?

BRAND STRETCHING

To determine where and how a brand can be stretched requires a good understanding of current and potential customers, good judgement about future market trends and inspiration.

Brands are often locked into tightly defined products, positionings and markets because of:

- Historical experience and past brand practice
- Conventional wisdom
- Resistance to change.

Shortfall against potential usually has less to do with problems of how the brand is perceived by consumers than how the brand is managed by those responsible for it. Instead of searching for ways to reinvent the brand for greater competitive advantage, management settles for initiatives that do little more than tinker with next year's marketing plan.

Once established, a brand can be used to embrace as broad a spectrum of products or services as is responsive to the identified brand values. As Figure 6.10 shows, there are three ways in which a brand name might be leveraged.

Line extension generally involves extending the scope of the brand within its product category, embracing products with functional, expressive and central values that reflect those of the original product brand. To be successful, a line extension should:

- be consistent with the core values of the original or 'parent' brand and ideally reinforce them;

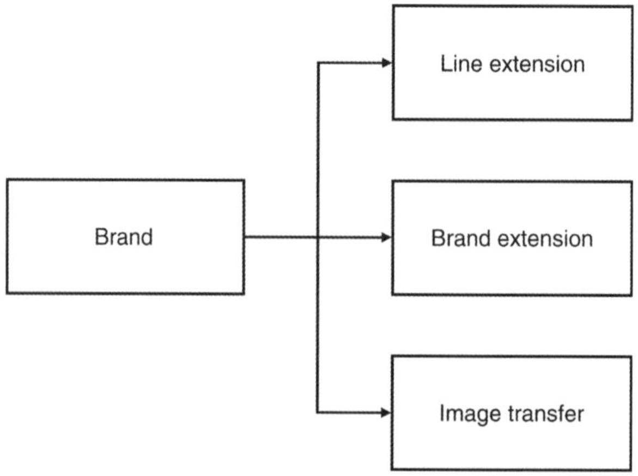

Figure 6.10 There are three ways in which to leverage a brand

Table 6.5 Varieties of brand extension for a manufacturer of prams and children's car seats

Feature	*Example*
Same products, different form	Prams, pushchairs, carry cots
Distinctive feature	Children's wheeled goods: push chairs, cycles
	Secure seating: high chairs, cots
Natural companions for usage	Prams, child restraints, booster seats, toys and games for long journeys
Same customer franchise	Children's goods
Perception of special expertise	For example, child safety, safety accessories, safety gates, monitors
'Owned' benefit	Robust children's products, toys

- not undermine the parent brand; it should not, for example, cannibalize sales of the parent brand but should bring in new customers of its own.

Brand extension involves extending a brand which covers a product or limited range into an umbrella brand. Here the process consists of taking the functional values of the brand and identifying other products where the consumer seeks the same values. See Table 6.5 for some examples.

Brand extension should:

- go in a direction where the functional values of the parent brand are just as important to the consumer as they are in the original category;
- be undertaken only when the parent brand is healthy, stable and (ideally) growing;
- reinforce the parent brand.

With image transfer, the brand's expressive and central values are what is important. They must be capable of transcending boundaries spanning a variety of product types. For image transfer to work:

- the brand must be credible in its new role;
- the greater the technical difference between the new product and the original, the more difficult it is to effect the transfer;
- the new target market must respond to the same core values as do the brand's consumers in its original market.

Distribution channels

The extent to which a business embraces new or different distribution channel options or how seriously it takes new channel players or channel formats are some of the most perplexing questions facing a business.

A company's channel strategy determines how it interacts with the marketplace and the routes through which goods, services and money flow between it and its customers. Simply put, it is about knowing how to get the right products to the relevant sets of customers effectively and efficiently, creating competitive advantage as you do so. Do it right and sales, market share and profits grow. Do it wrong and at best you stagnate. Channel members need to create customer value or their costs will sooner or later have to be met by the supplier. As value creators for the firm's customers they must therefore be seen as an extension of the target company's sales and marketing and not as some loose collection of independent businesses that happen to sell the target's products. CDD then must ask the obvious questions about the value created for the target by its channel strategy and whether it is sustainable. There are three questions:

- Can the existing channel strategy continue to deliver?
- Will existing channels continue to create customer value?
- Are there new channels that the target should be considering?

CAN THE EXISTING CHANNEL STRATEGY CONTINUE TO DELIVER?

The cornerstone of any channel review is an in-depth understanding of the sectors in which the target does business and those in which it does not. Many target companies think that a channel strategy begins and ends with channels, but that is the first major mistake. At the end of the day, both the target and its distributors exist because users allow them to; they choose to buy a specific product from the channel that meets their sourcing requirements. If the target addresses its market without knowing which customer segments are most attractive or understanding what is driving the customer's product and sourcing choices, it is taking a costly and ineffective scattergun approach and is leaving its business vulnerable to competitive threats. The difficulty is that, almost by definition, manufacturers are inward looking and focused on product and operations. They have a top-down view of the market, often seeing only as far as the invoice goes, most likely to a third party or channel. The manufacturer's view of the real customer is, therefore, limited. The sort of questions it should be asking (and so should you as part of CDD) are:

- Are the channels being sufficiently rewarded to keep them motivated?
- Are channel members tied into the target's processes to give maximum efficiency, for example, through the joint management of stock rather than each holding a buffer? Companies mistakenly believe that channels are customers themselves rather than routes to customers.
- Are there different channel options that lower cost or improve performance? User preferences and buying behaviour evolve continuously, markets mature and become increasingly competitive and the channel landscape grows more complex and sophisticated. Manufacturers often lag behind these developments and their channel strategies are out of synch with the marketplace. Finally, companies often forget to adapt their channel strategy in line with changes in company direction, depending on an old channel strategy to launch new products or to enter new markets.
- Can channel operation be improved? Efficiency can often be improved by gearing the interface between the target and its distribution channels. For example, most buyer–seller relationships are a mix of consultative and transactional selling. There is no need to tie up an expensive sales expert with transactional selling that can be done through the Internet or a call centre. Effectiveness is a function of the quantity and quality of dealer support, again going back to the principle that dealers are an extension of the target.

One of the problems of selling through distribution channels is that the target's sales can stagnate, either because it cannot sign up many more or because it is the channel partners' expertise that matters most to the end consumer, handing power to channel members. To prevent the trend to commoditization brought on by this state of affairs, target companies ought to be finding ways to keep contact with the end user. Kitchen work surfaces are distributed through wholesalers who have contact with the high street kitchen shops. Work surface manufacturers maintain contact with the high street through the normal promotional materials, including sample boards, with sales visits and by branding their products.

WILL EXISTING CHANNELS CONTINUE TO CREATE CUSTOMER VALUE?

The most common trend is towards familiarity and competition, leading towards price-based commodity buying and away from the consultative approach often provided by dealers. However, the trend can be the other way. If products become increasingly complex, they may outgrow the existing distribution system. The type of channel that makes sense depends entirely on the nature of the sale. A direct sales call can cost several hundreds of pounds, a telesales call costs under £10. Why, if a target is engaging in transactional sales that by definition involve experienced consumers buying well-understood products, would any firm even contemplate sending in a member of the field sales force in such circumstances? With transactional sales, what is needed are sales channels that minimize selling costs and maximize customer convenience. This will inevitably mean very lean sales management and as much information on pricing, product options and availability in the hands of the customer to increase convenience as well as cut costs.

Consultative sales are normally handled direct, but not always. Some customers are simply too small to handle. They still need a consultative approach, probably more so since they are small and relatively unsophisticated and therefore should sensibly be moved towards third parties who can profitably serve them in an appropriate manner. In many industries, the USA is markedly different from Europe, relying much more heavily on third-party distributors. The reason is that distances make direct consultative sales calls prohibitively expensive. Distributors fulfil that consultative role on a local basis. Typically they will handle a whole range of products used by their customer base and will be capable of bundling products to solve their customers' problems.

In contrast to transactional selling, consultative selling has intensive supervision to ensure that scarce problem-solving skills are properly deployed and for coaching the sales force. Studies show that coaching effort applied early makes the length of the selling cycle shorter than when managers become involved later on. To get the most out of an expensive sales machine, there should be a number of diagnostic tools to help identify customer needs and cut down on the amount of expertise sales staff need to accumulate. The need to maximize the application of knowledge should also mean sales and marketing efforts are focused on vertical markets.

ARE THERE NEW CHANNELS THAT THE TARGET SHOULD BE CONSIDERING?

New channels should be capable of bringing something new. The main possibilities are listed below:

- Do they reach a different type of customer? Some new channels can improve the target's penetration by reaching customers that other channels do not cover. Others can simply mean cannibalization of the existing arrangements, rather than bringing something new.

- Will they increase sales? Simply adding wholesalers in a mature market such as kitchen work surfaces will not add to sales unless these wholesalers can reach retailers not already stocking the brand. In other cases, more outlets will mean more sales.
- Does the channel offer real new value to customers? Simply ignoring an emerging channel because there might be a backlash from the existing distributors is not a viable strategy. If a new channel is offering new value and if it is here to stay, it ought to be irresistible. Raleigh bicycles established a chain of independent 'Five Star' dealers around the UK. These establishments were cycle retailers with professional repair capabilities. Once established, it was subsequently very difficult for Raleigh to sell to up and coming channels such as Toys'Я'Us and other big toy retailers.

New channels will inevitably bring channel conflicts. Companies can be reluctant to consider new channels because of conflict with existing channels. Often channel conflict cannot be avoided and it may well be better to accept conflict, but not miss out on a new winning channel. Channel conflicts can be managed by:

- offering different brands, products or services to each channel;
- reconfiguring commissions to make up for the any economic impact of new channels;
- for those companies with a strong market position, riding out the storms and accepting the risk.

New channels can also mean an opportunity, providing they satisfy a genuine need, as Case Study 22 demonstrates.

CASE STUDY 22

SECOND-HAND CAR DEALING ON THE INTERNET

This case is about a German Internet site on which car dealers advertised second-hand cars. The Internet would not replace dealers because 71 per cent of people want to test drive the actual car before purchasing and photographs are not the same as sitting in the car. New cars are different because quality does not vary.

Car dealers interviewed believed in the potential of the Internet as an advertising vehicle because they believed that the Internet would become ever more important, as it is so much more convenient for consumers:

- It is quicker and cheaper than traditional alternatives.
- Consumers believe that cars advertised on the Internet will be better value.
- It provides consumers with other useful car related information.
- There is no need to meet a dealer until the later stages of the buying process:
  - 73 per cent said they disliked pressure selling;
  - 62 per cent were worried about being 'ripped off';
  - 59 per cent didn't like 'showroom hassle'.

Most dealers expected to advertise more on the Internet in the future and if the German car site market broadly follows US trends:

- Most online consumers will use the Internet during the car buying process.

CASE STUDY 22 – *continued*

- Dealers will be adjusting their sales processes to cope with the Internet era.

HOW BIG IS THE NEED?

Figure 6.11 shows the potential demand from German car dealers.

Of those who are online, few are signed up with car web sites. US evidence suggests that dealers typically sign up with three sites.

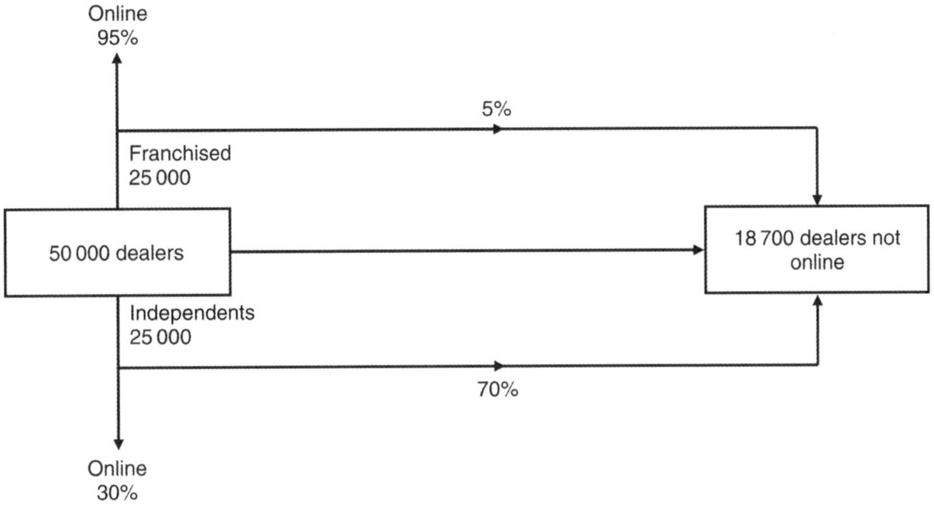

Figure 6.11 Potential demand for Internet car sites

The use of IT

IT and systems is a legitimate area for CDD. IT should go beyond the notion of faster data processing, but most companies view IT from a technical rather than a business point. It is still seen as a support function rather than as a competitive weapon, with companies unsure about how IT might be used as a competitive weapon.

Porter[24] suggests that technological change, and IT in particular, is amongst the most prominent forces that can alter the rules of competition because of the importance of information in most businesses. Porter and Millar[25] see IT as affecting competition in three ways:

- IT can change the structure of an industry and in so doing alter the rules of competition. For example, package holiday companies made use of IT to lower costs and compete more aggressively on price. The result has been an increase in concentration with larger companies gaining share at the expense of the smaller ones.
- IT can be used to create sustainable competitive advantage and provide companies with new competitive weapons. The application of IT in call centres is being used extensively to cut down on the need for people.

- IT can help create differentiation in a number of ways. McFarlan et al.[26] contend that IT offers scope for differentiation where:
  - It is a significant cost component in the provision of the product or service, as in banking, insurance and credit card operations.
  - It is able to affect substantially the lead time for developing, producing or delivering the product.
  - It allows products or services to be specially customized to appeal to customers individually.
  - It enables a visibly higher level of service to customers which may, or may not, be charged for. Keeping track of the jobs completed by outsourced providers of air conditioning servicing and maintenance is a major headache for the poor souls who are responsible for building maintenance in businesses where there is a branch network. Getting the invoices out on time is a major headache for the providers of such services. The problem for both stems from the fact that the operators out in the field are not the best or most timely form fillers. The solution is to issue operators with handheld devices which already contain most of the information on the jobs being completed, making it easy for operators to submit job updates quickly.
  - It can enable more and better product information to be provided to consumers. Like the maintenance men above, up-to-date information on the collection of outstanding debts is difficult to gather from numerous filed operators. They are paid to knock on doors, so not surprisingly this is their focus. On the other hand, information is key to the clients of debt collectors because the last thing they want is a collector to call after the outstanding debt has been paid. Issue the people in the field with personal digital assistants (PDAs) and a simple page to complete after each call and you might stand some change of getting half-decent information back and this has a tremendous marketing benefit.
  - It can also be used to target niches more effectively and segment individual products in ways that previously were only feasible for small, nimble, narrow market specialists.

Ability to compete over the industry life cycle

We discussed the industry life cycle as one of the determinants of internal rivalry in Chapter 5. The shifting patterns of customer requirements, technology and competition over the industry life cycle mean that different strategies are appropriate for different phases. Companies must adjust their strategies and their capabilities to take account of the key success factors of the future, which means that as well as assessing the appropriateness of the target's current strategy, CDD should also be assessing responsiveness to opportunities provided by external change. Information and flexibility of response are the keys to exploiting external change, which brings information systems, and other aspects of 'organizational hardware', organizational structure, such as decision-making systems, jobs design, and culture, into the ambit of CDD.

Table 6.6 reminds us of the evolution of industry structure and its implications for key success factors.

During the introductory stage, product innovation is the basis for initial entry and subsequent success. Soon, however, knowledge alone is not enough. Skills in product development soon need to be matched by capabilities in manufacturing, marketing, and

Table 6.6 The consequences of industry evolution

	Introduction	*Growth*	*Maturity*	*Decline*
Demand	Low. Buyers are early adopters.	Increasingly rapid as demand is taken up by the mass market.	Mass market. Replacement/repeat sales dominate. Customers knowledgeable and price sensitive.	Product is replaced by more advanced substitutes.
Technology	No standard. Rapid product innovation.	Standardization around a dominant technology. Focus shifts to process innovation.	Know-how well diffused. Focus shifts back to technological improvements.	Little innovation.
Products	Poor quality. Frequent changes. Wide variety.	Dominant designs emerge. Quality improves.	A tendency to commoditization leads to attempts at differentiation.	Commodity products. Differentiation difficult and the costs of differentiation are hard to recoup
Manufacturing and distribution	Batch/short run production. Skilled labour.	Mass production.	Overcapacity emerges. De-skilling. Long runs.	Overcapacity.
Distribution	Specialized.	Competition for distribution.	Distributors carry fewer lines.	Specialized.
Production	Producers located in advanced countries.	Producers located in advanced countries.	Production shifts to newly industrializing then developing countries.	Producers located in lowest cost countries.
Competition	A few companies	Entry and mergers.	Price competition leading to a shakeout of the weakest competitors.	Price wars.
KSFs	• Ability to innovate and establish a credible position in the market.	• Design for manufacture • Access to distribution • Branding and differentiation • Fast product development • Process innovation • High market share.	• Cost efficiency.	• Low overheads • Buyer selection.

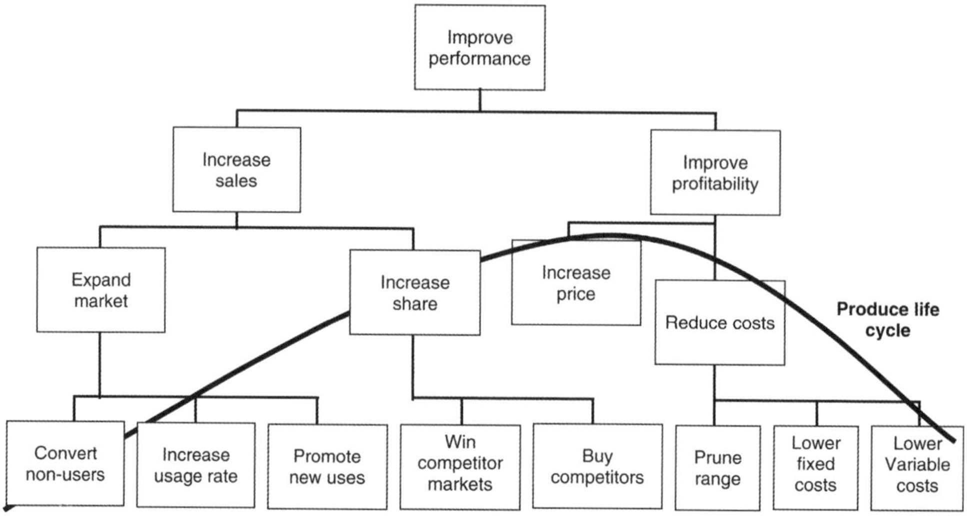

Figure 6.12 Strategic focus changes through the product life cycle

distribution. Once the growth stage is reached, the key challenge is scaling up. As the market expands, the firm needs to adapt its product design and its manufacturing capability to large-scale production.

To utilize increased manufacturing capability, access to distribution becomes critical.

With the maturity stage, competitive advantage is increasingly about cost efficiency and differentiation. The decline phase sees more price competition. Here, a competitive advantage is secondary to maintaining a stable industry environment to make sure price competition does not become fatal. Hence, strategies should focus on encouraging the orderly exit of industry capacity and building a strong position to capitalize on the remaining demand. Figure 6.12 shows which strategies are appropriate to which phase.

THE THREAT OF DISRUPTIVE CHANGE

The world has a habit of chugging along in a certain direction then suddenly, without warning, blasting off in some completely unexpected direction. The same is true of companies and markets. Continuous and adaptive change is effective only to a point. At some point, which Andy Grove[27] of Intel refers to as a *strategic inflection point,* a company must be willing to make a radical strategic shift. For Intel, such an inflection point occurred when it recognized that its future lay in microprocessors rather than its traditional business of designing and fabricating memory chips. Disruptive technologies are those that offer a very different package of attributes to what already exists. For example, early transistor radios sacrificed sound fidelity, but created a market for portable radios by offering a new and different package of attributes – small size, light weight and portability. But responding to radical product change is difficult for incumbent players because their research and experience always tells them two things:

- customers do not want the new technology;
- new technology does not perform as well as the existing technology.

And the reason is quite simply that they have become set in their ways, or, as the academic literature puts it, 'capabilities become embedded in processes and values ... [and] tend to be inflexible.'[28] There are three lessons from this for CDD:

- Beware the target company management that dismisses new developments on the grounds that they are not as good as what is already around and that customers do not want it.
- Applaud the target with two strategies – one for the present and one for the future. Target companies that are tuned into the future are maximizing the effectiveness of current resources and capabilities while simultaneously developing, extending, and augmenting them.[29] This will not always go down with the accountancy fraternity, who easily confuse operational effectiveness with strategy. The thing is that efficiency is desirable whichever strategy is adopted, but is not sufficient to save a company from fundamental strategic innovation in the market.[30]
- Recognize that these days competition comes from alternative business models and concepts as much as it does from products.

Conclusion

This chapter started with the assertion that a firm's ability to compete is more important to profitability than industry structure. In practice, distinguishing the profits associated with industry attractiveness from those associated with owning superior resources and capabilities is difficult. A closer look at Porter's Five Forces framework suggests that above-normal profits derive ultimately from the ownership of resources. Barriers to entry, for example, are the result of patents, brands, distribution channels, learning, or some other resource that incumbent firms possess, but that entrants can acquire only slowly over time or at disproportionate expense. A monopoly or oligopoly position in an industry is founded on the possession of reputation, know-how, manufacturing capacity, or distribution facilities that other firms in the industry cannot match.

The key issue of internal analysis is what the firm can do. This means looking at the resources of the firm and the way resources are brought together to create organizational capabilities. Our main interest is in identifying those resources and capabilities that give sustainable competitive advantage. Where firms possess very similar bundles of resources and capabilities, imitation of the competitive advantage of the incumbent firm is most likely. Where resource bundles are highly differentiated, competition is likely to be less direct. However, delivery is everything. Every company consists of hundreds of business processes that come together. The result is success if they come together better than those of the competition.

Competitive differentiation and positioning are neither vague nor academic; they are about delivering what the customer values.

Notes

1. Grant, Robert M. (1991) *Contemporary Strategy Analysis: Concepts, Techniques, Applications.* Oxford: Blackwell.
2. Berkshire Hathaway Annual Meeting, 1 May 2000.

3. Peters, T.J. and Waterman, R.H. (1982) *In search of Excellence: Lessons from America's Best-run Companies*. New York: Harper & Row.
4. McGregor, D.M. (1960) *The Human Side of Enterprise*. New York: McGraw-Hill.
5. Porter, L.W., Lawler, E.E. and Hackman, J. (1975) *Behaviour in Organisations*. New York: McGraw-Hill.
6. Prahalad, C.K. and Hamel, G. (1990) 'The Core Competence of the Corporation', *Harvard Business Review*, 90(3): 79–91.
7. Ohmae, K. (1988) 'Getting Back to Strategy', *Harvard Business Review*, 66(6): 149–56.
8. Hamel, G. and Prahalad, C.K. (1994) *Competing for the Future*. Boston, MA: Harvard Business School Press.
9. Stalk, G., Evans, P. and Shulman, L.E. (1992) 'Competing on Capabilities: The New Rules of Corporate Strategy', *Harvard Business Review*, 70(2): 57–70.
10. Thompson, J.L. (1993) *Strategic Management – Awareness and Change*. London: Chapman & Hall.
11. See, for example, Barwise, T.P. and Meehan, S. (2004) *Simply Better: Winning and Keeping Customers by Delivering what Matters Most*. Boston, MA: Harvard Business School.
12. *Management Today* (2003) 'Unzipping The Merger Myth', *Management Today*, February.
13. Grant, R.M. (2002) *Contemporary Strategy Analysis*. Oxford: Blackwell.
14. Cited in Johnson, G. and Scholes, K. (1997) *Exploring Corporate Strategy*. London: Prentice Hall, p. 251. Based on the work of Bowman, C. and Faulkner, D. (1996) *Competitive and Corporate Strategy*. London: Irwin.
15. Porter, M.E. (1985) *Competitive Advantage: Creating and Sustaining Superior Performance*. New York: Free Press.
16. Grant, *Contemporary Strategy* Analysis (see note 13).
17. Porter, M.E. (1996) 'What is Strategy?', *Harvard Business Review*74(6): 61–78.
18. Treacy, M. and Wiersema, F. (1995) *The Discipline of Market Leaders*. London: Harper Collins.
19. Barwise, P. and Meehan. S. (2004) *Making Differentiation Make a Difference*. New York,: Booz Allen Hamilton.
20. Peters, T.J. (1988) *Thriving on Chaos: A Handbook for Management Revolution*. London: Pan Macmillan.
21. DeChernatony, L. and McDonald, M. (1998) *Creating Powerful Brands in Consumer, Service and Industrial Markets*. London: Butterworth-Heineman and the Chartered Institute of Marketing.
22. Barwise, T.P. and Meehan, S. (2004) *Simply Better: Winning and Keeping Customers by Delivering what Matters Most*. Boston, MA: Harvard Business School.
23. Carlson Marketing Group (2003) *Relationship Builder Survey 2003*. Available from www.carlson-marketing.com.
24. Porter, *Competitive Advantage* (see note 15).
25. Porter, M.E. and Millar, V.E. (1985) 'How Information Gives you a Competitive Advantage', *Harvard Business Review*, 63(4): 149–60.
26. McFarlan, F.W., McKenney, J.L. and Pyburn, P. (1983) 'The Information Archipelago – Plotting a Course', *Harvard Business Review*, 61(1): 145–56.
27. Grove, A. (1996) *Only the Paranoid Survive*. New York: Doubleday.
28. Christiansen C.M. and Overdorf, M. (2000) 'Meeting the Challenge of Disruptive Change', *Harvard Business Review*, March/April.
29. Abell, D.F. (1993) *Managing with Dual Strategies*. New York: Free Press.
30. Porter, 'What Is Strategy?' (see note 17).

CHAPTER

7 Competitor Analysis

This is a relatively short chapter because many of the analysis techniques have already been covered and because a lot of the information is going to come from interviews and desk research, which is covered in the chapters that follow. Competitor analysis warrants a chapter of its own for two reasons. First, it is important. Buy a company and you are buying its future earnings. Its future earnings depend on it playing to its strengths and exploiting competitors' weaknesses. But strengths are relative to both customer needs and to the competition. What is the worth of our assessment if the target is going after the same customers with the same value proposition and the same marketing methods as strong, aggressive customers, but we have taken no account of competitor moves and reactions? Second, companies are notoriously bad at looking outside. A good piece of competitor assessment can add enormous value to a CDD exercise.

The competitive review is often left until the end of a CDD exercise because competitor interviews (see Chapter 13) are the most difficult and no one really wants to do them until they have a good knowledge of the market. There is nothing wrong with that except that the object should be to get inside the competitors' heads. When competitor analysis gets left behind, it can become a sort of sterile classification exercise.

Some common myths

Let us first start with a few home truths:

- Every organization has competitors. They may not always be direct and obvious, but they are there satisfying the same needs of the same customer base. Just because they might not be satisfying the needs of your customers, they are still competitors if they are satisfying the needs of those who could be customers.
- All companies always know who their competitors are. Just about every organization says this and an awful lot of them do not. Unfortunately, competitive myopia is a common condition.[1] Also, although the identity of current direct competitors is important, it is equally essential to identify future competitors. New entrants can cause considerable competitive disruption through improved price performance trade-offs, by bringing new skills to the market or by using cross subsidies.
- Small players, especially new entrants, are not worth looking at. Wrong. Pay particular attention the new entrants, especially the smaller companies that seem to be making headway because they will be the ones who will have come up with something new.
- Competitors are in the same industry. Target companies may very well identify competitors as firms from the same industry, that is, selling the same products produced in much the same way. But remember what was said in Chapter 3: industry and market are two very different things and it is the market which counts. Customers are not

interested in the 'industry', only in meeting their own needs. Competition is defined by the customer[2] and takes place on four dimensions, as determined by the customer:
- product competition – competition from the same product type;
- product category competition – competition from products that are similar;
- generic competition – includes substitutes (again as defined by the customer);
- budget competition – competition from all products and services that are bought from the same (limited) budget.

The real competition may therefore come from outside the industry. In outsourcing, the competition is from potential customers who at the moment prefer to do tasks that could be outsourced themselves.

- Competitors are unworthy. Rubbish. They exist because they have customers who think they do a reasonable job. They recruit from the same talent pool, have access to the same factors of production, and look at the market in much the same way. They and the target respond to the same market stimuli in much the same way.

What we want to find out

Competitor intelligence is not simply about collecting data. If it were, and if the target does it properly, the problem will be too much rather than too little information. The key is a systematic process that focuses on why certain data is required:

- Competitors' major objectives (see below).
- Assumptions about the industry. Competitor's strategic decisions are conditioned by their perceptions (of the outside world and of itself) and by assumptions concerning the industry and about business in general. Evidence suggests that not only do these systems of belief tend to be stable over time, they also tend to converge within an industry. As Sir Allen Shephard (ex Chairman of Diageo) said, 'there is a natural tendency for corporate behaviour to follow past momentum'. Thus, in trying to cover the ground listed here, start by talking to management and do some in-depth desk research – press cuttings from the last 2–3 years are a good start – and ask yourself: 'What big things have they done over the last couple of years? What links these things?' Such industry recipes may limit the ability of a firm, and indeed an entire industry, to respond rationally and effectively to external change.
- Marketing strategies. Segments pursued? How are they differentiating themselves? What is their value proposition? Product features? Where do they fit on the value map (see Chapter 8)? What is their supporting marketing mix?
- Strengths and weaknesses, defined as:
  - the ability to conceive and design new products;
  - the ability to produce the product;
  - the ability to market;
  - the ability to finance;
  - the ability to manage.
- Future strategies. Believe it or not, sometimes they will tell you their strategy either directly or through press statements. Otherwise, as mentioned above, the best way of doing this is identify their past actions and extrapolate them into the future.

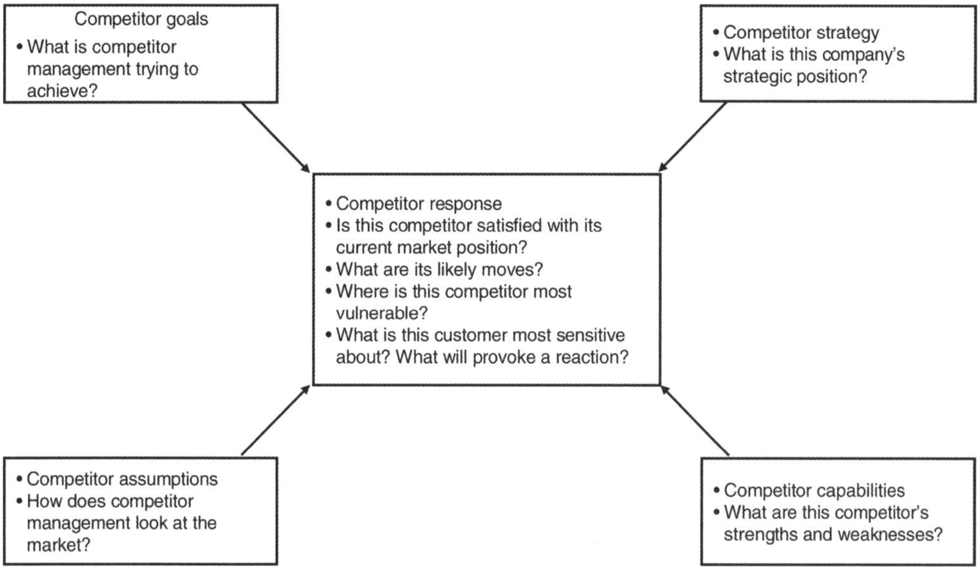

Figure 7.1 Understanding competitors
Reprinted from *Market-led Strategic Change: Transforming the Process of Going to Market.* N. Piercy. Copyright 1997, with permission from Elsevier.

This is summarized in Figure 7.1.[3]

There is no need to look at all of the competition, in fact it is often better to focus on a few competitors.

Identifying the competitor's objectives

To forecast how a competitor might change its strategy, some knowledge of its goals is crucial. Identifying basic financial and market objectives is particularly important. A company driven by short-term profitability is a very different competitor from a company that is focused on long-term market share goals. A company with market share goals is likely to be much more aggressive in responding to a rival's competitive initiative than one that is mainly interested in the bottom line.

Press[4] suggests that the culture of an organization is based on one or more philosophies, as shown in Figure 7.2.

The specific philosophies are determined by intersection of the two axes. One relates to whether the business is focused more internally or externally, the other is based on performance measures.

- The resource focus: concentrates on internal efficiencies and cost management.
- The shareholder focus: sees the business as a portfolio of activities that should be managed to maximize the value for the business for its shareholders.
- The people focus: emphasizes the skills and contribution of employees, and their needs and expectations.
- The market focus: stresses the importance of satisfying customers by adding value and differentiating products and services.

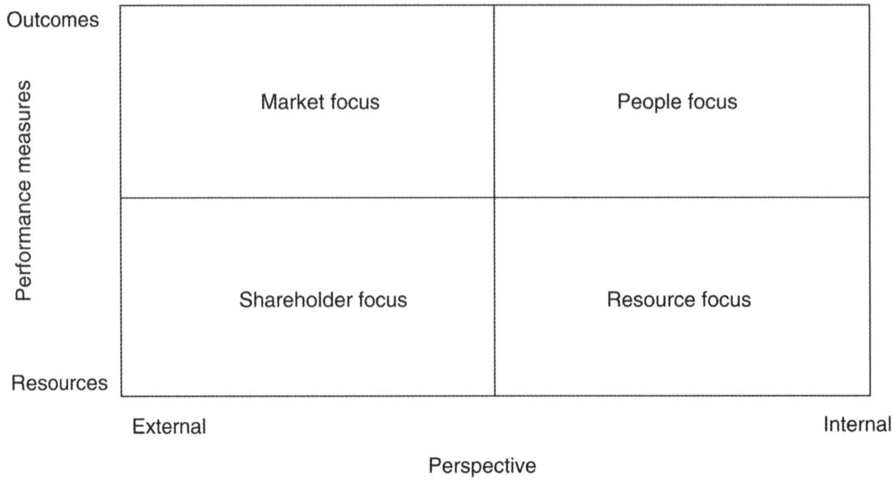

Figure 7.2 A philosophical basis for defining company culture

Table 7.1 Observing Porter's Five Forces in practice

	Cost leadership	*Differentiation*
Efficiency via	Driving out cost.	Doing things well.
Effectiveness via	Cutting out what is unimportant to customers.	Finding and sustaining different ways of competing.

None of these can be ignored, the question is how the four are prioritized.

Another way of thinking about the competition is how they choose to compete, as shown in Table 7.1. In terms of Porter's Five Forces, is their focus on efficiency or effectiveness? Cost or differentiation? And how does this focus compare with what the market wants?

COMPETITIVE DIFFERENTIATION

Use Porter's generic strategies as a framework for thinking about how the market players operate. Porter maintains that there are two sources of competitive advantage, low cost and differentiation and therefore only three generic strategies, as set out earlier in Chapter 3.[5] Porter's view is that competitors can adopt a broad or narrow approach and be either price leaders or differentiators. You can use the structure to see how groups of competitors are positioned, that is, group market players, according to the following categories:

- Broad scope/low price
- Broad scope/differentiation
- Narrow scope/low price
- Narrow scope/differentiation.

Other means of positioning the various players have already been covered in strategic group analysis (Chapter 3) and value mapping (Chapter 8). Chapter 8 also discusses how to measure key purchase criteria (KPC).

COMPETITOR PERFORMANCE

CDD thinks as carefully about competitors' ability to compete as it does about the target's. The whole of the previous chapter is therefore worth applying to the major competitors. In the next chapter we cover relative value (see Figure 8.3) and customer satisfaction. Figure 8.5 shows how to measure the target's performance relative to the competition. It measures performance against the reasons why customers buy the product or service KPCs. For competitor analysis there is a step beyond KPCs, and that is how they are translated into critical success factors (CSFs).

Contrary to popular belief, CSFs are not the same as KPCs, although the two are related and are often similar. As we have already noted, KPCs are the reasons (either conscious or subconscious) why customers buy a product or service. Customers select the offerings of one supplier in preference to another according to the suppliers' relative scores against the customer's KPCs. CSFs are what a target company has to be good at to survive and prosper in an industry. Surviving and prospering depends on getting just two things right:

- giving customers what they want;
- surviving the competition.

The firm must therefore:

- Identify who its customers are, determine their needs, and why they use one supplier rather than another.
- Examine the basis of competition in the industry. This may not be straightforward. For example, no matter how well differentiated the product might be and no matter that customers say they buy it on design and features and not on price, if competition is intense, a company still has to control costs to keep prices down.

The process is summarized in Figure 7.3.[6]

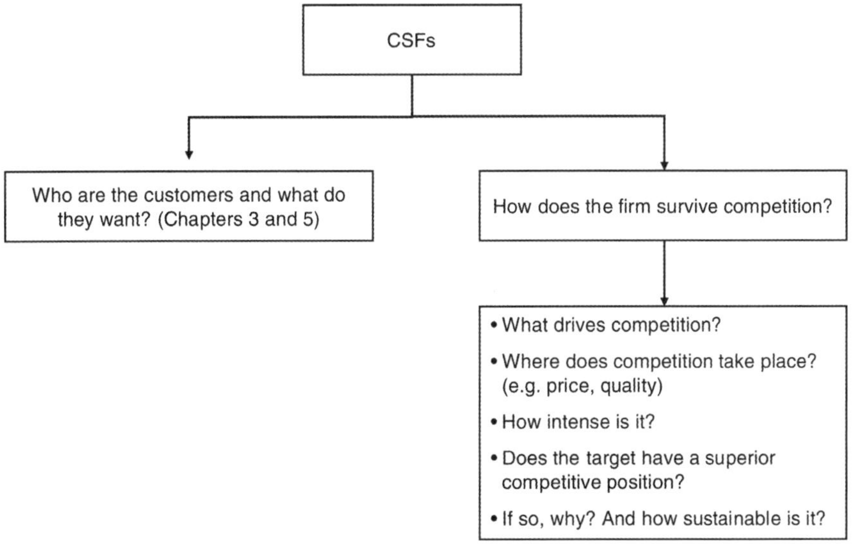

Figure 7.3 Identifying CSFs

Whereas KPCs are customer related and therefore external, CSFs are internal to the target company. They are the processes and systems that enable the company to deliver what the customer wants. Companies in the same industry often have different CSFs reflecting their different strategies. However, companies sharing similar strategies (that is, in the same strategic group) will share common CSFs. The CSFs for a segment will be linked to the KPCs for that segment.

Of course, as they are supposedly 'critical', there should not be too many of them – five to six seems to be the accepted limit.

Key performance indicators (KPIs), the last box in Figure 7.4, are quantifiable measures of the CSFs. Management use KPIs to monitor how well it is performing against their CSFs. KPIs therefore help management to answer the question, 'how well are we doing?' Because CSFs are often intangible, KPIs can be difficult to define and often end up as proxies for the CSFs.

The example in Table 7.2 illustrates the relationships and the differences.

You will avoid a lot of confusion if you have a standardized approach to analysing the competitive position of the target and the competition using both KPCs and CSFs.

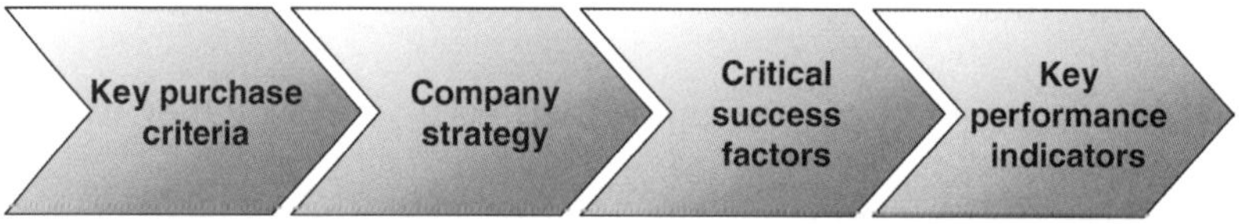

Figure 7.4 KPCs to KPIs via CSFs

Table 7.2 KPCs, CSFs and KPIs for bicycles

	Low end	*Mid range*	*Premium*
KPCs	• Price • Availability • Looks	Quality • Brand • Price	Performance • Design • Quality
Company strategy	Low-price bicycles sold through discount stores under the retailer's own brand	Medium priced bicycles sold primarily through specialist retailers under the manufacturer's brand	High-priced bicycles for enthusiasts and competition riders.
CSFs	• Global sourcing of components/manufacture in low cost countries • Supply contracts with major retailers • Supply chain efficiency	• Quality control • Cost efficiency • Distribution/dealer support	Research and development • Innovative design • Component and build quality • Brand management
KPIs	• Cost per unit • Sales volume • Stock levels	• Percentage returns • Brand recognition • Cost per unit	• Customer satisfaction • Brand awareness level • Percentage defect bicycles

FINALLY, CHECK WITH MANAGEMENT

You will discuss the competition with management at the beginning of the exercise and arrive at a view of their various strengths, weaknesses and strategies. At the initial meeting, you should make a point of asking them the two killer questions:

- Can you give us five reasons why customers would buy from you rather than your competitors?
- Can you give us five weaknesses that your business has in comparison to your competitors?

You should also check your analysis with them at the end and ask them to validate your assessments among their sales and support staff, those that deal with customers.

Conclusion

The objective of competitor analysis is to gauge the target's value based on its strategic position vis-à-vis existing and future competition. The focus will inevitably be on current, direct competitors, but you need also to consider the barriers to entry, the likelihood of entry and the threat to the target that entry represents. Once the competition is defined, the goal of CDD is to benchmark the target's relative strengths and weaknesses in meeting customer needs and to try and plot the direction in which competitors are going.

Notes

1. Piercy, N. (1997) *Market-led Strategic Change: Transforming the Process of Going to Market.* Oxford: Butterworth-Heinemann.
2. Johnson. G, and Scholes, K. (2002) *Exploring Corporate Strategy.* Harlow: Prentice Hall.
3. Piercy, *Market-led Strategic Change* (see note 1), adapted from Porter, M. (1980) *Competitive Strategy: Creating and Sustaining Competitive Advantage.* New York: Free Press.
4. Press, G. (1990) 'Assessing Competitors' Business Philosophies', *Long Range Planning,* 23(5): 6.
5. Porter, M.E. (1980) *Competitive Strategy.* New York: Free Press.
6. Grant, R.M. (2002) *Contemporary Strategy Analysis.* Oxford: Blackwell.

CHAPTER

8 The New Reality

The last two chapters encouraged the CDD analyst to deconstruct a complex set of market and competitive circumstances into their constituent parts: the market and the target's ability to compete. We then looked at factors impacting on market attractiveness and the factors that determine a company's ability to compete. A company's ability, we said, was far more important than market attractiveness. Ability to compete was defined as the ability to provide customers with more value than the competition. This is classical marketing theory that maintains that competition is not between what companies produce, but what they add in terms of extras – the packaging, services, advertising, customer advice, financing, delivery arrangements, warehousing and other things that people value – and it is the word 'value' that is the clue to customer satisfaction. The way it defines value is:

$$\text{VALUE} = \text{BENEFITS} - \text{COST}$$

If a target understands customers and what they want, it will understand benefits and will provide those benefits in one of two ways: it will either create additional benefits or reduce the cost of existing benefits. Whichever way it chooses to compete, providing it does this better than the competition it will have a superior competitive position. This is fine and logical, what is in all the text books and what all your clients will have been taught in accountancy school. But does it still apply? It is easy to get carried away with all the 'delight the customer' stuff that seems to be floating around these days, but given how demanding customers have become and how vicious and fast moving markets now are, is it not time for a new, cynical, harder-edged marketing textbook, a sort of Philip Kotler written by Quentin Tarantino?[1]

This chapter looks at the modern world and counsels that, while traditional marketing has still a part to play in CDD analysis, it may need to be supplemented by something a bit more modern.

The beleaguered company

There is a clinical logicality about the marketing and strategy literature. If only you can decide what you are really good at, knock up a product or service that builds on your strengths and segment the market to identify a bunch of customers who need exactly what you can provide, you can sell it to them (at a premium price of course) and gallop off into the sunset. Easy. I really don't know what all these businessmen have to complain about. I once witnessed a very senior consultant bounced around a board room when he had the temerity to suggest to the battle-scarred MD of a steel tube company that had not made a decent profit in a decade that there were only three strategies in this world and his tube company might do better if he followed one of them. The MD's situation is the situation now faced by most businesses. Steel tube is a mature business with a lot of experienced competitors all competing on the same terms for the same set of sophisticated customers. Because customers are so sophisticated, they have a lot of of product experience. They do not need technical advice and for them the product is easy to substitute. Their only concerns are price and availability and everyone will offer them just-in-time delivery, so that leaves only price.

Because the competitors are so experienced, they have more or less the same resources and competences. Any technical innovations are quickly copied. And if this lot ever did conspire to fix prices, there are plenty of producers in newly industrializing countries, particularly China and India, focusing on 'me too' forms of competition, ready, willing and able to exploit their cost advantage.

More and more markets are going this way despite what target management would have you believe. Customers are generally smarter and better informed than they ever have been and where they need information about products and services there is no shortage of impartial third-party sources around. Who would have predicted a decade ago that complex products like computers and stock broking would be sold like basic commodities with few value added services? Even so, target companies will try to convince you, and prospective acquirers, that they have an excellent reputation, a great brand and superb customer relationships. All of these are part of the target's value proposition. The value proposition is how the target company presents itself to the market – the 'why you should buy from me' bundle of explicit and implicit messages. This includes the use of key marketing assets like brands and messages about why the target is different from the competition – 'why you should buy from me and not from them'. It hardly needs saying that getting the value proposition to work depends crucially on responding to what customers want from the product or service. It is no good having an excellent reputation or a great brand name if all customers want is low price and immediate availability. Nor is reputation or brand or anything in the target's history going to be of much use if customer wants have moved on. This was illustrated in Chapter 3: Figure 3.10 contained a clear message for the client that operated in the solutions end of the market. This was, 'most of the market does not want a high cost/highly specified solution'. The analysis went on to show that the market was continuing to move away from the solutions sector and that the target needed to tailor its value proposition accordingly.

The easy riposte to all this is that the job of CDD is to advise on whether or not the proposed acquisition is any good. Clearly an acquisition of a steel tube company is not a great idea. If it has not made decent profits for a decade, it is unlikely to start doing so now, whichever of the three generic strategies are adopted. That is the right answer! But there is a lesson in here for CDD in less clear-cut cases and that is, 'do not forget to look not just from the market inwards but from the target outwards too'.

Customer segmentation

A target's present and future market prospects depend crucially on its customer base, so let us turn things around for the moment and consider how sophisticated B2B purchasers see their suppliers. The odds are they will segment their suppliers according to the extent to which their products or services contribute to the core competence and competitive advantage of the buying firm. This they will translate to cost and risk, where cost is the

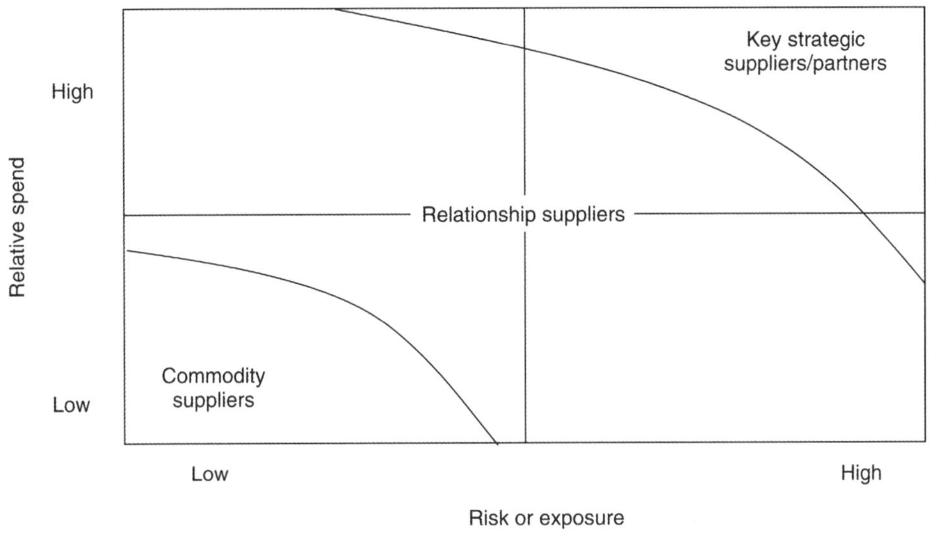

Figure 8.1 How professional buyers segment their suppliers

amount spent on the product and risk is the risk to the firm if the supply fails, as shown in Figure 8.1.

Commodity suppliers supply items such as stationery, basic services, the car fleet and basic desktop software. The nature of the products and services combined with the market for their supply (that is, lots of sources, easily substitutable products) means that there is no point the acquirer investing any time in developing relationships with suppliers. Do not forget that downsizing, re-engineering and benchmarking have fundamentally changed purchasing behaviour and that purchasing departments, just like any other central department, have to do more work with fewer people. Contracts will be short and e-procurement prominent. In contrast, the acquirer will manage relationships with the medium risk relationship suppliers, but those relationships will be nowhere near as close as they are with the strategic partners. Here the acquirer will attempt to work jointly to achieve a number of jointly determined desired outcomes.

Now let us look at the target's customers in the light of the above behaviour. We can think of customers in terms of the equation at the beginning of this chapter, as shown in Figure 8.2.[2]

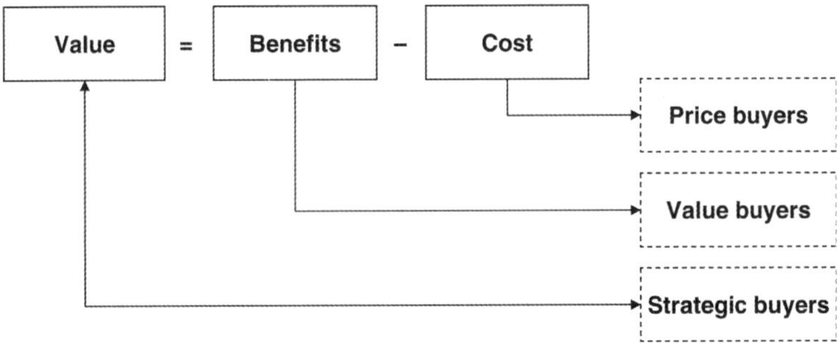

Figure 8.2 Analysing the customer base

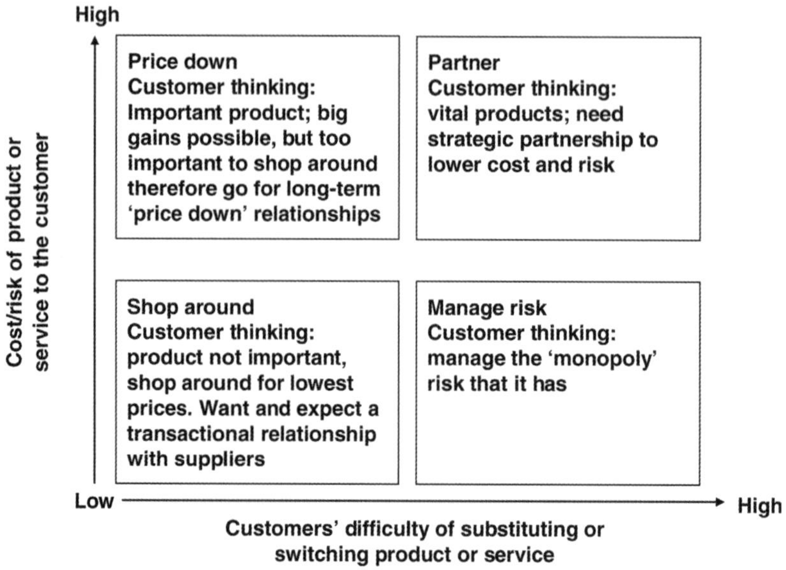

Figure 8.3 Customer behaviour is not always the same

And we can go on to segment them according to where they are on the two-by-two matrix set out in Figure 8.3. Not all customers will necessarily be in the same quadrant because mission criticality or the willingness to consider substitutes may be different.

Figure 8.3 is used in strategy analysis to understand how best to serve customers and where to expend marketing effort according to how they perceive and buy your products or services. For our purposes, in CDD, it is the ideal framework against which to judge the target's business plan. If the market is firmly in the bottom left, Shop Around quadrant, where price, availability and convenience of purchase are the main customer concerns, watch out for statements in the target's business plan such as, 'as competition increases we will maintain our margins by adding more value'. Not if the customer won't let you, you won't. In fact you should expect to find that most of the things that target companies push as their defining features, customers could not care less about. Customers in the bottom left of the chart will select the target's product as long as it does what it says on the tin better than any other for the price and is more convenient to get hold of. Buyers and suppliers often live in different worlds. On the other hand, as can be seen, the more the target lies to the top right in Figure 8.3, the greater the scope for selling value-added products or moving up market. Figure 8.3 should be prepared for each product-market. Placing your target's customers in the appropriate quadrant is a brilliant way of deciding what analytical theme(s) are the most appropriate for the rest of the CDD exercise. Research indicates that most suppliers, 50 to 70 per cent, fall into the top left (Price Down) or bottom right (Manage Risk) segments. Each of the four quadrants are described from the customer's point of view below. The differences between them are a question of relative buyer and supplier power.

SPOTTING THE QUADRANT

Before we look in more detail at each of the four quadrants, how do we know where to place the business? Clearly if the analytical direction of the whole CDD exercise is going to

Table 8.1 The output of a KPC interview with management

KPC		*Weighting (%)*
1	Price	50
2	Quality	10
3	Availability	20
4	Design	10
5	Reliability	10
		100

be based on segmenting customers, customer segmentation must be done early. One telling way is to track sales by customer over the past 5 years. How much churn has there been? (high = Shop Around quadrant?). Management interviews should shed some light as well. They should be able to come up with a weighted list of key purchase criteria as in Table 8.1.

By far the best solution is a few in-depth test interviews with market participants followed by some serious hypothesizing, which results in an initial view of where the product or service sits in relation to Figure 8.3. And I really do mean 'in-depth'. This is not the sort of stuff that is done easily in half-an-hour on the telephone. You really do need to sit down and go through thoroughly what the customer is buying and why. Does the customer really care that much about the product? Is the attitude: 'As long as it turns up in time and does the job at the right price, I am quite happy?' (Shop Around quadrant again). Or is it a case of: 'I spend a lot of money on this product, this product is important to me. I value the target's technical help, so I am more or less locked into the target, but I do not expect to pay more for it next year and I use the competition to keep Target Co honest' (Price Down quadrant). The result of these discussions and subsequent hypothesizing is shown in the Weighting column in Table 8.1.

THE SHOP AROUND QUADRANT

Customers in this group focus largely on price and availability (see Case Study 23). To them the product is a well-understood, readily substitutable commodity. It is widely available and/or easily substituted. They want it now at a good price, with the minimum of fuss. From their perspective, products in this group probably do not cost a lot individually, but may cost a fair bit in total. It makes sense for buyers to shop around.

Suppliers in this quadrant are faced with a transactional sell. Relationships count for little. All that interests buyers is cheap and easy acquisition of the product. They are not going to spend time and money developing relationships – time that they see better spent finding cheaper or more convenient alternatives

Many customer groups have had this outlook forced on them in recent years. Buying committees and even outside third-party buying groups, whose sole purpose is to drive down prices, have added further to buyers' focus on price as opposed to benefit. In many markets, the extensive use of price-driven purchasing staff is behind the drive to commoditization, which is why price-based buying is not restricted to commodity markets.

CASE STUDY 23

SELLING TO THE US HEALTHCARE INDUSTRY

The US healthcare market is the biggest in the world. Basic healthcare coverage has historically been funded by private insurers plus the two public healthcare schemes, Medicaid and Medicare. Until the early 1990s, patients who became ill went to the doctor and sent the bill to their insurer. This arrangement encouraged doctors to perform the most expensive procedures. Hardly surprisingly, insurance fees were rising at over 10 per cent per annum. Over the last 10 years this has changed dramatically. Today, private health insurance is dominated by health maintenance organizations (HMOs). An HMO contracts with selected physicians, hospitals and the like, which its clients must use. They can no longer use the facilities of their choice. An HMO pays contracted reimbursement rates, that is, fixed fees per intervention.

HMOs have changed insurance company buyer power dramatically:

- They use their muscle to secure discounts from their suppliers, including pharmaceutical firms.
- They control the provision of services for enrolled patients by:
  - cutting the number of unnecessary interventions;
  - making sure the most cost-effective treatments are used, using IT to determine what the best and most cost-effective treatments are;
  - encouraging cheap preventive care.

This has had a knock on effect to suppliers of healthcare products and services:

- Healthcare providers, hospitals and the like, have formed purchasing groups and developed IT-based access to price comparisons increasing price pressure on their suppliers.
- Distribution channel power has increased, facilitated by consolidation of channels and increasing professionalism of distribution companies. This adds to the price pressure on manufacturers, as distributors go own brand in response to the price pressure on them from healthcare providers.

The result for suppliers is that product differentiation is tiny and economies of scale are becoming the main competitive weapon both in manufacture and selling. And the old argument that medical buying groups only have an influence on 'non-special' products is breaking down too. In the USA, for example, it is evident that group purchasing organizations (GPOs) are now taking in the smaller more specialist items, not least by recruiting doctors to sit on their buying panels.

This trend to price down purchasing is taking hold across the western world changing the basis of competition across the healthcare industry and with it the resources and capabilities necessary to make a decent return.

At the same time, globalization and deregulation are conspiring to increase the number of suppliers. There is some very cheap Chinese product about these days. Faced with greater choice, customers have indulged in tougher, price-based buying. Any product differentiation has taken a back seat to price.

Technological advances are also making it harder and harder to maintain true product differences. While technology makes innovation much easier, it also considerably shortens the time it takes for competitors to copy and for production to move to cheaper locations.

Even call centres are not immune from cheap, offshore competition made possible by technological advances. Even where 'offshoring' has not been possible, in Holland for example, call centre prices have fallen as the markets have reached maturity. Once a market becomes price based, it becomes difficult to shelter from price competition. Even those call centres that have followed a strategy of adding value to their offerings have found it difficult to secure a price per call that reflects the value added.

Suppliers have aided and abetted their customers by meeting demand for common standards, open architectures and common specifications. This has resulted in opportunities for substitution by cheaper products, diminishing differentiation potential and pushing price to the top of the list of key purchase criteria.

However, all is not completely lost, all of the time, as the next quadrant shows. Buyers buy things that give them the best overall combination of benefits. It is only if they see no material differences that they buy the cheapest or the one they used last or the first they remember.

Shop around strategies

So now you have placed the target firmly in the Price Down quadrant. Does this mean you are in the land of the hapless steel tube company we met at the beginning of the chapter and the acquisition should be abandoned? Not necessarily. There are a number of strategies the target might try under the circumstances and success with any or all of them might make this a good deal – at the right price.

AUGMENTING THE TRANSACTION

The only things that count in the Shop Around quadrant are price, availability and convenience. A target in the Shop Around quadrant should be trying anything to improve the last two. This is where the Internet comes into its own – making purchasing that much more convenient for the informed buyer. This could also be the territory of the one-stop shop. Adding transaction products and making life even easier for the customer would certainly be a viable strategy.

The other augmentation strategy is to turn the transaction into a revenue earning opportunity in its own right. Having rationalized their branch networks, the clearing banks have tried to woo selected customers by providing them with a personal service via 'Premier Accounts' and the like. Customers pay a small fee, for example, £10 a month, for a personal financial manager, access to a call centre, enhanced overdraft facilities and a few trinkets such as special cheque books. Charging customers for a service you used to give them for free and at the same time giving yourself privileged access so that you can sell them insurance and other bank-assurance products is a very nice trick indeed if you can pull it off.

DIFFERENTIATION

It may be possible for the target to create new value and in so doing move towards another quadrant. Most transactions do not involve a single product or a single service, but are a combination of products and services. In analysing differentiation, we therefore have to look for differentiation of the product and ancillary services. There are four transaction categories as shown in Figure 8.4.[3]

Moving towards another quadrant is easier said than done, but one strategy that has worked in the past is to augment the product and in so doing get a bigger share of the

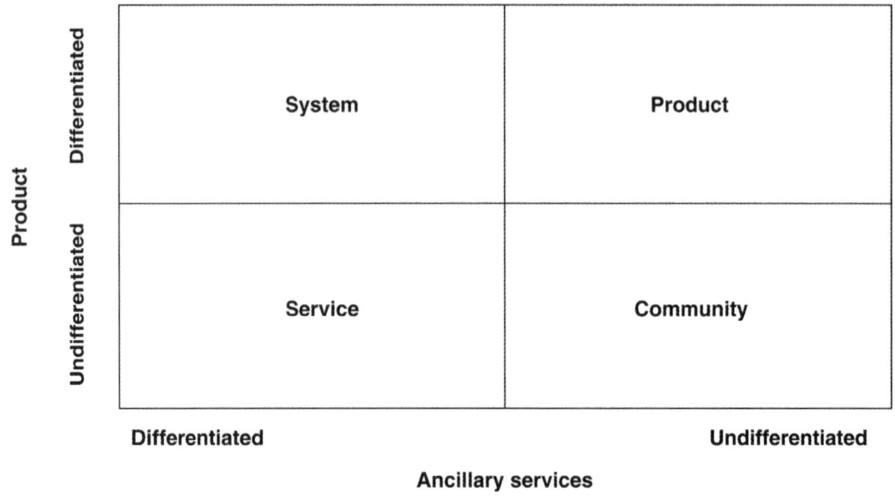

Figure 8.4 The categorization of transactions

customer. Augmenting the product frequently means selling a system rather than a product. The hoped for effect is to lift the target out of the Shop Around quadrant and put it firmly in the Partner quadrant. However, three-quarters of companies that move to a systems-based business model fail to see any benefit. The reason for this is that they do not think the systems proposition through properly, in particular they do not:

- distinguish between selling systems/solutions and merely bundling products;
- understand the customer's business economics, what diseconomies they suffer as a result of buying products, how systems can add value and therefore what capabilities and resources the target must add;
- appreciate the different selling process required by a systems approach especially, how a target company persuades customers to allow it to play a wider role in their businesses.

Also, as is suggested in Figure 8.4, both the product and the service need to be differentiated for a truly successful shift to a systems sell.

TAKE COST OUT

Transactional buying is cold and businesslike with price the dominant factor. A third way in which a target company might deal with the Shop Around quadrant is to adapt to the situation by lowering costs. Customers are not interested in paying a higher price for additional benefits. They want lower prices, which for the firm means stripping out cost. If a product feature or marketing activity does not provide customer value, it should be eliminated. The objective is to find the cheapest way of delivering the required bundle of benefits to the customer. This is not fine tuning, it is cost deconstruction. It involves taking drastic action to any cost that the customer is not prepared to pay for. Think, for example, about how PCs were sold in the 1990s compared with now. As the customer has become more knowledgeable, the need for salespeople with product and application knowledge has diminished, the product has moved increasingly into the bottom left transactional segment to the point where Dell and others now sell direct to the customer, thus stripping out transaction costs that deliver no benefits to the customer.

Performance measures

Many of the traditional sales measurements apply to transactional selling. The target should be monitoring internal costs such as sales cost per customer, sales cost per transaction – any investments in sales must lead to cost savings or improvements in customer service. For example, a manufacturer of washrooms for offices, schools and hospitals changed its sales approach from sales representatives on the road to telesales because it recognized that contractors bought washrooms at the last minute with little pre-purchase screening. The target had recognized that the chances of a sales representative arriving just as the contractor was about to place an order were nil and the contractor certainly would not remember a sales visit when the time did come for an order to be placed. The 'machine-gun' telesales approach was a much more cost-effective way of selling this product to their customer base. Given the fickle nature of the customers involved, transactional sellers will avoid customer investments with a long-term payoff and will look very carefully at discounts and other loyalty investments because again with such a fickle customer base, discounts, in fact, do not buy loyalty. One of the best sales managers I have encountered was asked by a very large acquirer in a near commodity market how much his company charged for the fastest-moving range of products. When told the price, the response from the would-be customer was: 'I can get those 30 per cent cheaper from the competition.' 'Well in that case why don't you buy them from the competition?', the sales managers replied. 'Because they haven't got any,' said the would-be customer. 'In that case the price just went up 20 per cent'. This might sound like terribly bad practice but it is exactly the right approach in transactional selling, where everyone knows the score.

The target should also be measuring performance to ensure maximum convenience and availability. This will include delivery time, percentage of orders 'on time and in full'. Measures must reflect customers' perspectives. There are numerous examples of how these two may differ. For example, when customers order a product and are promised a 3-week delivery, they expect it to arrive in 3 weeks. Typically, what happens inside the factory is that the Sales and Production departments agree a delivery date that may or may not be 3 weeks hence. Measuring factory performance against customer expectations is what counts and not against what the factory agreed.

THE PRICE DOWN QUADRANT

Products in this quadrant are more important to purchasers but are still substitutable, therefore price matters and the customer has negotiating power. Buyers' overriding aim will be to manage prices down, by playing suppliers off against each other. This is not to say that buyers will switch suppliers as readily as in the Shop Around quadrant, but it does mean that they will invest in making sure they get the best possible deal.

For suppliers, it is still a price-based, transactional sell where they will be played off against other suppliers, but non-price factors become important. However, differentiation is easier because these 'value based buyers' look beyond the physical product to its use. As their buying is motivated by solutions and applications, they expect suppliers to understand their needs and help apply that understanding to getting the best out of the product. They will tend to buy only from organizations that are willing to invest the time and resources in

Table 8.2 Measuring relative value perception

Non-price attributes affecting customer choice		*Weight given to attribute %*	*Target's score*	*Competitor scores (out of 10)*			
				1	*2*	*3*	*4*
Product attribute	A						
	B						
	C						
Quality attribute	A						
	B						
	C						
Range attribute	A						
	B						
	C						
Service Attribute	A						
	B						
	C						

understanding their needs and as they put a premium on advice, they are prepared to pay for extra value. They tend to build relationships with suppliers. They value a technically based field sales force.

CDD should be measuring customer's perceptions of relative value. The winners will be those, like UK supermarket Tesco, who can craft superior customer value propositions.

Understanding relative value perception

More than in any other quadrant, competing in the Price Down quadrant means providing maximum customer value. It is about out-performing the competition on the non-price attributes affecting customer choice and selling at what is seen as a satisfactory price; what the motherhood statements in this discipline refer to as 'value for money' without really thinking how to measure it. Here's how to measure it. Table 8.2 shows the data that needs to be collected.

For a piece of software, you might come up with the scores set out in Table 8.3. Figure 8.5 shows the results graphically. As can be seen, the target is offering superior value to this quadrant.

Value mapping

Figure 8.5 illustrates what is known as a value map. A value map defines the relative position of different companies in an industry along a cost–performance axis. The value frontier defines the maximum performance currently feasible for any given cost to the customer. Plotting where it lies, as we have seen, is a matter of identifying what market players offer in terms of performance and cost. The value frontier should encompass all ways of fulfilling core needs – that is, it is applied to the market as defined in Chapter 3.

Successful market leaders create unique positions on the value frontier. If all the competitors converge toward a similar point on this frontier, the industry faces

Table 8.3 Relative value perception of a piece of software

Non-price attributes affecting customer choice	*Weight given to attribute %*	*Target's score*	*Competitor scores (out of ten)* 1	2	3	4
User friendly	26	9	9	8	6	8
Logical screen layout	21	3	5	2	2	4
Helpful helpdesk	14	4	6	2	2	8
Modularity	9	6	9	9	8	1
Full suite available	8	8	5	9	2	1
Frequent updates	8	9	5	1	9	6
Easily upgraded	6	5	2	6	1	6
Influential user group	5	7	8	3	5	9
Fully integrated	3	9	7	1	1	6
Weighted score	100	6.35	6.57	4.93	4.25	5.68
Price (2 most popular modules £ thousands)		45	74	50	41	66

commoditization and potentially reduced margins. The way to escape the commoditization trap is either to extend the value frontier or shift it. Ryanair has extended the value frontier in the airline industry at the low end while Concorde shifted it at the high end. Shifting the value frontier is about positioning yourself to the right of the existing line. Dell anticipated the commoditization of the PC business and created a value proposition based on better

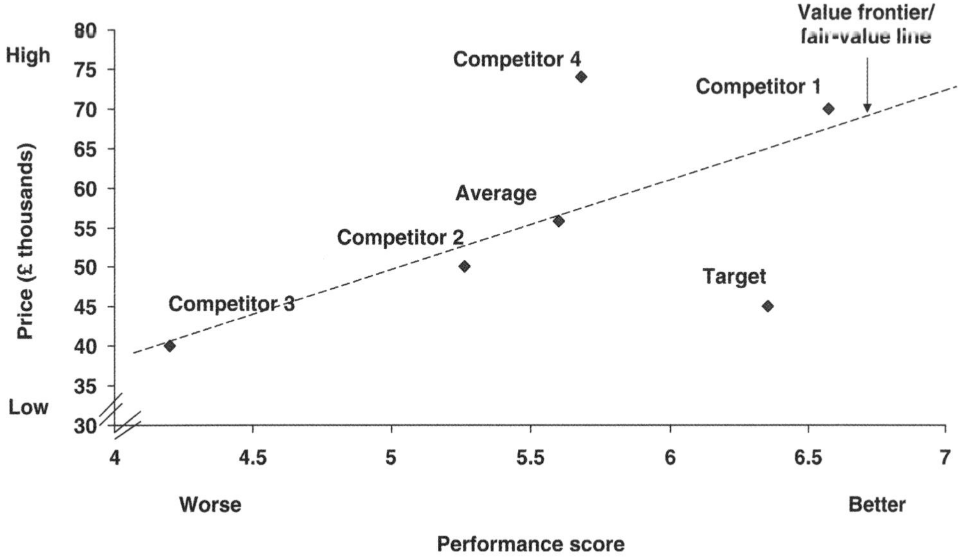

Figure 8.5 How professional buyers segment their suppliers

Table 8.4 Classifying customer needs

Attributes category	*Description*
Basic	Mandatory for the product or service to serve its purpose.
Expected	Attributes typically delivered by the competition that have to be matched.
Desired	Those that customers would like but which no-one delivers for the price they are willing to pay.
Unanticipated	Those that customers would value but do not ask for. Usually only come to light when someone applies serendipity, vision and technological innovation to come up with something new.

performance at a lower price than the rest of the industry. Points to note about value are:

- Many companies try to come up with 'The' value proposition. Value is in the eye of the beholder and must be tailored to each customer group and it needs to change with customer needs.
- Value based solely on a product feature, functions, performance and pricing is not sustainable because the competition will always catch up.
- The greatest value often lies in the intangibles that go with the product, such as the relationship the customer has with the sales team, the responsiveness of the target, its flexibility, the ease of doing business with it, the trustworthiness of its staff or their ability to find solutions.
- Elements of value may be business or personal. Many people just focus on the business but it may be the personal that is more important. One former colleague and star salesman in the food industry was very successful because he recognized that what his customers, supermarket buyers, valued most was someone who could get them out of trouble when they made a mistake and that is exactly what he did.

The following three sections describe non-price attributes, price and customers in more detail.

NON-PRICE ATTRIBUTES

Non-price attributes measure how many customers need the attributes of a product and how well it fulfils them. Table 8.4[4] sets out a classification map of attributes and customer needs.

PRICE

Price can be measured in a number of different ways too, as shown in Table 8.5.[5] This is the theorists' way of measuring price. For CDD it usually best to stick to 'pound notes parted with' as the definition of price and include risk and effort as non-price attributes.

CUSTOMERS

Customers can play up to four roles in the buying process. The same person may play all four or there could be four different people involved. It is important to bear these in mind because the price/performance trade-off will differ depending on the customer role. Traditionally, suppliers concentrate on satisfying the needs of customers in the user role. As can be seen from the examples in Table 8.6, some companies deliberately formulate their product attributes to link with the different customer roles. As the market converges on

Table 8.5 Defining product price

Dimension	*Attributes*	*Definition*
Price	Direct cost	The price paid
Risk	Physical risk	The actual risk of using the product
	Financial risk	The fear that the price will go down in the near future
	Selection risk	The risk that the product will not be the best for the job
	Delay risk	The risk that the product will not be delivered in time
	Functional risk	The risk that the product will not perform as expected
	Psychological risk	The risk that poor product choice will reflect badly on the purchaser
Effort	Acquisition effort	The time needed to search for, evaluate and get the product
	Operations and maintenance effort	The effort needed to learn to use the product, maintain it and dispose of it
	Complementary effort	The time and cost of acquiring complementary products; providing a one-stop shop is a way of packaging the product and all its complementors under one roof to increase customer convenience

Table 8.6 Customer roles

Role	*Description*
Buyer	The buyer role defines how a customer determines needs, assesses suppliers, orders, pays for and takes delivery of a product and service. Dell understood the importance of acquisition as PCs became commodities.
User	The user role describes how the end-user derives the expected performance from a product or service to satisfy a specific set of needs.
Co-creator	The co-creator role refers to how customers co-operate with their suppliers to produce the expected value.
Transferer	The transferer role defines how customers dispose of a product.

satisfying the needs of users, companies should focus on satisfying all of the customer roles as a way of adding value to the customer's core needs.

DRAWING THE MAP

In thinking about performance and cost, it might be as well to score each customer element separately as in Table 8.7.

GETTING THE INFORMATION

There is a whole section to follow on getting information in CDD; however, it is worth pointing out here that the data-relative perception measures come from the target's customers and the competitors' customers. The initial list of non-price attributes affecting customer choice and their weighting is going to come from management and the in-depth customer interviews if you can schedule them at the beginning of the process. The initial list will be modified in the course of interviewing.

Table 8.7 Scoring the four customer elements

	Buyer		*User*
Performance		Performance	
Cost		Cost	
	Co-creator		*Transferor*
Performance		Performance	
Cost		Cost	

Price down strategies

The Price Down quadrant calls for a consultative approach to sales and marketing by providing technical and applications advice that helps the customer understand how to solve its own problems or improve efficiency. This approach requires a technical field sales force that understands the customers' needs and can link the target's resources to satisfying those needs and thereby differentiate their offering from those of competing solutions. Be warned, though, the consultative approach only works in circumstances where:

- the product or service is differentiable and can be adapted to customer requirements;
- the customer is not an experienced acquirer or is not completely clear about how the product or service can add value;
- the product or service can provide customer benefits that justify a premium to cover the relatively high sales support costs.

Case study 24 illustrates how two seemingly similar products can fall into two very different quadrants.

CASE STUDY 24

TWO VERY DIFFERENT TYPES OF SCIENTIFIC INSTRUMENT

As we saw in Chapter 3, rheometry is the science of measuring runniness. Rheometers are expensive machines and are bought by highly specialized scientists. Given that the machines are so expensive and their buyers so knowledgeable, one might expect them to be in the Shop Around quadrant. They are not, they are in the Price Down quadrant. Because every buyer has a different application and therefore a different set of problems, technical support is very important to sales and does generate a premium. This can be compared with scientific microscopes, which is a lower margin business because techniques are broadly similar whatever the subject matter under examination and therefore buyers shop around.

As well as demanding a high level of investment in selling and sales support, the consultative approach also demands a culture in which time horizons extend well beyond a single transaction. For CDD, this means understanding that the investment in understanding customer requirements is unlikely to be recouped from a single sale, but having made that investment, the marginal cost of subsequent transactions is small. The target's sales must therefore be judged in terms of the potential revenue over the life time of customer relationships.

A consultative approach puts the sales force at the centre of things. This is not a transactional sell where the fast-talking and persuasive techniques of the used car salesman might win a sale, rather it depends on a technically qualified sales force that is conditioned to listen more than it talks. Their job is to create value, not to communicate value. Sadly, listening is not a core skill of most salespeople. The saving grace for many target companies is often that the competition's salespeople are just as bad.

The one or two 'rainmakers' who do understand how to do it properly will be crucial to the target's future. CDD needs to identify these people, assess their commitment, assess any success the target may have had in any attempts to transfer value creation from the sales force to the company and quantify the target's vulnerability should these star salespeople leave after the transaction.

Also telling is how the sales force is managed and supported. Monitoring sales calls per day is not the best way of encouraging a consultative approach. Nor is requiring the sales team to fill out detailed call reports after a sales visit when all they can do is report what happened, but not do much about it. It is far more effective to put the same time and effort into planning the calls. Finally, product literature is fairly useless in consultative sales. Sure they communicate potential solutions, but far more rewarding are sales support tools that allow salespeople to diagnose customer needs and help them identify the products and customization that will match them.

Measuring performance

What is measured is what gets done. Measurements should be few and simple concentrating on the critical tasks not the urgent tasks. They should measure results not activities. Sales calls may lead to more sales, but what really counts, and what should be measured, is not sales calls but results. Measuring sales calls is more or less asking the sales force to make easy and quick calls rather than focus on potentially large, strategic sales that require time and effort. This is a general rule. Again on the grounds that what gets measured gets done:

- Rewards should be aligned with measurements.
- They should measure what matters, not what can be measured.
- Salespeople should be able to influence the outcomes and have a hand in their design.
- They should be designed to get improvement.

Measures will encourage the sales force to concentrate on each of the stages (see Chapter 3, Figure 3.8) of what can be a long and complex process. Because this is a team effort, rewards will probably be team based.

THE MANAGE RISK QUADRANT

Buyers in this quadrant do not see the target's product or service as 'mission critical', but because there are not a great many substitutes, power has shifted to the supplier. Purchasers are aware of this and will recognize their vulnerability. This makes them keep an eye on competitive alternatives. For suppliers, maintaining some differentiation while keeping pricing and service competitive (so as not to give the buyer an excuse to look around) are the keys to success. If a supplier performs, then it will remain as a supplier. Such habitual usage

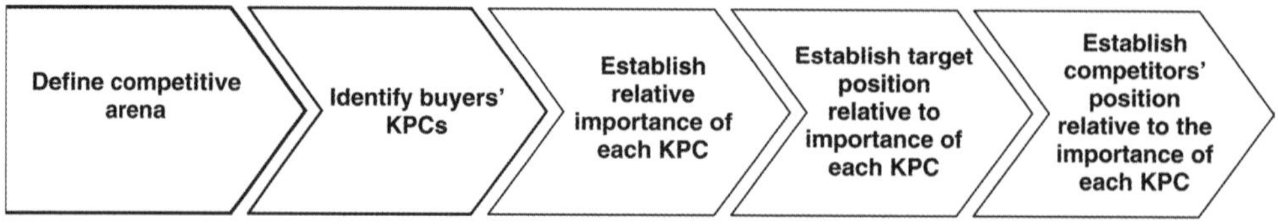

Figure 8.6 Defining performance relative to KPCs

is great because it gives quality of earnings and it takes other companies a lot of time and money to pry away satisfied customers. Why should they take the risk of change when they already have certainty that they will get what they want? It is important to get the basics right, what is known in the trade as providing the category benefits. These are routine purchases, which means the target's day in, day out performance must be better than anyone else's. This is exactly what underlies Tesco's success. Tesco has skilfully managed to deliver the generic category benefits of price, quality, range and service that appeal to all supermarket shoppers through superbly implemented operational programmes. As unexciting as it might be and difficult as it is to capture in those 2 × 2 matrices we all love, in this quadrant, execution is more important than strategy.

Measuring satisfaction

For a target in this quadrant, the strength of its customer relationships is key; we therefore have to measure customer satisfaction. There are two angles to this: we measure satisfaction against what customers want and against what the competition can provide. Figure 8.6 shows a schematic of the process.

Figure 8.7 shows the how customer satisfaction is normally presented. As can be seen, it is an alternative way of presenting some of the results that went into producing Figure 8.5.

Along the X axis are the factors that customers see as being the most important in their decision to purchase, or KPCs. These are scored out of 5 (or 10 if your prefer) for their importance and ranked in descending order, as shown by the bars. The target company is

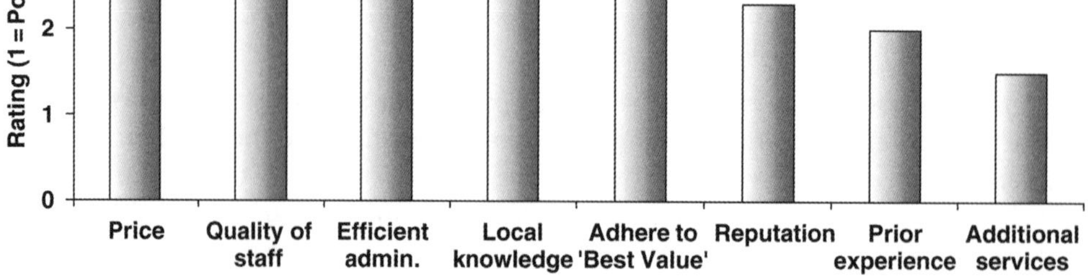

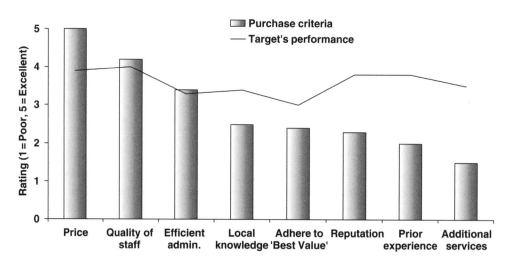

Figure 8.7 Measuring customer satisfaction

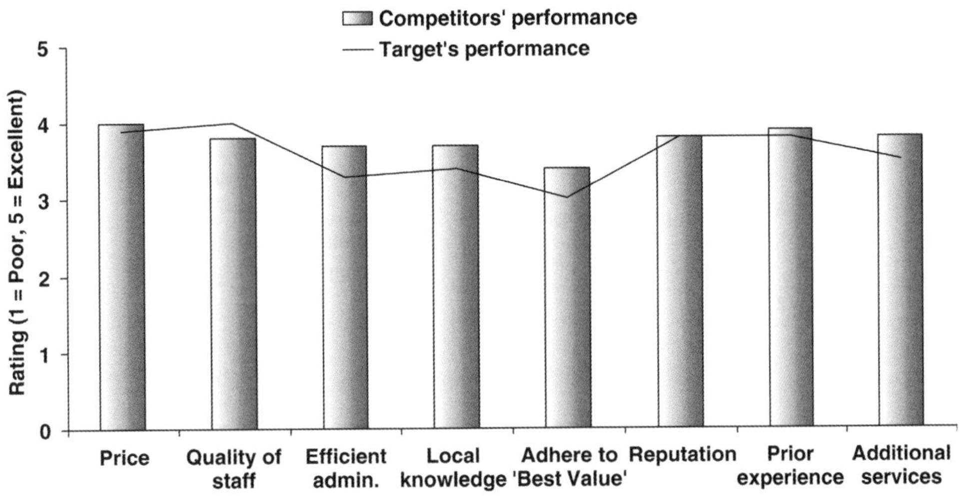

Figure 8.8 Customer perceptions of the target's performance versus the competition

then rated, again out of 5 (or 10), for its performance against each of these criteria. The result is the line. If the line is below the bar, the target is not performing against the KPC in question. If the line is above the bar, the target is over-performing against the KPC. Under-performance on the left-hand side of the chart is of the greatest concern.

These charts are compiled as above (see also Checklist 7 in Appendix A) by first asking management what they think are the KPCs, their relative importance and how they are likely to change in the foreseeable future, then confirming this in the first few interviews and amending as necessary. Thereafter, it is a case of asking each interviewee, in a consistent manner, to score each of the KPCs and to rate those competitors with which they are familiar. Again it is worth asking how the KPCs will change and how each company will be able to respond. This should give us a clue as to how the market is moving, for example, the danger of it slipping towards the Shop Around quadrant as well as telling us about competitive position.

It is important to determine the KPCs early on, so that a common interviewing template can be adopted. If not, it becomes impossible later on to aggregate interview results because the factors selected by every interviewer will be different and inconsistent.

However measured, performance against KPCs tells only part of the story because customers often have an ideal in mind when scoring KPCs regardless of whether or not the market can deliver this level of performance. The second element of the customer satisfaction rating must be perceived performance over the competition. Figure 8.8 shows that this takes exactly the same format as the rating against KPCs, but this time the bars represent the competitors' performance.

The theory is that market share gains will come about if the target is better than the competition at meeting KPCs. This may well be the case, but there are a number of issues with this as a measure of future success:

- KPCs have a habit of changing. All products and services have a tendency to commoditize with time as consumers become accustomed to their relative performance

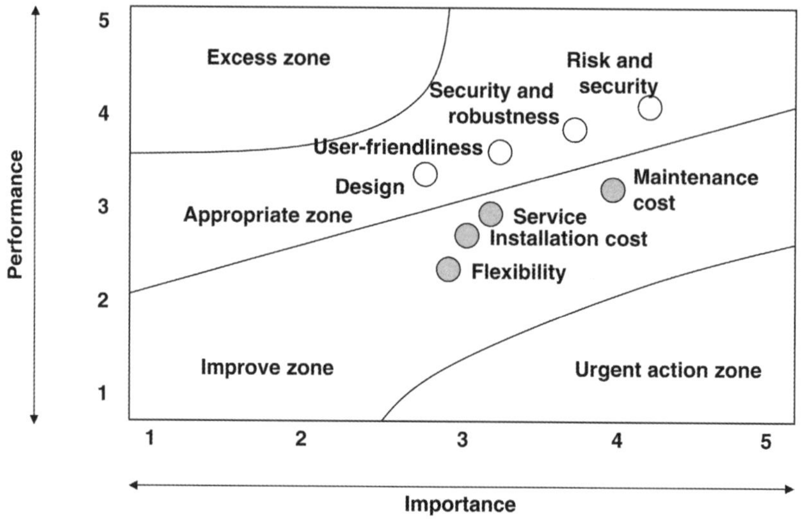

Figure 8.9 Customer perceptions and target company performance

and increased competition changes the way in which the market works. This is why it is important to ask about the future and how customers think KPCs will change and over what time period.

- The competition has a habit of changing, developing capabilities that can improve their performance relative to the market. This needs to be a feature of competitor analysis (Chapter 7).
- The charts above are the result of talking to customers. The bulk of the target's future revenues will come from the customers it already has, which makes these ratings extremely important. However, customers are customers for a reason and the reason is not because they see the target as a poor supplier! They will be open about what they say, but nonetheless their comments are biased. You still need to speak to non-customers and lapsed customers.
- KPCs are not the end of the story. KPCs must be translated into action, that is, CSFs and KPIs (see Chapter 7). The problems organizations have stem from the way they are run. In an acquisition, future earnings come about through management focusing on finding better ways of doing what the customer values and concentrating on being better than the competition at the few key internal skills that really matter for the creation of customer value.

Figure 8.9 is yet another alternative way of presenting KPC/customer satisfaction ratings, this time with the aim of prioritizing strengths and weaknesses against KPCs. Figure 8.9 could also be used to compare the target against the competition.

THE PARTNER QUADRANT

This is the Nirvana. Mission critical products, which are not easily substituted. With such seller power, why on earth would any supplier even contemplate a partnership? Partnerships in this quadrant only make sense for the buyer. Partnership for the seller means throwing away negotiating advantage and compromising its ability to deal with other customers.

Sellers are always dead keen on forging partnerships with their customers. In most cases, these will be companies who find themselves in the left-hand quadrants of Figure 8.3, where their products are substitutable, as a way of tying in their customer. Certainly the aim of every cleaner, caterer and air conditioning maintainer in Figure 3.7 is to reach the apex of that triangle. Why? Because it is their perception that having got to the point where they are working in partnership with their customers, strategically managing their property portfolio, their position as cleaner of choice is guaranteed. How naïve. What our earnest floor mopper is failing to understand is what partnership really means, that is, what the buyers see it as. Buyers in this quadrant are a few very large customers who demand an extraordinary level of commitment from all levels of the supplier's organization. The cleaning contract is not guaranteed; far from it. But over and above best-in-class cleaning, what these strategic buyers want is a partnership that creates benefits over and above what can be achieved in a normal supplier–buyer relationship. It is no accident that the few Total Facilities Management contracts that have been awarded have been given to financial engineers who buy in the basic services, such as cleaning, from third parties. Cleaning is a 'shop around' product and always will be. Many partnerships are set up with the sole objective of reducing costs. For example, close partnering so that a supplier can save on order processing or physical distribution costs is still a transactional relationship. The fundamental difference between this arrangement and a true partnership is that it has a very narrow set of objectives. In a true partnership, both parties will be seeking to create new value by whatever means possible, not just reducing costs. Take, for example, outsourcing the recruitment process. This is a partnership where customers keep hold of the strategic elements of the recruitment process, job description and selection, but outsource the grunt work of finding the candidates, screening them, writing rejection letters, arranging interviews and sending out offer letters. It is a partnership because the outsourced team become indistinguishable from the client's staff, the outsourced activities are seamless and outsourcing delivers a better process at less cost than the transactional alternative.

CASE STUDY 25

PARTNERSHIPS REQUIRE BOTH SIDES TO MAKE THEM WORK

A leading supplier of automotive paint, with a dominant share of the UK market, recognized the way the market was changing due to insurance companies' attempts to lower costs and increase service to their customers. Insurance companies wanted to deal direct with suppliers of crash repair products. When one of its customer's cars was taken to A1 Paintshop Ltd for repair, this meant a change in distribution arrangements for the paint supplier so that it could get products to targeted crash repair shops rather than rely on its hitherto more general selling through paint wholesalers.

The paint supplier approached a leading automotive wholesaler specializing in crash repair products. What it wanted was an exclusive partnership. It would be able to supply targeted bodyshops while the wholesaler would get a reliable supply of market-leading paint. The partnership was never formed because the wholesaler could not change the way it had always done business, which was to shop around for the best prices. A partnership was an anathema to them.

Partnership strategies

As we have already seen, partnerships will only happen if customers want them to and they will only work to the benefit of the supplier if the balance of power is in the supplier's favour. Partnership is an arrangement between equals working together to create value for the customer's customers. It is a shared mission, shared, that is, by the whole enterprise, which goes beyond solving problems. It is about creating maximum productivity by fitting functions together, as illustrated by Figure 8.10.

The theory is borrowed from enterprise re-engineering and assumes that the greatest potential for productivity gain lies at the boundaries between different functions in different organizations. This is partly because the gains inside functions have already been captured, but is mainly because this is where the big inefficiencies creep in. For example:

- supplier and customer schedules are not co-ordinated so that the supplier is either over-producing leading to excess stock, or under-producing leading to sales problems for its customer;
- duplication and waste because of different IT and logistics systems;
- each company doing its own thing rather than concentrating on what it is best at and leaving all other activities to competent partners.

Is there sufficient potential for new value creation that would not be possible from a transactional or consultative relationship and have both parties made the changes necessary to create value? Given half a chance, suppliers, seduced by the prospect of a strategic partnership, will not have asked the searching question, 'what, specifically, do we have to do differently for the partnership to create new value?'[6] for fear of upsetting progress towards a partnership agreement. Any agreement that fragile is doomed to failure. At the same time, customers wanting a partnership must be prepared to share their innermost strategic thoughts with suppliers. Finally, companies are not good at changing their ingrained ways of thinking about and doing things and, as most are pretty dire at getting their own departments to work together, it is hardly surprising that most partnerships fail.

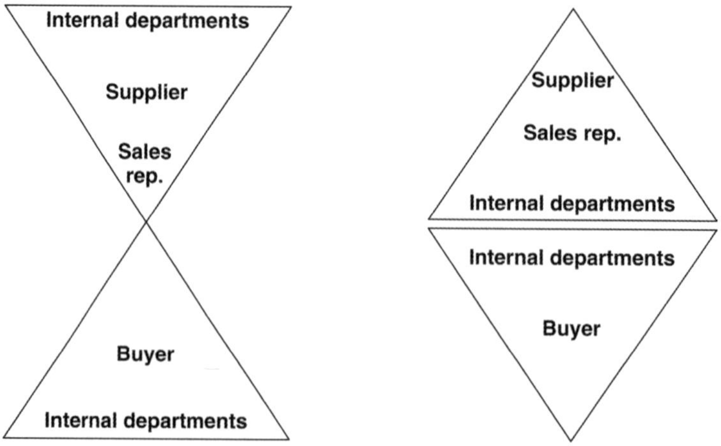

Figure 8.10 A partnership means all departments have customer contact

Measuring performance

A partnership business is just that – a business. Because partnerships depend on the entire organization working with each other, any strategic partnerships should be seen as separate business units. The business has its own assets base and its own cost base in the shape of the investments in people and resources to make this business work. Investments have been made by both sides and should be made clearly visible to all, as indeed should value created, if only to be able to judge whether or not to continue with the relationship. But the complication is that the aims of such partnerships are strategic. Measuring strategic gains is not easy. Even where partnerships do not have agreed success measures, a regular review of performance goals and measures are crucial to understanding whether the partnership is bringing the planned mutual benefits.

The target's approach

Figure 8.11 looks at the lessons learnt from Figure 8.3 from the inside. What it says is that companies should understand the buying motivations of customers and organize their marketing efforts accordingly.

There are two lessons from this. First, in many markets, it is simply not possible to move up market when the going gets tough without creating something fundamentally new that the customer values and is willing to pay for and often, if it is, everyone else will do the same thing at the same time thus keeping margins down. Second, not only does the product and service offering have to be tailored, but so does the sales and marketing approach. Any target you examine must be completely clear on the customer value proposition appropriate to the served market and design a business system that delivers that value proposition to the highest level. The partnership quadrant is the one area where the purchaser has freedom of choice. Partnerships might sound like a good idea, for example they bring a constant stream

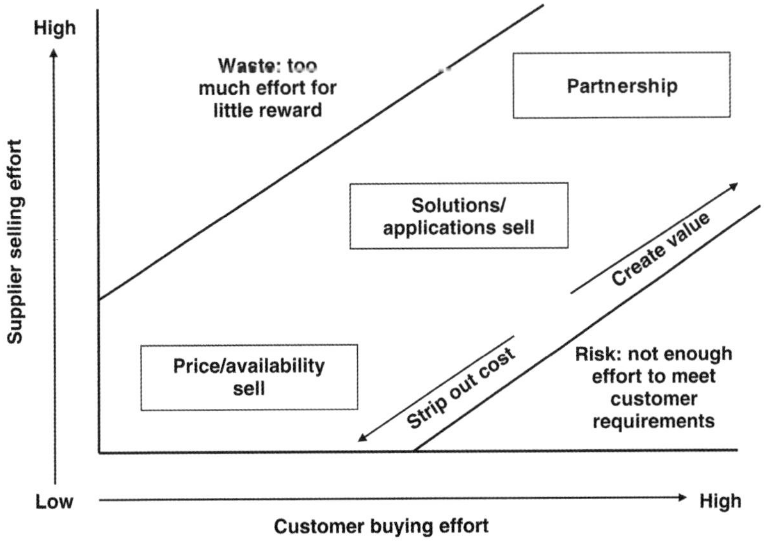

Figure 8.11 What is the different approach to use with different customers?
Source: Rackham, N. and DeVincentis, J. *Rethinking the Sales Force: Redefining Selling to Create and Capture Customer Value*, 1999, New York: McGraw-Hill. Reproduced with permission of McGraw-Hill Companies.

of new work and there is no need to 'make' every sale. They also bring an expectation of continual improvement and demand exclusivity of supply. Quite rightly, many suppliers take the view that partnerships seriously undermine their market power and compromise with a consultative or relationship approach instead.

The sales force

The field sales force should not be seen as a bunch of order takers. It is a strategic resource and source of competitive advantage that, in industrial companies, can cost three-quarters or more of the total marketing budget. In a wide variety of industries, the salesperson has a major influence on the buyer's motivation to continue the supplier relationship. On top of the direct role, the sales force also has a strong indirect influence on the customers' perception of the supplier and the value of its good and services. The other side of the coin is that, as we have already seen above, market strategies that are not consistent with what is expected of the sales force in the field are doomed to failure. It is no good having a transactional sales force if what the customers want is a partnership.

For all quadrants except transactional sales, the sales force should be pursuing one or more of the following four strategies:

- differentiating their products and services by building on their inherent advantages;
- building business solutions by selling a package of products and services to solve customer problems, not selling single products or services;
- understanding the customer's business in order to identify customer needs and develop acceptable solutions;
- providing service as part of the package.

According to a major recent study, the world-class sales force will focus on benefit or business results, utility and ease of use, not on products.[7] There are eight processes that must be benchmarked.

- Customer satisfaction: the most important measure of success. Measures are used to prove value to the customers, for example for paying the price demanded, as well as to reward the sales force. These are not just the soft measures but hard measures such as money saved or cycle time improved.
- Market segmentation: taken down to the sales level when customers require specialist attention, such as products tailored to particular industries.
- Recruitment and selection of salespeople.
- Training and development: as customers demand more added value and more knowledgeable salespeople, training and development becomes a continual process for all sales personnel.
- Compensation: world-class sales organizations were found to use all combinations of compensation methods across the spectrum from totally fixed to totally variable. The more the tendency towards transactional sales, the more likely variable rewards are to be used.
- Integrated sales service and support systems: the lone salesman is no more. Members of the sales force are now is supported by a team of professionals, applications engineers for

example or transport and logistics, who may work either directly with the client or through the salesperson, depending on how many customers there are on each salesperson's patch.

- Direct customer feedback: direct customer feedback measuring customer satisfaction is found in the best sales organizations:
  - evaluation of transactions from how well customer needs are evaluated, to how well they were satisfied, to what can be done to improve the relationship between supplier and customer;
  - extensive use of IT to help the customer, the sales staff and management.

Beyond satisfaction ratings

Customer satisfaction measures are not a good indication of the underlying strength of the target's relations with its customers. Customer retention is much more important than satisfaction because customer satisfaction does not automatically lead to customer loyalty. Although there is a positive link between customer satisfaction and repurchase intentions, empirical studies[8] have found that satisfaction explains less than half of the variation in repurchase intentions, clearly showing that factors other than satisfaction are important in determining whether or not a customer comes back. And in any case, as customers become ever more sophisticated, satisfaction is an entry qualification for doing business. It is not, by itself, sufficient to retain business. Strategic acquirers might therefore want to go further by trying to look into the future and think about customer loyalty in a similar way to the way in which Figure 8.3 encourages us to think about products and buying behaviour.

The idea of seeing customers as a portfolio of assets to be managed just like any other portfolio of assets is not new. For example, Shapiro and Bonoma[9] classify customers in two dimensions based on their sensitivity to price and the cost to the organization to service the customer. Other writers choose different axis labels,[10] but the point is not which label is right or wrong, but that there are important differences between customers. This reflects the fact that while many industrial buyer–seller relationships are mutual and long-lasting, many are not.

Existing customers come in the four varieties shown in Figure 8.12. The customer satisfaction equals customer loyalty assumption is box 1 and this is where we would like to see the majority of the target's customers. However, as can be seen, there are another three possibilities and CDD should attempt to determine how much of the top line is coming from each. It has been suggested that in a typical company today, customers are defecting at the rate of 10 per cent to 30 per cent per year.[11] The happy wanderers in box 2 ought to be loyal because they are satisfied, but they are not. They will give the target top marks in the satisfaction ratings, but will take their business elsewhere for all sorts of unrelated reasons, for example, because people or policies change. The hostages in box 3 may be some of the most loyal customers, at least for now, but they are also highly dissatisfied, perhaps because they are tied in by economic or emotional factors. Too many customers in this box and the target's sales may be at risk (see for example Case Study 16 in Chapter 4). The dealers in box 4 are loyal to no one except the best deal – wherever it may be.

CDD should attempt to analyse customers according to their 'type' and their value to the target company. This requires systematic classification of customers in terms of their

Figure 8.12 Customer satisfaction and customer loyalty

historical or likely loyalty. In general, the following factors would be relevant in calculating the value of each customer and therefore the value of each segment:

- Annual sales revenue
- Cost of sales
- Marketing and selling cost
- Distribution costs.

Case Study 26 illustrates the utility of this level of analysis.

CASE STUDY 26

THINKING ABOUT WHAT REALLY MATTERS

Customer churn is an important proxy for how well a target company's product or service appeals to its customers. The higher the churn, the worse the target's ability to compete – except when the customer does not matter. It is rare that customers do not matter, unless if the customers that are deserting the target are small and never likely to return. This was the case with an IT trade show. The customer churn was a heart-stopping 70 per cent. Each year 70 per cent of the customers were lost. However, when these customers were properly understood, it was clear that they were very small IT companies, the bulk of whom were bankrupt before the next show took place. What was much more serious was the defection of two of the five very big IT companies, because that could be a signal that something had gone wrong with the show.

The classification in Figure 8.12 should also encourage us to look again at KPCs and how customers rate the company against them. Different types of customer will have different KPCs and different ideas of what is important, which, if properly understood, may well lead to different conclusions about the target's relative performance.

Looking further forward, the reality of modern markets is that customers are becoming increasingly cynical. More and more customers will compare suppliers to the best in the world.[12] For example, if Fedex can absolutely guarantee overnight delivery to anywhere in the world, how come airlines cannot even keep your bags in the plane? How come South West Trains still cannot run my trains on time, expects me to endure considerably longer journey times and cannot guarantee me a seat even after the most fundamental revision of the timetable since 1967 designed to reflect changes in travelling patterns? Could it be that it does not really care about its customers? The truth is, as Niel Piercy observes[13] about the privatized rail system, 'adding commercial trappings to a hostile bureaucracy simply produces a hostile bureaucracy with better excuses'. Why is it that my local fish and chip shop cooks everything to order, keeping customers hanging around for as long as it takes to deep fry a piece of cod? Is it not familiar with the concept of fast food? The point is not just the incompetence of these outfits, but that I am a sophisticated consumer who expects certain minimum standards, such as a train timetable that bears some passing resemblance to reality and food that I can collect on the way home because I am hungry and in a hurry. I, like many of my peers and most business-to-business customers, know what I want, am not easily fobbed off, will not put up with spin and deception and certainly do not believe advertising messages.

Alan Mitchell[14] produced a schematic model of customer behaviour based on customer loyalty and customer sophistication. This is shown in Figure 8.13.

Traditional marketing is designed for boxes 3 and 4 – that is, situations in which the customer is seen as unsophisticated. The reality is that boxes 1 and 2 are becoming the most common. Understanding where the target's customers lie within this matrix and probing for a new approach to customers that treats them according to their degree of sophistication and pushes them to the right-hand side of Figure 8.13 is one of the areas where CDD can add real value.

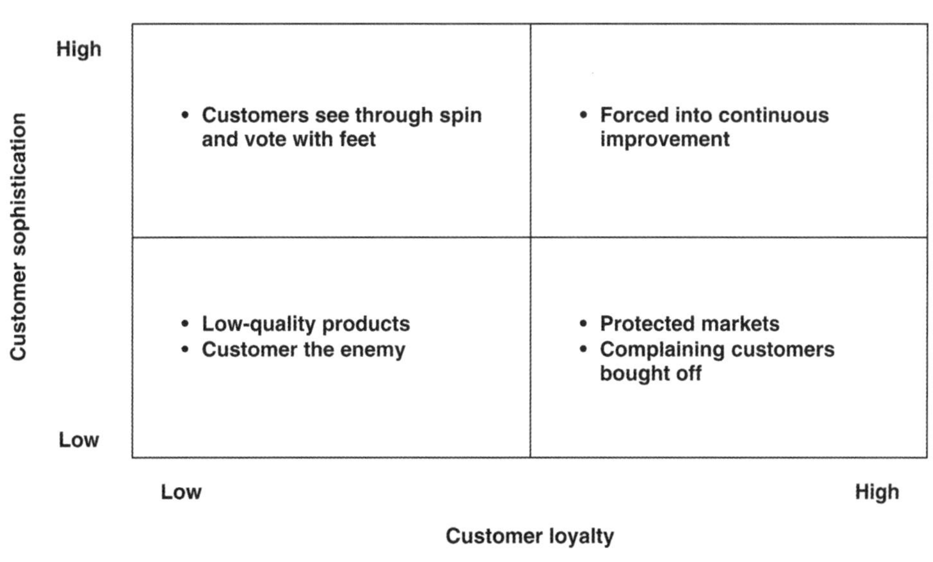

Figure 8.13 Customer loyalty and customer sophistication
Source: Mitchell (1997) 'Evolution'.

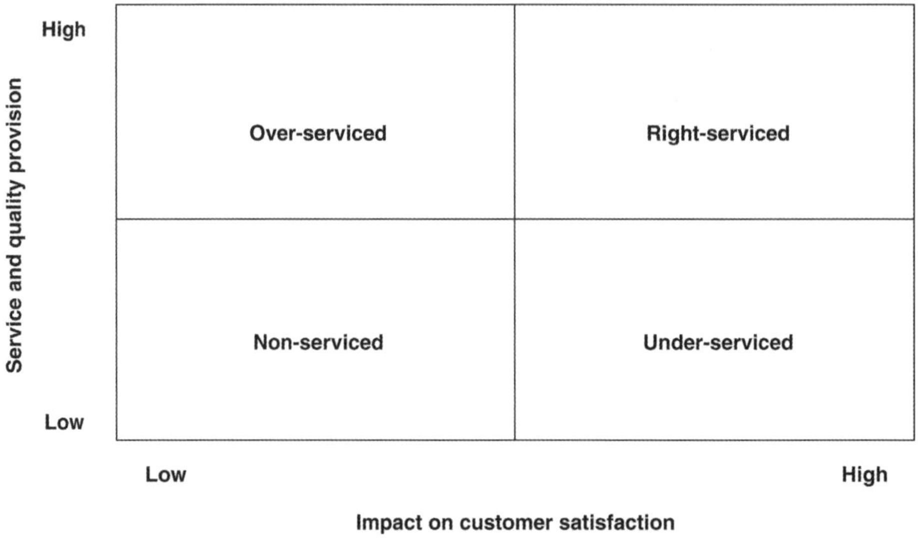

Figure 8.14 Service and quality vs. customer satisfaction

Another thing to bear in mind is that customer satisfaction should be appropriate to what the customer actually wants – again in line with the sort of analysis that would come out of Figure 8.3 above. Having collected and analysed the data that goes into Figure 8.7, it is not a bad idea to look at which firms are doing best and ask to what extent this has to do with service and quality provision – if at all. At the same time, CDD should ask if the target is over- or under-servicing and/or whether there are low service opportunities or indeed high service opportunities that it is missing out on. Figure 8.14 provides the framework for such analysis.

Using the target's customer satisfaction measures

Some target companies will keep a log of customer complaints. It is obviously worth combing through this to see if themes emerge. However, CDD must go further because silent customers are not necessarily satisfied customers Only 4–5 per cent bother to complain, besides, something like 90 per cent of customer care programmes are used as the latest, plug-in quick fix, which brings no change in management behaviour,[15] used to treat symptoms rather than the disease. Measuring customer satisfaction is not what counts, but what companies do with the output. The experience with many companies is that customer care surveys become a game in which beating the system rather than improvement is the name of the game, with questionnaires even filled in by managers who do not want to bother their customers! On top of this, the usual concern is with measuring and data collection, when the real concern should be with setting targets for customer service, then working out how to attain them.

Customer care needs to pervade the whole organization – it is not just about adding a bit of customer service; it is integral to market strategy. People buy from people, but people do not always deliver the perfect service all the time because:

- they do not always know what 'right' is;
- they do not always know if they are being effective or not because they do not get the right feedback;
- they are not always rewarded for doing the right thing;
- they have conflicting demands, for example, spending time with customers or spending the same time on administration;
- they are stuck in their ways;
- they do not understand what is needed.

Also it is no good a target company training the front-line staff if the messages they get from the rest of the organization are inconsistent with customer care.

Therefore, just because a target carries out regular customer satisfaction surveys does not mean it is customer focused. Customer satisfaction surveys have great potential, but done badly can do more harm than good. Before being seduced by a target's attempts to measure customer satisfaction, check that it has carried out the research for the right reasons and has done it carefully. Much of the expenditure on market research is to help clients satisfy and impress their bosses and investors, rather than to understand what is going on. As everyone in consulting knows only too well, managers use research results to justify already formed positions. To paraphrase Lenin, they use research to support their position and not for illumination. A classic example of the use of market research to justify an already formed position cropped up a few years back at the height of the Internet boom in a venture capital house with an investment in a PKI provider similar to Baltimore (see Case Study 11 in Chapter 1). The request was: 'What we need is a market survey because if management know where the hot buyers are they can clean up.' The fact that a recent market study had conclusively shown that PKI was never going to be widely adopted fell on deaf ears.

Contract-based businesses

Ideally, a lending bank wants to see certainty for as long a time period as possible. In reality, this is not possible. As we saw in Figure 4.8, the bank's main focus will be in the first two years of the investment's performance. If the target is in a business where fixed-term contracts are the norm, banks will want some reassurance that an acceptable proportion of contracted revenues will still be present 2 years hence. The only way to do this is to ask! For example, Armor Group supplies security in 'high fright' areas of the world. In most cases it has a 3-year contract with its customers. The business was floated on the London Stock Exchange in 2004. As part of the due diligence for that transaction, the CDD team contacted each of the 100 or so firms with which it had a contract to confirm the size of the contract and to ascertain the chances of it being renewed. This is the same approach as used in Case Study 7 (Chapter 1) to confirm the forecasts of a target company supplying very large pieces of expensive equipment to the construction industry. The business in question put together its forecasts by listing all the contracts for which it had bid, assigning a probability of success for each and multiplying this by the contract's value. The only way to confirm the robustness of the forecasts was to speak to each contract awarder and ask the same questions.

Conclusion

The winners in any market are the suppliers that truly understand what it is that the customer wants, and provides exactly that. Providing quality or service that is not valued by the customer is a waste of time. Being best counts for little if the customer only wants products cheaper.

The importance of understanding where and why the target adds customer value cannot be underestimated. Its importance derives not just from the fact that the long-term health of the sales line depends on it, but also because what is important in value creation should be the theme that runs through the entire organization, from the context in which we judge management right through to the operational due diligence, which asks whether the technology, plant and equipment, production and logistics systems are adequate for the future.

There are four broad types of customer and therefore four generic approaches to serving the market, as summarized in Table 8.8.

Except with transactional purchasers, the product is not the only factor in perceptions of value. This means designing the entire system so that the required value is delivered, starting with the customers' needs and working backwards. For example, if customers require an application focus, then one would expect to see the target company have a direct sales force organized on an industry basis backed by a specialist R&D function and a production system with a high level of customization capability. For companies that target more than one type of customer, the same principles apply, but organization is a lot more complicated with separate and distinct approaches for each customer type. The most

Table 8.8 The four basic sales approaches

Product/service type	*Buyer's approach*	*Seller's approach*
Straightforward, basic, well-understood, easily substituted	Price based	Transactional, based on price, availability and convenience. The seller needs to add value by focusing on the transaction itself, making it as cheap and as easy as possible
Complex or fast changing, but easily substituted	Value based	Consultative: the seller needs to provide the customer with insights into their buying problems or uncertainties and create innovative solutions. Sellers should focus sales and marketing efforts on the early stages of the buying process, especially on the need recognition phase (see Chapter 3, Figure 3.10).
Low importance, not easily substitutable	Satisfaction based	Meeting customer price and service expectations. These are routine purchases where the buyer feels vulnerable because substitution is not that easy. The seller needs to differentiate and provide the buyer's required price and service levels in order to 'stay under the radar' so that the buyer does not feel it is being badly served and starts to investigate alternatives. The is no 'silver bullet', it is just a case of being better.
Very high importance, not easily substitutable	Partnership	Partnership: alignment of seller's strategic interests with those of the buyer in a trust-based arrangement between equals.

appropriate seller's approach is determined by the product and buyer. It is not possible to 'move up' from say a transactional approach to a consultative approach without doing something different to the product or service to create value. Simply changing the approach gets nowhere because there is no value to be created and, in fact, trying to do so may destroy value. Delighting one's customers by performing better than expected may sound a great slogan to writers of self-improvement books, but for everyone else it is the route to bankruptcy.

Having shown how to measure the target's performance, we went on to discuss satisfaction ratings and customer loyalty. To really understand the target company and its prospects, customers should be classified according to their degree of loyalty. Too many potentially lost customers should set alarm bells ringing. Another way of looking forward is to gauge customer sophistication because a majority of sophisticated customers might mean increased pressure on prices and margins.

Notes

1. Philip Kotler is the S.C. Johnson & Son Distinguished Professor of International Marketing at the Kellogg School of Management, Northwestern University, Evanston, IL. One of his many publications is *Marketing Management: Analysis, Planning, Implementation and Control* (1991, Englewood Cliffs, NJ: Prentice Hall), the most widely used marketing book in graduate business schools worldwide. Quentin Tarantino is an American screenwriter, film director and actor who rapidly rose to fame in the early 1990s as a fresh and gritty storyteller. Tarantino's movies are renowned for their sharp dialogue, graphic violence, splintered chronology and pop culture obsessions. He took Hollywood by storm in 1992 with the cult hit *Reservoir Dogs* and his trademark combination of clever dialogue and brutal violence hit a new peak in 1994 with *Pulp Fiction*.
2. Rackham, N. and DeVincentis, J.R. (1999) *Rethinking the Sales Force: Refining Selling to Create Customer Value*. New York: McGraw-Hill.
3. Mathur, S. and Kenyon, A. (1997) *Creating Value*. Oxford: Butterworth-Heinemann.
4. Albrecht, K. and Bradford, L.J. (1990) *The Service Advantage: How to Identify and Fulfil Customer Needs*. Homewood: Dow Jones-Irwin.
5. Kmabil, A., Ginsberg, A. and Bloch M. (2004) *Re-Inventing Value Propositions*. New York: New York University Stern School of Business.
6. Rackham and DeVincentis, *Rethinking the Sales Force* (see note 2).
7. The H.R. Challey Group (1996) *Benchmarks for World Class Sales Success*. Dayton, OH: H.R. Challey Group.
8. Söderlund, M. and Vilgo, M. (1999) *Customer Satisfaction and Links to Customer Profitability*, SSE/EFI Working Paper Series in Business Administration. Stockholm: Stockholm School of Economics.
9. Shapiro, B.P. and Bonoma, T.V. (1984) 'How to Segment Industrial Markets', *Harvard Business Review*, 64(May/June): 104–70.
10. See, for example, Elliott, G. and Glynn, W. (n.d.) 'Segmenting Industrial Buyers by Loyalty and Value', paper presented at the 16th IMP Conference, Bath University, UK. Elliott and Glynn segment customers according to their loyalty and their value to the seller.
11. Söderlund and Vilgo, *Customer Satisfaction* (see note 8).
12. Piercy, N. (1997) *Market-Led Strategic Change*. Oxford: Butterworth-Heinemann.
13. Piercy, *Market-Led Strategic Change* (see note 12).
14. Mitchell, Alan (1997) 'Evolution', *Marketing Business*, March: 29–33.
15. Clutterbuck, D. (1989) 'Developing Customer Care Training Programmes', *Marketing Intelligence and Planning*, 7(112): 34–7.

CHAPTER 9

CDD in Special Situations

This chapter deals with six special cases that are often the subject of CDD, but where the ways of analysing target companies covered in the previous chapters either do not apply or may need some modification. They are:

- New technologies
- Diversification
- New business models
- Joint ventures (JVs) and strategic alliances
- Declining industries
- Recovery plays.

This chapter looks at each of these in turn, discussing how CDD needs to be adapted and what it should be looking out for.

New technologies

Innovation and invention are always a bit tricky from a CDD perspective. They are the best ways of creating competitive advantage, but it by no means always follows that they will or that a strategy of innovation leads automatically to success. In some industries such as test equipment, R&D is essential for long-term survival and growth. Pearson[1] argues that outstanding companies are consistently innovating in ways that create value for their customers. Their approach is to search for new opportunities and package and present them in such a way that they deliver customer satisfaction. For the record, the empirical evidence (PIMS data) shows R&D intensity and the rate of new product introductions to be negatively related to profitability.

The term innovation covers a wide variety of product and market developments, including:

- new products – products that are either radically new or that extend the product life cycle;
- process innovation leading to reduced production costs;
- marketing innovations which increase differentiation;
- organizational changes which reduce costs or improve total quality.

Innovation, then, can involve fundamentally new products stemming from years of research or it can be the result of new ways of carrying out activities more efficiently or effectively.

No one has an infallible means of telling which innovations will succeed and which will not. If you get it right half the time, you are doing well. Typically, the success rate is much,

much lower. Only 2 per cent of patented inventions earn more than the cost of developing and patenting.[2] Allowing for all those patents filed by big companies for products that never get to market, around 5 per cent of inventions that are patented earn more than the cost of their patents.

This is an area of CDD where shooting the messenger is particularly popular. Inventors fall in love with inventions. They assume their invention is perfect and that everyone else will think so too. They also have a tendency to skip over the answers to basic questions such as:

- How much will the product cost to manufacture?
- Who are the companies most likely to be interested in the product?
- How many units of the product can the company expect to sell?
- How is the product different or better than similar products and, if it's more expensive than similar products, why is it worth the higher price?
- Is it patentable? Does it even need to be patented?

Either that or they patent products before determining the likelihood of their success. Unless there's a market, what good does it do to patent products?

New technologies are risky. There are two main sources of uncertainty:

- Technological uncertainty that arises from the unpredictability of technological evolution and, in particular, whether or not the technology under consideration will become the standard.
- Market uncertainty. Will there be a market for the product? If so, how big, will it grow? If so, how quickly?

The CDD questions that need answering about a radically new product or service are:

- Does it work?
- Is there a market?
- How profitable will it be?
- How is it best commercialized?
- Is this the right time to invest?

Because the businesses under consideration are by definition new, there is very little history to guide us as to whether the new technology business is worth backing. As a starting point, Table 9.1 sets out the characteristics of successful new products.

IS THERE A MARKET?

A useful frame of reference for thinking about whether or not a new product has broken the mould is to ask whether it brings alternative technologies or methods that:

- give a superior way of satisfying buyers' needs;
- gives the buyer additional functions that have a value;
- focuses product functions on the needs of one particular group of buyers and possibly lower costs by so doing;
- appeals to non-users of the product or service.

Table 9.1 Characteristics of successful new products

Factor	*Explanation*
Provides easily comprehended benefits that existing alternatives do not provide	An obvious statement, but one that definitely needs checking out in CDD. A new product that is not just a 'me too' item and is the first product of its kind on the market will command an enviable position. In business-to-business (B2B) markets it is often a question of assessing how well a new product fits in with customers' processes.
Responds to 'pull marketing' rather than requiring 'push marketing'	Pull marketing means pull from the consumer which comes because the consumer understands the product as something that they need or want, or that they very quickly recognize as fulfilling a well-defined need or want that has not been fulfilled previously. The problem with most of the 'hot' Internet businesses of the early 2000s was that they were merely reinvented mail order businesses badly done. Push marketing is required when a product fills a need or want, or solves a previously unsolved problem, but that need, want, or problem is vague, weak, suppressed, denied (it won't happen to me), or not compelling until legislated. Products that need to be pushed need a lot of explaining before the potential buyer understands and agrees that they need it, should want it, or that it solves their problem.
Is timely	An invention that is long overdue can create wealth due to the easy and rapid recognition of its utility value.
Does not require a change in established modes of operation	For example, although the 'QWERTY' was invented to slow typists down so that typewriter keys would not jam, it would be a waste of time to come up with something faster because it won't stand a chance of being accepted. Successful inventors go with the flow but they do not offer alternatives to things that already work well because on top of the usual resistance and problems of product launching they must also convert the would-be customer to a different way of doing things.
Does not require legislation or governmental approval	Seat belts were shunned until legislation compelled them because people think that nothing that will happen to them. It is always the 'other guy' who gets hurt or killed.
Is not intended for large companies	If in doubt about the wisdom of this statement, see James Dyson's book.[3] The attitude of big companies is that independent inventors simply cannot come up with inventions that their own engineers haven't already thought of because they are certain that no one knows more about their field than they do. Any idea or invention that is submitted to them, whether patented or not, must be accompanied by an agreement signed by the submitter. This agreement is entirely one sided.
Has an established distribution channel that can be penetrated	It is not feasible to create a new product and set up a new marketing channel at the same time. Therefore always identify the channel(s) through which the new product will reach the ultimate user. Equally challenging is the economics, meaning that the manufacturing costs must be low enough to support all the people who will demand a chunk of the selling price and still leave enough for re-investment and profit. Manufacturing costs are often only a small percent of the retail price. Established items have costs of raw material and labour that are a quarter or less of the retail price.
Quality	Quality in a product is not only that which modern quality control methods help to achieve, but also that which customers somehow perceive that the product possesses. While the quality of a product does improve its chances of success, it in no way assures that success.

As Case Study 27 illustrates, CDD should not just be thinking about the 'better mousetrap syndrome'. As is discussed below, the world will not necessarily beat a path to the target's door just because it has developed a good product. Commercialization is always a big issue. It helps greatly if new products have been developed in consultation with prospective customers, as in the case study. Likewise, competition should be a big part of the investigation. CDD should cover both direct competition and indirect competition, by identifying other commercially available products that might compete with the new product.

CASE STUDY 27

GAS SENSORS FOR OIL RIGS

The product was an infra-red device (IR LED point) that detects gas leaks on oil rigs. The product satisfies the oil industry's need for a solution to pellistor problems. Pellistors are the old gas detection technology. They use the catalysts that react with gas to set off a reaction. The chemical reaction produces an electrical signal that is transmitted to a control panel on the rig. Since 1988, when an explosion occurred in the gas compression module on the Piper Alpha platform, 176 km north-east of Aberdeen, gas detection requirements have been tightened considerably. The target's unit can be swapped directly with a pellistor and is the only available 'plug and play' IR gas sensor for pellistor replacement. Products were on trial with Shell and BP (British Petroleum) in the North Sea.

The target's IR product gives superior performance. Pellistors are unreliable:

- Catalysts are prone to what the industry refers to as 'poisoning'. This is when salt water rots the precious metal catalysts in much the same way that gas would, thus setting the detectors off.
- Pellistors are prone to 'fail unsafe'. This is when salt residue coats the catalyst meaning that it would not sound the alarm if there was a gas leak. It is very difficult without a manual inspection to tell if a pellistor is not working, and there

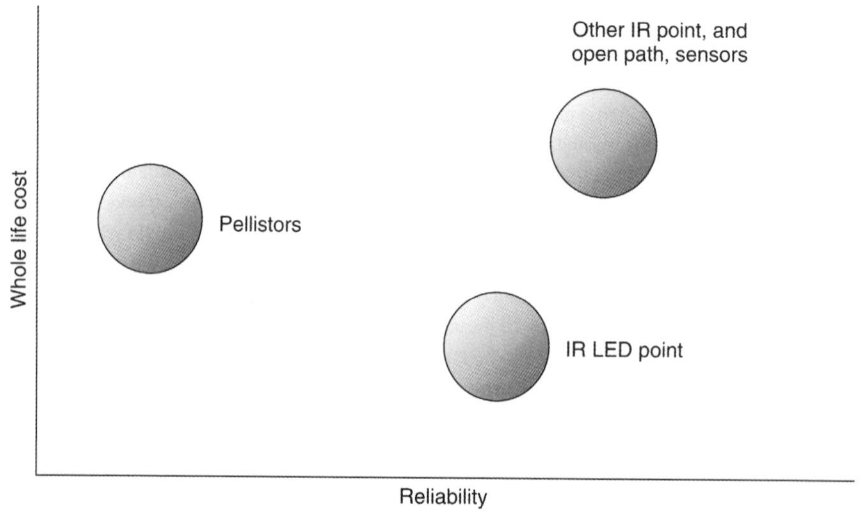

Figure 9.1 The relative positioning of different gas sensing technologies

CASE STUDY 27 – *continued*

can be as many as 400–600 pellistors on a single oil rig. Since the Piper Alpha disaster, just installing detectors is not enough. They must now be shown to be performing to required standards. Pellistors are therefore high maintenance and as they can fail within a few days of installation, they require regular inspection. Although they are relatively cheap, the cost of getting engineers to the rig for maintenance makes pellistors an expensive option.

- Pellistors do not last long because they degrade through their life and they degrade every time they are re-calibrated.

There are alternatives and a trade-off between reliability and cost. Figure 9.1 shows the trade-off between reliability and whole life cost among the three different technologies now available for gas detection.

Compared with pellistors, IR LED point sensors are more durable, reduce replacement costs and provide higher accuracy, resistance to contamination and more reliable measurements. They also produce better diagnostic information. A similar technology is fitted to new and refurbished rigs, but this 'Open Path' system is not suitable as a replacement for the pellistors fitted on older installations. The attraction of the target's product, therefore, is limited to where there are already pellistors in place.

MAKING MONEY FROM NEW PRODUCTS

Even if an innovation satisfies all seven of the characteristics in Table 9.1, there is still only a fair chance the target will make any money from it. A key determinant of the profitability of an innovation to the innovator is the share of the value created that it can keep (or in the jargon, appropriate). The value created by an innovation is distributed among a number of different parties as is shown in Figure 9.2. The same applies to entrepreneurs trying to build or sell their businesses. The reason why they regularly fail to develop a business to its true

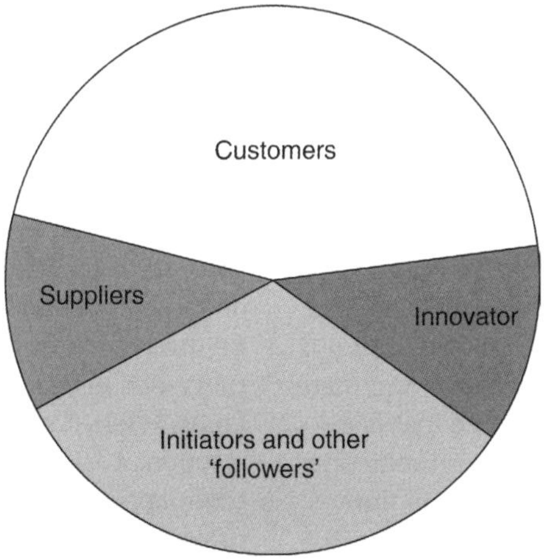

Figure 9.2 Who benefits from innovation?
Note: Illustrative only

potential is that they underestimate how much they must give to others in order to make the pot bigger for themselves.

Three factors determine the extent to which innovators are able to appropriate the value of their innovation:

- property rights that prevent or slow down imitation;
- complementary resources that may have to be bought for the product to succeed;
- those characteristics of the technology that influence its imitability.

Property rights

Property rights give a legal basis for enjoying the benefits of innovation, although their effectiveness depends on how easy it is for imitators to get round the protection they give. The legal profession tends to get very excited about patent and other protection in the due diligence process. This is a very interesting area of law, so who can blame them? What all acquirers should bear in mind is that research shows that patents are less effective at protecting both process and product innovations than are lead time advantages, learning curve advantages, and sales and service networks. The time it takes competitors to duplicate new products and processes tends to be short, with patents offering little lead time advantage at all. Property rights are certainly nice to have, but the key is not so much having them but in getting on and exploiting them before everyone else catches up.

Complementary resources

Getting new products and processes to market requires more than invention; it requires additional resources and capabilities to finance, produce and market the innovation. These are referred to as complementary resources. The presence of specialized complementary resources means that innovators have to share their gains with the suppliers of these assets. As is demonstrated in Case Study 28, the division of value between an innovator and the suppliers of complementary resources depends on their relative power.

CASE STUDY 28

LOW-COST THERMAL IMAGING CAMERAS

Developments in IR technology means that it is now possible to produce low-cost thermal imaging cameras. The picture is not as good as the image from conventional IR cameras used as night sights by the military, but it is good enough to detect whether or not there is an object in the near distance that is a different temperature from the surrounding area. It has potential applications in fire fighting, to allow fire fighters quickly to detect the presence of a person in a burning room, in building management, to save energy by detecting when a room is empty and switching off the lights, in intrusion detection, to detect the presence of a person rather than just detecting something that moves as is the case with current technology, and in production maintenance, where it can be used to measure the temperature of wear parts such as bearings and to detect electrical faults. While it is an excellent technical solution, it is one part of a system in all of these applications, all of which are the province of large multinationals who are in a powerful position to beat down the price of the new technology.

Case Study 28 is an example of market power, but similar principles apply to supplier power. A key determinant of relative power is determined by the extent to which components (or any other complementary resource for that matter) are specialized. For example, the gas sensor in Case Study 27 used a specialized IR unit developed in Russia for use in MiG fighters. The manufacturer of this unit captured a significant share of the IR LED point's value (but unique access to a specialized complementary resource created a barrier to imitation). On the other hand, the final product was a direct replacement for pellistors, fitted into any pellistor socket and interfaced with existing monitoring systems. If it had required specialized fittings and interfaces, it is likely that the suppliers of the specialized fittings would also have captured part of the value of the sensor innovation.

Imitability

The extent to which an innovation can be copied depends not just on legal protection, but also on the extent to which the knowledge contained in the innovation is codifiable. Codifiable knowledge can be written down. If someone does write it down and it is not protected by patents or copyright, it is easily copied. Sustainable competitive advantage comes only if the innovation relies also on complementary resources such as the know-how, intuition and insight of employees, or on sheer complexity. This is not to say it will not be imitated, but barriers to imitation buy the innovator time that can be used to build capabilities and a market position that will give leadership.

CASE STUDY 27 REVISITED

GAS SENSORS FOR OIL RIGS

Management claimed their product would sell for £800+ each. Research showed that customers were able to appropriate more of the value than management had thought possible. Likely pricing of the sensors was checked in three ways:

- Talking to the bigger customers. Detailed price negotiations had yet to be completed, but the signs from the bigger customers were that £600–£750 was a more realistic price for volume sales.
- Comparisons with similar products. The offshore IR sensor market had been suicidal. IR sensors could be bought for as little as £450 plus £100 for the interface. An IR detector that cost £2800 in 1990 could be bought for £700 to £800. There were more than 10 companies supplying them for the North Sea. The target's product would have to be priced below existing IR units (£750).
- Cost/benefits for the customer. At a unit price of £500, a large operator with a short field life would make savings of between £50 000 and £60 000 per rig over the remaining life of the platform. If the unit price was £600, the saving would be £20 000 per rig, a figure that would be much more difficult to sell internally.

In addition, the target needed to share some of the value it had created with the larger operators in order to capture the rest of the market quickly. The oil industry is cautious when introducing new technology. However, other oil companies would buy the target's sensor if Shell and BP went for it in a big way.

It is never easy to draw firm conclusions from a jumble of numbers such as these, but at least there was a consistency about them.

CASE STUDY 27 REVISITED – *continued*

The price ceiling seemed to be £750 for small volumes and £600 for large volumes. The floor was £500. Prices around the £500 level would give rapid penetration of Shell and BP and open up the rest of the North Sea and indeed the world, A price of around £550 looked a sensible number for volume sales.

STRATEGIES FOR EXPLOITING INNOVATION

How should an innovating firm maximize the returns to its innovation? Several alternative strategies are available. Table 9.2 ranks them according to increasing involvement by the innovator in commercialization.

The choice of strategy depends on:

- The characteristics of the innovation
- The resources and capabilities of the firm.

Characteristics of the innovation

The key issue here is the extent to which the firm can establish property rights through patents. Licensing can only work if there are patents in place, because only when there is proprietary knowledge is there something to licence. The advantages of licensing are that:

- The licensor does not need to develop the full range of complementary resources and capabilities needed for commercialization.
- The innovation can be commercialized quickly.

The problem, however, is that the success of the innovation in the market is totally dependent on the commitment and effectiveness of the licensees.

Resources and capabilities of the firm

The organizations that are best at innovation are often small firms and start-up enterprises that do not possess the range of resources required for commercialization. In biotechnology and electronics, the commercialization of innovation is a two stage process:

Table 9.2 Alternative strategies for exploiting innovation and relative risk/return

Licensing	*Outsourcing certain functions*	*Strategic alliance*	*Joint venture*	*Internal development*
Small risk and small return; only viable where an innovation has clearly defined patent rights	Limits capital outlay but may create depen-dence on supplier	Benefit = flexibility; risk = informal structure	Shares investment and risk; risk of partner disagree-ment and culture clash	Biggest risk and biggest potential return; benefit of full control

- The technology is developed initially by a small, technology-intensive start-up.
- It is then licensed to a larger concern.

IS THIS THE RIGHT TIME?

Timing an investment in an emerging industry or in a new technology depends on the extent of first-mover advantages (or disadvantages) associated with pioneering and on the capabilities and resources of the target company. There are four factors to examine:

- The degree of protection: the longer an innovation can be protected through patents or copyrights or a lead time advantage such as learning, the more the advantage falls to early movers.
- The importance of complementary resources: the more important complementary resources are in exploiting an innovation, the greater the costs and risks of getting in early.
- The potential to establish a standard (see below): markets differ as to whether they will converge towards a technical standard or not. The greater the importance of product standards, the greater the advantages of being an early mover in order to influence those standards.
- The resources and capabilities of the target company: if the target is a small start-up with not much in the way of complementary resources, it has no choice but to be a pioneer. It has to grab first-mover advantage and develop complementary resources before somebody else enters the market.

Case Study 29 brings together some of the issues in exploiting innovations.

CASE STUDY 29

REVOLUTIONARY GARMENT CLEANING SYSTEM

At risk of sounding like an advertisement for soap powder, this was a revolutionary new garment cleaning system developed by a small company, which removed hard-to-shift stains, such as grease, at low temperatures. It was a unique, top-secret formula that appeared to be better than anything else on offer. It does not involve dry cleaning the clothes. A major cleaning company were considering buying the know-how.

Its primary use would be not so much in getting wine stains out of expensive silk jackets, but for cleaning luminous clothing such as reflective jackets. These tend to be used in places where they attract more than their fair share of dirt, but they should not be washed at high temperatures because this shortens the life of their reflective parts. If they are cleaned at all, they go in with the family wash typically at 60 degrees or are subjected to something a bit less technical, typically involving a hose-pipe in the back yard back at base. This does not get the oil and grease out. The type of grease that gets on this clothing is very heavy. The process removed it and restored the clothes to looking almost as good as new. The price per jacket was £10.

Although £10 per clean is relatively expensive, the process can work out to be very cost-effective because it extends the garment's life. Without proper care, even high-quality garments have to be thrown away after only 2 to 3 years. Cleaned this way, they last over 2 years longer because they still have their reflective capability. When they are discarded, it is on purely aesthetic grounds.

CASE STUDY 29 – *continued*

WHY IS THERE A NEED?

The driver for increased use of this new cleaning process was a growing market for high visibility clothing (HVC). The HVC market was growing at something like 10 per cent per year because of tightened health and safety legislation. Analysis showed that most expansion was taking place at the cheap end of the market, where employers supply HVC to their employees only because they have to and want to spend as little as possible. This part of the market had become commoditized. Providing the HVC meets the required visibility standards, price becomes the only issue. Jackets cost about £6 each and because the cost of new HVC jackets has reduced so much, they are now seen as disposable.

Interviews with users showed that jackets costing less than £20 each are not worth cleaning. As well as getting dirty, they get a lot of wear and tear. It is rare that they become unusable simply because of dirt. As a result, users wait until they are worn out and then throw them away. However, a jacket costing more than £70 is definitely worth cleaning because of the extended life. The jackets in between could go either way, but there are not many of them. Below £20 covers most of the HVC used on construction sites and the like; above £70 you are into the more specialist applications such as fire fighter's outfits. The reality of a fire fighter's daily routine is that they can be cleaning up a diesel spill one minute and forcing their way into a burning building the next. The suit has to be cleaned in between. The performance end of the market is more interested in cleaning because HVC can cost £250 each. Cleaning and maintenance is much more of an issue than at the low end.

The potential market, therefore, was confined to specialist HVC, as used by police forces and fire services. The potential European market for specialist HVC cleaning is around £80 million.

WHAT ARE THE ALTERNATIVES? HOW DOES THE TARGET RATE AGAINST THEM?

This process is unique, but there are substitutes even though none of them can clean to the same standard. Alternatives include:

- Local cleaners: cleaning HVC at less than 40 degree gets rid of most of the dirt and costs about £3 per jacket. For more stubborn stains there are spot and stain removal services that cost about £5 per jacket.
- Self washing: many fire stations have their own washing machines and the individual fire fighter can take the suit home and wash it if they want. Fire stations use a special type of washing liquid and have specially modified machines that can cope with re-waterproofing. The problem with self-washing is that apart from damaging the material, other clothing could become contaminated. There are also issues around clothes being worn when not completely dry.

COMPLEMENTARY RESOURCES

The problem with introducing this technology is the fragmented user base. As well as launching a cleaning service, some sort of infrastructure for getting HVC to the cleaners also needed to be built. Organizing a cleaning service such as this would cause a lot of administrative problems because the jackets would have to be picked up from each individual fire station or police station. But it is not just a question of picking up and cleaning. There needs to be a system in place that starts with pre-inspection, includes tagging and tracking, cleaning (decontamination, cleaning, disinfecting and deodorizing), water repellent treatment, inspections and

CASE STUDY 29 – *continued*

whatever repairs are needed. Then there has to be a detailed final inspection and packaging. In addition, anyone cleaning high performance HVC has to be incredibly careful about what it is they are offering. If they take an HVC item, clean it and then return it guaranteeing that it will still perform to the required legal standard, who will measure the performance? Who will guarantee the performance? Whose liability will it be if the HVC does not perform after cleaning? Potentially, there is a whole minefield of risk assessment and legislation that needs to be managed. As if that was not enough, getting the jackets cleaned would mean users either investing in spare jackets or the cleaning service providing them because staff cannot work without them.

However, new regulations are pushing fire services towards putting in place proper care and maintenance policies and therefore driving the market towards a 'total care' concept. Total care involves repairs as well as cleaning. Total care is attractive to users because it means that the onus to make sure that the clothing is up to the correct standards is taken out of their hands. Providing a total care package is not the province of a cleaning company, but it could be if it could form a joint venture with a clothing manufacturer. But would the manufacturers be interested? Cynics say that HVC suppliers are not motivated to make easy-to-clean garments because they will sell less. However, some manufacturers already offer a service where they hire HVC and run lifetime and inventory policies, enabling them to keep a record of repairs and cleaning. Such leasing contracts were becoming more and more important with fire brigades and indeed all manufacturers trying to go down the total care route.

CONCLUSION

This requires an awful lot of effort and there is a big risk that the rewards will not be that great.

FORECASTING DEMAND FOR NEW PRODUCTS

Forecasting demand for new products is hazardous, since all forecasting is based on some form of extrapolation or modelling based on past data and with new products there is no past data. The first thing to say is do not be tempted to use conceptual models such as the product life cycle. As Figures 9.3–9.6 show, the product life cycle is never quite as smooth and predictable as one might believe.

One approach is to use analogies. For example, for services the USA is usually at least a couple of years ahead of the rest of the world. In other examples, it is usually possible to think of industries or markets that have the same feel as the one under discussion. The rise of nail bars, for example, is a good analogy for retail beauty products.

However rigorous you are with the use of proxies and analogies, new technology always presents a risk. Target companies that are managing risk properly should be:

- working with lead users to develop the product;
- limiting their exposure to risk;
- maintaining the highest levels of flexibility.

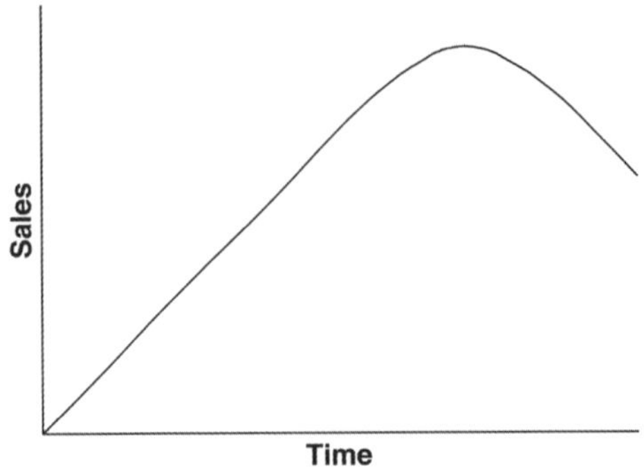

Figure 9.3 Product with slow adoption

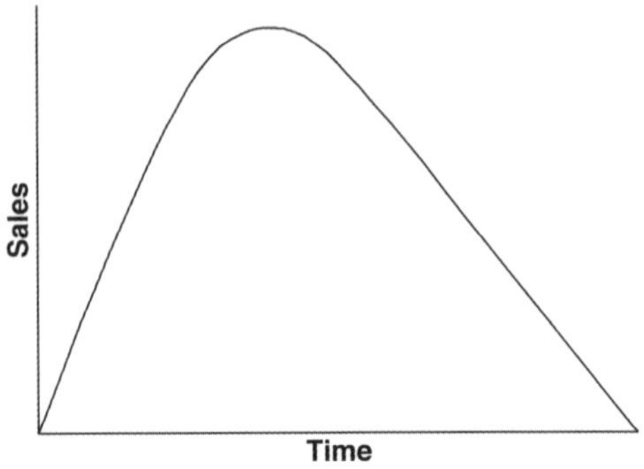

Figure 9.4 Product with fast adoption

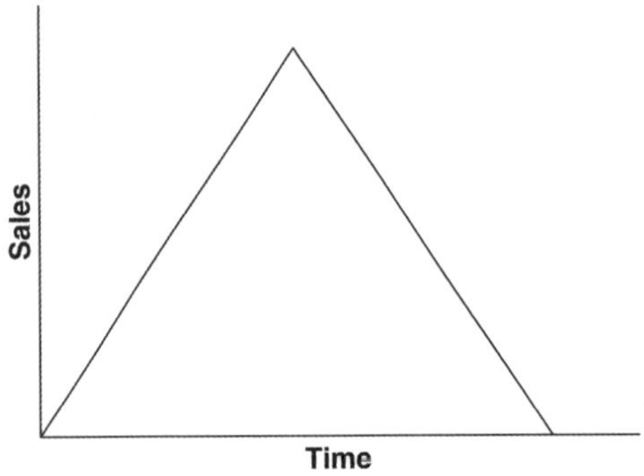

Figure 9.5 A fad product

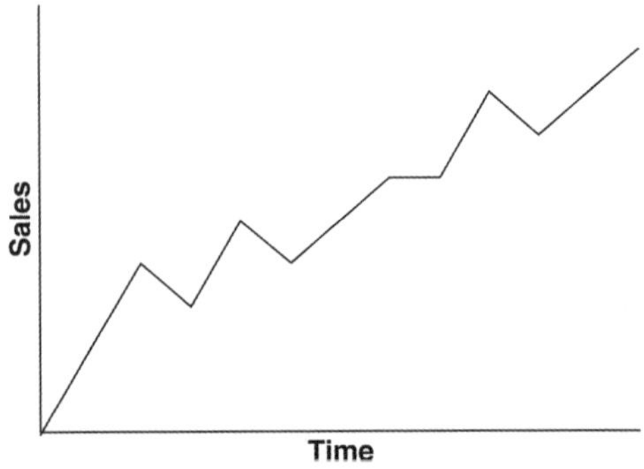

Figure 9.6 Product with frequent revitalization (for example, semiconductors)

Working with lead users

- Lead users are the innovator's friend and by co-operating with them, a pioneering company gets not just a source of market data, but a source of inspiration for new developments. Nayak[4] argues that that most good ideas come from customers. This is the reason why the computer industry releases beta versions of new software to enthusiasts for testing. In areas such as software, an independent user group is well worth supporting. Made up of thoughtful customers, it can be an incredibly effective means of generating new ideas and, being independent, a powerful marketing weapon when prospective customers need an unbiased perspective on a product's performance.

Limiting exposure to risk

- The last thing any company in an emerging industry should be doing is betting everything on success. This means keeping capital expenditure and other fixed costs to a minimum, as well as concentrating resources in areas where they are likely to yield the most. This is why smaller players in high-risk industries concentrate on R&D and license their discoveries to larger firms for manufacture, marketing and distribution.

Maintaining flexibility

- The high level of uncertainty in emerging industries means that target companies should be:

- Trying different approaches until a successful formula becomes evident. Learning from the failures is very often the key to success.
- Keeping an eye out for changes in the market and responding accordingly.
- Keeping options open and delaying commitment to a specific technology for as long as possible. During the Internet boom, private equity houses recognized that this was an important technology but had no idea who the winners would be. Their strategy, therefore, was to make a lot of small investments in the hope that by spreading themselves widely enough, they would pick up enough real winners to make a good overall return.

THE EMERGENCE OF STANDARDS

The more the value of a product to an individual customer depends on the number of other users of that product, the more likely a new technology is to converge around a standard. This is why Microsoft® has captured virtually all of the PC operating system market. At the other end of the spectrum, there is no standard for ladies' evening wear for precisely the opposite reason. If just one other woman turns up at a function in the same outfit, the value of the very expensive evening dress rapidly becomes negative. Standardization does not require everyone to use the same product, only that products are compatible with one another. Everyone using Microsoft Windows® is not using a Dell PC.

What tends to happen with new technologies is that a virtuous circle builds up whereby the product with the largest installed base attracts more new buyers because of the benefits of going with the market leader. Rival technologies co-exist for a time, but once a company appears to be gaining the upper hand, the market 'tips' very quickly and you end up with a winner-takes-all market. Once established, standards are highly resilient to the point where even when the standard is inherently inferior, switching to a superior technology may not occur. For example, Betamax was technically a better video cassette recording (VCR) system than VHS but Matsushita's superior market approach quickly established VHS as the industry standard.

If a company operates in a market where there is a customer need for standards, setting them has huge implications for competitive advantage. The single most important strategic issue in standard setting is to establish early leadership and, by so doing, creating a bandwagon. This requires a company to:

- get as much support as it can from consumers, suppliers of complements and even competitors through JVs and alliances;
- get ahead of the market through penetration pricing and rapid product development;
- build expectations – if you can convince the market that you will emerge as the victor, you probably will.

The lesson that has emerged from the classic standards battles of the past is that in order to create initial leadership, a company must share the value created by the technology with other parties (customers, competitors, complementors and suppliers). If a company attempts to appropriate too great a share of the value created, it may well fail to build a big enough bandwagon to gain market leadership. One of the secrets of Matsushita's victory over Sony was licensing its technology early on. Similarly, IBM was the first PC manufacturer to encourage other manufacturers to produce IBM clones. Adobe® gives away Acrobat® to encourage its use and makes its money on the software needed to produce PDF documents.[5] However, winning a standards war is a long drawn out and expensive business and the best strategy may be just to pool knowledge and agree a standard with the competition.

WINNER TAKES ALL IN NEW TECHNOLOGIES

The above has another side to it: the economics if digital technologies veers towards the extreme levels of economies of scale. The initial cost of creating a piece of software or information content is very high, but, once created, the product can be replicated at negligible cost. Market share and the ability to amortize development costs over a large sales volume is therefore the key to profitability and all market rivals will fight for share. The effect of such extreme scale economies in driving competition is exacerbated by two further factors. First, where the value of a product or service to a consumer depends on the number of other users of the product, firms have to fight for share so that they emerge as the dominant supplier and therefore survive. The second is that shortening life spans for technologies means a new product has to be pushed for all it is worth. The result is intense competition in emerging markets for information-based products creating 'winner-takes-all' markets, where each competitor is willing to incur substantial losses in the hope of emerging as the industry winner.

Diversification

Target companies' business plans may be relying on new products or new markets for some or all of the projected growth. The chances of success should be evaluated using the analytical techniques covered in this section. There is just one extra piece of information to add which is that, as shown in Figure 9.7,[6] the further the diversification from the existing business, the lower the chance of success.

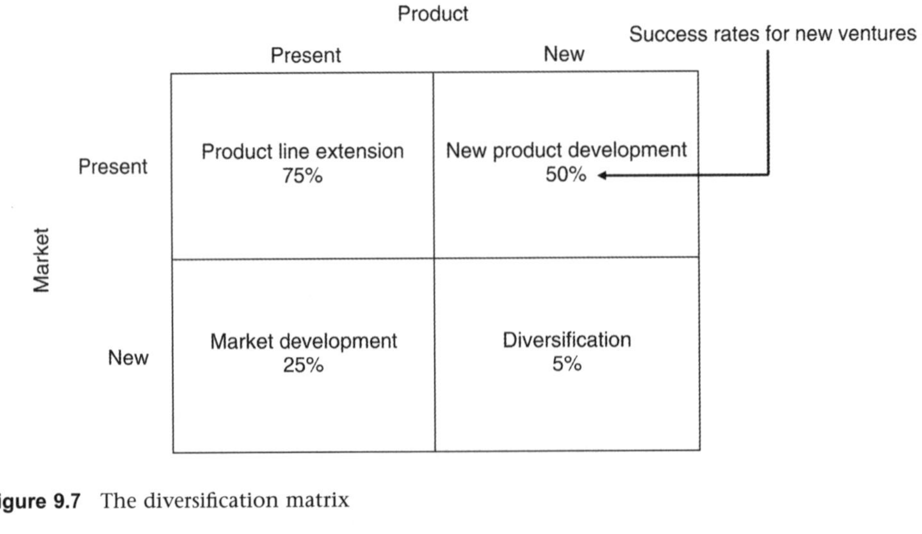

Figure 9.7 The diversification matrix

Assessing new business models

'The greatest opportunity for creating competitive advantage often comes from new ways of segmenting because a firm can meet true buyer needs better than competitors or improves its relative cost position.'[7] A problem in many industries is that there is little to distinguish the products or service features of the different players. The upshot is increasing commoditization, which in turn brings falling profits. There are, nonetheless, companies in many unpromising markets that have successfully broken away from and outperformed the pack. These companies have created:

- new ways of putting together product and service features to meet customer needs better than anyone else (value propositions); and
- new ways of delivering those product and service features to customers (value architectures).

The question for CDD is: Will a new business model work? The way to think of this is in terms of the value frontier outlined in Chapter 8. The aim of a new business model is to place the target to the top, bottom or right of the value frontier (shown in Figure 8.5). This means a value proposition that differs from the rest of the market.

Extending the frontier to the low end is worth it if:

- customers would value a low-value/low-cost offering;
- the industry can compete with the high end of another industry.

The converse applies to extending the frontier upwards, that is:

- customers would value a high value/high cost offering;
- the industry can compete with the low end of another one.

If neither of these makes sense, the only option remaining is shifting to the right of the frontier. This is about innovating to reduce price, risk and effort across all the multiple roles customers play. One way of doing this is removing or adding to the non-basic product attributes (see Table 8.2). One way to isolate the absolute essential is to think about attributes that would still need to be delivered if customers paid half the current price. This is prime focus group territory (see Chapter 13). The same principle applies to eliciting desired attributes. Ask potential customers what they would demand if they had unlimited resources. Is the target providing these attributes at a price consumers are willing to pay? However, new attributes are not everything because often they are easily copied. What is more difficult to copy is the means of delivering value. Think back to Tesco in Chapter 8. Implementation is king.

Case Study 30 is an example of CDD on a new business model whose proposition was to deliver minor medical procedures more quickly and cost effectively.

CASE STUDY 30

MOBILE OPERATING THEATRES

The target was a provider of a mobile operating theatre, fully staffed for minor, 'day treatment', operations. Normally such operations are carried out in fixed facilities inside hospitals. This is a new business model which met the UK National Health Service's (NHS) requirement for additional capacity by carrying out minor operations where they are needed.

The demand for such a business arises because the UK government has made a strong commitment to eliminate the backlog of patients waiting more than 6 months for an operation. Meeting targets is made all the more difficult because of an ageing population (more demand for treatment) and better technology (more conditions can be treated). Existing operating theatres work at 90–99 per cent capacity, which leaves no room for the proper scheduling required to reduce in-patient waiting lists. Taking day-cases out of existing theatres reduces capacity utilization and gives the breathing space required to reduce waiting lists.

DO THE PROSPECTIVE PURCHASERS HAVE THE MONEY TO BUY?

Whether or not prospective purchasers have the money to buy is an important consideration that is often overlooked in CDD. For example, there are some 5 million lamp-posts in the UK, around 80 per cent of which technically need replacing. There will, however, be no mass replacement because local councils do not have the funds to do it. In this case, health and the 'War on Waiting' was a key pledge for the government and the top policy area within the Labour Party. By the time this CDD investigation started, the NHS had already spent £20 million on purchasing capacity from the private sector under its new 'Concordat' arrangements.

WHAT WERE THE ALTERNATIVES? HOW DID THE TARGET RATE AGAINST THEM?

The target's mobile concept was attractive to purchasers requiring a quick, total solution. A key factor was that the target offered a complete solution, as buyers are unwilling to package a solution themselves:

- The target rated well on future KPCs versus alternatives. Alternatives ranged from using private hospitals to exporting patients.
- Although the NHS was going to build additional capacity, new theatres would only supply part of the planned capacity increase.
- Modular suppliers (that is, supplying prefabricated buildings equipped as operating theatres) were aggressive competitors over whom the target had few advantages. They posed the major threat.
- Barriers to entry were high for imitators of the target's solution because:
  - The NHS would only accept a unit whose design had been proven extensively with demonstrable results.
  - A new entrant would lack the relationships inside the NHS necessary for success, especially as the purchasing system was devolved to Primary Care Trusts (PCTs). A 'good word' from other NHS staff who have developed relationships with the target was key to getting a foot in the door with the PCTs.
  - The target's units cost around £1 million each. Any imitator would require at least this amount to construct each unit.

WOULD THE TARGET MEET ITS BUSINESS PLAN?

Yes the target would meet its business plan because:

CASE STUDY 30 – *continued*

- there was little pressure on price;
- it only needed a 5–8 per cent[8] share of all non-acute 'day case' operations and it did have a unique advantage in some market niches.

THREATS

- Delayed restructuring of the NHS budget would hamper decision-making and budget allocation.
- There was a reluctance within the general practitioner community to refer patients to new surgery providers.
- The target had difficulty sourcing enough credible NHS staff to provide complete geographic coverage.
- The NHS could expand its fixed surgical capacity.

JVs and alliances

There has been an explosive growth in JVs and alliances because they are seen as a cheaper and more effective way of acquiring key resources and capabilities without the risks inherent in an acquisition. The term 'joint venture' can capture a wide range of business relationships, from contractual agreements and licensing right through to common ownership of a separate legal entity JV vehicle. They can cover specific functions (R&D, marketing, manufacturing) or specific markets (China).

There are five features that work together to create a JV:

- Collaboration
- Shared participation in decision making
- Parent firms who remain separate entities
- A combination as opposed to an exchange of assets
- Complementary assets.

They tend to be short term or goal specific. To be successful, a JV has to add to the business plan and it is important for both partners to have a very clear view about what exactly it is for. As average lifespan is 3.5 years; exit rules should be determined right at the outset. Most are undertaken as related diversifications for at least one of the parties. Parent companies continue with their normal businesses, often competing with the JV.

As with acquisitions, due diligence should be used as a tool that helps ensure a successful venture and not just something to uncover pre-deal risks.

Alliances require great skill. The problems they bring stem from one source: that there is more than one parent. As every child knows, parents can, and will, disagree on just about anything. Differences in priorities, direction and so on cause confusion, frustration and slowness in decision making. The failure rate is somewhere between 36 and 70 per cent.[9] Precise measurement of success is hard because it depends on the original objectives of the partners, which are often different. Besides which, even JVs that have been wound up could be considered successes! The key to JV success is trust. Alliance strategies enable companies to get protection from business risk, but only by taking on relationship risk. Hardly surprisingly, therefore, due diligence must concentrate on the relationship and this will mean an emphasis on the soft due diligence issues.

There is no excuse for poor CDD in JVs. With acquisitions, greed and lust get in the way. Not so with JVs, which are goal specific. Partner selection is key and having found a partner, much of the CDD will focus on the partner's ability to contribute to the goals of the venture. What is important in CDD will differ according to the reasons for the JV. The reasons for using JVs include:

- A more rapid route to global marketing capability
- A route to speedier innovations
- Flexible access to complementary resources
- Sharing the risks/costs of R&D
- Technological systems convergence
- Pre-emption of the competition
- Overcoming local trading barriers
- A precursor to something more permanent
- Eventual divestiture of non-core assets.

The differences in emphasis required are set out in the sections that follow.

A MORE RAPID ROUTE TO GLOBAL MARKETING CAPABILITY

If a JV is relying on one partner to provide marketing skills, then self-evidently an important part of CDD will be assessing the prospective partner's ability to do just that. A strong US pharmaceutical company wanted to break into the Japanese market and so partnered with a Japanese company. The main attraction of the Japanese partner was its large sales force. However, the venture failed because:

- the Japanese sales force was poorly managed;
- the partner did not have the contacts, clout or experience to push the US products through Japan's development and approval process;
- it lacked the management resources and capital to invest in commercialization.

The Japanese partner was incapable of providing the marketing capability the US company needed.

A ROUTE TO SPEEDIER INNOVATIONS

CDD here is similar to the case above. If your aim is speedier innovations, the main focus of CDD must be on the innovations that will have the biggest market impact and whether or not the partner has the capabilities needed.

FLEXIBLE ACCESS TO COMPLEMENTARY RESOURCES

Again, CDD here is similar to the above. What resources are required? Does the prospective partner have them?

SHARING THE RISKS/COSTS OF R&D

The chances are that the partners in a JV will be competitors in some products in some parts of the world. If the aim of a JV is the joint development of new products and processes, the focus of CDD, apart from the usual concerns with the partner's motivations and capabilities, must be on what happens when the JV ends and both partners are free to compete with jointly developed intellectual property (IP).

TECHNOLOGICAL SYSTEMS CONVERGENCE

Convergence is where two or more industries converge to form a new market. One of the biggest losses in acquisition history was AT&T's acquisition of NCR. AT&T forecast the convergence of computers, communications and consumer electronics. It saw itself as a communications company (which is arguable) and bought NCR to give it a capability in computing. NCR was a manufacturer of point of sale systems, it was not a computer company. At the time, the involvement it had with computers was the manufacture of 'me too' PC clones. There are a number of lessons for CDD here. First, convergence, like cross-selling and one-stop shopping, is nice in theory but often illusory in practice. Consumers prefer best in breed. Second, if a partner is supposed to bring certain capabilities, check that it does.

PRE-EMPTION OF THE COMPETITION

Ferodo, the manufacturer of brake pads, set up a number of JVs in South East Asia in the 1980s. Experience in Europe taught that the first to supply the car manufacturers in a geographical market had a continuing advantage. The issue for each of their JVs was what to do in the decade or more before car production began in earnest and this should have been one of the main focuses of CDD. In Thailand, there was an obvious solution because the Thai partner had the tooling to supply the Australian replacement market. The story in India was very different. The plan here was to supply the replacement market until car manufacturing took off. This would never have been viable because the replacement market was price based and the local competition used asbestos as the main raw material. Asbestos is a cheap and highly effective binding ingredient in brake pads, but very dangerous. Ferodo would not use asbestos, meaning that it would have to import safer materials at a cost that would make the JV highly uncompetitive.

OVERCOMING LOCAL TRADING BARRIERS

Some countries stipulate that a company must have a local trading partner. The Ferodo JV in India had such a partner. The venture got into trouble because of differing expectations between the two sides. The Indian partner thought the business would float on the Indian stock exchange within 5 years, when the British knew that this was highly unlikely. The British thought their partner would manage the venture for the long term whereas its early decisions on where to site the plant suggested it was more motivated by short-term profit through property speculation.

A PRECURSOR TO SOMETHING MORE PERMANENT

Effectively this is using a JV as due diligence. The key is to make sure that is exactly what the JV is used for and not to drift into buying out the other side simply because that is what is expected.

EVENTUAL DIVESTITURE OF NON-CORE ASSETS

British Steel and GKN put its special steel assets into a JV, United Engineering Steels (UES). British Steel had to simplify its structure prior to privatization, GKN wanted to exit the steel business. The work leading up to the formation of the venture was around the valuation of each side's contribution. Neither partner paid much attention to what the venture was supposed to do beyond the rationalization of assets, principally the closure of the GKN mill in Wales. As a result, the venture drifted. Management retained their original loyalties and long-term decisions were never made. The venture was eventually bought back by British Steel, at an opportune moment in the cycle, after GKN had paid its share of the rationalization costs.

WHY JVs ARE SUCCESSFUL

Having vetted the prospective partner in the context of what the JV is designed to do, CDD should go on to tackle the more general issues around partner selection. These are:

- Both sides have a well-thought-out strategy.
- There is complementarity between the parties.
- The partners are of equal strength.
- Flexibility is built into the agreement.

These are considered in more detail in the following sections.

A well-thought-out strategy

A successful joint venture must begin with a sound, well-articulated business strategy. Before moving forward, companies must be able to explain:

- why they wish to enter a JV;
- what they hope to achieve;
- why they have chosen their particular partner or partners.

So, a good starting point for CDD is some 'self due diligence' by both sides as they are about to enter serious JV negotiations. Why a JV and not something else? What are our motivations (this will help later in running the venture)? Why this partner?

The partners also need to be clear on the strategy for the venture. The sort of questions that need clear answers are:

- What will each side's involvement be (management, capital, and so on)?
- How long will the JV last?
- What will cause the venture to end?
- What is the preferred exit strategy?

- What operational strategies will be employed (for example governance, accountability, conflict resolution procedures)?

Complementarity

JVs work extremely well when expanding existing businesses into:

- New geographic markets
- New or related businesses.

The research shows that some 62 per cent of JVs that involve partners with different geographic strengths succeed. Credit Suisse–First Boston, a joint venture formed in 1978 to expand both companies' positions in the Eurobond market, shows the benefits of using JVs to leverage complementary geographic strengths. First Boston provided access to US corporate issuers of bonds and possessed the skills for structuring the new financial instruments such as convertible Eurobonds. Credit Suisse provided the capability to place issues with investors in Europe. This combination allowed the JV to assume a leading role in the rapidly expanding Eurobond markets in the early 1980s.

The Corming/Siemens fibre optic cable JV, started in 1977, succeeded for many reasons. For one thing, the parents brought complementary skills and capabilities. Corning had developed and patented processes to manufacture high-quality optical fibres. Siemens had capital, scale, and worldwide distribution of telecommunications cable. Siemens also brought the manufacturing technology and equipment to produce cable from fibre.

CDD should therefore assess the degree of overlap between the two partners. The less the better.

Partner strengths

While it is important that partners have complementary skills and capabilities, an even balance of strength is also crucial. This is especially true in product-for-market swaps when one partner brings product technology and the other brings access to desirable markets. There is often a certain amount of suspicion in this situation with each partner fearing the other will try to usurp its proprietary advantage. Such fears are hardly unwarranted, since it is quite likely that the two parties will compete somewhere. JVs work best when the partners are of equal strength – and the stronger they both are, the better. What often happens is that:

- strong companies seek smaller or weaker companies with which to partner in order to control the venture;
- weaker companies seek a stronger partner to get them out of trouble or to build their skills.

These strategies do not work well because the weak link drags. For the weak partner, managing the venture is too great a distraction from making the improvements needed in other parts of the business.

Partner flexibility

Flexibility is important because things are bound to change. Some two thirds of JVs run into trouble in their first two years and therefore need flexibility to evolve. JVs frequently have

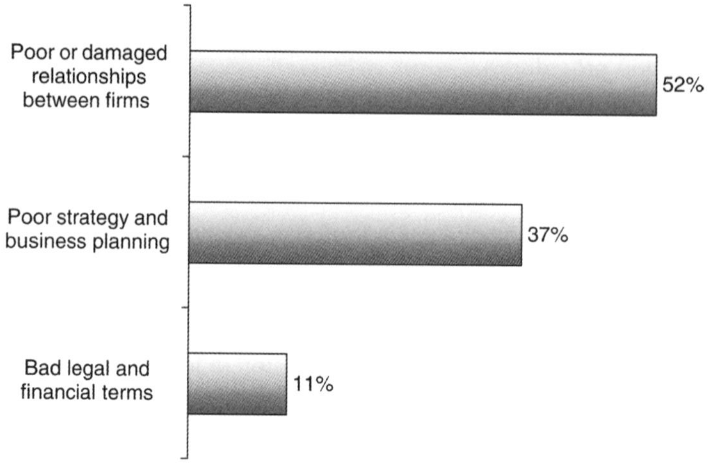

Figure 9.8 Why partnerships fail
Source: Eaves, D., Weiss, J. and Visioni, L.J. (2003) 'The Relationship Relaunch: How to Fix a Broken Alliance', *Ivey Business Journal*, 67(5). Copyright © 2003 Ivey Management Services. One time permission to reproduce granted by Ivey Management Services on 27 February 2006.

trouble meeting their initial goals, often because expectations or projections at the outset were too optimistic. JVs need to be able to refine and broaden their initial charter. One JV to sell minicomputers in the USA failed because, when faced with a rapidly changing market and the need to adapt the hardware to meet customers' specific requirements, its scope was not broadened from purely sales to include product development.

Flexibility cannot be negotiated into the contract. What is needed are resources and strong management.

REASONS WHY JVS FAIL

Having dealt with the partnership issues, CDD should then tackle the issues that lead to JV failure. Figure 9.8 shows the results of some research into partnership failures.[10]

As can be seen in Figure 9.8, the two major causes of JV failure are poor partnership relations and poor business planning. We have dealt with many of the partnership issues above. Unfulfilled market expectations can be traced to:

- the partner's capabilities turning out not to be what was wanted (see above);
- the partner's vision of the future being radically different from what was understood;
- market potential not meeting expectations because:
  - the original strategy was not valid;
  - clashing cultures;
  - bad management of the JV.

Two of these merit further discussion.

Clashing cultures

The importance of relationship risk means that cultural issues are very important. A typical example was the US/British JV where there was considerable disagreement about how much data was required in decision making. The Brits could not understand why the Americans wanted loads of numbers, while the Americans thought the Brits were flying blind.

Cultural differences make JVs that draw functional staff from both parents more difficult to manage. It is not just language barriers. Different attitudes to time, job performance, material wealth and the desirability of change can all play a part. One US–Iranian venture only worked when all the Americans were sent home. They could not adapt to dealing with a poorly (by their standards) educated workforce. Such differences can have a huge impact. A group that shares basic assumptions or is used to operating in certain ways is going to work a lot better than one that does not.

JV management

There are basically two types of JV structure:

- Dominant partner
- Shared management.

JVs are routine and successful in many industries, for example in property development and oil and gas exploration. These tend to have a dominant parent. This means that they:

- are managed by one parent (just like a wholly owned subsidiary);
- have a board, with representatives from both sides, which plays a largely ceremonial role.

In shared management ventures, the board has a real decision-making function; both parents manage the enterprise and usually both provide functional personnel. They tend to be a feature in manufacturing industries where one partner is supplying the technology and the other knowledge of the local market. As shared management ventures are more difficult to get right, companies should think very hard about using them. The question in due diligence is: Will the extra benefit of having a partner who is helping to run the JV outweigh the resulting disadvantages? The amount and type of help needed from a partner changes over time, which complicates this decision. In most markets, technology or market expertise will only be needed in the early years until the venture learns for itself. A JV between the UK engineering company TI Group and the Japanese manufacturer of automotive suspensions, Kayaba, recognized the reality of this. The JV was set up to re-configure a Spanish manufacturing plant and supply the European market with a new suspension technology. TI would bring the sales and marketing expertise – a long term activity – and Kayaba would bring engineering skills, the bulk of which were confined to the early stages of the venture when the re-configuration of the plant was taking place. Accordingly, the venture was structured 75 per cent TI and 25 per cent Kayaba.

If, therefore, a partner is chosen for reasons other than managerial input – for example, financial backing, access to resources, patents, or because it is a big consumer of the product being made – a dominant parent is best. The same is true when a company takes on a partner because local regulations say it has to. Clearly, in this situation any passive partner that is supplying large sums of money or important technology but exerting very little influence must trust the competence and honesty of the dominant parent. But perhaps this is one of the areas where CDD can add the most value.

To sum up, CDD for JVs should focus on the partner's motivations and capabilities to deliver what the venture needs, but it should not end there. Having a successful JV means attention must be paid to each stage of the life cycle and CDD has a part to play in each of the critical pre-deal stages, which are:

1 developing the strategic rationale;
2 selecting the partner;
3 thinking about exit early;
4 negotiating the best structure and governance.

Declining industries

As some venture capitalists have found, it is possible to make a great deal of money from declining industries. It is also possible to lose a great deal. In declining industries, the ability speedily to adjust capacity to the current level of demand can be a major source of cost advantage. During the 1980s and early 1990s, British steel was Europe's most profitable steel producer partly because it reduced capacity faster than its rivals. The key to such adjustment, however, is the ability to distinguish cyclical overcapacity – common to all cyclical industries, from semiconductors and construction to hotels and railways – from the structural overcapacity that affects the steel industry.

Maturity has two main implications:

- it reduces the number of opportunities for establishing competitive advantage;
- the opportunities that exist are cost-based not differentiation-based.

Fewer opportunities for competitive advantage in mature industries stem from:

- experienced buyers, which means that there is less scope for differentiation;
- experienced producers – diffused knowledge means that there are few cost advantages to be had through superior processes or more advanced capital equipment;
- powerful distributors and a developed distribution system make it easier for competitors to attack market niches and therefore more difficult for companies to pursue a niche strategy;
- standard products and powerful distributors make mature industries vulnerable to attack by overseas competitors with either an exchange rate advantage or lower costs.

In addition, as markets mature, so 'systems' (see Chapter 8, Figure 8.4) tend to be 'unbundled', with products increasingly becoming commodities and services being provided by specialized companies. The Internet has reduced buyers' transaction costs further, allowing them to assemble their own bundles of goods and services at low cost. Against this, firms will seek higher margins through bundling and providing a 'one-stop shop'. A critical issue for CDD is whether such bundling really creates customer value. One-stop shopping is always presented by target companies as an advantage they have over the competition, but is it really?

ASSESSING COMMERCIAL PROSPECTS

The commercial prospects of target companies in mature industries depend on five factors:[11]

- The nature of the decline
- The causes of decline
- The speed at which decline is taking place
- Whether specific segments survive that offer differentiation and niche marketing opportunities
- The ability of the company to target these segments.

Two factors determine whether or not a declining industry remains structurally attractive:

- The demand/supply balance – or more correctly the demand/capacity balance
- The degree to which demand is disaggregated.

The demand/capacity balance

As is clear from the discussion in Chapter 4, the more excess capacity, the greater the potential for destructive competition. Capacity is taken out of an industry most easily where:

- decline can be forecast – the more cyclical and volatile the demand, the more difficult it is for firms to see the trend of demand through all the market noise;
- barriers to exit (see Chapter 4) are low;
- stronger firms facilitate the exit of weaker firms by taking them over.

The disaggregation of demand

If demand is disaggregated, some segments will survive and even prosper, despite the general decline across the rest of the industry.

Targeting niches

Less overall scope for differentiation means that to survive and prosper, target companies in mature industries must look that much harder to find it. With cost leadership so difficult to sustain, differentiation is really all there is to go for. Segment selection is therefore key. Markets must be disaggregated much further than is implied in Chapter 5. Maturity demands that target companies segment right down almost to the level of the individual customer with IT playing a key part in identifying customers that contribute most profit and all management effort going into targeting the more attractive customers and transforming the less valuable ones into more valuable ones. Standardization of the physical attributes of a product and convergence of consumer preferences means concentrating on finding new approaches to uniqueness in terms of marketing, product design, product features, customer service, organization, image, distribution, complementary services and (despite the above) bundling. The new approach may also involve redefining markets and market segments, embracing new customer groups and adding products and services that perform new but related functions (like, for example, putting supermarkets in petrol stations). The ability to break away from conventional wisdom and establish a unique positioning or novel forms of differentiation is critical in mature industries.

Recovery plays

Occasionally CDD is used to evaluate businesses that collapsed. It is the job of CDD to pronounce on whether the crisis has been brought about by the management or the market. The analysis is no different from normal CDD. Given what we discussed in Chapter 8, the questions to ask are self-evident:

- Can the causes of the decline of the firm's sales of profits can be tackled?
- Does the industry, or particular segments of it, remain attractive?
- Is there is potential for creating or enhancing competitive advantage?

The problem is that time is against in-depth enquiries even more so than it usually is because either the business is in free fall or the receiver wants to do a quick deal before things deteriorate further. Short-cuts are definitely called for. One of them is to make a quick decision about the odds of salvaging the business. Slatter[12] maintains that there are essentially four types of recovery situation, as shown in Figure 9.9.

Given what you can find out about the business and its markets in a very short time, you have to make a quick decision about the most likely of Slatter's four recovery paths:

- Non-recoverable: the business has declined so far because of a poor competitive position in a declining industry.
- No sustained turnaround: a temporary recovery only is made, perhaps through reduced costs or extra sales in an essentially unattractive industry.
- Sustained survival: a turnaround but with little or no further growth. The industry may be in slow decline or generally competitive or unprofitable. The business will survive and there will be limited profit opportunities, but that is all.

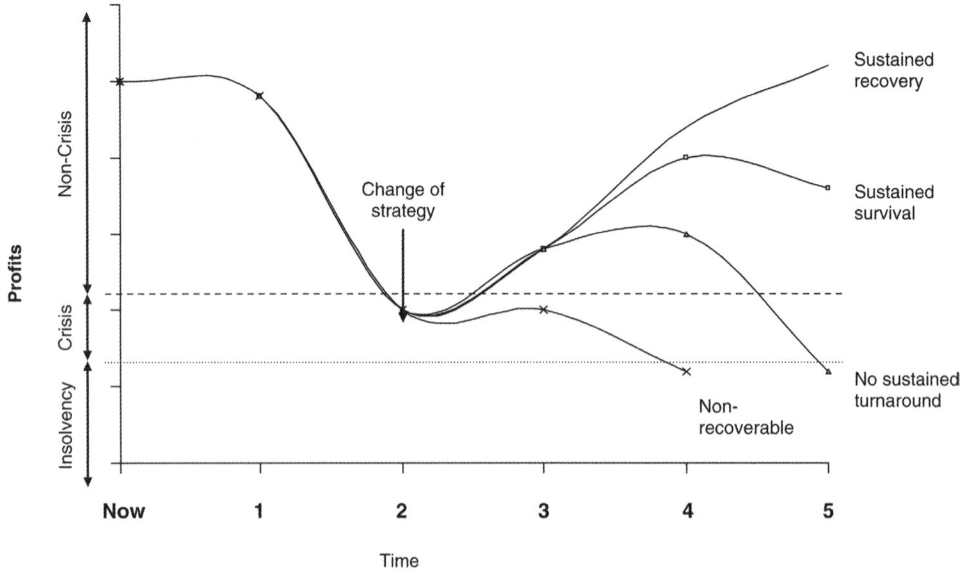

Figure 9.9 The feasibility of recovery
Source: Slatter (1984) *Corporate Recovery.*

- Sustained recovery: this is most likely to be brought about with new products and/or new market positioning. The recovery is helped if the industry is strong and attractive and the company's decline has been caused by poor management rather than industry decline.

There are usually three factors present where recovery strategies are not going to work:

- The company is not competitive and the potential for improvement is low.
- The company lacks both the resources or access to the resources to remedy the weaknesses.
- Demand for the basic product or service is in terminal decline.

CDD in turn-arounds must focus just on these three factors.

Conclusion

Innovation must deliver benefits that consumers actually care about. Segmentation, differentiation, technical or design excellence are often distractions. Business ideas and new products fail mainly because the need they satisfy turns out to be so trivial or applies to so few customers that the resulting marketing opportunity is not worth the effort. The type of radical innovation that places a company in uncontested territory can bring spectacular rewards if the strategy succeeds but the reality is that once an innovator proves that a new product or new approach does have a big potential, others with better resources and better execution pile in and dominate the market. The test for innovations and inventions is: Do they enable the company to improve its offering to customers either directly, say through better customer service or indirectly, say through lower prices? This holds true for new business models as well as new products.

CDD in JVs needs to concentrate on what it is the JV is designed to achieve and, like CDD in M&A, because of the importance of the JV partners and the venture's management, CDD will inevitably focus more on the softer issues.

CDD in declining industries is all about the assessment of islands of demand where differentiation is still possible. In a recovery situation, CDD needs first to understand the reasons for the target's collapse and then assess the chances of a sustained recovery. As with CDD generally, the chances of recovery will depend on market attractiveness and the target's ability to compete.

Notes

1. Pearson, E.A. (1988) 'Tough Minded Ways to get Innovative', *Harvard Business Review*, 66(May/June): 99–106.
2. Mosley, T.E. Jr (1997) *Marketing Your Invention* (2nd edition). Dearborn, MI: Dearborn Financial Publishing.
3. Dyson, J. (2000) *Against The Odds*. London: Texere Publishing.
4. Nayak, P.R. (1991) 'Technological Change' (report), Arthur D. Little.
5. Grant, Robert M. (1991) *Contemporary Strategy Analysis, Concepts, Techniques, Applications*. Oxford: Blackwell.
6. The percentages in Figure 9.7 are from Johnson, G. and Scholes, K. (2003) *Exploring Corporate Strategy*. London: Pearson.

7. Porter, M. (1985) *Competitive Advantage: Creating and Sustaining Superior Performance*. New York: The Free Press.
8. Depending on how the figures for market size are calculated.
9. Heatfield, L. and Pearce, J.A. II (1994) 'Goal Achievement and Satisfaction of Joint Venture Partners', *Journal of Business Venturing* 9(5): 423.
10. Eaves, D., Weiss, J. and Visioni, L.J. (2003) 'The Relationship Relaunch: How to Fix a Broken Alliance', *Ivey Business Journal*, 67(5): 1–8.
11. Harrigan, K.R. (1980) *Strategies for Declining Businesses*. Lexington, MA: Heath.
12. Slatter, S. (1984) *Corporate Recovery: Successful Turnaround Strategies and Their Implementation*. Harmondsworth: Penguin.

CHAPTER 10 Assessing Management

A target company can have the best position in the best market, but without good management it will go nowhere. In contrast, great management can work wonders with a weak business. Great people substantially out perform good people. The difference can be staggering: a 250 per cent over-performance is not uncommon. Worse, no proper succession planning can severely disrupt a business; 50–75 per cent of key managers leave of their own accord within 2 to 3 years of a company being acquired. A good rule of thumb is that the cost of replacing someone is 2.4 times total annual compensation. Getting the right management in place is critical to the success of an acquisition. The starting point is assessing incumbent management as part of due diligence. The market interviews conducted during CDD can provide excellent insights to management, but they should be supplemented with the formal management appraisal methods described in this chapter. Of course, experienced acquirers use due diligence to deepen their knowledge about and links with the target's management. Every such interaction offers an opportunity to assess people's abilities and personal agendas. Does the target's management have command of the company's operational details? Do they work well as a team? Are they easily flustered or hostile when challenged? Are they enthused by the transaction or are they more concerned about their personal futures? Many acquirers continue to rely on their judgement and intuition to assess management. The argument for a rigorous process of evaluation is that it gives new insights into managers' capacity to deliver what the deal requires by providing an impartial external perspective on management. It uses disciplined methods to evaluate management, both as individuals and as a team. This is a process that takes us well beyond initial impressions or self-reports by the managers themselves. Formal management due diligence appraisals evaluate management's ability to meet the challenges facing the business and provide an external benchmark with which to compare more intuitive judgements. An external benchmark is important because the capabilities required to succeed vary according to the nature of the business and the market it is in. A high tech start-up is going to require different skills from a rationalization acquisition in a mature industry.

Objective

When a would-be acquirer asks, 'What do you think of the management team?' what is the question they are really asking? Is it 'What does each person bring?' Or, 'What is their motivation?' 'Do we really need all these people?' 'Are there gaps?' 'Can they cope with change?' Answering these questions is the objective of management assessments. They provide:

- an assessment of human capital against new organizational demands;
- a benchmark of human capital against the market;

- a comparison with executives across geographies;
- an objective evaluation of the top leadership (generally one to two levels below the CEO/ main board);
- a pragmatic assessment of executives' potential within the context of the business;
- a clear recommendation and options for filling key positions;
- a basis for strategic human capital planning and development.

Management assessment should be a two way process. The process should be non-threatening and enjoyed by the participants. It should be used to give the participants the opportunity to:

- talk about their own achievements;
- register their aspirations;
- get personal views off their chest with a neutral third party;
- receive feedback – the output should be made available to individuals so that they get feedback on strengths and development needs;
- think about their own development.

EVALUATION METHODS

Figure 10.1 shows the evaluation methods most commonly used to assess future performance and behaviour and those most valid as predictors of performance. Management assessments use structured interviews and reference checks.

STRUCTURED INTERVIEWS

To be truly useful, interviews must be properly planned and properly carried out. They are not cosy chats, but controlled situations in which one person, the interviewer, is in charge and directs proceedings. As a rough guide, this means the interviewee doing about 85 per

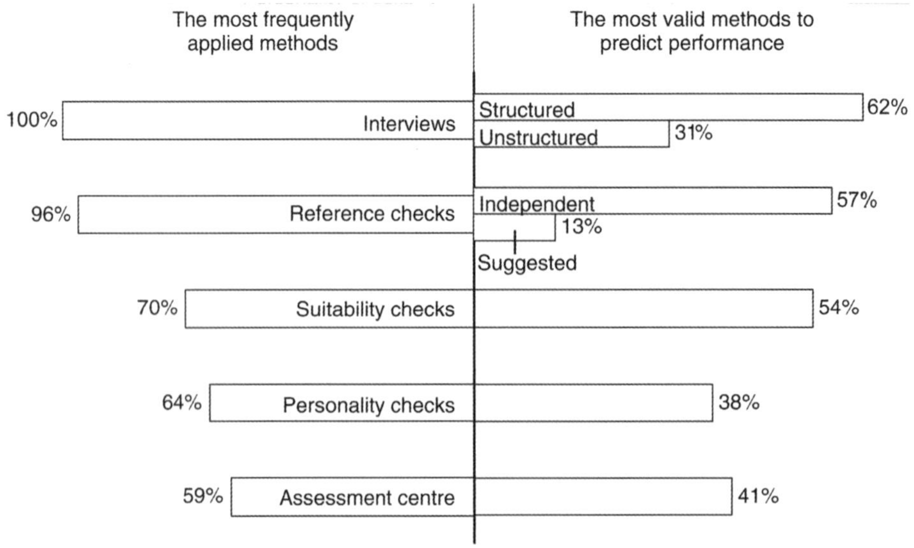

Figure 10.1 Methods used in management appraisals and their effectiveness

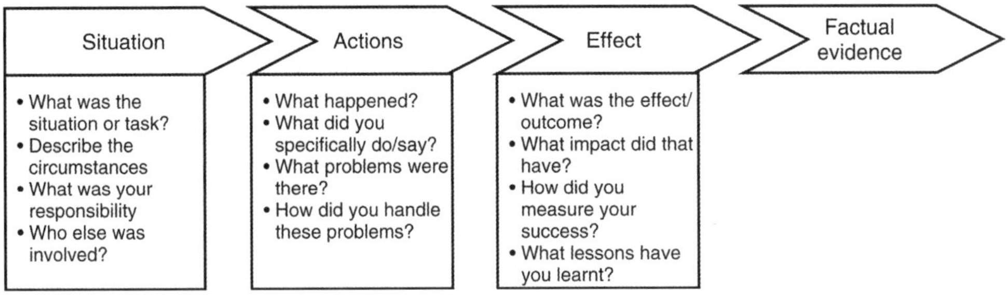

Figure 10.2 Competency-based interviewing

cent of the talking. Management assessment interviews typically last about 2 to 3 hours. This is the minimum time required to really understand individuals' achievements and capabilities. Before interviews begin, the assessors must first be clear on what skills, resources and experience are needed for an acquisition to be successful. Checklist 8 in Appendix A lists the commonly sought management competencies. The aim is, then, to collect data in order to be able to judge the degree to which target managers (and maybe also managers in the acquirer's company) possess the attributes needed. Interviews are past-orientated, fact-based, structured interviews in which the interviewer gathers data on past performance in order to assess the interviewee's competencies. Figure 10.2 demonstrates how competency-based interviewing works in practice. This is amplified by Checklist 9 in Appendix A.

Competencies are the building blocks of structured interviews because research shows that structured competency-based interviewing is the most effective selection and evaluation method.[1] Past behaviour is the best predictor of future behaviour and performance. Competencies are definable, measurable and distinct. This means that they can be tailored to the specific requirements of the acquisition under consideration, tested and scaled across organizations. The interviewer starts at the beginning of the candidate's career and works through to the latest job. Questions for each of the different positions held will be along the lines of those in Checklist 9 (Appendix A).

Interview style

The aim in assessment interviews is a dialogue with the interviewees. This is the style adopted mostly by head-hunters and selection consultants in one-to-one interviews. They see themselves as operating as an honest broker. The aim is to establish a genuine dialogue where both parties put themselves forward honestly but in the best light. Real opinions are expressed and if difficulties are encountered, both parties talk them through in a genuine attempt to solve them.

Interview structure

There are two facets to structuring an assessment interview:

- Data gathering
- Pacing.

DATA GATHERING

As mentioned above, an interview will last between 2 and 3 hours. The rough apportionment of time is shown in Table 10.1.

Table 10.1 Structuring a 3-hour interview

Activity	*Topic*	*Percentage of time*	*Minutes*
1	Career to date	20	30
2	Degree to which current and future job demands are fulfilled	50	75
3	Background on references given and to be checked later	20	30
4	Personal issues	10	15

PACING

Interviews have a beginning, a middle and an end. Because first impressions are so important the assessor has to be careful to avoid early judgements. Voice, appearance and body language are all important influencers of the interviewer's attitude and all occur on first contact. The antidote is to explore favourable impressions and not be biased by unfavourable ones.

The early stages are also where interviewer and respondent develop 'rapport'. 'Rapport' is a difficult term to define, but is important because it is what creates the comfortable, co-operative relationship necessary for best results. Rapport is developed by a combination of factors:

- Opening niceities: most people do not want confrontation. They want their dealings with others to be pleasant, they want to be liked and seen as likeable. Empathy and normal standards of politeness help develop rapport.
- Scene setting: the respondent needs to be told what the interview is to be about, the credentials of the interviewer, what is going to be done with the information, whether the interview is confidential, and, if so, how that confidentiality is going to be guaranteed.
- Removing anxiety: anxiety manifests itself in many ways; hostility, forgetfulness, incomplete responses, responses aimed at pleasing the interviewer. Careful scene setting, beginning with the least threatening questions, calm and time all help lessen anxiety.

Having established rapport, the relationship has to be maintained as the interview proceeds. Things to watch for are:[2]

- The effect of the content of the questions
- The order in which they are presented
- Bias
- Emotion and other threats to good relations.

Questions

Checklist 10 in Appendix A gives a list of suggested competency questions that will be used mainly for activity 2 in Table 10.1; but for this, and the other three activities, it is not just a question of sitting back and listening to the answers. Questions have five functions:

- Collection: this is to fill in blanks in the CV/resumé. They will usually be of the straight forward closed or yes/no type.

- Exploration: exploration aims to gain an understanding as to what lies behind the words on a CV/resumé and is the main purpose of the questions listed in Checklist 10 (Appendix A). Questions are open ended. This is the most common format because it allows the respondent complete freedom to reply without suggesting what the answer should be.
- Search: this is different from exploration in that we are no longer just trawling to see what comes up, but instead we are on the trail of something we know to exist but which may not come to the surface unless we dive in and get it. Search is very important in management assessments because it allows us to get to what really makes the managers tick.
- Probe: used to dig deeper when the interviewer is not sure that what has been heard is correct or complete. Probe is also used to counter evasion. Evasion is not uncommon in management assessments and given the levels of experience of the average interviewee, this should not be surprising. Questions might include:
  - Can we just go over that once again?
  - I am sorry, but I must be clear on this one. Why exactly did you do that?
  - We seem to have wandered off the subject.

Effective probing can also be silent or near silent. A nod of the head or a 'I see' or 'go on' to give encouragement or a slightly raised eyebrow to indicate surprise may be all that is needed to dig deeper.

- Check: a check aims to do just that, to check that the interviewer has understood correctly. The most effective means of checking is to paraphrase what the interviewee has just said. Another is to ask the same question some time later.

Body language

Answers to questions do not tell everything. Body language can often tell a lot more and, because it is hard to disguise, it can often be nearer the truth. For these reasons, it is important to be on the look out for subtle, spontaneous reactions. Few interviewees at this level will blush, but many will look away, or at their shoes, when not wholly convinced by the answer they have just given. Similarly, the assessors must avoid body language and verbal messages saying different things or body language revealing what they really think of the manager or the answers given. On the other hand, body language can be a great help in encouraging the interviewee to talk.

Context

Do make sure the context of the appraisals is taken into account. For example, it would be wrong to expect miracles of management sophistication from stable, mid-market companies. Not only do they not have the resources, Mintzberg[3] is right, managers do not spend a great deal of time planning work. Rather they respond to situations and needs as they arise. Although information is available, judgement and intuition are more commonly used. Management is basically about problem solving, producing results and controlling tasks. However, if companies require constant innovation, entrepreneurship and quality improvement, something more is required. Companies also need to cope with change, which calls for leadership as well as just management. And according to Peters and Austin[4] such leadership is accomplished and demonstrated through:

- Caring for customers and constant innovation. Innovation is the result of listening to customers and being constantly adaptive to their needs and monitoring the competition and constantly adapting to competitive moves.
- Motivation of people by soliciting their ideas and encouraging greater involvement in their implementation.

REFERENCE CHECKS

The starting point for reference checks is the CV/resumé. The CV/resumé will provide the basic background information of the individual(s) concerned. Reference checking seeks to expand and verify the information contained in the CV/resumé. This is done through a mixture of desk research and primary information sources. Typical questions include:

- Are the qualifications and job/education history accurate?
- How has the person performed in the past? Is this as claimed?
- Is there any evidence of fraud?
- How honest are they? What is their reputation as far as integrity is concerned?
- What is central to their motivation? What makes them perform?
- Where do they want to go?

Desk research will include:

- Address: confirmation that the manager lives at the address claimed. Brief assessment of the residence. Yes, go and have a look.
- Credit: find out if there any county court judgements or other bad credit associated with either the person or the address.
- Media checks: look for any past media articles that may cause concern.
- Past experience check: carry out interviews with previous employers to confirm information on the CV/resumé (dates, remuneration, responsibilities, and so on), reasons for leaving, and to try to elicit any information on past performance and character.
- Verification of professional membership.
- Industry enquiries: these are to try and establish whether there is anything in the manager's background that might cause concern. Is the individual seen as competent, honest and respected? Ex-colleagues are particularly revealing sources.
- A list of current directorships and shareholdings.
- Is there a record of any criminal acts?

Interviews with current and former associates and colleagues are used to verify the personal information. These discussions are with people who have seen the manager in action. Current and former colleagues, 360-degree feedback sessions, analysts, investors, advisers, customers and suppliers are the most obvious sources. Under certain circumstances, the audit can also include experienced practitioners watching the team in action and so observing the quality of their interactions and of their relationships with each other. This involves shadowing managers for a day.

PERSONALITY CHECKS

If interviews raise particular concerns about an individual that could be clarified in a more intensive assessment, psychometric tests may be used to give a deeper insight into that individual's predispositions, attitude, leadership style, and so on. They are also particularly useful in putting together effective management teams.

Psychometric tests are self-reporting questionnaires that are used to uncover aspects of personality. They ask about preferred ways of behaving and of relating to other people. Although there are many different forms of personality questionnaire (there some 1200 on the UK market alone) they all tend to fall in to one of two psychological camps:

- Type: these assign the respondent to a specific personality type.
- Trait: these categorize according to personality trait, where a trait is an aspect of personality that the respondent possesses to a greater or lesser extent.

Remember that psychometric tests are not a substitute for interviews. They can only supplement them. What they can do is:

- predict how a person is likely to behave generally, but not how a person will behave in a specific situation;
- build up a picture of the person (although note that they rely on that person's self-perception) but they cannot determine whether or not that person has the critical skills needed or what they have done in the past and what the results were;
- help if you have a footprint of what profiles will work well in the target company or merged entity.

Personality type

By far the most widely used type of questionnaire is the Myers-Briggs Type Indicator® (MBTI). Type questionnaires owe their structure to the work of Swiss psychologist Carl Jung. At their most basic, they categorize human behaviour into four base types, hence the term 'four quadrant behaviour' (4QB), although many of the commercially available tests go well beyond this, breaking the basic four types into many more sub-types.

Jung's work, published in the 1920s, developed a theory to describe the predictable differences between the ways in which people behave in different situations. His theory says that variations in behaviour are caused by the way we *prefer* to use our minds. The word 'prefer' is key because Jungian theory is very much based on an 'either/or' view of personality. All psychometric tests measure preference rather than give descriptions of behaviour.

Jung starts with the proposition that there are two ways in which our mind reacts to information:

- we receive it (perceiving); or
- we process it (judging).

There are, according to Jung, only two ways of perceiving:

- sensing
- intuition.

And two ways of judging:

- thinking
- feeling.

Thus, there are four key processes that we use to understand the world around us. These are shown in Figure 10.3:

- Thinking–feeling: thinkers take a detached and logical approach, but may overlook the human side of things. Feelers are the exact opposite. They base their decisions on their likely impact on other people. At work this translates into a desire to please.
- Sensing–intuition: sensors are usually practical and take things one-step at a time. These are the ones who prefer dealing with facts and detail. The intuitive types prefer the big picture. They tend to follow their noses rather than rely on their senses. They work in short inspirational bursts rather than make steady progress.

Finally, Jung overlaid two further divisions, extrovert and introvert, to give 16 main personality types in all.

These days, Jung's basic ideas are still used, although the descriptions to identify the four main quadrants seems to have moved to DISC:

- Dominant or Driving (D)
- Inspiring or Influencing (I)
- Supporting or Steadfast (S)
- Co-ordinating or Compliant (C).

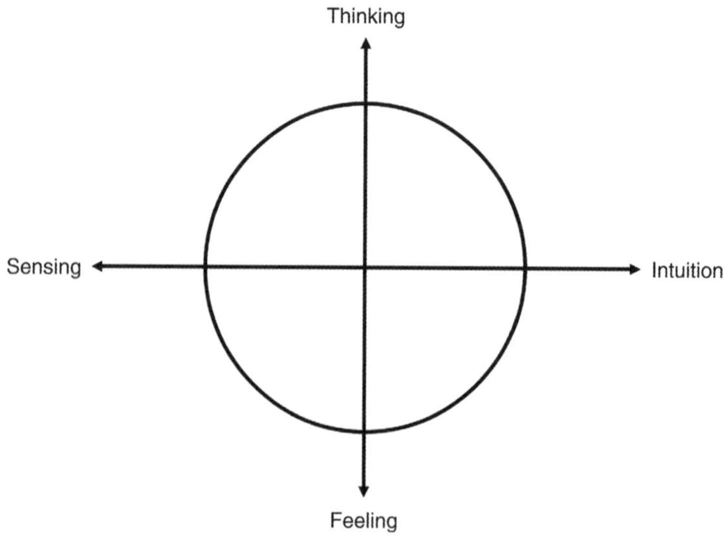

Figure 10.3 Jung's personality types

Under normal circumstances, type questionnaires are best used for development and training purposes, although they can be used to select people for jobs if the questionnaires are designed to capture the amounts of a particular characteristic a respondent possesses, so that comparisons can be made between candidates. As far as management assessments are concerned, they can be very valuable because of the insights they can give in team building. Type tests can help show the sort of environments in which people prefer to work, the way in which they are likely to go about their work and the ideal personality of any colleagues with whom they would work best.

Personality traits

Trait questionnaires measure the different amounts of personality characteristics that we all possess. The theory is that the traits are predictive of behaviour. Questionnaires set out to measure between 3 and 30 of the 20 000 or so personality traits that are said to exist. For example, two of the most commonly used psychological tests in the UK are 16PF (Sixteen Personality Factor Questionnaire), which, as the name suggests, measures 16 personality traits, and the Occupational Personality Questionnaire® (OPQ), which measures 30. There are only five personality traits that really count and some experts maintain that three dimensions underpin all observable behaviour. The five dimensions of personality, often referred to as the 'Big Five', are as follows:

- Action: this dimension is all about an individual's attitude towards others. At one end are the type 'D', tough-minded, do it and do it now, individuals, who are results orientated, have little time or patience for those needing support and who tend to work best with other 'D' types. At the other end of the dimension are the warmer, people-focused, individuals. They have a genuine concern for other people and achieve results by listening and through consensus.
- Thinking: this dimension is about structure. The 'high structure' person is tidy, systematic and leaves nothing to chance. The 'low structure' person does not worry too much about formal structures or schedules, as long as things get done, and has a much greater preference for the big picture rather than the detail.
- Relating: this dimension refers to how a person relates to other people. The extrovert hogs the limelight, is sociable, outgoing and impulsive. The introvert has a tendency to take a more cautious and restrained approach and does not relish open competition with other people.
- Feeling: feeling is about self-assurance. The high self-confidence individual is relaxed and optimistic, calm under pressure, enjoys responsibility and being put to the test. Low self-confidence individuals are more pessimistic, cannot take pressure well, question their abilities and prefer predictability to challenges.
- Conformity: conformity is about the way in which an individual responds to change. The conformist is happiest operating within the status quo, solves problems by applying well-tried methods and is better at implementing plans than creating them. The non-conformist is much more change orientated, innovative and concerned with individual expression to the point, sometimes, of resenting structure and order.

ASSESSING TEAMS

In the 1960s, John Adair developed a leadership model to identify the requirements for leadership when advising on leadership training at the UK Military Academy at Sandhurst. This model drew on the work of MacGregor, Maslow and Hertzberg and resulted in three overlapping areas of needs – those of the task, the team and the individual.[5] He likened them to three interactive and overlapping circles, as shown in Figure 10.4.

Each circle has an influence on the others, but should never overwhelm them. Each has a set of needs that need to be met for the team as a whole to be successful; any imbalance will mean failure:

- Individuals all have their own social, personal and professional needs. If one or more individuals selfishly assert their needs to the detriment of others, the team is divided and the task is unlikely to be accomplished.
- The task must be clear and completed, but must not overwhelm the individual or the team. Many organizations are task driven and there is nothing wrong with that. The problems come when teams and individuals feel undervalued. The result is high staff turnover, with the consequent cost of recruiting and training, and only shallow experience resulting in bad decisions and lower standards.
- The team must be co-ordinated and operate efficiently, but, like the task, must not overwhelm the individual.

Although focused teams are invaluable in certain circumstances, the more common is the balanced team. A task-driven organization will probably naturally tend to recruit dominant 'D' types. The problem with 'D's, and for all the other types, is that for every strength there is a weakness. Assertive, decisive, direct high 'D' types are also aggressive, impatient and insensitive. Two or three high 'C's running a business would result in immaculate sets of accounts, a first-class reporting system and brilliant sales literature. On the other hand, the sales effort would be laughable.

Questionnaires like the MBTI and Belbin's Team Role Inventory® can provide considerable insight into the way a person interrelates with others, their preferred role in

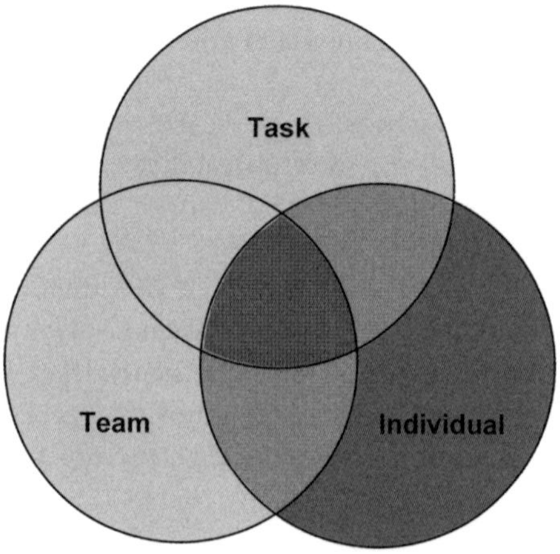

Figure 10.4 Team dynamics
Source: Adair (1986) *Effective Team Building.* Reproduced with the permission of John Adair.

group situations and their favoured work environment. This can help understand the strengths and weaknesses of a team.

Belbin suggested that there are eight primary roles that people adopt in teams:[6]

- Shaper: the driver, the agenda setter.
- Chairman: the team's controller: the person which makes the team cohere and shapes how it moves towards group objectives.
- Monitor-evaluator: the analytical, tenacious one whose role is to evaluate ideas and suggestions.
- Plant: an unorthodox, imaginative ideas generator.
- Team worker: a sympathetic diplomat who supports team members and builds team spirit.
- Company worker: a stable, cautious, organizer who translates ideas into action.
- Completer-finisher: the person whose role is to get the job done. Tends to be disciplined and conscientious.
- Resource investigator: the communicator with the outside world. The extrovert, enthusiastic, 'life and soul of the party' type.

CASE STUDY 31

HOW MUCH DIFFERENCE DOES AN INDIVIDUAL MAKE?

The founder and managing director of a publishing company claimed that management would not be a problem if he sold the business to a buy-in candidate because he only came in to open the post and left at 10:00 AM most days. According to him, the business could function perfectly well without him. While this was factually accurate, it masked most of the truth. First, there was no real management at all. The finance director was part time, contracts administration was managed by the founder's secretary. Only the sales manager was a seasoned professional and he was far too stretched with a sales force of 100 and a churn rate of 60 per cent. Closer investigation revealed that on the days when the founder did not leave at 10:00 AM, he put in a couple of full days training new salesmen in his sales techniques – techniques that he had successfully used to build a business now worth £10 million in as many years. Second, it does not take a genius in psychology to work out that the founder of a business does not have work 9 to 5 to keep a firm hand on the tiller. His mere presence every day, being seen by the workforce, was enough to make sure everyone kept their heads down and it was enough for him to spot problems and deal with them. Finally, no one but him had any idea how much each contract was worth and only he and the finance director knew what the profits were. Self-evidently there was no management strength in-depth in this business and the transaction did not go ahead as a result.

Reporting

Reports should give an insight into individual managers and into the capabilities of the senior management team, as a team, but above all they should describe what is really going on (see Case Study 31). They should contain the elements described below.

For individuals, an executive summary on each of the key managers assessed that:

- profiles their capabilities against a broad range of general management competencies;
- matches these against the managerial challenges that will need to be addressed over the next few years;
- highlights their strengths and weaknesses;
- benchmarks them against senior managers in other organizations;
- indicates what areas of development or support would compensate for their weaknesses;
- provides the behavioural evidence to back up these conclusions.

For the team, or proposed team, a profile that:

- maps out the overall strengths and weaknesses of the management team as a whole;
- identifies where individuals' strengths complement each other;
- exposes any specific experience or capability that may be lacking in the team.

Reporting on individuals will probably be against some or all of the following 10 attributes. These 10 generic competencies generally cover 95 per cent of all observed behaviours. For a more detailed checklist of management competencies see checklists 3 and 8 in Appendix A.

- Strategic vision: here the measure is the degree to which the candidate is able to formulate and articulate a vision of the business several years down the road. To do this requires the candidate to show an entrepreneurial streak coupled with a realistic understanding of the environment in which the business operates. In turn, this requires more of an external than an internal focus.
- Results orientation: evidence of delivering, for example, profit or sales growth (or both) and a personality that sets and communicates firm business goals and tracks performance against them.
- Market knowledge: understands how the market works, what is important, what is not important. See checklist 3.1 in Appendix A for possible questions.
- Customer knowledge: able to demonstrate empathy with customers and their needs. Candidates will be able to respond to and anticipate change and be able to build the same customer dedication in the staff. See checklist 3.2 in Appendix A for possible questions.
- Functional competence: this usually boils down to technical knowledge, if the candidate is a professional such as a production or finance director, or industry knowledge, if knowledge of an industry is more important than technical skills. How good is this person at the technical demands of their role. Is the finance director, for example, au fait with the latest standards? Can the production director articulate their vision of the production process?
- Collaboration: how well does this person work as part of a team? Do they understand colleagues' roles?
- Team leadership: the evidence would point to a candidate who has confidence and conviction, someone who can build and motivate teams.
- People development: is there evidence that this person is someone who sets goals and objectives, guides staff towards them and who is quick to confront any performance problems?
- Teamwork: does the person work well with other members of the team?
- Change orientation: someone not uncomfortable with change, uncertainty, ambiguity and complexity.

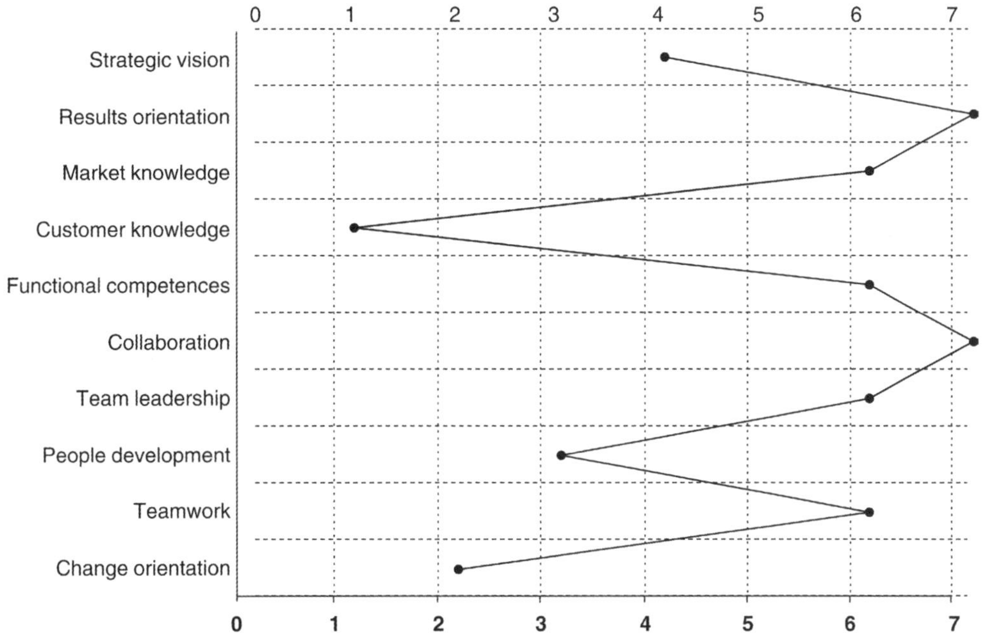

Figure 10.5 A typical competency profile

Figure 10.5 shows how scores against the above competencies are scored, although often the above topics are rolled into broader headings.

You will note that the competencies in Figure 10.5 are marked out of 7. Table 10.2 interprets the scoring system.

Typically, the CDD will report on each individual and the team as a whole. Minimum acceptable performances for various Board members would be:

- Chief Operating Officer 4
- Finance Director 5
- Chief Executive 6

Figure 10.6 shows how the combined abilities might be summarized in diagrammatic form. Each member of the management team would be plotted on the chart and an assessment made of the team's overall balance.

Table 10.2 Scoring individual managers on each competency

Score	*Summary*	*Meaning*
1	Unsatisfactory	Does the job
2	Weak	Wants to make things better
3	Below expectations	Works to specific goals
4	Meeting expectations	Drives beyond goals
5	Exceeding expectations	Introduces incremental improvement
6	Excellent	Creates significant improvement
7	Outstanding	Transforms a business

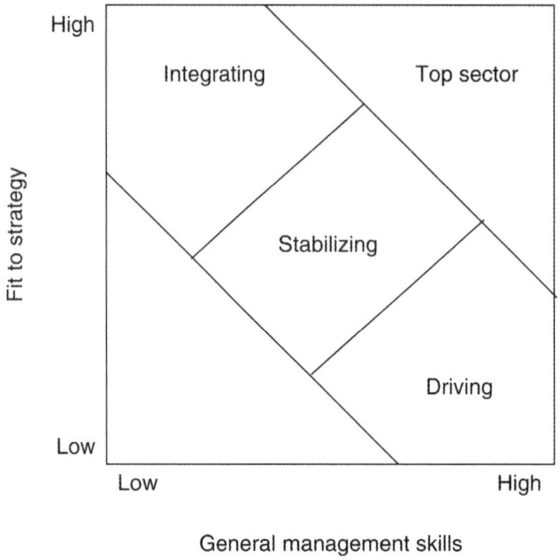

Figure 10.6 Assessment of the management team

As well as the diagrammatic representation there should also be a commentary on the manager's rating against each attribute and an assessment of the strengths and weaknesses of each.

The point to remember is that management assessments are just that. They are assessments. Even with the help of psychometric testing, this is not an exact science, which is why it is so important that the consultant has wide business experience. Case Study 32, however, is a summary of a real interview with the owner of a target company where the outcome of the assessment is obvious even to those who do not have extensive business experience.

CASE STUDY 32

A MANAGEMENT INTERVIEW

STRATEGIC VISION

Dr John Pringle, the Managing Director of ABC Ltd, also leads the sales team and the finance function. This does not leave him a great deal of time for strategic development. The evidence of development that exists is confined to tactical considerations around new products and new product launches. Dr Pringle is more focused on sales growth than on profit. His package includes a sales-linked bonus.

RESULTS ORIENTATION

Dr Pringle has significant ambitions. His comments include: 'I would like to run a big public company', and 'I would like to run a company with 25 000 or 30 000 people ... I could see myself running a company with 50 000 – but not anything as big as Shell or Unilever.' Dr Pringle expects a seat on the successful bidder's board (even if it is a financial acquirer!). He does not expect a successful bidder's manager to sit on the board.

CASE STUDY 32 – *continued*

MARKET KNOWLEDGE

Dr Pringle leads his business with intense commitment. He commands great respect for his technical product knowledge and is rated as a keen negotiator. He is also highly regarded as an international business partner. Dr Pringle's personable, 'hands-on' style of management is underpinned by a positive 'can-do' attitude.

CUSTOMER KNOWLEDGE

Dr Pringle has developed close relations, built over many years, with key suppliers and customers. He is held in high esteem.

FUNCTIONAL COMPETENCE

Dr Pringle's scientific achievements are matched by his charismatic management style. But Dr Pringle is arrogant. He says: 'I have done MBA classes, but they did not teach me anything.' The target has few management controls. Dr Pringle accepts that an acquirer will require that major expenditures are approved. There is no budgeting and Dr Pringle contends that he could not write a budget for his business as it is so unpredictable. This excuse probably hides the desire to remain flexible and his view that budgets are not very necessary. Dr Pringle admits that the company's bookkeeping is poor and says: 'I hate finance people ... they never come up with anything positive.' There are only two meetings scheduled each week as Dr Pringle does not like 'meeting to death'. This is evidenced by the fact that the meeting room has now been turned into an office.

COLLABORATION

Dr Pringle is motivated by power over money. He comments that he does not pay himself as much as he might: 'If I just wanted to fill my bank account I would have done so ages ago.' Dr Pringle would expect to operate unfettered once the transaction is complete. He now accepts that he should implement systems in his own business. He is confident that the new project management system will satisfy needs.

TEAM LEADERSHIP

Dr Pringle is criticized for not having effectively transferred responsibility to middle management. He has no external source of advice or sounding board for ideas, as he himself readily admits: 'I guess that I discuss some things with my wife – but she knows that I take no notice of the advice she gives.' Dr Pringle admits that his staff are probably reluctant to speak their minds in full. He admits to not wanting to cede power to any of his people and that 'it took me a long time to get up the courage to hire the sales lady'. Once a year, the company takes a 5-day weekend trip to Mallorca to discuss the business, as well as to play golf.

PEOPLE DEVELOPMENT

Up to now management issues have largely been sorted out in Dr Pringle's head or written out in pencil notes in a Filofax® planner. A new organization chart has been sketched out in Dr Pringle's Filofax. It shows a more complete organization, but it does not recognize the need for top management. Nonetheless he recognizes the top management problem and says: 'Yes – I accept absolutely what you say ... it is something that I will have to work on.' Staff are not highly paid. Pay rises are not given automatically, they are granted when staff summon up the courage to request them. Dr Pringle's pay rise philosophy is easily defined: 'I think that pay rises should be deserved – so if someone thinks that they have done something good, they can ask for a rise.' In one exceptional case, Dr Pringle has given a

CASE STUDY 32 – *continued*

rise to one technician who would otherwise not had the courage to request one.

TEAMWORK

Dr Pringle admits that everything is done in a rush. He readily admits that he should plan further in advance and take on more staff, which would avoid some of the last minute panics. He does not delegate, both because it is not in his nature and as he lacks the people to delegate to. Until he turned his mobile off, he received three calls in the first 30 minutes of our meeting. On the Friday and Saturday before our meeting Dr Pringle had been testing products in Turkey. He admits that as Managing Director, Sales Director and Finance Director he should not be doing this. At the same time, he justifies the decision by stating that he must keep close to the product.

CHANGE ORIENTATION

Dr Pringle does not have it in him to change.

Communication with management

Inevitably, management will be nervous about management assessments. All that can really be done about this is to tell the truth. The script might go something like this:

- A management audit has been commissioned as part of the commercial due diligence.
- The aim is to confirm that there is a balanced team in place that can deliver.
- Everyone has their relative strengths and weaknesses, but in a balanced team these are compensated for.
- This process is a rigorous, disciplined and independent way of establishing the strengths and weaknesses of team members, identifying where, if at all, development or support is needed and of confirming that the team as a whole has the necessary blend of skill and experience.
- The process is also an opportunity for management to demonstrate their capabilities.

As mentioned above, assessments should be a two-way process. Reports are confidential, but feedback to managers can usually be arranged. Feedback will normally consist of a run through the main conclusions of the assessment, exploring the implications of these to individuals and/or for the team as a whole.

Culture

Company culture is difficult to define but easy to observe. It is formed from all those networks and intra-company interactions that turn resources into capabilities. As was hinted at in Chapter 6, it is these networks that prevent competitors copying what look like easy to copy strategies. A competitor can buy the resources, but it cannot always replicate how they are turned into capabilities.

Some of the key questions about the target comapny in M&A are:

- Have they performed well in the past?

- Will they perform well in the future?
- Could they perform better with us?
- Will they perform better with us?

Table 10.3 Organization culture and strategy

Type	*Characteristics*	*Strategy formation*
Defenders	• Conservative beliefs	Emphasis on planning
	• Low risk strategies	
	• Secure markets	
	• Concentration on narrow segments	
	• Considerable expertise in a narrow areas of specialism	
	• Preference for well-tried resolutions to problems	
	• Little search for anything really new	
	• Attention given to improving efficiency of present operations	
Prospectors	• Innovative	Entrepreneurial
	• Looking to break new ground	
	• Search for new opportunities	
	• Can create change and uncertainty, forcing a response from competitors	
	• More attention given to market changes than to improving internal efficiencies	
Analysers	• Stable: formal structures and search for efficiencies	Planning
	• Changing: competitors monitored and strategies amended as promising ideas seen	Adaptive
Reactors	• Characterized by an inability to respond to change pressures; adjustments are forced on the firm to avert crisis	Adaptive

This last point is largely a question of cultural fit and it is a question that needs to be covered in due diligence with the same rigour as finance or legal issues. However, if the assessment is to be based on extensive questioning of the employee base, it cannot be done until the transaction is announced. However, it is possible to do some initial cultural assessments along with senior management assessments.

Miles and Snow[7] have suggested a typology of organizations that can be looked at in relation to culture and strategy formulation (see Table 10.3). Miles and Snow argue that their typology can be used to predict behaviour.

Deal and Kennedy[8] concluded from research among US companies that those companies that are most successful over the long term are those that believe in something; where a common set of beliefs has permeated the entire organization.

Successful companies maintain flexibility and adaptability and focus on the external environment. The dominant values are entrepreneurship, creativity, autonomy and willingness to experiment. The opposite is the bureaucratic hierarchy. Hierarchies tend to be inward looking, rigid and prioritize order and routine. Although one might expect them to perform well in mature industries and stable markets, evidence suggests that the more bureaucratic the organization, the less likely it is to be commercially successful. But there should not be an undisciplined free-for-all either and decision making has to be data driven.

In successful companies, management interaction is different too. There are open disagreements, but nothing is taken personally; there is a focus on facts, on building multiple alternatives and extensive use of humour to defuse tension. Less successful teams rely on opinions, wishes and guesses. They focus on only one or two alternatives, have an autocrat (or no one) running them and in general are a pretty miserable bunch.

The role of a good leader is as a genuine chairman. If there is no consensus, the chairman uses the casting vote and everyone is happy with that as long as they feel they have been listened to. This limits conflict and leads to fast decisions. Good managements have clear top-down guidance without detailed prescription. Detailed prescription is the norm in poor companies. One Chief Executive felt it necessary to dictate the size of the annual price rise despite having sales directors in the various subsidiary companies who were much closer to their markets than he was (but who were clearly relieved that the responsibility for deciding by how much to raise prices was not theirs!). Needless-to-say, the Chief Executive got it wrong and the company lost market share. In good companies, challenge and debate are seen as forces for good. Discussion of conflicting ideas and views based on facts and objective observation encourages people to share learning and build judgement and requires people to make a strong case, something which is often missing in poor companies where managerial discussions are made in advance of debate and handed down.

Finally, beware complacency due to security, or inactivity due to insecurity. One company in deep trouble drew up a plan for survival. It spelt out five alternatives, any one of which would have been better than doing nothing, but insecurity drove them to do nothing and it was left up to the company that acquired them from the receiver to put their plan into action.

CULTURE AND INNOVATION

In Chapters 4, 6 and 9, it was suggested that creativity was one of the keys to company success. A culture of creativity requires an organizational structure and management systems that are quite different from those appropriate to the pursuit of cost efficiency. Table 10.4[9] contrasts some characteristics of the two types of organization.

Although innovation requires creativity, creativity needs to be stimulated by and directed toward need, which explains why customers are such fertile sources of innovation – they are most acutely involved with matching existing products and services to their needs – and why it is critical to collaborate with them on the development of new products (see Chapter 9).

Table 10.4 Operating versus innovating organizations

	An operating organization	*An innovating organization*
Structure	Hierarchical organization based on specialization and division of labour.	Flat based on task orientated project teams.
Processes	Control and coordination from the top based on capital allocation.	Processes based around the generation of new ideas. Loose control.
Reward systems	Compensation, promotion and status.	Autonomy, recognition and equity.
People	Recruitment based on the need to fill specific slots. Management by command.	Employ technically qualified creative idea generators. Managers are enablers.

Innovation upsets established routines and threatens the status quo. The more stable the operating and administrative side of the organization, the greater the resistance to innovation.

Hence, in an emerging industry, firms need to support their innovation with a broad array of vertically integrated capabilities.

Conclusion

Structured, competency-based interviewing is the most effective method of assessing management. This could be supplemented with psychometric tests. Management assessment reports may reinforce opinions already held or expose specific risks to be plugged. On the other hand, their conclusions might come as a complete surprise, in which case there may be a case for revisiting the data and checking things out in more detail. The fact is that management is too important for it not to be systematically assessed. The main way of doing this is through structured, competency-based, interviewing and reference checks. Psychometric testing may be used where there is a need to dig deeper, but should not be used as a matter of course. CDD should assess the individuals as well as the team. CDD may also look at culture to assess likely fit and the target's ability to innovate.

Notes

1. Smart, Geoffrey H. (1999) 'Management Assessment Methods in Venture Capital', *Venture Capital,* 1(1): 59–82.
2. Keats, Daphne. M. (2000) *Interviewing: A Practical Guide for Students and Professionals.* London: Oxford University Press.
3. Mintzberg, H. (1975) 'The Manager's Job – Folklore and Fact', *Harvard Business Review,* 68(2): 163–76.
4. Peters, T. and Austin, N. (1985) *A Passion for Excellence.* London: Collins.
5. Adair, John (1986) *Effective Team Building.* Aldershot: Gower.
6. See www.belbin.com.
7. Miles, R.E. and Snow, C.C. (1978) *Organization Strategy, Structure and Process.* New York: McGraw-HIll.
8. Deal, T. and Kennedy, A. (1982) *Corporate Cultures. The Rites and Rituals of Corporate Life.* Boston, MA: Addison Wesley.
9. Based on Galbraith, J.R. and Kazanjian, R.K. (1986) *Strategy Implementation: Structure, Systems and Processes.* St Paul, MN: West.

CHAPTER 11 *Using the Output*

You have defined and analysed the target company's market, assessed its company's ability to compete and thought very hard about its customers and their motivations. You are now at the stage where you have to bring it all together. Like so much in due diligence, this is not an exact science and as said in the opening chapter, CDD is not just about the cold, rational application of analytical techniques. Analytical techniques are a short-cut that provide a framework for putting a report together. Beyond that, it is your ability to sense what is going on with a company in a market that is going to create the magic in your analysis. Case study 33[1] is a beautiful illustration of sensing in action.

CASE STUDY 33

THE IMPORTANCE OF MARKET SENSING

When Disney transferred its Disneyland format to Paris – Euro Disney near Paris – the company lost $921 million in the first year. The decision to enter the European market was well supported by research. Figures showed the growing number of European visitors to the US theme parks. In the conventional Disney way, the location was based on modelling population figures – 17 million people live within a 2-hour drive of the Paris site, and 109 million people live within a 6-hour drive, which are much better figures than those for the US parks. The figures were encouraging, but the launch of Euro Disney was an expensive lesson in the importance of market understanding. The company ignored the failure of amusement parks in France, it dismissed anti-Disney demonstrations as insignificant and it ignored the fact that European holiday patterns are completely different from those in the USA – people in Europe have longer holidays and spend less on each. Myopia also led the company to ban alcohol from its park – you try telling the French they cannot drink wine at lunchtime and see what happens! Excellent research that ignores the things that really matter (because no one asks the right questions) is no better than no research at all.

The primary purpose of the CDD investigation is to decide whether or not to buy the company. If the CDD is heading towards a negative decision, this must be communicated as soon as possible. You will get no extra points for turning up at the end of the assignment with a perfect report that is full of deal breakers. It is rare for CDD to be commissioned if the acquirer is not reasonably certain that the deal will go ahead, but it does happen sometimes, as Case Study 34 shows.

CASE STUDY 34

TELL THE CLIENT IMMEDIATELY YOU IDENTIFY DEAL BREAKERS

In many respects, businesses that rely on contracts for the bulk of their sales are easy to evaluate. You do this by looking at the company's success rate in winning new work and by talking to the customers who awarded the existing contracts to gauge the likelihood of renewal. Evaluating a company that has only one or two customers is also fairly straightforward. As we saw in Case Studies 8 and 21 (see Chapters 1 and 6 respectively), it is a question of focusing on benefits sought and benefits provided. It should, therefore, be fairly easy to come to a view on a business that relies on two large contracts from the same customer. It is not when, as in this case, that customer is the government, the contracts are due for renewal at about the time of the next election, and the criteria for awarding them are inconsistent and likely to change – but nobody yet knows how. It would be a brave analyst who gave an opinion on future prospects in those circumstances and the would-be acquirer needs to be told that it is impossible to form a view on the business one way or another. For the analyst, it is very tempting to go on and look at company performance against contract expectations and such like, but in this case, there was no point because even had the target been a perfect performer (which it was not by a long way), this would have counted for nothing at contract renewal time There is every chance that once given the news, the acquirer would stop the CDD and any other due diligence going on at the same time, but better that than spending a lot of time, energy and money getting nowhere. This case also illustrates the wisdom of doing CDD first. If the commercial side of the deal does not make sense, the process can be stopped and money will not have been wasted on the legals and financials.

Always keep the bigger picture in mind

Figure 11.1 summarizes the competitive position element of CDD and should be kept in mind at all times. A target company is being bought for its returns. In evaluating a target company, the main focus of CDD is whether it can outperform its rivals by establishing a difference it can preserve. The other focus is, of course, market attractiveness.

The more a target company can give customers what they want in a way that is better than the competition, the higher those returns will be. The same is true for the merged entity. As far as post-acquisition success is concerned, has the deal created a sustainable competitive advantage by giving customers what they want in a way that is superior to the competition's offering? If not, the acquisition is being made for the wrong reason (and plenty are).

Excellent companies use M&A as a component of corporate strategy. The strategy comes from a thorough understanding of the forces acting on the market and the desire of the company to make the most of those forces (see Table 11.1). They recognize that growth is the result of superior customer value and the creation of long-term customer relationships over long periods of time. For them, acquisitions create value by contributing to the strategy and they spend a lot of time thinking about whether the target is the right company and how, when and how much it will contribute. In contrast, poor companies have an M&A strategy shaped by opportunism, a partial understanding of markets, a desire to buy their

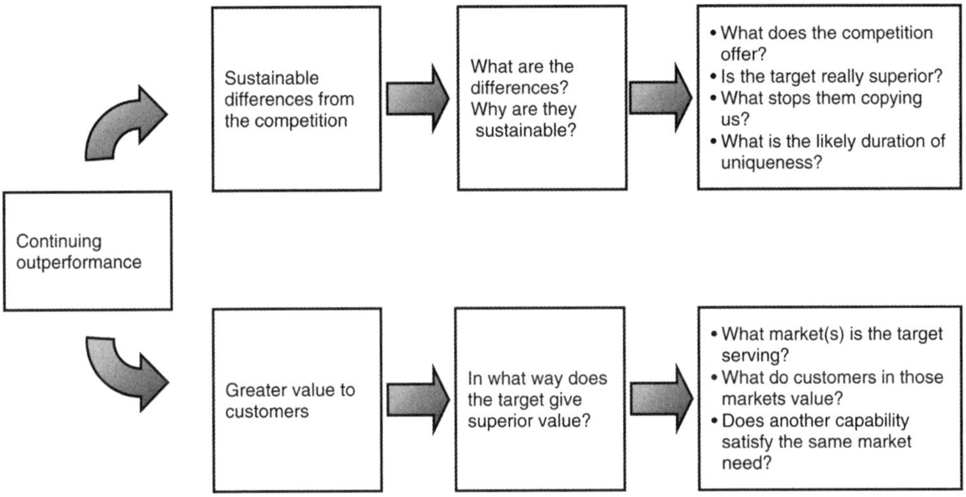

Figure 11.1 A company can only outperform its rivals if it can establish a difference it can preserve

Table 11.1 The forces acting on most markets

Force	*Consequence*
Globalization	The emergence of global or pan-national customer segments and with them the emergence of pan-national competition. Use acquisitions to create a pan-national offering and sufficient scale to survive the competition.
Rapidly maturing markets	Differentiation is more difficult to maintain, if at all. Economies of scale become the dominant theme. Use acquisitions to create scale and/or broaden the range of products/services offered.
Increasing buyer power	Improved IT (enabling better price comparisons), increased product experience, customer sophistication, consolidation and organization, and market globalization combine to make customers more price sensitive. Use acquisitions as above to create scale and/or broaden the range of products/services offered so that you can capture more value.
Increasing channel power	As above.
Product convergence	Product categories combining as technological and business developments cater for customer demand for better value propositions. Use acquisitions to broaden the range of products and competencies.
New technology	New technology from both within and outside the industry altering product capabilities much more rapidly.
New segments opening up	Market being segmented ever more finely, or in different ways, because of new business ideas and changing customer needs.
Higher stakes	Market sophistication, technology and regulation increasing firms' investment requirements.
Changing sources of value-added	Increased product familiarity means previous sources of value-add are now entry qualifications. They are necessary to compete but not a source of value or differentiation. The need now to provide services alongside the product is a good example of value-add shifting from product quality/functionality to delivery.
Demographics	An ageing population has a knock-on effect for most businesses.
Customer expectations	Customer expectations have increased significantly in the past decade.

way out of trouble and a focus on just getting the deal done. Any company that thinks that by making an acquisition it can somehow manipulate market forces has lost the plot. Market forces cannot be manipulated, but they can be exploited and that is where acquisitions come in. Table 11.1 lists the forces acting on most markets.

Companies always fail to appreciate when the effective life of a particular strategy is coming to an end, as much as anything because it had proved so successful in the past. The current market and competitive situation could endure for some considerable time, but both will change sooner or later. If the target is successful and profitable, it will attract the attention of competitors who will seek to take over its position in the market. However good the target is now, it must have sufficient creative capability to stay ahead of the game.

SPACE

Rowe et al.[2] have developed a positioning model that can sometimes be adapted as a useful checklist for the areas in CDD that need the most attention and/or what you should expect to see in the business plan or produce as part of your CDD report. It uses three of the four variables used by Rowe et al.:

- The relative stability or turbulence of the environment
- Industry attractiveness
- The extent of any competitive advantage.

The company's financial strengths is Rowe et al.'s fourth variable. This is less appropriate to CDD, although using it could be useful in assessing the combined entity. The company's position is plotted on each of these axes. Table 11.2 shows the generic strategy appropriate for the various combinations of the four variables.

ASSESSING PROSPECTS

Marketing strategy is the set of decisions made about which customers to target and what to offer them. The core competency of any company is its strategy-making process. Every single other process can be outsourced. Each set of marketing decisions is specific. Despite what you might think from the text books, there is no one single right way. In fact, the weakest strategies are usually formulated by those who have read the text books and are trying to apply a process rather than creative thinking. Checklist 3.4 in Appendix A summarizes the difference between strong and weak market strategies.

At the root of all strategy analysis is where a company lies on the 2 × 2 matrix 'attractiveness versus ability to compete' (see Figure II.1). Table 11.3 gives a systematic way of thinking about where is a company is on that matrix.

This analysis needs to be done for each individual market served by the target company. The overall picture can then be analysed according to Figure 11.2 and characterized according to Figure 11.3.

With reference to Figure 11.3:

- Core businesses are those attractive market areas that fit the target's capabilities and resources.
- Peripheral businesses are areas where the market is less attractive for the target (there is no growth, competition is tough, margins are low, and so on), but where it can maintain

Table 11.2 SPACE – Strategic Position and ACtion Evaluation Implications for CDD

Environment	Stable	Unstable	Stable	Unstable
Industry	Attractive	Attractive	Unattractive	Unattractive
Competitiveness	Strong	Strong	Weak	Weak
Financial position	Strong	Weak	Strong	Weak
Appropriate strategies	Growth. Innovate to sustain competitive advantage. Consider further acquisitions.	Business plan/CDD must identify cost reductions, productivity improvements, and opportunities to strengthen competitiveness	Business plan/CDD must identify cost reductions and opportunities for product/service rationalization and at the same time identify new products, services and competitive opportunities	Avoid
Target's strategic thrust				
	Aggressive	Competitive	Conservative	Defensive

a strong position. These are areas where the target will continue to do business, but where profit growth will be hard to come by and quite possibly profits will decline. At the extreme, businesses in this quadrant suffer from the same wishful thinking as we saw in Case Study 11 (see Chapter 1). PKI was a solution looking for a problem.

- Illusion businesses are the attractive areas of the market where the target's capabilities and resources mean that it cannot compete effectively. Unless the target invests to improve its position, profits from this quadrant should be considered opportunist and likely to disappear if the market turns. The target only has a position because the strong players let it have one.
- No-hope businesses are those bits of business where the market is not attractive and the target has a weak position.

Where a target has a portfolio of businesses or competes in a collection of businesses, the BCG growth share matrix may be a useful tool also.

Portfolio analysis

The BCG growth share matrix can be very useful for positioning products in relation to their stage in the product life cycle. The growth share matrix (Figure 11.4) suggests the following strategies for products or business units falling into certain categories:

- Cash cow: run for cash.
- Dog: liquidate or divest.

Table 11.3 Plotting market attractiveness and ability to compete

Market attractiveness				*Ability to compete*		
Factor	Weight	Score		Factor	Weight	Score
Market size				Relative cost		
Market growth prospects				Relative market share		
Degree of rivalry				Rating on KPCs		
Power of suppliers				Innovation record		
Power of customers				Management ability		
Total	100			Total	100	

- Star: Strengthen competitive position.
- Problem child: invest as appropriate to secure and improve competitive position.

This is a simplistic analysis, but at least is a starting point for thinking about product strengths and weaknesses and for looking for linkages. It is simplistic because it is too black and white. As we saw in Chapter 9, there are many low growth markets in which companies make reasonable profits. This does not automatically make these businesses 'dogs', as some of the very healthy returns that venture capitalists have made on management buyouts

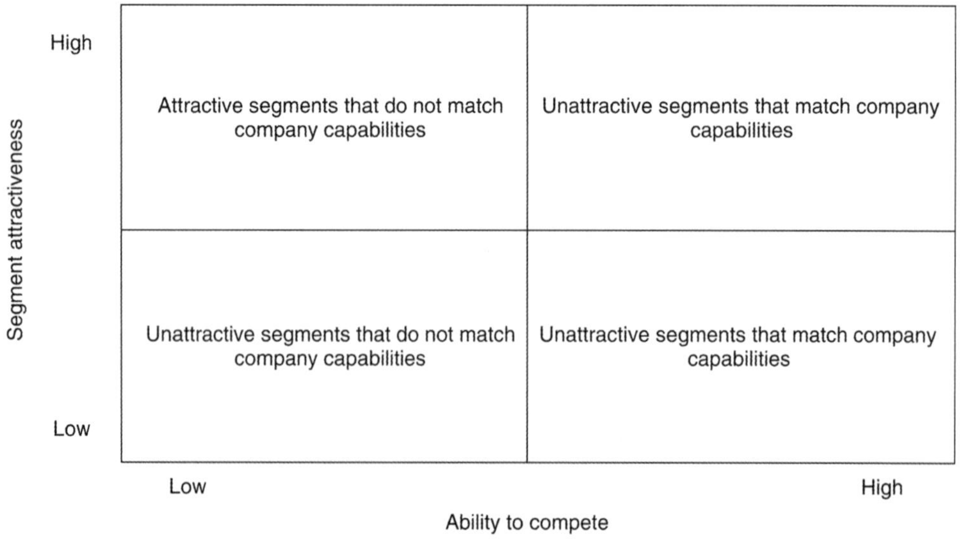

Figure 11.2 Understanding the target's market position

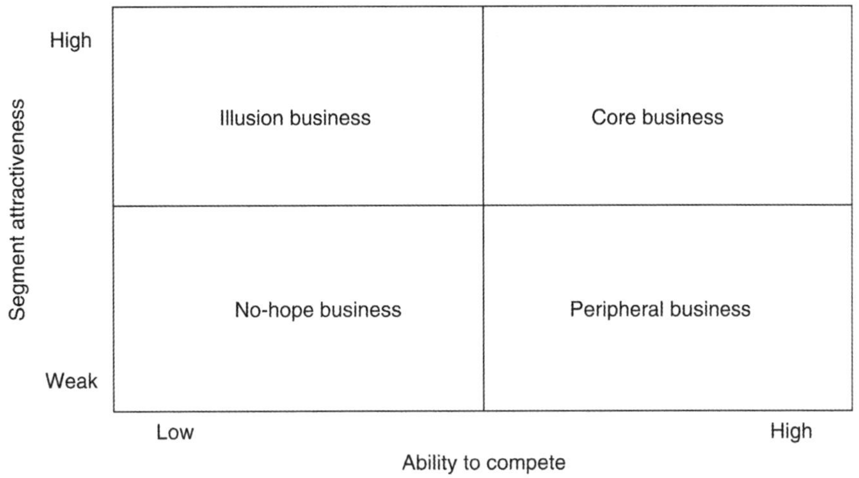

Figure 11.3 Segmenting the target's business streams

demonstrates. Companies or products that have a strong market position, even though they may not be the market leader, and that have a distinctive competitive advantage, can have a healthy cash flow and good profitability. These are sometimes referred to as 'cash dogs'. Similarly Hamermesch[3] maintains that many businesses that are classified as cash cows should be managed for innovation and growth, especially if the industry is dynamic or volatile or can be made so.

Looking only at portfolio positions may also ignore crucial issues of interdependence and the synergy benefits of having a number of different but related businesses in a portfolio. Just like Ansoff's matrix, the basic BCG growth share matrix has been developed over the years, most notably by Shell and GE. Figure 11.5 shows the directional policy matrix developed by Shell.

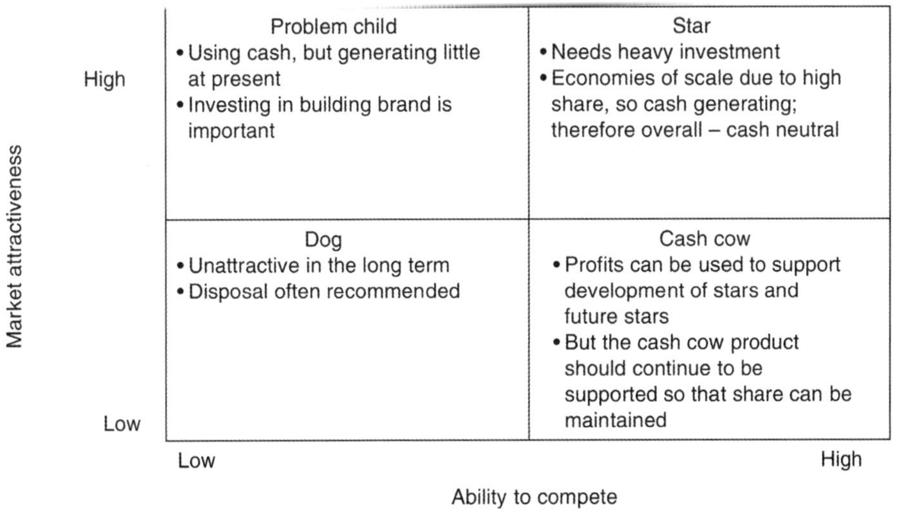

Figure 11.4 The growth share matrix

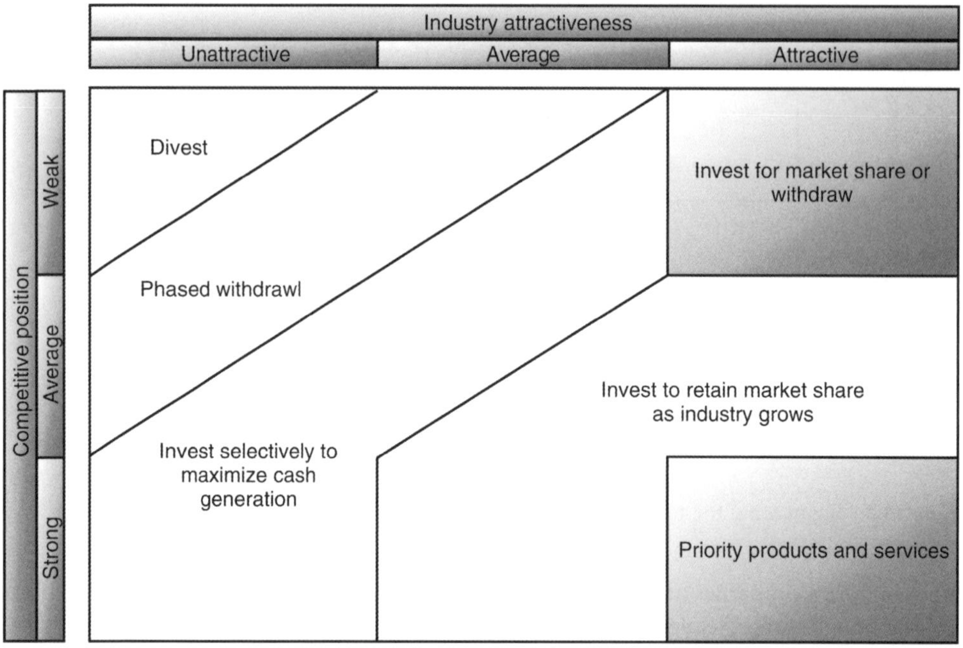

Figure 11.5 Directional policy matrix developed by Shell

As can be seen, the Shell model goes to a finer level of detail than the original BCG model:

- Priority products, in the bottom right-hand corner, are those that score highly on both axes. As a result they should receive priority for development.
- Products bordering on the priority box should receive the appropriate level of investment to ensure that share is maintained and all the advantages of market growth are captured.
- Products with a weak competitive position in an attractive industry are placed in the top right of the matrix. These are evaluated according to their potential to establish and sustain real competitive advantage.
- Products across the middle diagonal should receive custodial treatment.
- Currently profitable products with little future potential should be withdrawn gradually.
- Products for divestment, in the top left-hand of the matrix, will most likely be losing money.

At this stage, we have segmented the target's business, we understand segment growth rates, competitive forces and such and we understand customer purchasing behaviour and the target's ability to compete in each segment. Now is the time to turn this into numbers, which inevitably involves the use of spreadsheets. Time pressures mean it is essential for the CDD team to adhere to at least the basic spreadsheet disciplines.

Spreadsheet modelling

The spreadsheet is an indispensable tool, but there is a lot more to spreadsheet modelling than opening Microsoft Excel® and hoping for the best. Unfortunately, most modellers have no formal training in good modelling techniques and most organizations do not have even rudimentary internal standards. It will not surprise many to learn that the standard programme management manuals used in 'grown-up' IT stand waist high when stacked on top of each other. Spreadsheet modelling neither needs nor deserves anything quite so outrageous, but it does require more discipline than it is usually given because, with a bit more discipline, spreadsheets can achieve so much more.

A best practice model is:

- easy to use, so that it can be used for analysis and not just as a means of 'getting the answer';
- focused on the important issues, so you do not waste your time in unnecessary development;
- easy to understand both by you and your colleagues;
- reliable.

A spreadsheet goes through a number of stages in its development.

The typical design stages for a spreadsheet are as follows:

1 Scope
2 Specify
3 Design
4 Build
5 Test
6 Use.

SCOPE

This is frequently an informal stage where you assess the nature, scale and complexity of the model required. During the scope stage you should:

- state what the model will do;
- be clear on what it will not do;
- understand in outline how the model will work;
- decide what needs to be included in the model;
- decide on the level of detail required in the input and output;
- work out where the data is going to come from.

SPECIFY

This stage is frequently glossed over in our quest 'to get on with it'. At this stage, you should define the logic of the model in sufficient detail to provide an unambiguous statement of how the results will be calculated. The discipline of producing a model specification ensures that you produce a definitive statement of what the model should do and how it will do it. It allows you to tackle the most difficult problems associated with the model before you have started to build it.

Failure to write a model specification leads to difficulties later on. An inadequate specification leads to:

- more time being spent building the model, because the issues that could have been resolved during the specification come back to haunt you;
- numerous late changes to the model logic – perhaps the greatest single cause of errors in completed models;
- vague objectives: it is easy to start with a small model that aims to solve one problem – and end up with a large model that solves all sorts of other problems, and solves them badly.

The process of model specification

Logically, all spreadsheet models should flow from inputs through calculations to the model results. As shown in Figure 11.6, the process of model specification should run the other way around, because it is model results that are most important and these should determine the structure of the model.

Try to avoid letting the availability of input data determine the output that you produce. The model objectives should drive the results required, the results should drive the calculations and the calculations should drive the required inputs. Do not allow the fact that relevant data is available to create additional complexity in the model that is not really required.

Defining model outputs

The first stage in the model specification process is to refine the broad output requirements that were defined from the scope stage into defined outputs that the model will produce.

Defining calculations: Techniques for model specification

Because the calculation rules that define the workings of a model can be difficult when your understanding of the problem to be modelled is vague, the process of defining the model

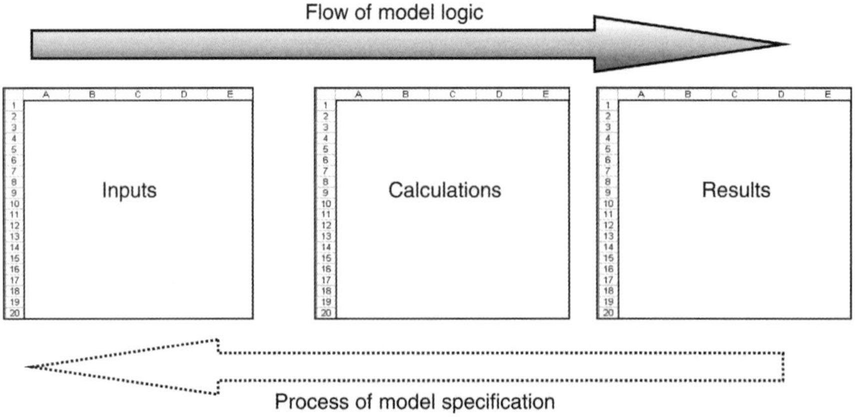

Figure 11.6 The process of model specification
Source: Institute of Chartered Accountants

specification is usually iterative. More than one attempt is required before you get it right. There are three techniques for developing a model specification:

- Bubble diagrams
- Calculation tables
- Prototype models.

BUBBLE DIAGRAMS

A bubble diagram, as in Figure 11.7, shows the logical flow of the model. It indicates the required inputs and which calculations are required for each output from the model.

Bubble diagrams are fairly quick and easy to produce and can be updated as your thinking develops. Finished bubble diagrams make an excellent method of communication to explain the overall structure of a model. They can be constructed at a variety of levels, depending on the detail required. For example, a high-level bubble diagram can be used for the overall structure of a model together with more detailed diagrams for particular parts of the model.

CALCULATION TABLES

A calculation table is a detailed statement of the inputs and calculations in a model. It documents unambiguously the detail of how the model will work.

It should be possible to read the calculations from top to bottom down the page and understand the logic of the model. Therefore, all calculation rules should refer to reference numbers further up the table. This practice enforces a 'top to bottom' structure for the final spreadsheet model, which is good design practice.

Calculation tables are the most rigorous way of defining how the model will work. They are particularly useful when the relationships to be defined are complex or unusual. They are, however, time consuming to produce.

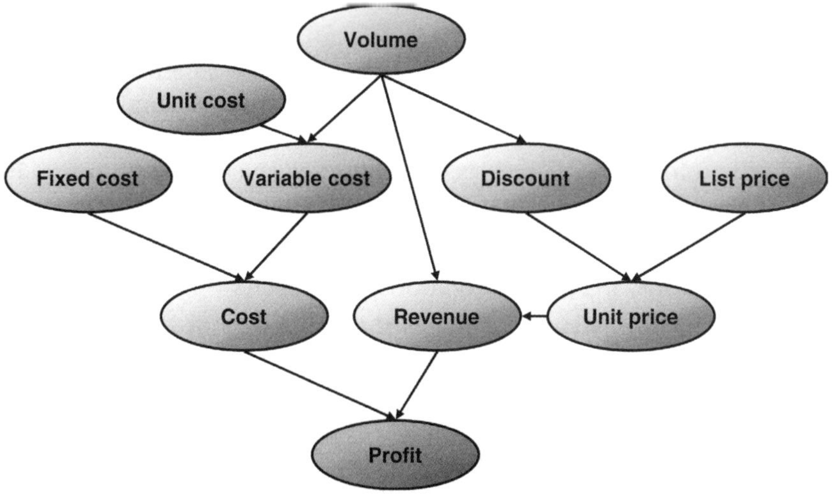

Figure 11.7 A bubble diagram
Source: Institute of Chartered Accountants

PROTOTYPE MODELS

A prototype model is an experimental model used to clarify calculation definitions prior to the development of the eventual model. As a technique for developing the model specification, it is most appropriate when understanding of the problem is vague and therefore a 'try it and see' approach is needed.

Although it is a useful technique, there are some risks associated with an over-reliance on prototyping. For example, developed too far, a prototype model can have all of the problems of bad layout, lack of clarity and errors in formulae that are typically associated with skipping the preparatory stages of the modelling life cycle and diving straight into the build stage.

DESIGN

The design stage involves producing the most effective structure for the model. By following some simple guidelines, it is possible to make spreadsheet models easier to use and less error prone. Careful design means you are less likely to make errors while using the model and more likely to spot the mistakes you do make, and a well-designed spreadsheet is easier for another person to pick up. The are 10 golden rules of spreadsheet design:

- Always have one source, and only one source, of data in the spreadsheet.
- Separate assumptions, inputs, calculations and results.
- Use one formula per row or column.
- Design spreadsheets to read like a book.
- Use multiple worksheets.
- Use each column for the same purpose throughout the model.
- Use nominal prices.
- Always have a units column.
- Build checks into the model.
- Avoid hard coding constants and assumptions into formulae.

One source of data

Because numbers change as the investigation goes on and because the same numbers are used for a number of different purposes, you should input raw data only once and read it across to where it is used. Then, if a number changes, you need only change it once. You do not have to go hunting round a complex spreadsheet and change it everywhere it is used. You can also sleep easy knowing that the competitor turnover figure you have used to calculate market share is the same as the one you have used in your market size calculations.

Separate assumptions, inputs, calculations and results

Assumptions, inputs, calculations and results should be separated. Keeping assumptions together in a separate part of the model means that they are easy to find and change when, for example, generating scenarios. Separating inputs helps to avoid confusion in using and maintaining models. It reduces the risk that parts of the input data are overlooked or that calculations are overtyped with input figures. Inputs should be separated physically on the sheet, but can also be separated by clear labelling and colouring of the spreadsheet. Figure 11.8 shows two different ways of keeping these four separate.

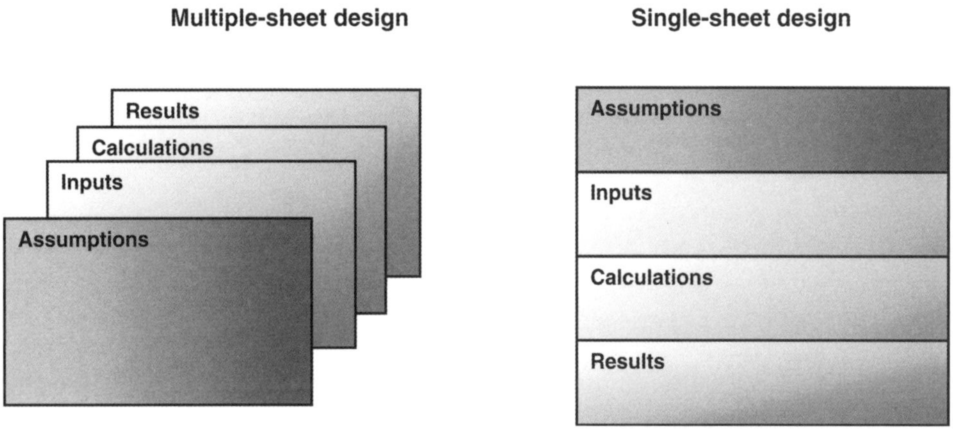

Figure 11.8 Two ways of separating assumptions, input, calculations and results
Source: Institute of Chartered Accountants

An exception to this rule is when calculations are used to make providing inputs easier. For example, a checksum on a row of input values is more usefully placed in the input section of the spreadsheet than anywhere else.

Use one formula per row or column

As far as possible, formulae should be written so that a single formula can be copied across the entire row of calculations, or down the entire column, because:

- it speeds up model development because every formula can be written in a single column, then copied;
- it is more reliable – every time you change a formula in a cell you know that it should be copied across the rest of the row. One of the most common causes of errors in formulae is when a change is made, but old versions of the formula are left lurking unseen somewhere in a row.

Producing a design with only one formula per row requires careful thought but the benefits of the design far outweigh the extra work required. However, beware: not all calculation rules are automatically the same for each time period. For example, in a quarterly model some costs may be calculated only once a year. This problem can be solved using an IF statement.

Another inconvenience when using a single formula per row is trying to include sub-totals, or other intermediate calculations. This is commonly approached as in the top half of Figure 11.9 where the intermediate totals are placed next to the inputs. A much better design is to produce two separate blocks of calculation, as shown in the bottom table in Figure 11.9.

Design spreadsheets to read like a book

A well-designed spreadsheet can be read like a book: from front to back, top to bottom and left to right. This makes the spreadsheet easier to understand and reduces the risk of introducing circular references.

Poor design

	A	B	C	D	E	F	G	H
1			1999	% of sales	2000	% of sales	2001	% of sales
2		Sales	100	100%	120	100%	115	100%
3		Cost of sales	60	60%	65	54%	65	57%
4		Profit	40	40%	55	46%	50	43%

Better design

	A	B	C	D	E
1		Units	1999	2000	2001
2	Sales	£	100	120	115
3	Cost of sales	£	65	65	65
4	Profit	£	40	55	50
5					
6	As a percentage of sales				
7	Cost of sales	%	60%	54%	57%
8	Profit	%	40%	48%	43%
9					

Figure 11.9 Including intermediate totals

Use multiple worksheets

Multiple worksheets are best for two reasons. They allow easy expansion and make life much easier when modelling 'repeatable blocks'. Repeatable blocks occur when a model contains sections that can usefully be repeated, such as a model of a company with a number of similar business units. The best way to present them in a spreadsheet is to use one worksheet for each repeatable block.

When the models for a number of subsidiaries in a business are similar, but not quite the same, it is still a good idea to use separate worksheets for each subsidiary. If some subsidiaries require more detail, the best thing is to develop a worksheet for the most complex example and then blank out the relevant sections for other subsidiaries. Just blank them out, do not delete any rows or columns because then the common elements on the different worksheets can still be edited together.

Use each column for the same purpose throughout the model

However many worksheets you use, it is good practice to always use the same layout for all columns on all worksheets. For a discounted cash flow (DCF) model, an example column layout might be:

- Column A and B: labels
- Column C: units
- Column E: first time period
- Columns F: onwards, subsequent time periods.

Use nominal prices

Nominal prices are the ones with inflation in them. Using nominal prices is more accurate for any calculation involving monetary values over more than one time period. You should always use nominal prices for calculations of debt and interest, depreciation, tax, stock and other assets and liabilities on a balance sheet. However, real prices can be useful for input assumptions or for some results. So, the steps to go through are:

1 Inputs, often in real prices
2 Conversion of any inputs into nominal prices
3 All required calculations carried out in nominal prices
4 Conversion of results back to real prices, if required
5 Presentation of results.

To make conversion between real and nominal prices easy, it is a good idea to place the calculation of a retail price (RPI) index in the assumptions section.

Always have a units column

A units column on every worksheet will tell you what is expected in each and every input cell and what is being presented in calculations. It is particularly useful when different units are being used in different places, for example, if the price per widget is input in dollars, but the annual turnover is presented in millions.

If the model uses a mixture of real and nominal monetary values, make sure the units column always specifies which is required. To avoid confusion, always make it clear in prices of which year real inputs are required.

Build checks into the model

Testing should be built into model through the use of check totals. When modelling company accounts, it should be compulsory for the cash flow statement to be calculated from the P&L (profit and loss) and balance sheet (rather than input) and the resulting cash balance input into the balance sheet. Then, if the balance sheet balances, you know all the signs are the right way round and that you have not omitted anything.

Avoid hard coding constants and assumptions into formulae

Avoid using hard-coded numbers in the definition of a formula. For example, the formula:

$$\text{Sales price including VAT} = \text{Sales price excluding VAT} \times 1.175$$

assumes that the VAT (value-added tax) rate is 17.5 per cent. This works fine until the VAT rate changes.

To avoid having to search through every formula in the model for calculations that assume the VAT rate, set up an input cell for the VAT rate and refer to that instead. For a single cell of this sort, it is useful to create a range name, say 'VAT rate', so instead of typing the constant you use the formula:

$$\text{Sales price including VAT} = \text{Sales price excluding VAT} \times (1 + \text{VAT rate})$$

If there is any change to the input assumption, or you want to run a sensitivity test, the constant can be changed throughout the model instantly. Even if the constant never changes, the new formula is much simpler to read and understand.

Consolidating and connecting worksheets

There are three common methods for consolidating data or connecting worksheets:

- Multiple sheets within a single spreadsheet
- Separate spreadsheets with external links between them
- Macros.

MULTIPLE SHEETS WITHIN A SINGLE SPREADSHEET

Imagine you are consolidating the results of market size calculations from nine European countries. Probably the most obvious consolidation method is to have one worksheet per country on nine worksheets and a front consolidation sheet that contains formulae to sum through the other nine sheets and calculate the totals. The advantages of this method are that:

- it is easy to understand, with all of the calculations and data visible;
- it is simple to build;
- inserting an additional country will be fairly easy provided that you do not want to insert the country at the beginning or the end.

However, by using this method you will create quite a large spreadsheet, especially if there is a large quantity of information to consolidate for each country. For presentation purposes, you may also need new rows or columns to introduce the highlights from, or summaries of, the inputs from each country into the consolidation sheet.

SEPARATE SPREADSHEETS WITH EXTERNAL LINKS BETWEEN THEM

This method is best when there is a lot of information per country. This might be the case with a detailed DCF model for a company with a large number of subsidiaries where each subsidiary has been modelled individually. For anything less detailed, it is not worth the effort, as most PCs now have the capacity to cope with large spreadsheets.

With externally linked spreadsheets, you have one spreadsheet for each country and a tenth for consolidation. Each formula in the consolidation spreadsheet contains a reference to each country's separate spreadsheet. A typical formula might look something like:

='C:\Countries\[Austria.XLS]Results'!$C$3 + 'C:\Countries\[Belgium.Xls]
Results'!$C$3 + 'C:\Countries\[France.Xls]Results'!$C$3 + . . . (six more countries)

The advantages of this method are that:

- it is reasonably easy to understand;
- none of the spreadsheets will be particularly large;
- it provides a method of extracting values from a number of separate spreadsheets.

The disadvantages are that:

- when a large number of files are involved, the formulae become long and unwieldy;
- it is awkward and time consuming to add an extra country;

- it is easy to introduce errors by making changes to the individual country files and failing to update the links;
- it is likely to be slow to update the links.

MACROS

The third method is to use macros to copy and consolidate the individual countries' spreadsheets automatically. The consolidation model contains a list of all the files for individual countries. A macro will then go through the list of files, extract the data for that country and add it to the consolidation table.

The advantages of this method are that:

- the consolidation model is small and will run quickly;
- if the macro is well written, the model is easy to use;
- by leaving room for expansion on the list of files, adding an extra country is easy.

The disadvantages are that:

- writing the model will require a detailed understanding of programming macros;
- the calculation method is not transparent, so you have to be confident that the macro contains no errors.

Finally, before we move onto the build phase of modelling, always include a documentation sheet so that any other users know how the model is structured, who developed it and which version they are using.

BUILD

The build stage is where we get stuck into the actual building of the model. This is where we normally start, with little or not attention paid to the pre-build stages outlined above. It is always tempting to start coding the model too soon, especially when you are under pressure to produce results from the model quickly. It may seem like a good idea to omit the planning stages but do not be fooled. As time effective as it may seem, it leads to:

- a model that is more complex than required;
- a model that takes longer to build;
- assumptions being made that were not part of the original brief;
- a lack of common understanding about what the model is doing.

Taking time to understand the problem and how you are going to solve it makes building the model quicker and easier, less prone to errors and less likely to have to be reworked. There are four rules to keep in mind:

- keep formulae simple;
- use named cells and ranges;
- build in error traps;
- use headers and footers.

Keep formulae simple

To make your spreadsheet as easy to understand as possible, keep the formulae simple. Just as a clearer writing style can be achieved by breaking up long sentences, a clearer model can be achieved by breaking up a long formulae.

Use named cells and ranges

Allocating meaningful range names to areas or cells within a spreadsheet can speed up the development process, make the model easier to understand and reduce the risk of errors due to referring to the wrong cell.

Build in error traps

As mentioned twice already (which is a good indication of its importance especially in complex models), include checks for errors in a model. These can be set up either to check for errors in the input data provided or for errors in the model formulae.

Use headers and footers

Putting key information onto report headers and footers makes it much easier to keep track of different model runs. Without them, it is easy to mix up out-of-date versions of model output with the correct version. Include the following in the header or footer:

- The model file name and/or the model name and version number
- The date and time of printing.

TEST

To test a model is to root out errors and inconsistencies and to increase confidence in the results that the model produces. While it is never possible to test a complex model to the extent that you can guarantee it to be error free, this stage does provide the confidence that the model is producing reliable results. As already noted, testing should be built into model through the use of check totals.

Why test?

If testing is skipped or done poorly, errors are likely to be discovered after the model has been put into use. If there is an a error in the model, you can bet it will be spotted by someone not as close to the numbers as you, most likely at the presentation stage of your CDD. Errors at this stage are not a good idea as they can undermine the credibility of the model, its developer and the rest of the CDD report.

Who should test?

The objective of testing a model is to demonstrate that the model does not work as intended, not that it works correctly. It is impossible for model builders to be sufficiently critical of their own work. As a result, testing should always be carried out by an independent third party. Table 11.4 summarizes the most common tests.

Common errors

The most common errors in spreadsheets are:

- not copying formulae;
- using the wrong references;

Table 11.4 The most common types of spreadsheet test

Type of test	*Questions to ask*
Specification test	Does the model specification make the agreed logical assumptions about the business problem?
Formulae test	Has the model specification been appropriately coded in the model?
	Have formulae been copied appropriately across rows or down columns?
Numeric tests	Can you reproduce some part of the model results independently from the model itself?
	Is it possible to reconcile the results with another source, such as a previous model?
	What are the most surprising conclusions of the model results?
Robustness tests	Does the model work on all of the computers where it will be used?
	How does the model cope with a wide range of differing input values?
Macro tests	Can the macros cope with all of the situations that might arise?

- using the wrong range in @SUM;
- temporary fixes left in the model;
- using relative instead of absolute references (or vice-versa);
- mixing up units;
- misusing functions.

NOT COPYING FORMULAE

There is not much more to be said. Sticking to the 10 golden rules of spreadsheet design above will help.

USING THE WRONG REFERENCES

Nearly every formula in a spreadsheet refers back to another input or calculation. With the quantity of references in any large spreadsheet, it is inevitable that you will make mistakes and refer to the wrong cell. Sometimes, the resulting formula will produce meaningless results making it easy to spot with some simple numerical testing. If you are unlucky, the error in the result will be more subtle. The only way to check for wrong references with any confidence is to go through a formula map, checking every unique formula. In Excel, checking references is made easier if you use the auditing toolbar, which allows you to trace the relevant cells graphically.

USING THE WRONG RANGE IN A 'SUM'

A similar mistake is to include the wrong cell reference in a SUM formula. It is particularly easy to introduce this error when you insert an extra row in a block of cells that are being summed. If you insert a row in the middle of the block, the formula will automatically adjust to include the extra row, but if you insert a row immediately above or below the block the new row will be omitted from the formula.

You can build internal checks of the SUMs in a spreadsheet by using cross-casting. Cross-casting is the process of checking that the totals in the rows and columns of a spreadsheet are consistent.

TEMPORARY FIXES LEFT IN THE MODEL

Sometimes in model building you will insert formulae as part of the build process. Do not forget to take them out and replace with the developed formulae if necessary.

USING RELATIVE INSTEAD OF ABSOLUTE REFERENCES (OR VICE-VERSA)

Another commonly found error is caused by confusion between relative and absolute references. Remember that a cell reference in a formula of the form '=D4' will change if you copy the formula across the row to E4, F4 and so on. Copied down a column it will change to D5, D6, and so on. If you use the reference '=$D$4', it will not change when copied across or down. You can also use semi-absolute references of the form $D4 or D$4.

The most common mistake is to use a relative reference instead of an absolute one, such as when calculating percentages row by row with the total in a single cell used as the denominator. This is quite easy to spot numerically, but if you use an absolute reference in place of a relative one, it can be much more difficult to spot.

MIXING UP UNITS

Mixing up the appropriate units for the elements in a calculation is another frequently occurring problem. Especially common is confusion between the order of magnitude for inputs, such as £s versus £000s.

MISUSING FUNCTIONS

Certain functions are frequently used incorrectly. In financial models, the most commonly misunderstood is the NPV function, used to calculate net present values. The NPV function takes the form =NPV (rate, value1, value2, ...) where rate is an appropriate discount rate and value1, value2, and so on, are a stream of cash flows to be discounted. One common error with the NPV function is using an inappropriate discount rate, especially when the model contains calculations in a mixture of real and nominal prices.

Another common mistake concerns the timing of cash flows. By default, the NPV function assumes that all cash flows occur at the end of the time period you are considering. It is more realistic to assume that cash flows occur in the middle of each time period. For a model based on annual time periods, using a discount rate of 10 per cent and an end year rather than a mid year assumption decreases the present value calculated by 5 per cent.

You can work around these problems by making an appropriate adjustment to the NPV function. Alternatively, it is often easier to calculate present values from first principle and use the Excel add-in function XNPV, which allows you to explicitly state the dates on which cash flows occur.

Other functions that often cause errors are:

- lookup and reference functions, such as VLOOKUP, HLOOKUP, INDEX and MATCH;
- complicated IF statements, especially when the model developer creates over-complex formulae by nesting a series of IF statements.

These functions are often very useful, but make sure that you understand exactly how they work before using them in your model. By making the formulae in your model easy to understand, you reduce the risk of introducing errors and increase the chances that a tester will find your mistakes.

USE

Getting the best out of your spreadsheet is about more than getting the sums right. A great spreadsheet is also about:

- presenting useful information to help make decisions, not just printing out the numbers;
- presenting sensitivities and scenarios to understand the important drivers in the business;
- controlling the evolution of the model as it develops and further changes are required.

Presenting useful information

Good presentation leads not just to easier communication of the results, but also improves the perception of the quality of the underlying model.

In general you should try to do the following:

- Establish a standard look for all reports from a model (or family of models), so that the reader immediately knows the source of any new reports. It also saves you time when developing additional reports.
- Group lines into blocks of about five rows, so that the results can be understood in digestible blocks.
- Use one, or at most two, typefaces. Achieve emphasis with sparing use of bold, italic or underlined text,
- Draw boxes around cells to visually separate different results and remember that shaded cells can become illegible if they are photocopied or faxed.

Spreadsheet models are powerful tools for analysis. A successfully developed model can analyse a variety of alternative situations and inform the decision-making process. Using a model to produce useful information requires skill. Section B.3 in Appendix B sets out in detail how best to present numbers and graphs.

DATA TABLES

One of the most powerful ways that a model can be used to improve understanding of a problem is by illustrating the sensitivity of the results to varying some of the key input assumptions. It is very easy to understand how your input assumptions affect the results by using data tables.

Data tables are quick and easy to draw up and can be produced in one or two dimensions to show the effect on the key results of varying one or two of your input assumptions, as illustrated in Tables 11.5 and 11.6.

Table 11.5 Example of a one-dimensional data table

Sales growth (%)	*NPV (£ millions)*	*Cash positive (year)*	*Equity funding (£ millions)*	*Year 3 value (£ millions)*
2	278.9	2010	111.6	358.6
5	287.1	2009	114.9	369.2
7	292.6	2008	117.0	376.3
9	298.1	2007	119.2	383.2

Table 11.6 Example of a two-dimensional data table

NPV (£ millions)		*Discount rate*	
Sales growth (%)	5%	7.5%	10%
2	278.9	201.6	160.1
5	287.2	207.5	164.8
7	292.6	211.4	167.9
9	298.1	215.4	171.1

CONTROLLING THE EVOLUTION OF THE MODEL

As your understanding of the target business develops the model will usually need to change. If you fail to keep track of changing model versions, it is easy to mix up old and new models. As a result, you can present results that do not include the latest corrections to the model or waste time typing the latest input assumptions into an out-of-date version of the model.

Valuation

Acquisitions create value when the value of the businesses combined is greater than the sum of their stand-alone values. The difference between the value of the combined businesses and the value of the sum of the parts is the value of the synergies as shown in Figure 11.10.

Where there are synergies, the target is worth more to the acquirer than it is to the seller, but because sellers know this, you are almost certainly going to have to pay a premium for the control of a company.

The first thing to remember is that deal pricing is not an exact science. There are many methods of pricing a business – none are particularly right and none wrong. Where you

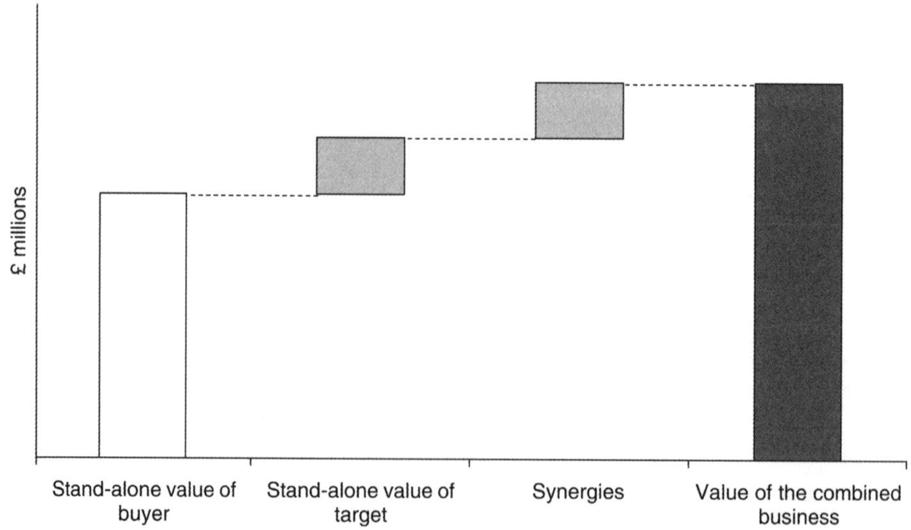

Figure 11.10 Synergies in M&A

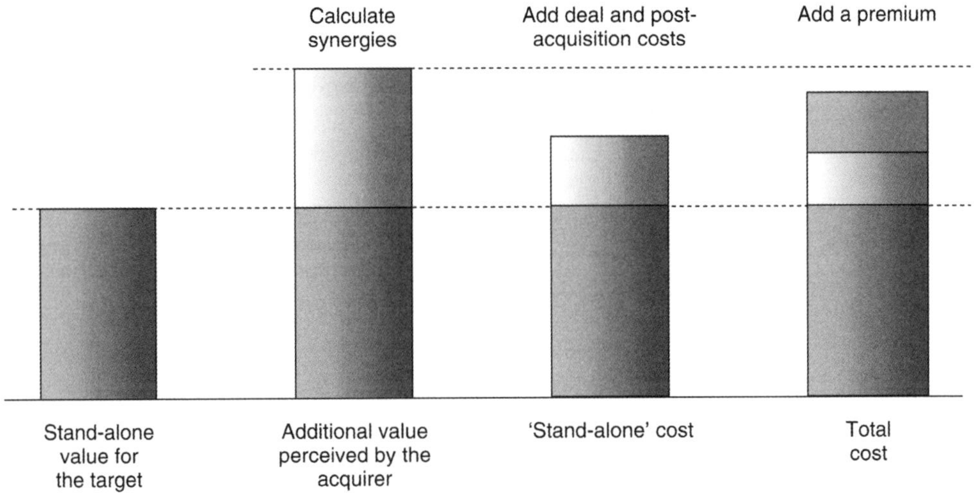

Figure 11.11 The valuation process

come from – that is, whether you are a acquirer or a seller – is certainly going to shape your perspective for a start. Also timing and negotiating tactics play an enormous role. In one deal that spanned the 1987 stock market crash, the parties had agreed on a price of $35 per share in September 1987. The acquirer subsequently pulled the deal and reopened discussions the following February. By then the management had worked out that they were the only game in town, had hired a Wall St Investment Bank and given themselves golden parachutes. Result? $43 per share. What had changed? Nothing. Intrinsically the business was still worth the same.

Figure 11.11 is very simple but a good way of thinking through the strategic aspects of deal pricing.

The stand-alone value of the target sets the lower price limit. No seller in their right mind should accept less than this, although it does happen a lot, as the size of the private equity industry around the world testifies. The stand-alone value of the target plus synergies sets the upper negotiating limit. No acquirer in their right mind should pay more than the maximum a business is worth, although it does happen a lot, otherwise the failure rate in acquisitions would not be between the 50 and 75 per cent. In addition to paying a premium above the stand-alone value of the target, you will also have deal costs. Your job as a negotiator is to make sure that the synergies are big enough to more than cover the costs of the transaction.

The first task is to assess the value of the business as a stand-alone entity. Valuation is an art, but one valuation method will almost certainly be a DCF, because it calculates cash flow and the value of any business is determined by the cash inflows and outflows, discounted at an appropriate interest rate, that can be expected to occur during the remaining life of the asset. Common yardsticks such as price earnings ratios have nothing to do with valuation. One of the key outputs from CDD should be the construction of a financial model of the business in question. This will contain forecasts of the operating and financial performance given certain assumptions.

To some DCF stands for Deceit by Computer Forecast. While it is true that values can be moved by many millions with a simple change of assumptions, this is by far and away the

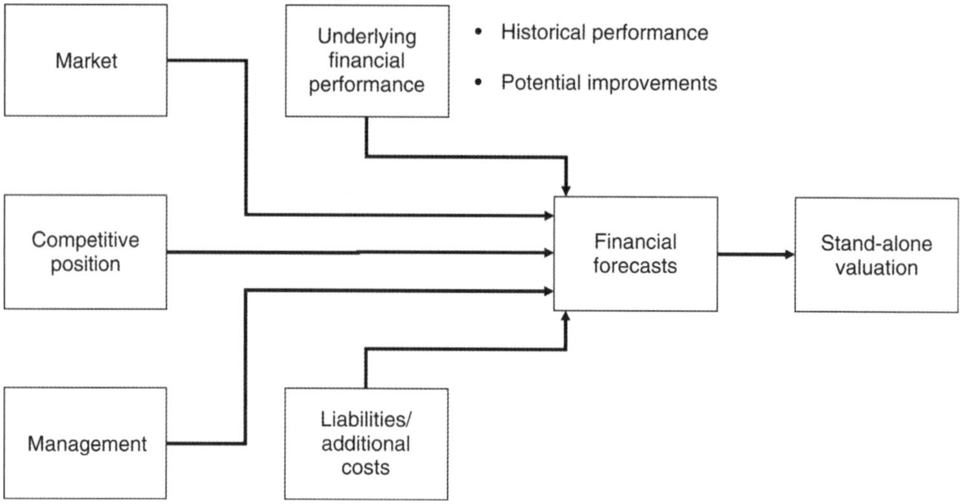

Figure 11.12 Stand-alone target assessment

best means of valuation there is and because doing a DCF means assessing the future cash flow of the business, it forces acquirers to think in a systematic way about the drivers of the business. This in turn is done by analysing the state of the market, the company's position within it, sales and margin history, future prospects and taking a view on liabilities. Figure 11.12 shows this schematically.

Figure 11.13 shows how the outputs of CDD link into the financials.

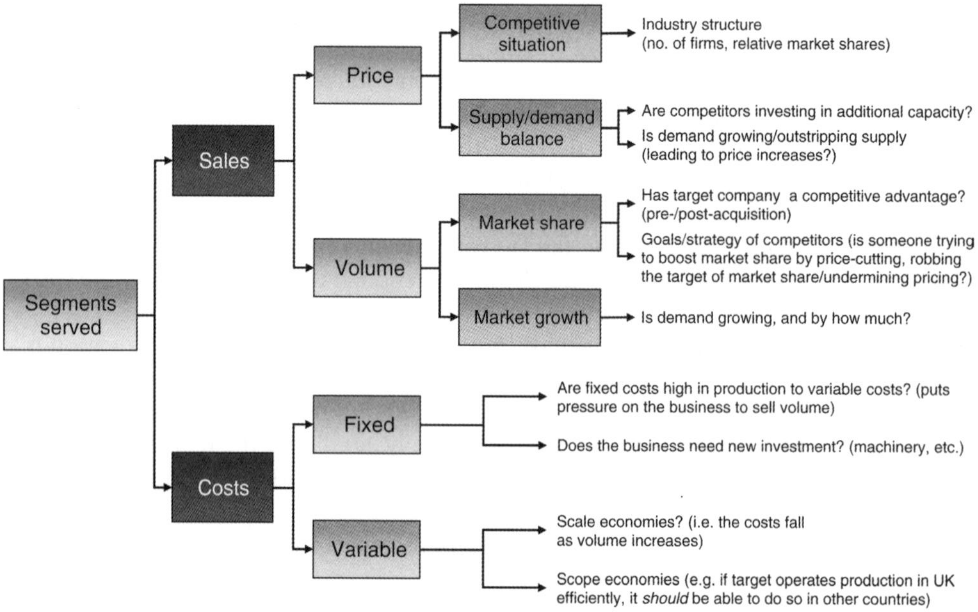

Figure 11.13 CDD and financial analysis

Assessing synergies

Next comes working out where the synergy benefits are going to come from. Stripped down to the bare essentials, synergies come from:

- Lower costs
- Higher sales.

Companies are bought either because they are cheap compared with their potential or because of the synergies that are available by combining the acquired company with another one. Where an acquisition is being made for the synergies, CDD will need to comment on their achievability either directly, or indirectly, via comments on a business plan. The major sources of synergy are:

- Manufacturing, administrative and other operational synergies
- Marketing, sales and distribution synergies, such as overcoming buyer power in distribution, economies of scale in the sales force and advertising, and through cross selling
- Research development and regulatory synergies
- Management, cultural and human synergies.

The importance of each of these will vary with the industry and their realization will depend as much on the preparatory phase of the acquisition as it does on the integration phase.

Financial acquirers

If CDD is being undertaken for a financial acquirer, there will be no synergies. Financial acquirers make their money when they sell the businesses in which they have invested. As we saw in Chapter 1, typically private equity houses want to make a minimum IRR on their investments of 25 per cent on exit. This is roughly equivalent to doubling their money over 3 years. These days they do not play the arbitrage game of investing in unfashionable sectors on low multiples and selling at a higher multiple. We saw in Chapter 1, Figure 1.1, how venture capitalists make their returns. Taking Figure 1.1 into account, a target must add roughly 14 per cent to sales to get to the 25 per cent IRR.

Whether you are a corporate or financial acquirer, if you can increase revenues you are in great shape. What drives revenue is innovation, so if you get synergies through cost savings, they should not be seen as an end in themselves but as a pot of money that can be invested in innovation. Cost reduction should not be the sole goal. Cost savings are one-off benefits, whereas sales gains come from strategic change and therefore last for a very long time. In fact, it could be argued that acquisitions fail for just one reason – failing to capture additional sales. If you follow this logic, as acquisitions are a tool of strategy, the test for whether or not an acquisition is a good idea is its, or the merged entity's, ability to grow. It is essential, therefore, to use CDD to prepare a detailed quantification of synergies. Two final points on Figure 11.11. Do not forget:

- The deal and integration costs: these are often underestimated and indeed often forgotten, but can be very large indeed. BP, for example, spent over £100 million in advisors' fees in the AMOCO deal. After the deal is done, all sorts of additional costs start to appear: the new computer system, the additional costs of coping with one more

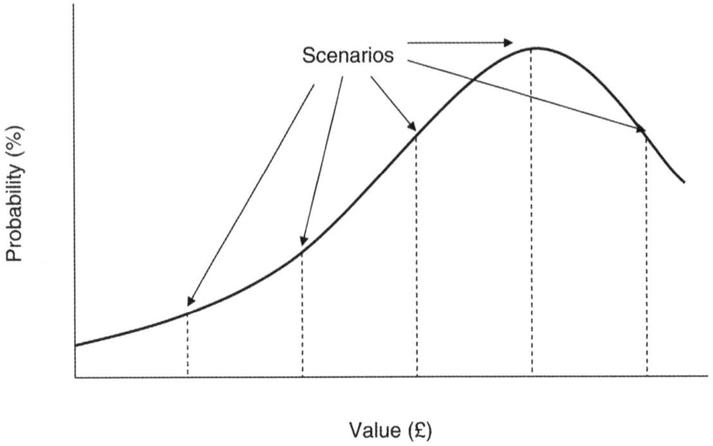

Figure 11.14 A value probability distribution

subsidiaries, the cost of new management because the old lot could not deliver what was expected of them and so on.
- To factor in the premium you are a going to have to pay.

Scenario analysis

DCF relies on forecasts, often as far as 10 years out. The only thing you know for certain about any forecasts you construct is that they will be wrong. Scenario analysis is a means of working out the range within which sales and profits might lie. It involves Identifying and quantifying events that may favourably or unfavourably impact the target's value and assigning a probability to each. As more and more scenario values are calculated, a value probability distribution can be constructed, as shown in Figure 11.14.

The benefit of financial modelling for DCF calculations and the use of scenarios is two fold:

- The seller's aspirations can be modelled. If the seller wants £X million, what has to be true in terms of synergies for the business to be worth this and what do we think are the chances of achieving them?
- The likely walk-away price of other bidders can be estimated.

Sensitivity analyses should not be limited to 'base', 'best', and 'worst' case scenarios. Such simplistic scenarios involve guessing point estimates for key assumptions. A better technique for managing uncertainty is to use range estimates, rather than point estimates, for input assumptions. This avoids having to get people to agree on point estimates, which is notoriously difficult to do, but also allows you to start thinking about presenting forecasts as probability distributions.

GAP ANALYSIS

Financial projections are always difficult to evaluate. Most people are over-optimistic about the degree to which they can control events stretching into the future. For example, something like 80 per cent of entrepreneurs think that the success of their ventures is

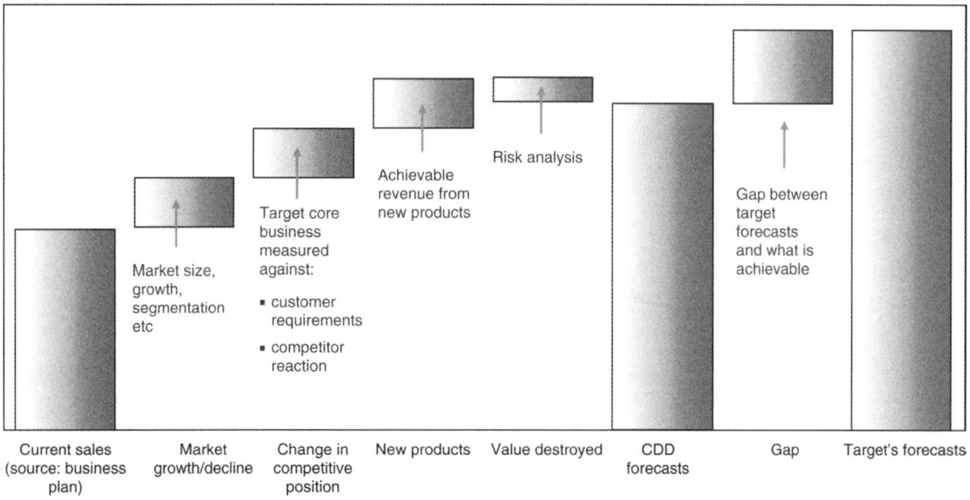

Figure 11.15 CDD versus the business plan

guaranteed, whereas the actual success rate for new ventures is 35 per cent. In an acquisition, the difficulties are compounded because deal sponsors are always doubly over-optimistic.

Nonetheless, it is the job of CDD to provide an assessment of a target company's business plan. The technique is to disaggregate the plan's various elements and plot any gaps between it and the CDD findings. Figure 11.15 shows one way of presenting it.

Filling the gaps

Filling the financial gaps is all about filling gaps in capabilities and resources. CDD must, therefore, come to a conclusion on whether or not the acquired company has the necessary capabilities and resources. Thus, once the analysis has evaluated the target's market and competitive positions, the next step is to compare its desired relative position with its actual position, then determine whether resource and capability gaps can be filled and, if so, how and at what cost. When looking, for example, at repositioning a target, it makes sense to start by building on existing strengths. Once you look at exploiting key strengths more effectively, critical gaps in certain complementary resources and capabilities may soon become apparent. But do not be naïve about the time and effort that may be needed to fill any gaps. Additional resources will either have to be purchased or, if they are not transferable, developed internally. Developing resources is a difficult, long-term task and target companies with highly developed capabilities will find change difficult. Studies of new product development, for example, show that although core capabilities are essential they can also be a drag on innovation because they inhibit companies' ability to access and develop new capabilities. Why do you think the most successful firms in most new industries tend to be start-ups?

In addition to missing capabilities and resources, a big issue here is risk. Risk in a business plan is directly related to the extent to which future products and markets are related to existing ones. Figure 11.16 shows a second way of presenting any gaps in the business plan. This presentation puts the issue of risk centre stage.

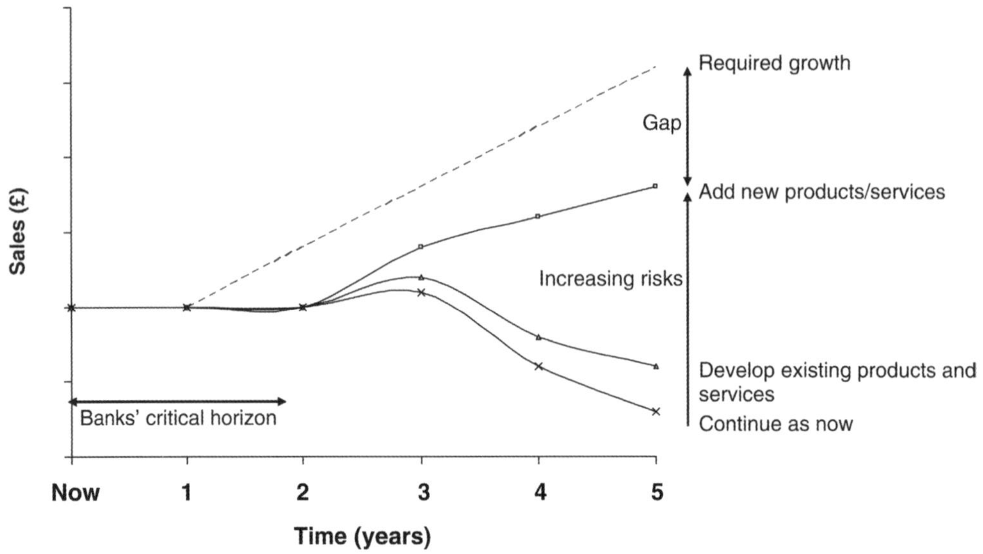

Figure 11.16 Gap analysis highlighting risk factors

THE ANSOFF MATRIX

Organizing thoughts around how the gap may be filled could start with an Ansoff Matrix,[4] as shown in Figure 11.17. As we saw in Figure 9.1 (see Chapter 9), the Ansoff Matrix picks up this idea of risk increasing the more the future depends on quadrants away from existing products and markets.

Ansoff classifies growth plans according to which of four boxes they lie in:

- Box 1: Market penetration. Sell more of the same to existing customers.
- Box 2: Market development. Sell existing products to new customers. This could be geographic diversification or even the exploitation of new market segments with new products possibly being modified to provide increased differentiation.

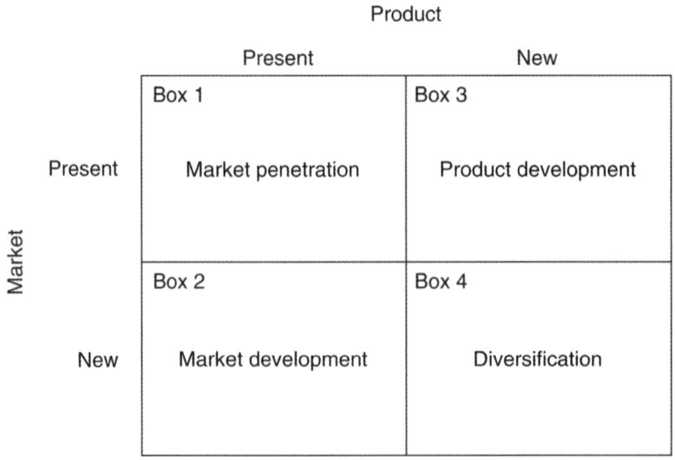

Figure 11.17 The Ansoff matrix

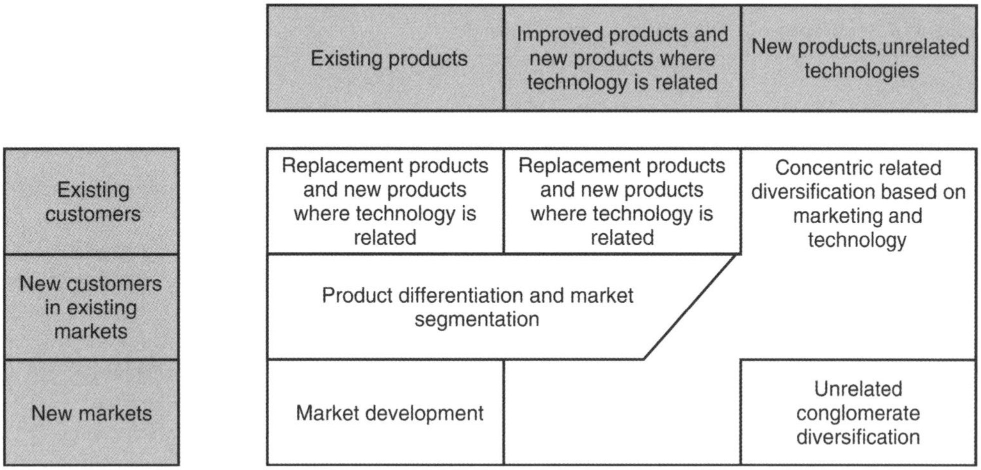

Figure 11.18 An extended Ansoff matrix

- Box 3: Product development. Sell new products and services to existing customers.
- Box 4: Diversification.

Figure 11.18 further develops Ansoff''s basic framework and distinguishes between the following:

- Replacement products and product line extensions that are based on existing technologies and skills and that represent improved products for existing customers.
- Concentric diversification that is new products based on new or unrelated technologies and/or on marketing skills that are sold to either existing or new customers but that are nonetheless related to existing products/markets/technologies rather than being completely unrelated.
- Completely new and unrelated products for sale to new customers. This is conglomerate diversification and is the highest risk strategic alternative.

The integration plan

Planning integration early on in the deal process is essential to a successful deal. The value of using CDD in integration planning has only recently been fully realized by many acquirers. However, perhaps because, rightly, the emphasis now seems to shifting away from cost cutting and towards revenue growth, CDD is a vital input to the integration plan. And so it should be because:

- You only get one chance at revenue enhancement but you can have several goes at cost.
- Without preparing the integration plan in advance it is difficult to value the business with any accuracy. As we have seen, valuation depends first on the stand-alone performance of the target and then on the synergies brought by the acquirer. In order to work out the synergies – which can be positive as well as negative – an integration plan needs to have been developed.

Table 11.7 Examples of CDD inputs to integration

Topic	*Example*
Product	Product and service weaknesses that need to be addressed to maintain or improve competitive advantage.
Distribution	Whether or not to integrate the distribution channels. Feasibility of selling through each other's channels.
Sales and marketing	How to communicate ownership change to customers and the message to communicate. Preservation of brand and brand positioning. Co-ordination of sales efforts between acquirer and the acquired company.
Pricing	Opportunities for price increases.
Business development	Feasibility of new product launches and new market entry opportunities.
Management	Identifying the key team members who must be motivated and retained. Management weaknesses/areas of under-performance. Skills which can be transferred to the acquirer. The desirability, or otherwise, of cultural convergence.

- A focus on growth helps build a positive climate that makes it easier to achieve other integration objectives, including cost cutting.

There are six critical requirements for successful integration:

- the creation and communication of a clear strategic vision;
- a focused programme of value creation opportunities;
- the use of implementation teams to make sure the value creation opportunities are realized;
- the selection of the best people and practices from both sides;
- continual monitoring of factors critical to performance;
- execution of a comprehensive communication plan.

Table 11.7 sets out the integration that can be informed by the CDD process. The CDD inputs to integration are more pertinent to business development issues than to cost-cutting opportunities.

Conclusion

Bringing the results of CDD investigations together is not a cold rational science. Sure you need to collect and analyse the facts, but you also need to apply common sense and the fruits of experience. In CDD, you are looking for the positive as much as the negative, but if negative findings emerge, they should be communicated immediately. CDD is all about future earnings. Decent earnings over the long term come from competitive advantage in a benevolent market. Competitive advantage is all about taking advantage of market forces. The analysis of market attractiveness and ability to compete must be carried out for each of the target's business streams without losing sight of the fact that there may be linkages between various parts of the target's portfolio and that it is still perfectly possible to make good returns in low growth markets.

Bringing CDD findings together inevitably means the use of spreadsheets to analyse and manipulate the data. Good planning, such as scoping out what the spreadsheet will do and specifying how it will do it, will make life much easier in the long term. Adhering to a few simple disciplines, such as having only one data source, separating calculations, data, assumptions and output and having a logical flow throughout the file, to name but three, are essential to avoiding confusion and error.

CDD should feed into valuation. The valuation process can be simplified by breaking it down. The value of the target as a stand-alone entity plus deal costs plus the premium paid (above intrinsic value) should come to less than the value of the target plus synergies. Valuation is an art that can be improved by running a number of different scenarios with CDD providing the market related range estimates used in these scenarios.

CDD should highlight any gaps between what the sales line in the target's business plan says and what is realistic. Positioning the business so that these gaps can be filled requires new capabilities and resources. CDD should be able to provide a judgement on what is needed and how quickly (if at all) it can be developed. Some gaps will be easier to fill than others and CDD should be able to provide an assessment of the risk/reward trade-off in any gap filling.

Finally, do not forget to think about integration early. Early integration planning is central to deal success and CDD is uniquely placed to help in that planning.

Notes

1. Piercy, N. (1997) *Market-led Strategic Change: Transforming the Process of Going to Market.* Oxford: Butterworth-Heinemann.
2. Rowe, A.J., Mason, R.O., Dickel, K.E. and Snyder, N.H. (1989) *Strategic Management: A Methodological Approach* (3rd edition). Boston, MA: Addison Wesley.
3. Hamermesh, R.G. (1986) 'Making Planning Strategic', *Harvard Business Review*, 64(4): 115–20.
4. Ansoff, H.I. (1987) *Corporate Strategy*. Harmondsworth, Penguin.

PART III
Collecting and Presenting the Data

PART III Introduction

To many this is the most important part. Without good data, any analysis is built on sand; without presenting the data in a way that is logical, credible and easy to understand you might as well not bother to do any of the research and analysis.

It is important to have read and understood the contents of Part 2 before moving to Part 3 because if you can apply some of those models to the target company you are looking at, you will be able to structure your enquiries that much more efficiently. Planning and structuring the work is the subject of Chapter 12, which tells us that we will be most successful if we first make sure we understand the question we are addressing (obvious, but so often overlooked), then systematically map out the issues that must be covered to come up with an answer and have a hypothesis to prove or disprove the sub-question that each issue is asking us to answer. With good planning it is easy to draw up a concise yet comprehensive work plan, something that is essential given the deadlines involved in CDD, including where and from whom to collect the data. Chapter 13 deals with interviewing, including question design and competitor interviewing. Good interviewing goes to the very heart of CDD yet *good* interviewing needs preparation and practice as well as few tricks. This, therefore is a very important chapter. Finally Chapter 14 tells us how to bring it all together in the form of a final report. In many respects, Chapter 14 is a continuation of Chapter 12, as indeed it logically should be given that any report needs a logical structure that answers the question. It then goes on to discuss the techniques needed to produce a report that is clear, concise and to the point.

CHAPTER

12 *Structuring and Planning*

The core of CDD is collecting useful data. There is a wealth of free information available to anyone who cares to ask for it, but to collect it in the most cost effective manner means using a structured approach. As my old boss used to say (with depressing regularity): 'If you don't know where you are going, any road will do.' The chapter looks at structuring a CDD investigation and particularly at the pre-research planning needed to ensure an excellent result. The topics covered are:

- Understanding the question
- Issue analysis
- Collecting the data
- Dealing with obstacles
- Other planning tips.

Understanding the question

Nothing in the final report will be of interest unless it answers a question the audience has in mind, such as: Will this company make its forecasts? Or: Will this company return 25 per cent compound equity growth over the next 3 years? The first task, therefore, is to understand what the question is. This sounds obvious, but getting the question right is one of the trickiest issues in consulting. This is further complicated in CDD because the question usually changes as the work proceeds.

CDD differs from strategy consulting in that it sets out to answer more or less the same question every time: Is this business worth investing in? That simple question hides a multitude of sub-questions. In order to answer the top-level question, you must work out what prospective investors are most nervous about, what would persuade them to invest and

CASE STUDY 35

WHAT IS THE REAL QUESTION?

The target company concerned had something like 80 per cent of the UK market for bus ticket machines. These are the machines that bus drivers or conductors use to issue tickets but, with the right micro-chips inside them, they are capable of a lot more besides. The venture capitalist thinking of buying this business had been persuaded that the future of the business depended on the adoption of smart cards by bus companies. This is hardly surprising since management had built its strategy on exactly this. Roughly 5 years before, the UK bus market had been de-regulated. There was a fair degree of consolidation following de-regulation, which prompted bus companies to invest in new

CASE STUDY 35 – *continued*

ticket machines. As a ticket machine lasts over 10 years, sales of new machines would be relatively low for the next 5 years or more. The company had to find new sources of revenue. Expansion overseas was one way and new technology 'add-ons' (smart card readers, GPS (global positioning satellite) navigation cards and associated systems) were another. The only problem was that our first five calls to the big UK bus companies to validate management's vision of the future elicited the same answer: 'No, we would never invest in smart cards because we cannot make a business case.' The case looked hopeless except for the fact that the target company had sold smart cards in the previous 5 years, so somebody must have been buying them. Who? The answer is that the equipment is bought when public transport is being upgraded. These schemes are financed by local government, which in turn is given grants by central government. Local government like smartcards because they give much a much better picture of concessionary fares.[1] This was not about ticket machines or smart cards, it was about local government finances and public transport modernization.

what would cause them to walk away. The average client is not always that good at articulating what it sees as the main issues at the beginning, but you can bet your life that it will by the end. Although the client may have asked very detailed questions about the market and demanded a profile of the competition, you can bet this is not what is really wanted. As Case Study 35 illustrates, to do CDD well you must find out what the real question is, answer it and incorporate answers to all the side questions as you do so.

All the writings on this subject recommend the 'S–C–Q' approach to identifying the client's key question:

- Situation: where the client is now and where it wants to go.
- Complication: what is stopping it.
- Question: the critical question that really needs to be addressed.

Table 12.1 shows why different main questions can arise from identical situations which, as can be seen, are very different, depending on where the client is coming from.

Given the above, you should always push hard at the initial briefing with the client, to find one to three very high-level questions that will guide the rest of the work. Those questions must then be translated into issues to be addressed by the work programme.

Table 12.1 Recognize that there can be different possible S–C–Q profiles

Situation	*Complication*	*Client's question*
Client wants to enter the US market	Uncertain whether acquisition is the best route.	Should we acquire at all?
Client wants to enter the US market	Concerned about risks of acquiring in the US.	What should our entry strategy be if not through acquisition?
Client wants to enter the US market	Does not know whether the target represents the best acquisition opportunity.	Which segments have best fit with our strengths and who serves them in the US?

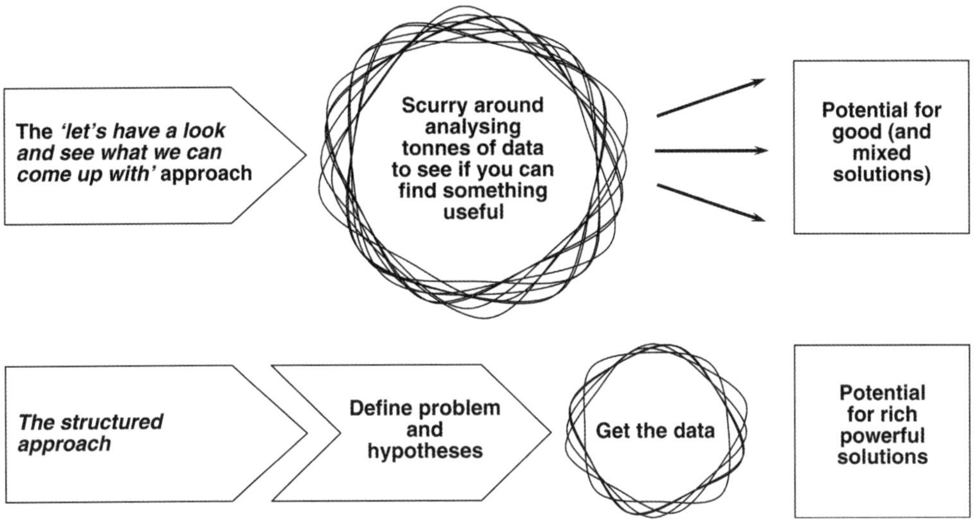

Figure 12.1 There are two approaches to approaching CDD

Issue analysis

Identifying the issues that need to be explored in CDD, issue analysis, is a vital step in the CDD process. As shown in Figure 12.1, there are two ways to go about planning a piece of CDD.

There is nothing wrong with the first approach except that there is normally not enough time to do CDD this way. In order to cover the ground in the time available, you must structure the work for maximum efficiency. If you do not, you will end up going down all sorts of blind alleys and run the risk of reporting the interesting, rather than answering the question. Figure 12.2. summarizes the process.

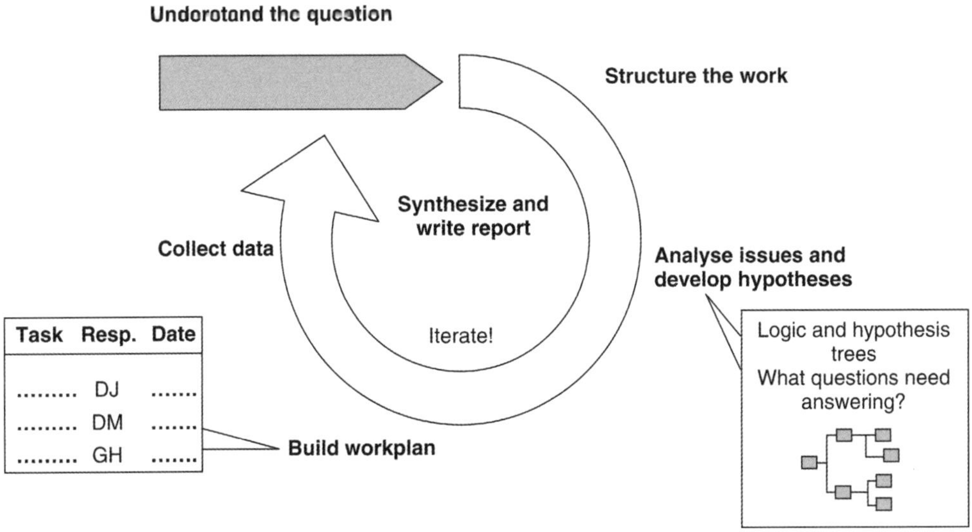

Figure 12.2 A hypothesis-driven and iterative approach to problem solving

Structuring CDD means following (a 'lite' version of) the classical scientific method, which is:

1 Hypothesize a structure that could explain the result.
2 Devise an experiment that will confirm or exclude the hypothesis.
3 Carry out the experiment to get a clear yes or no answer.

ISSUE TREES

Most analysts would have no trouble breaking return on capital down into a pyramid of financial ratios. This is done in Figure 12.3.

Constructing an 'issue tree' is exactly the same. Working down from the key question, the aim is to cascade a hierarchical tree of all the questions that must be answered in order for the main question to be answered. This was the approach in the second half of Case Study 2 (see Chapter 1). CDD will always be concerned with the hierarchy of issues shown in Figure 12.4.

This sort of structured thinking is also important because at the end of the assignment you are going to have to explain your findings to a variety of people who may know nothing about the target business but will in all probability have a thousand preconceptions and the attention span of a goldfish (approximately 3 seconds, since you ask). The report needs to be simple, clear and logical and the best way to achieve that is to have a simple, clear and logical analytical framework from the start. We will see in Chapter 14 how a report needs to consist of logical groupings of evidence, each of which cascade up to the next level. Figure 12.5 shows how reporting and issue analysis join up.

Mutually exclusive, collectively exhaustive

The skill is to identify the importance of each question and to drill down until all important questions have been identified. The acronym MECE (mutually exclusive, collectively

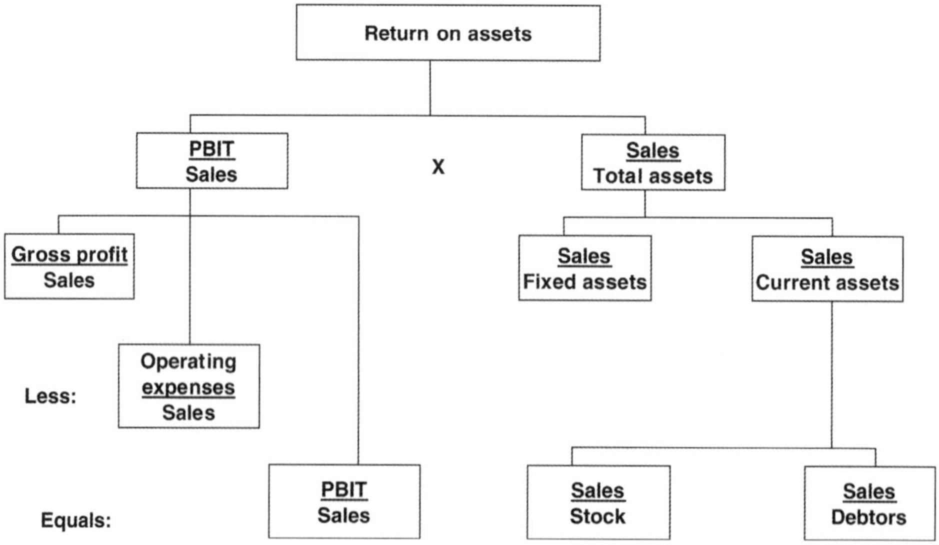

Figure 12.3 Return on capital ratio tree

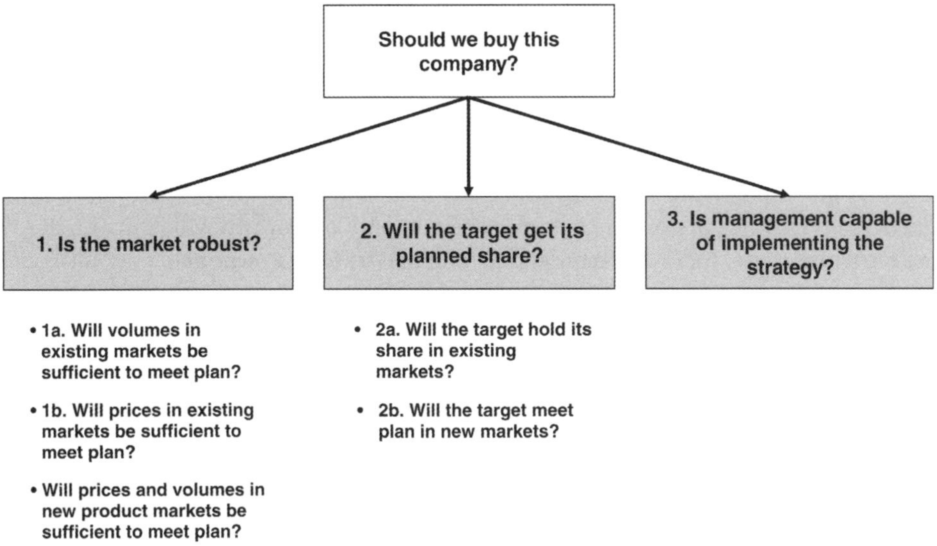

Figure 12.4 CDD top issues

exhaustive) is used to summarize the end result:

- Mutually exclusive (ME) means making each question separate and distinct from the others. For example, if we want to understand where a target's turnover is going, we would look at volume and pricing. Obviously we are going to cascade down the list of issues that feed into volume and price, but these are the only two 'top' issues. Anything else – the effectiveness of the sales force for example – is a subsidiary of one of these two. Three to five top-line mutually exclusive questions at each level is what to aim for.
- Collectively exhaustive (CE) means you have thought of everything and every aspect of the problem comes under one (and only one) of these questions. This is where we cascade questions down to lower levels. Under questions about sales volume would come issues

Structured investigation
• Key question: Should we buy this company?
• Issue 1: Is the market growing at over x% p.a.?
• Sub-issue: Is German market growing over x% p.a.?
• Sub-sub issue: Is Product 2, Germany, growing over x% p.a.?
• Hypothesis: Yes
• Evidence: Expert forecasts
Report structure
• Overall answer (buy)
• Level 1: Market is growing at ... %
• Level 2: German market is growing at ... %
• Level 3: Product 2, Germany, is growing at ... %
• Level 4: Average of three experts is ... %
• Expert says ... %

Figure 12.5 A structured investigation leads to a structured report

such as: 'Is the market growing?', under that 'Why, what is driving the market?', and under that 'What is going to happen with these drivers?'

A word of warning, though. This is fine if you are on a 6-month strategy consulting assignment. However, with CDD you do not have the luxury of time. For the sake of good discipline, go through the MECE routine, but in a simplified form. There are a million influences on business performance, but in the end only one or two will really matter. You must recognize these, focus on them and avoid analysis for its own sake.

TURN QUESTIONS INTO ISSUES

The typical questions that need to be addressed in CDD, as set out in Appendix A, are not issues. In order to apply the scientific process, we need to rephrase those questions so that they only elicit a 'yes' or 'no' answer. An issue is a question phrased so that there can only be a 'yes' or 'no' answer. Taking some examples from Appendix B, the question is, 'Is the product important to its acquirers?', not 'How important is the product to its acquirers?' and 'Are there distinguishing advantages of the products/services?', not 'What are the distinguishing advantages of the products/services?' Once you have framed the issues in terms of a 'yes/no' question, it is much easier to frame the sub-issues. Table 12.2 shows how the first few questions in Checklist 2 (see Appendix A) are turned into issues when applied to the market for recruitment process outsourcing.

Having drawn up the list of questions and turned them into issues, we can now formulate hypotheses.

HYPOTHESES

Having a hypothesis about each of the top-line issues is the only way to get through a CDD assignment in the time available. As already mentioned, 3 weeks (if you are lucky) does not give enough time to charge about in the hope that something will turn up. You simply have to have an idea of what the answers are going to be before you set off.

This may sound slightly odd. After all, surely the job is to find out the facts, not collect the 'facts' to fit some theory. In fact it is not 'some theory', but a guide as to where to go, just like the map that shows you, and my old boss, which road to take. The reason that hypotheses matter is that they keep your efforts:

- On target: they explicitly tie your analysis to your problem definition. You and the client know you are tackling key concerns.

Table 12.2 Turning questions into issues for recruitment process outsourcing

Question	*Issue*
Define the market in terms of customer benefits/the role of the target's products in the value chain.	Are there are benefits to the customer of outsourcing their recruitment processes?
What are the substitute products/services?	Are there are close substitutes? Are these are unsatisfactory for some customers?
What are the geographical boundaries of the market?	Is there is a geographical boundary?
What is the size of this market?	Can the market size be accurately calculated?
What is the market growth rate?	Is the market about to take off?

- Accurate: they help define the level of accuracy that matters.
- Focused: they ensure you analyse no more than is needed to disprove hypotheses within a reasonable doubt.
- Actionable: hypotheses allow quick checks before massive data collection and number crunching – 'If we confirm our belief in the hypothesis, will we be able to act on it?' Team members know where their contribution fits in.
- On time: you can draft the final report pyramid on day one, then refine it as data comes in.

Generating hypotheses

As Figure 12.6 suggests, generating hypotheses is a three-stage process:

1 Start with proven processes.
2 Apply general validity checks.
3 Iterate using lateral thinking.

START WITH PROVEN PROCESSES

There are three routes to generating initial hypotheses:

- talk about the problem;
- brainstorming;
- asking five whys.

Talk about the problem The best way to start generating hypotheses is to have an informal chat with someone who works in the target's industry.

When researching certificated bailiffs (these are the people who collect unpaid local authority taxes, such as Council Tax in the UK, and unpaid parking fines) a couple of hours firing questions at a revenue officer in the local council was time well spent because it painted a picture of what the people who hire and instruct the bailiffs think about the local authority revenue collection process and bailiffs' role within it. As long as everything was

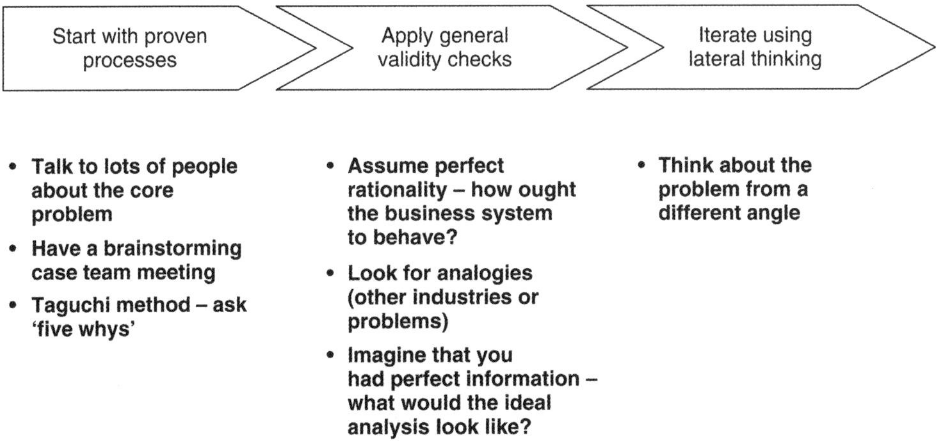

Start with proven processes
Apply general validity checks
Iterate using lateral thinking
• Talk to lots of people about the core problem
• Have a brainstorming case team meeting
• Taguchi method – ask 'five whys'
• Assume perfect rationality – how ought the business system to behave?
• Look for analogies (other industries or problems)
• Imagine that you had perfect information – what would the ideal analysis look like?
• Think about the problem from a different angle

Figure 12.6 How to generate a good hypothesis

going OK, the revenue collection people did not give much thought to bailiffs. This is because:

- bailiff services are free (bailiffs collect their fees from the debtor not the creditor) and therefore not subject to the normal tight local authority scrutiny;
- the number of unpaid bills that require bailiff action is relatively small;
- bailiffs only collect on half of these anyway.

Bells start ringing when one of two things happen – either the collection rate falls below an acceptable level or the number of complaints reaches a worrying level. The last thing the average local authority employee wants is either the auditors or a councillor giving them a hard time.

Similarly, when looking at a company that owned and ran homes for children in local authority care, quizzing a local social worker on the various options open to social services departments in the various circumstances when they needed to buy childcare paid dividends later.

Both of these were dream starts, but they are by no means typical. Normally the best available source is the managing director of the target company. This is better than nothing, obviously, but at deal time, management's time is precious and in any case they take an awful lot of the detailed workings of their business for granted. If possible, it is a good idea to talk to the sales director as well as the managing director or, even better, have an initial face-to-face interview with a friendly customer.

These initial discussions are designed to do nothing more than allow the team leader to be thought leader, too but generating hypotheses should not be a one-person job. As all further work, as well as the final report, is going to depend on the quality of the ideas generated at this stage, it is worth getting the whole team together to generate ideas and hypotheses.

Brainstorming Brainstorming is about generating lots of ideas quickly. This means not getting bogged down in the detail of each one. Create an atmosphere that makes idea generation happen. The following are to be avoided in any brainstorming session:

- Silence
- All the old ideas
- Team members agreeing with each other
- Team leaders flouncing in and saying, 'right this is the answer'
- Sessions that last more than 2 hours.

The most junior team member is just as likely to come up with a good idea as the team leader. Everyone needs to participate to the full which means:

- No deference
- No hierarchy
- No such thing as a bad idea
- No such thing as a stupid question
- No sacred cows.

Asking five whys The 'five whys' is a technique used in Six Sigma methodology. Six Sigma is a disciplined, data-driven approach for eliminating defects. By repeatedly asking the question 'Why' (five is a good rule of thumb), you can peel away the layers of complication. Very often the answer to one question will lead to another. The process works like this:

1 Write down the issue because this helps you formalize it and describe it completely. It also helps a team focus on the same thing.
2 Ask what the answer to the issue is likely to be and write the answer down beneath the problem.
3 If the answer you just provided does not identify the end result of the issue that you wrote down in step 1, ask 'Why?' again and write that answer down.
4 Loop back to step 3 until the team is in agreement that the hypothesis generated answers the question.

APPLY GENERAL VALIDITY CHECKS

Do not be frightened to apply patterns from one industry, that you know about, to others. What, for example, does using an outside payroll processor have to do with the development options for a Guernsey-based manager of investment funds? The answer is that many of the customer decisions are similar. For tax reasons, Guernsey is useful for some funds with certain investor profiles, but if a Guernsey-based management company wants to develop beyond Guernsey, the benefits it must provide to fund managers are very similar to the ones the payroll company provides to its customers. Some potential customers are too small to have a payroll function of their own, some want to concentrate only on their core competencies, others know their own true costs for running a payroll department and appreciate that a specialist can often do it cheaper and better and yet others do not outsource payroll because they value the flexibility of having it in-house. Much the same psychology applies to fund management. Strip away the sophisticated financial products, global custody, tax avoidance and you are back to the same basic customer thought processes as to whether or not to outsource payroll.

ITERATE USING LATERAL THINKING

You will have to think of the issues and hypotheses at least twice:

- to prepare the work plan;
- to refine the work programme once data starts coming in.

This is on top of whatever issue analysis has gone into preparing the proposal.

FROM HYPOTHESES TO WORK PLAN

The next step is to decide whether the answer to a sub-issue is 'yes' or 'no'. If the answer is 'yes', then the answers in most of the sub-issues below should also be 'yes'. After that, you must figure out what evidence would confirm or refute the hypothesis and from there devise specific tasks, responsibilities and deadlines for data collection. Table 12.3 shows the process.

Table 12.3 From issue to hypothesis to work plan

Issue:
Are there are benefits to the customer of outsourcing their recruitment processes?

Hypothesis:
The benefit to the client of outsourcing recruitment is that it can use experts to run a critical process which it is not good at while retaining control. Answer, 'Yes'.

Sub-hypothesis	*Evidence?*	*Source?*	*Who?*	*How long?*	*When due?*
Recruitment is a critical process for companies of a certain size and type.	Skills shortages.	Questions to HR directors	Fred (telephone)	1 week	16 February
	Rapid company growth.	Questions to customers	Peter (face to face)	2 weeks	23 February
Recruitment volumes are not big enough in these companies to have a devoted resource.	Who are the big recruiters?	Desk research	Mary	2 days	14 February
	What is the recruitment set-up for big recruiters?	Questions to HR directors	Charlotte (telephone)	1 week	21 February
	Evidence from HR professionals.	Questions to customers	Peter (face-to-face)	2 weeks	23 February
The previous recession led to HR departments downsizing.		Professional bodies	Nick (telephone)	1 week	16 February
		Questions to HR directors			
		Questions to customers	Peter (face-to-face)	2 weeks	23 February

Keep a perspective

There is too much data out there. You need to collect and analyse only enough to prove or disprove the hypothesis. You have to be selective, otherwise you will end up doing a lot of work for little reward. Remember the 80/20 rule. Remember also how a report can balloon if you let it. A typical report structure could easily consist of five issues per sub-point as follows:

- 1 top issue
- 5 first-level issues
- 25 sub-issues (1st tier)
- 125 sub-issues (2nd tier)
- 625 sub-issues (3rd tier) ...

That is about 10 times as big as a typical report should be and needs drastic pruning. CDD does not have the same burden of proof and depth of creative thinking as that found in strategy consulting. It is a piece of market and competitive analysis and issue analysis needs to be adapted with that in mind.

Remember also that problem structuring is not problem solving. Structuring is an essential start. Time spent planning the work is seldom wasted; however, at some point you need to go and get data. Do not use structuring as an excuse not to get started.

Finally, problem solving is iterative. As your knowledge increases, the issues will change. Issue analysis and hypotheses cannot be a blueprint but a guide. Be prepared to theorize again once you have some data and make sure you build time for this into the timetable.

Collecting the data

There are four sources of data:

- Target company management
- The acquirer
- Desk research
- Primary sources.

TARGET COMPANY MANAGEMENT

As we saw in previous chapters, most CDD projects will start with discussions with the target's management. Management interviews perform five functions:

- collecting basic information;
- opening a line of communication;
- reassuring management that this is not going to be a painful, time-consuming process that will damage customer relationships;
- agreeing ways in which to approach customers and other contacts;
- obtaining a list of contacts for primary research – ideally the target should provide names and telephone numbers of customers and others in the market that it is worth the CDD team contacting.

Checklist 3 in Appendix B is a detailed list of questions for management. One of the key issues in CDD will be customers' KPCs – the criteria used (either consciously or subconsciously) by customers in selecting one supplier over another. As mentioned in Chapter 8, talking to management is the first step in understanding what KPCs are, although you must always bear in mind that operational management have an altogether different timeframe from the CDD consultant; they are not that good at monitoring their market and are certainly not used to conceptualizing about the market forces they deal with every day. This is not to say that they do not know what is going on; of course they do. What it means is that they take so much of what the analyst conceptualizes for granted that it has to be dragged out of them and because their jobs are about solving problems and getting things done, in depth knowledge of what customers and competitors think of them is normally lacking. Three advertising companies were pitching to the board of a medium-sized engineering company. One of these companies had taken the trouble to call half-a-dozen customers and presented its findings as part of the pitch. The effect on the board was mesmerizing. Here were neutral outsiders telling them what their customers really thought of them. It was not a particularly scientific study and being an advertising agency the questions did not all focus on the central business issues, but it was very valuable to the management because they never got feedback at this level. Whenever they spoke to their customers, the conversation was about prices and discounts and nothing fundamental and, in any case, as their definition of the long term was tomorrow afternoon, it never entered their heads to have deep and meaningful discussions with their customers about long-term needs.

The main questions to ask management are:

- How does the market segment?
- What are the top five KPCs used by customers in each market segment?
- What is the relative importance of each KPC?
- Are KPCs or their order of importance likely to change in the future?
- What is the management's strategy (value proposition) for each segment?
- Who are the competitors/how do they compete?

How confidently they answer these questions (and how robust their answers subsequently prove to be) can also contribute to management assessments.

THE ACQUIRER

Any information the acquirer has should be shared with the CDD team. On top of this, the CDD team should be encouraged to talk to any relevant internal contacts. Confidentiality is an issue, but salespeople and others with day-to-day contact in the market can be invaluable sources of information and can assist greatly in framing the overall direction of the study. Furthermore, companies often recruit from their competitors, so it is entirely possible that there are former employees of an acquisition target on the payroll.

DESK RESEARCH

'Secondary' sources are published, or publicly available. There is no comprehensive list of what these might be. These days, the Internet is the usual starting point. Trade journals are a must in most cases, brokers' reports can be very good, if a little broad brush, published market reports (for example, Keynote, Mintel, Frost & Sullivan, Datamonitor) are a good means of getting a broad outline of a market, its size, growth and the relative market shares of its participants.

The problem is that secondary sources are general, rarely up to date and often wrong. It is surprising just how often market research appears to be wrong. Frequently the problem can be traced to definitional issues. You should talk to the authors and clear up any inaccuracies, misunderstandings or definitional points and always cross-check secondary data.

Apart from giving an overview on the industry, secondary sources should be used to give background information about the industry as a prelude to primary research. The more CDD researchers know about an industry before they start their work, the better their questions will be. Secondary sources can also be a good way of tracking down contacts to supplement the list given by management.

As mentioned above, desk research provides:

- useful background information for formulating the questions used in primary research and bringing researchers up to speed so that they can talk knowledgeably about the industry;
- ideas about who to call for primary research;
- market and company data that can be checked by primary research.

Before you start, it is worth checking how much data is already held in-house and do not think the Internet is the only information repository to use. Good old reference libraries, for example, often have all sorts of extra information that is not available for free on the Internet.

Table 12.4 below covers the areas that commonly need exploring. The list is not exhaustive and not all of it will be relevant to every project. The team should scope what is required at the start of the project part of its issue analysis.

Table 12.4 Common issues for desk research in CDD

Data commonly needed	*Notes and comments*
Market size for target's market and possibly those of its suppliers and customers	1 Check geographic area that data is required for, e.g. UK, Europe, global, etc. 2 Get the most up-to-date information you can. 3 If recent information is not available, old information is usually better than none; be prepared to extrapolate. 4 Be careful about definitions – e.g. the 'consultancy market' may, or may not cover a variety of activities; 'Europe' may also mean different things (e.g. EU?, Western Europe? 'Old' Europe?). Check the definition of the figures you collect coincide with definitions you are using elsewhere. 5 Sanity check your figures – if the market size figure for Europe is smaller than the combined turnover of the main players (and they don't have other activities outside of that market), something is wrong! 6 Record sources of all data, as thee will have to be listed in the final report
Market growth for target's market and possibly those of its suppliers and customers	As above.
Turnover/profit/employees/other financial data is often required for the target and its main competitors; sometimes the data will need to be broken down by business unit, but mostly company-wide data will suffice	• Try and get data for the last three to five years, if possible. • Be sure to pick the right company – sometimes a 'company' might comprise a holding company and tens of subsidiaries. Looking at a subsidiary's accounts rather than the parent company's could be a mistake! • If recent info is not available, old information is usually better than none.

Table 12.4 Continued

Data commonly needed	*Notes and comments*
	• Make sure you understand what the data relates to, e.g. is it just for the UK subsidiary of a global company or for the whole world?
News and press releases	• Check how far back in time you should search and which geographic areas to look at.
Qualitative market research reports	• Check how far back in time you should search and which geographic areas to look at. • Market reports are often expensive, but it is often possible to buy only selected extracts or even selected tables. identify relevant reports and what they can provide rather than just buying them! • Some of the large management consultancies place 'white papers'; i.e. free research reports, on their websites.
Annual reports	Obtain the annual report of any listed companies – either the target or its main competitors – you can get paper copies direct from the company, or via the FT reports service in the UK. You can often download an electronic copy from the company's website.
Exhibitions and directories	Trade shows are a superb opportunity to speak to competitors and other market players. Search for any relevant forthcoming tradeshows, exhibitions or conferences and even if you cannot visit them, download the brochures, as they may contain a list of key industry players, and details of trade associations.

PRIMARY SOURCES

The key information for running a company is not what spews out of the management pack every month, but the information you get from customers. Asking customers about the target company is invaluable. Obtaining information from primary sources is the core of CDD. It is the only way of getting relevant up-to-date information on the target and the market in which it operates. This means talking to people operating in the target's markets. Teasing out the best from industry participants requires semi-structured and free-flowing discussions, rather than highly structured questionnaire-based interviews. This in turn calls for a lot of planning and skilled researchers who:

- can get to the right people;
- have the experience and know-how to build on previous discussions;
- are prepared, and confident enough, not to stick to the script because:
  - they already know what is being said and therefore need to alter the direction of the conversation to get the most out of the contact;
  - they are experienced enough to recognize when an unexpected avenue is worth pursuing;

- ask intelligent, stimulating questions;
- can keep the discussions focused.

There is really no need to be frightened of asking for information from other people. There is a huge amount of free information available for the asking. If approached properly, people are usually only too glad to help.

Unfortunately, there is not one proven ideal information source. Information should also be cross-checked. The researcher therefore has to speak to as many different sources as possible in order to find the best source of information. It is a question, therefore, of 'surrounding' the target company by speaking to anyone and everyone who might be able to shed some light on the target and its market. It is also a question of talking to as many people as possible to eliminate bias and emerge with a consistent message. The types of respondent typically spoken to (in rough order of importance clockwise, starting with customers, although this tends to vary with industry) are shown in Figure 12.7.

Customers

Customers are the most important group of people to talk to; after all they know the target pretty well. However, they are customers for a reason. Asking customers about the target's performance is almost guaranteed to prove a high degree of customer satisfaction. Why should existing customers own up to being stupid and buying the wrong product? They will also say that the target's prices are too high – but which customer would not have a moan about price if given the chance? Does this tell you anything reliable about the target's value for money relative to the competition? Not really. Far more revealing are ex-customers who

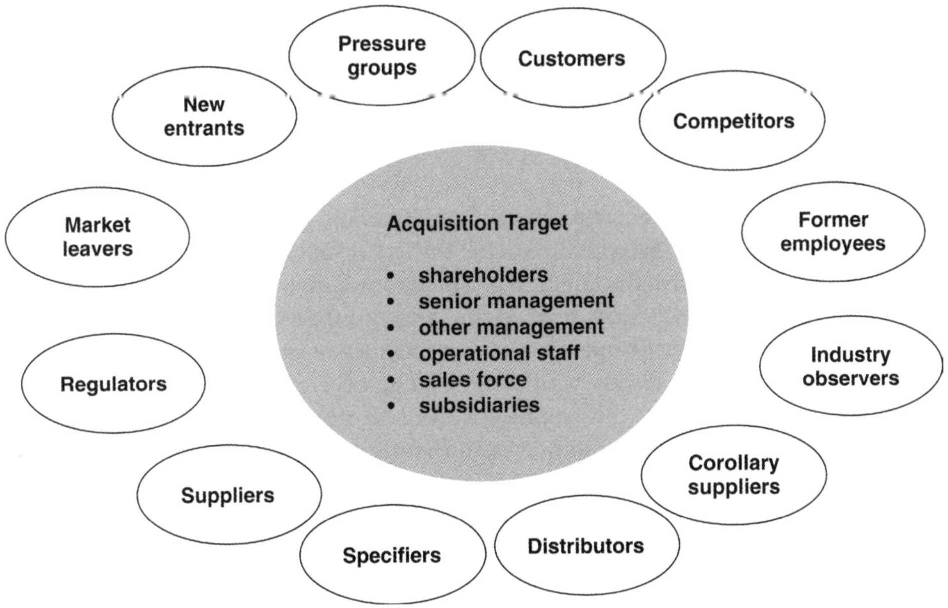

Figure 12.7 Primary information sources

left or those who have never tried the target. Therefore, remember:

- Customers come in three varieties:
  - past;
  - present;
  - non-customers.
- It is important to speak to a good mix of all three.

Past customers should be asked why they are no longer buying from the target. Present customers will be able to talk in depth about the target's current performance, how it rates against the competition and whether it is improving or getting worse, whether the customers' purchase criteria are changing, how well the target is keeping up and so forth. The main problem with current customers is keeping them focused on the big picture rather than with more mundane issues like problems with last week's deliveries. The bigger the company and the more senior the interviewee, the better. Prospective customers will give yet another perspective on the market, especially how the target rates against competitors.

Any business-aware researcher who conducts enough good interviews with a cross-section of customers can be confident of coming away knowing at least as much as target management about the way the market works.

Management will often hand pick the sample so that you speak only to the most loyal customers. This is not always a bad thing. What target management never realizes when picking only 'friends and family' for interview is that friends and family usually have a pretty secure relationship with the target. This makes them talk much more freely than other contacts.

Competitors

Competitors are the second most important source of primary information. Approaching customers is always problematical, so much so that some researchers will not do it at all. Given their proximity to the target and its markets, discussions with competitors have to be a feature of CDD. The experienced CDD researcher will either get the competitor into sales mode or exchange information to open discussions, but more on this in Chapter 13 when we come to competitor interviewing.

Former employees

Former employees are an invaluable source of information – if they can be found and the right truth filters applied. Be careful to check their testimony, though, because target management is apt to rubbish information gleaned from former employees. Test equipment needs to be upgraded every 5 years to keep the range fresh and up to date. While carrying out CDD on a test equipment manufacturer, a member of the research team got into a discussion about technical trends with a design engineer at one of the target's biggest competitors. It turned out that this engineer worked for the target company until about 18 months previously. Further discussion revealed that the whole design team had worked for the target company until about eighteen months previously, when they were made redundant. It then became crystal clear what had gone on. The target, in an effort to flatten its bottom line pre-sale, had cut back on R&D. Given the 5-year product cycle, this was a course of action that could only have short-term benefits. In another assignment, a former employee was able to give a first-hand opinion on the skills and deficiencies of the entire management team. In another piece of CDD, in a fairly specialist sector of the packaging market industry, talking to ex-employees of the target benefited the study greatly. All the contacts were found through technical articles they had written in the packaging trade press. Furthermore, approaching them on the basis of, 'I saw your article on such and such and just wondered how the various companies in that part of the market differed ...' yielded a much better response than the alternative approach of, 'You used to work for target co, please can I talk to you about them?'

Industry observers

Trade journalists usually have a tremendous knowledge of their own sector and the players within it, which they will gladly share with anyone who is interested. Other industry observers such as trade association officials, academics, and consultants are more of a mixed bag. Consultants usually want payment and it is sometimes worthwhile buying their time. Academics are rarely useful sources in a CDD enquiry, although they may be of help in understanding technical aspects of a product or service. As trade associations must remain impartial, they are reluctant to offer opinions, but are helpful in providing lists of further contacts.

Corollary suppliers

A corollary supplier supplies a product or service that is related to the target's product or service. For example, compounders and rubber suppliers are both suppliers to rubber moulders and suppliers of bolts for conveyor systems know an awful lot about conveyor belt manufacturers.

Distributors

Distributors are crucial in many industries, especially in North America where there is often an extra, distributor, level in the route to market. The same shift in buyer power that has happened in the grocery market over the past 30 years is now happening in other more mundane markets. Manufacturers of adult incontinence products used to supplying hospitals and old peoples' homes at decent margins are now subject to tremendous price pressure from distributors who have the direct link and therefore influence with the customer and the ability to substitute own brand to bolster margins. Like former customers, former distributors can also be an excellent source of information, as can non-distributors. The best suppliers tend to attract the best distributors, so it pays to talk to distributors who do not handle the target's products as well as those that do.

Specifiers

In some industries, construction for example, specifiers are central to the buying decision. While it is difficult these days for specifiers to dictate who will and will not supply and while their power is more pronounced with some products than with others, their importance needs to be understood. With some products, it is much easier for the specified product to be substituted with something cheaper than it is with others. Some products are almost an afterthought or a necessary inconvenience, which says a lot about how the target should be handling the sale and how important it is to talk to specifiers!

Suppliers

Sometime suppliers can know a lot about the market and if they are introduced by the target, will talk freely to keep their customers pleased. They are usually better at giving a *tour d'horizon* of the industry than they are at talking about the strengths and weaknesses of their major customers.

Regulators

The future plans of regulators are only a factor in a minority of CDD reviews, but on occasion they can be critical. For instance, many of the European health and safety laws and recycling/anti-pollution regulations can have a profound effect on entire industries.

Market leavers

A company that has left a market should not be overlooked. Given the agony it would have gone through to reach the decision to exit, the quality of its information and analysis will be excellent.

New entrants

In theory, companies intending to enter a market are a good source of information because they have carried out a considerable amount of independent research and are hungry to trade information. In practice, however, they are all but impossible to find.

Pressure groups

Pressure groups such as Friends of the Earth are playing an increasing role in some markets. What they have to say must be treated with care and verified because of their biases, but knowledge of markets in which they have an interest can be very good indeed.

COST AND DURATION

Apart from the breadth of the original scope, the main variables that affect the cost of a CDD programme are:

- The number of discussions
- The seniority of the people to be contacted
- The method of contact
- The degree of access
- How willing the industry is to talk.

Each of these is discussed in turn below.

The number of discussions

There is no 'right' number of discussions. The complexity of the target company, the number of products, the number of markets, the acquirer's existing knowledge and where the perceived risks lie all play a part, as does the deadline. The typical timetable for a piece of CDD does not usually permit an exhaustive study of every aspect of a large business, so discussions have to be limited to critical areas.

The real confidence that enough research has been done only comes when the level of knowledge and understanding feels right. The core of CDD is not market research, CDD is not about rolling reams of numbers or building complex models. What it is all about is understanding – understanding the customer, understanding market changes and understanding competitor moves, all of which can make or break the acquisition. As illustrated at the beginning of Chapter 11, it is about market sensing, not about information as such. It is about is creating a picture of the world that the target faces. When you have that understanding, you have done enough.

As a rough rule of thumb, fewer than 30 interviews in one product/market would be unlikely to cover the ground. For each additional market or product, add another 20 and for obscure markets or demanding information requirements, add 30 per cent to these numbers.

SELECTING THE SAMPLE

A sample is the sub-set of each group that you choose to contact. There are two issues to consider here:

- Which companies?
- Which contacts within each company?

Which companies? With many of the groups listed above, there will only be a few companies to choose from and time pressure will normally decide for you – the ones who are willing to speak are the ones you will talk to. Not very scientific I know, but realistic. Customers are a different matter. How do you select from a customer list? You want a representative sample, but you also want an articulate sample. Sometimes size will determine both. The bigger customers do normally have a better, well-articulated perspective than the smaller ones. Sometimes the objectives of the research will decide for you. For example, if one objective is to gauge the effect of time on customer churn rate, you will want to speak to a number of respondents who have been using the target's services for, say, under 2 years, 2 to 4 years and more than 4 years. Apart from these, common sense, rather than science, plays the biggest part in selecting the customer sample, with one important exception. Those customers with the closest relationship normally turn out to be the ones who are the most honest and forthright about the target. It is bit like taking up references on someone. A sibling will tell you all sorts of things that a colleague either does not know or would not be willing to disclose.

Which contacts within each company? The easy answer is, the most relevant. It is no good talking to the facilities manager about the provision of managed services – managing services is their job so they will totally biased against third-party one-stop shop facilities management. Talk to the finance director, whose remit is to cut costs, and you may get a different perspective.

Talking to the right people might mean talking to more than one person in the same organization. For example, if you are evaluating an HR software company that also provides outsourcing solutions you will want to talk to the HR director about how well the software performs and the financial director about the customer's propensity to outsource.

The seniority of the people to be contacted

Talking to salespeople is easy. Talking to the marketing director is more difficult, but the more senior the respondent the better because senior people are more likely to have thought through the issues. They are also less guarded, less stressed and less political, more thoughtful, more confident and more open than junior people. Their contacts will be better, more widespread and carry more clout and if they are any good, they will also have more time. They will also be more challenging. The ones with the best information are the ones that ask the most questions up front. Starting at the top can only work to your advantage because even if you get referred on you have the perfect opener: 'Your boss told me to talk to you.'

Getting thorough at a senior level means dealing with the PA. PAs are your best friend, so be polite and professional and involve them from the start in matching the bosses busy schedule to yours. They will also know who else it might be worth talking to.

The method of contact

All CDD programmes should try to use a mixture of face-to-face meetings and telephone discussions. Face-to-face discussions are undoubtedly the best, but time pressure always means the bulk of interviews are by telephone.

The degree of access

When the person carrying out CDD gets through on the telephone, they have to have a story. The nearer that story is to the truth the better. In most acquisitions it is not possible to tell the whole truth. If a stranger calls out of the blue, says they got your name from one of your suppliers and claims to be carrying out a customer care programme or to be researching the market on behalf of that supplier, the chances are that you will co-operate. Contrast this with the other end of the spectrum. A stranger calls out of the blue claiming to be researching the market. What is the typical reaction? Usually suspicion. It gets worse. The caller really wants to ask you about your biggest supplier, but cannot say so openly. Calls like this tend at best to be circumspect, quick and superficial. The researcher typically ends up doing a lot more calls and taking a lot longer to get decent information and this is on top of the extra time that must be taken to find the right person. Imagine how long it takes to find the person in charge of specifying rubber door seals in a giant automotive company. The more access a researcher can have, the better.

Target companies are always wary about letting consultants talk to their customers, fearing that they will either give the game away or, worse still, mess up commercial relationships carefully built up over many years. Persuading them otherwise is where the experienced project leader comes in. Three things usually count:

- The composition of the team: a team that has genuine empathy with the management will fare much better in persuading them to give access to customers and other sensitive contacts. CDD is best carried out by seasoned business brains rather than process-driven analysts anyway.
- The experience of the team: a track record of not having messed up sensitive relationships helps a lot.
- Reminding the target of the PR benefits of canvassing customers and the useful market intelligence it yields: good CDD should be useful to the business irrespective of the transaction. It is not unusual for CEOs of target companies to find that CDD has revealed a great deal more than they already knew about the market and what customers think. There is one CEO who admits to consulting the CDD done on his company every time they bid for new work.

How willing the industry is to talk

Some industries are incredibly open. Others, such as many parts of the IT industry, are over-researched. It can, therefore, be difficult to find enough of the right type of respondent willing to talk. The automotive industry automatically assumes that anyone calling is on a spying mission from a competitor. Many automotive companies make it company policy not to talk to researchers.

INTERVIEWING

If you interview 50 knowledgeable people with an average of 10 years' experience, you are getting 500 years' experience. That should be enough for anyone. The question is how to get them to give you the benefit of their experience.

Why do people talk?

There is absolutely no reason for anyone to talk to a due diligence researcher. But they do. Why? There are a number of reasons:

- Respondents go into sales mode and, when they do, stopping them from talking is often more of a problem than getting them to open up.
- People who carry out CDD are usually pleasant, persuasive, people and therefore good interviewers.
- In general people do like to help. This may well be a trait of the human psyche with deep-rooted Freudian reasons. Maybe it makes them feel wanted. Think what happens when somebody stops you in the street to ask the way. Is your instinctive reaction to say, 'No, go away'? Not usually. The same generally goes for people on the receiving end of a due diligence call.
- People like talking about themselves. Ask people to talk about their jobs and really you are asking them to talk about themselves. For most of us this is our favourite subject. Preface the questions with, 'I got your name from so and so who tells me you are the world's greatest expert on tubular steel lamp-posts', and again the problem will be ending the conversation.
- It helps to clarify the interviewee's own thinking. Explaining something often forces you to get your own thoughts on the subject in order. In so doing you re-evaluate your notions as you go along. Very often you come up with new ways at looking at old problems.
- You might get something in return. Experienced consultants are practised at analysing an industry or a sector in a short space of time. A desk research exercise combined with introductory briefings from the client and some friendly contacts will often enable a good consultant to make some observations which even the most experienced market participant will find valuable. Good CDD exercises are a two-way street, not simply a process of sucking information from unwitting victims.

These last two points are very important. Imagine carrying out due diligence into a target that makes vibration monitoring equipment. Vibration monitoring equipment tends to be used to protect big pieces of rotating equipment. Big pieces of rotating plant are found, for example, in steel and paper mills. Paper mills tend to be found in fairly remote locations where there are lots of trees. They run 24 hours a day, 7 days a week. The plant is worth millions and if it ever stops, the cost is millions too. It is the job of the maintenance engineer to keep the plant running. To help, the mill has invested in vibration monitoring equipment that is going to tell the engineer when preventive maintenance is required. The engineer has researched the market and chosen what seems to be the best equipment for the job. But can that engineer ever be 100 per cent certain? Someone who seems to know what they are talking about calls the engineer to discuss vibration-monitoring equipment. This person seems genuinely interested in why this mill chose the system it did. Suddenly the respondent has to articulate the reasons for buying one system over another. This, in turn, will justify the decision in the engineer's own mind, and therefore make the decision more comfortable. There is also the chance to ask what everyone else is doing and thinking and therefore learn if, for example, there are other matters the engineer should be thinking about.

But like many things in this world, preparation is the key to getting the best out of respondents. They are busy people, protected by secretaries, who will talk only if they perceive some advantage for them along the lines listed in the bullets above.

Platforms

The CDD consultant can never pick up the telephone and say: 'Hello, I am working for company A, which is buying company B.' Some form of subterfuge, or platform, is called for. Secondary sources can be good for platform ideas, but the best are those that give the interviewer a legitimate reason for calling and asking impertinent questions about the target company. The ideal is to persuade the target to let the CDD researchers say they are working on its behalf, say carrying out a customer care programme or collecting data for a market report. Management must also go along with the platform if anyone calls to check (which they will). This platform has the great benefit of giving the researcher a legitimate excuse for calling in the eyes of the person on the receiving end of the call. This helps minimize suspicion and therefore improve the quality of the responses. If the target can be persuaded to contact the customers first to warn them of the impending call, even better.

Dealing with obstacles

It almost goes without saying that throughout the acquisition process, the acquirer and its advisers should be sensitive to the stress due diligence places on its relationship with the seller:

- Due diligence is a major disruption.
- In non-Anglo Saxon countries, due dilligence is often seen as a sign of mistrust by the seller.
- Sellers will always be afraid of the consequences for the future of the business and/or its sale to someone else if the deal does not go ahead.

It would be nice if acquirer and seller could draft Heads of Terms, shake hands and then spend a couple of months helping the acquirer's advisers find, comb through and make sense of the mass of information they will inevitably want. It never quite works like that. Even with a perfect relationship between acquirer and seller, there are a number of obstacles to contend with.

CONFIDENTIALITY AGREEMENTS

The fact that negotiations are taking place probably gives rise to an implied obligation on the part of the acquirer to keep everything confidential that the seller and its advisers disclose. Nevertheless, sellers usually require the comfort of a signed confidentiality agreement before they release any information. CDD relies heavily on information from the seller and access to the target's management and customers; therefore, nothing very much is likely to happen until prospective acquirer and seller have agreed on confidentiality undertakings. Just make sure the agreement does not contain a clause that says the prospective acquirer cannot speak to the target's customers.

Although notoriously difficult to enforce, sellers, or more likely their legal advisers, take confidentiality agreements unbelievably seriously. As a result, they are tending to become excessive in their demands. This in turn means that these agreements have to be negotiated, which in turn adds delay to what is usually already a fairly tight timetable. The thing to remember is that rarely do parties go to law over breaches of confidentiality agreements, so it is better to sign them and get on with the due diligence than waste a disproportionate time quibbling. Restricting the due diligence programme is definitely something that is in the seller's interest and a protracted fight over the terms of the confidentiality agreement could be exactly what the seller had in mind.

CROSS-BORDER CONSIDERATIONS

Many of the obstacles listed below, and throughout the rest of the book, arise because of an inherent conflict between acquirer and seller. The acquirer wants to see and understand everything before being bound to a deal. The seller wants to give nothing away until the acquirer is bound. These natural differences are often exaggerated in cross-border deals:

- for cultural reasons;
- to gain a tactical advantage.

The technical issues in cross-border deals are usually quite straightforward, especially with good local advice. Cultural difficulties are the real problems to be overcome, especially since the doctrine of *caveat emptor* and therefore the idea of due diligence is not a feature of most non-Anglo Saxon legal systems. Standard approaches will not work with cross-border transactions.

SENSITIVE INFORMATION

For understandable reasons, the seller will often not reveal sensitive commercial information until the last possible minute. Sellers do not want to hand potential (or in many deals, existing) competitors information that damages the business if the deal does not go ahead. The profit made on each product and from each customer, gross margin by product by customer, is not something a seller wants outsiders to know. Unfortunately, late disclosure may lead to last-minute changes to the CDD conclusions, especially if the information turns out to be different from what the acquirer had expected.

AN AWKWARD SELLER

Many sellers now accept that customer research is a necessary part of the sale process. If they are surprised by this requirement or uncertain about its consequences, it can be sold to them on the following basis:

- It is a normal part of the acquisition procedure.
- CDD can be dressed up as a customer care programme.
- Change of ownership will not be implied or discussed in the interviews.
- The results will be provided to the seller even if the deal does not go ahead.
- Unlike many other forms of due diligence, this is more than a tyre-kicking exercise. Most targets use the CDD results long after the deal is done.

An experienced CDD project leader should persuade the seller that a customer survey will not damage the target's business but that, on the contrary, it has a positive benefit among customers. They may accept it, but that is no guarantee that they understand it. Acquirers, sellers and the target management are in a difficult relationship. On the one hand, there is a natural conflict, with both sides negotiating hard for the best deal and the seller worried that if the deal does not go ahead, the target will be soiled goods. On the other hand, there is a tendency towards co-operation with acquirer's and seller's management planning integration, working out how to run the businesses together. During the course of a deal, the pendulum swings from one extreme to the other on a weekly basis. At some point, the target is bound to get worried about strangers talking to customers or to start complaining about some aspect of one CDD interview. It is amazing how perfectly innocent questions such as, 'What factors did you take into account when choosing your present supplier?' can get blown out of proportion and in the re-telling become something like, 'Why on earth do you buy from this lot?' One target company even had the nerve to complain that the interviewers were asking about its performance! It is a sensitive time. If the target does start complaining, do not get angry, but do not back down. You are here to do a job. Your client, the acquirer, has asked you to carry out CDD. The bottom line is that if the seller wants to do the deal, it must co-operate, which means providing access to management and customers.

RESTRICTED ACCESS TO CUSTOMERS

In the first instance, sellers often react negatively to the prospect of CDD and this needs to be built into the timetable. They are often anxious about any contact with their customers. It can take a couple of weeks to persuade sellers you thought had 'got it' to hand over even a restricted list of customers. On one occasion, even a company commissioning a CDD report on itself refused to allow access to customers. Selling a company is a stressful time and due diligence generally knocks the price down. It can even stop the deal. The seller is also wary of any damage CDD will do to the business. The CDD team should emphasize that change of ownership need not be included in any customer survey. Ideally, the results of the CDD programme should be fed back to the seller, whatever the outcome, to provide something positive.

It is absolutely reasonable for a vendor to wish to protect the confidentiality of the discussions; indeed, it is in the acquirer's own interest to avoid any rumours in the market that may harm the target's relationships with its customers. Nor does a seller want customers' suspicions aroused by a sudden volley of telephone calls from consultants purporting to be studying the market or carrying out a customer care programme on behalf of the target. The seller will have to live with these customers afterwards if the deal does not complete. What is not reasonable is for the vendor to seek to prevent a would-be acquirer in exclusive negotiations from talking on a confidential or undisclosed basis to the people who know the real strengths and weaknesses of the company and/or the company's technology or products, and it is a point worth pushing very hard. By denying access to customers, the seller may only be playing a negotiating game. Test this. It is also worth getting whatever help you can from the acquirer and any acquisition-side corporate financiers at this stage. Both have a vested interest in getting the deal done, yet often do not fully understand the CDD process so may not have pushed the seller too hard on customer access. CDD is not impossible without being able to tell customers that you are carrying out a customer care exercise for the target, but it is more difficult, takes longer, costs more and the results are not as good. However, if you do not get customer access, remember that not even the most difficult of sellers can prevent consultants finding and talking to customers on an undisclosed basis. Just allow extra time.

RESTRICTED ACCESS TO MANAGEMENT

Sometimes sellers, or their advisers, attempt to restrict access to top management. This is less serious, but should ring alarm bells because there is no justification for it.

If you do get access, make sure you and your team treat management with respect. Do not mess them about or make life difficult for them, do not make unreasonable or silly requests and remember they also have a business to run. Make sure their life is as pleasant as possible and you will get a lot more out of them.

RESTRICTED TIMETABLES

Every seller will do everything possible to convince a would-be acquirer to accept the shortest possible due diligence period. Corporate finance firms, in particular, are very good at creating time pressure. It is in both their interests to do so. The more time an acquirer has, the greater the chance of it finding something it does not like. If the timetable imposed on an acquirer is unfeasibly tight, alarm bells should ring. Most timetable issues are moveable and indeed by the time discussions get round to due diligence timetables, the seller is so close to a deal it would be foolish to alienate a prospective purchaser for the sake of a couple of weeks' extra investigation – especially if the business is as good as it appears to be from the seller's sales pitch. Most advisers will need 3 weeks to carry out their work and more if they come across unexpected issues or problems that need further investigation. Add to this time to digest their findings and you can see that due diligence needs a month at the absolute minimum. If the seller or the seller's advisers will not budge, you should seriously consider walking away. If not, try to negotiate a break fee; at least then due diligence costs will not be wasted if the work is not completed in time.

It is not always the seller's fault that the timetable is tight. Many acquirers hold off from briefing advisers until the very last minute, just in case the deal does not happen, only to find that they have ended up not leaving anywhere near enough time for proper investigations.

DATA ROOMS

The objective of a data room is to give potential purchasers enough information for them to submit indicative bids. It is in the seller's interests to put in as much non-sensitive information as possible and especially information about all the problems. If a seller gets all the problems out at the beginning of the sale process while there are a number of interested parties, it leaves itself much less vulnerable to purchasers chipping the price. If there is only one bidder left, the seller is much more vulnerable to a 'take it or leave it' type of negotiating stance if the acquirer comes across unexpected problems. For CDD, data rooms rarely contain anything of interest, but it is always worth reading through the monthly management reports for details of lost customers, lost contracts or market down turns.

Other planning tips

There are five other things to take into account while drawing up the plan of campaign:

- Do not overlook the importance of good project management.
- Plan for an interim report.
- Maintain a close relationship with the target.
- Remember who the client is.
- See the wood for the trees.

PROJECT MANAGEMENT

Good project management is making sure that everyone on the team knows what is expected of them when, and in what form. It depends on them being briefed properly (Checklist 1 in Appendix A would be a good start), on knowing the timing of the interim and final reports, on knowing what format the report will take and what the rules are for its production. Checklist 11 in Appendix A lists the things that can go wrong. Good project management can avoid many of the blights on management consultancy, such as people working stupid hours. It is also the route to good quality, good morale, a sense of achievement from doing an excellent job, and with all of these, working the magic mentioned at the beginning of this book. If you are in charge, be the mid-field general who sees, hears and communicates everything while working tirelessly to plug the gaps.

PLAN FOR AN INTERIM REPORT

Always build an interim report into the project plan, even if it is not going to be presented. Interim reports are a pain, but if there is time they are a great benefit to the quality of the final report. The reason they are a pain can be seen in Figure 2.3 (see Chapter 2). The analysis cannot start until the interviews are completed and without the analysis there can be no conclusions and, to make matters worse, the team has used up two or three valuable interviewing days. However, life is never quite as linear as a two-dimensional diagram might suggest. What typically happens is that within a week of starting, answers to most of the questions will have been answered pretty consistently, but two or three really key questions will have suggested themselves. There is no point continuing with the same set of questions if you already have the answer to most of them. This is what I call mindless interviewing – easy to do if you are not managing the process properly. It is far better to 'bank' those answers in an interim report, then concentrate on bottoming out the key issues in the remainder of the time available. Why write an interim? It is simply that it writing down what you know forces you to think hard about what you do not know. In any case, clients prefer a 'taster' before the final presentation, as Case Study 36 shows.

CASE STUDY 36

BANKING THE EASY WINS WITH AN INTERIM REPORT

In 2000, a firm of venture capitalists commissioned some CDD on a target company that wired up computer systems. Their job was to lay the cables that connected PCs with servers. They specialized in the really big installations for financial institutions. One of their biggest contracts, for example, was wiring 42 floors of Canary Wharf in London. At the half-way stage, the CDD team had answered the operational questions the venture capitalists were asking, such as: What was the state of customer relationships? (excellent); How did the target compare to its competitors? (far superior). Writing an interim allowed them to bank these 'easy wins' and spend the final week concentrating on the two big strategic questions:

- Where was the customers' market going?
- What would be the impact of new wireless technology?

These were not easy questions to answer, especially the first. There was a City of London recession. Every day the headlines announced thousands of job losses at yet another financial institution. How much longer would it go on and how deep would it be? Focusing on these two sub-questions was far easier without the clutter of the banked issues.

An interim, even if it consists of a conference call to update progress, is also a good way of making sure there are no surprises at the final presentation. If the number of computer users in the financial institutions looks like being the big issue, flag it at the interim so that the target does not get the chance to rubbish your conclusions at the final presentation by presenting something you did not know it had.

MAINTAIN A CLOSE RELATIONSHIP WITH THE TARGET

The seller is at least as anxious as the acquirer to obtain a positive result from the transaction. If the seller is an entrepreneur, they will be very sensitive, as their future personal fortune is at stake. Maintaining close contact with the seller has two advantages. It helps to:

- smooth the relationship so that misunderstandings are avoided and any difficulties that arise can be addressed in a level-headed way;
- assess the calibre of management by monitoring the way in which they manage the process and react to events.

If the seller is a corporate, these points remain important, but the atmosphere may be less emotional.

REMEMBER WHO THE CLIENT IS

It is easy when conducting CDD to become a fan of the company you are investigating or enter into some sort of conspiracy with the seller or target company management. If you are doing your job properly, you will get very close to the target company. Such proximity can on occasions cloud judgement. In addition, you will rely on information from the target to shorten timescales and help clear up uncertain findings. It is far easier to rely on this information and write it into your report than it is to go out and verify it. Furthermore, if the client is doing things properly, they will be asking all sorts of detailed questions as you get towards the end of your assignment. The easiest course of action to get the client off your back is to ask the target for an answer. Do not be tempted to get too close to the seller, however much easier life might become as a result. The team conducting the CDD project must be clear for whom the project is being conducted and what their objectives are. It is also important to keep the would-be acquirer objective. No one commissioning CDD should judge the output on the extent with which it agrees with their own personal agendas and viewpoints. Sadly, this is often the case, especially with financial investors who are rewarded on the basis of getting deals done rather than the success of those deals.

SEE THE WOOD FOR THE TREES

A common due diligence problem is sheer volume of material available during the process leading to useful information becoming concealed in irrelevant or unfocused data. Focus is paramount. The two most common mistakes for a CDD team to make are to remain too rigid in its approach or to be distracted by detail. You must validate data and consider its relevance as it comes in. You must also recognize that a CDD programme will cover a wide range of issues and the focus changes as the reality of the target's position within its market unfolds. Every time the programme becomes more tightly focused or redirected due to unforeseen events and opportunities, make sure that the team keeps its eye on the ball. We have already said that hypothesis generation is an iterative process. This applies not just in the initial hypothesis generation phase, but right throughout the process as is represented diagrammatically in Figure 12.8.

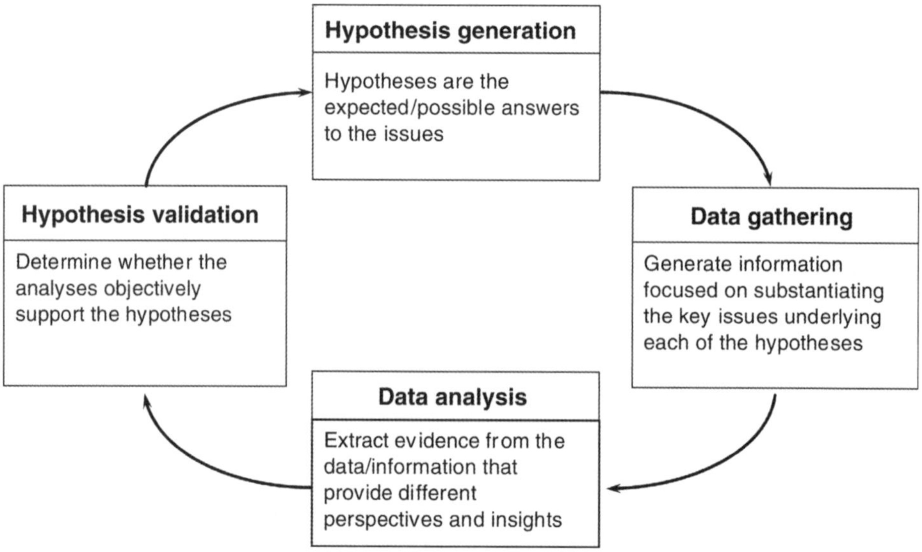

Figure 12.8 Hypothesis generation and testing is an iterative process

Conclusion

Issue analysis is a vital first step in the CDD process because it identifies the work that should be done and can then be expanded to include the sub-issues that define the work programmes for each team member. It also forces a logical structure on the work right from the start and therefore greatly aids the structuring of a logical report. You do not have the time simply to collect data and then see if something interesting pops out. Just like the scientist, you form a hypothesis and then design an experiment that will help prove or disprove the hypothesis. However, be careful not to get too carried away. This is CDD, reporting on the market and competitive position of an established commercial concern. It is not the blue sky consulting of many a strategic consultancy assignment.

Having used a 'lite' version of issue analysis to identify the issues you need to explore, you will then turn to collecting the data. There are four main sources:

- Target company management
- The acquirer
- Desk research
- Primary sources.

Each complements the other. In most assignments, though, market interviews will be the main source of data. Finally, do not forget to plan for the inevitable obstacles right from the start and to proceed in a way that forces you to make the maximum use of the limited time available, especially by scheduling in an interim report to make sure that you bank the easy wins while leaving enough time to cover the really critical issues.

Note

1. UK citizens over 60 years old are entitled to a free bus pass issued and paid for by their local government.

CHAPTER

13 Interviewing

We noted in Chapter 12 that the bulk of the data for CDD comes from interviews with knowledgeable managers in the target's market. However, you cannot simply pick up the telephone and start firing questions at some unsuspecting respondent. You only get one shot at each call, so a great deal of planning needs to go into preparing for the discussions. Each call is a demanding exercise because the researchers must achieve three things simultaneously:

- They must maintain the interest of the person they are speaking to. This means being polite (perhaps even charming), but more importantly it means asking intelligent, stimulating questions, and occasionally providing interesting information or ideas in return.
- They must keep the discussion directed towards the areas of interest without appearing manipulative.
- They must constantly evaluate the information they are receiving and assess it in the context of the information they already possess. The direction of the conversation may be radically affected by what is said during it.

The hard work is getting past the switchboard and the secretaries. Having managed to get the interviewee on the telephone, do not run the risk of blowing it. You will not get the chance to speak to this person again. You must know what you are going to ask, so write an interview guide. Questionnaire design in market research is a huge topic. Because the approach in CDD is less structured, there is no need for the same rigour, but a CDD team will do itself no harm by borrowing the market researcher's approach when planning discussions. However well the questionnaire is designed, the data collected by interviews can be improved with the application of a few simple tips, while competitor interviewing requires special attention and this too is covered in detail below.

Questionnaire design

Questions need to be very carefully thought through and need to be ordered and asked in such a way that the person contacted is not intimidated or alienated. Remember, you are collecting information for strategic analysis not conducting market research. You are gathering opinions, so you do not need a long list of 'yes/no' questions. These are not questions, they are topics for discussion.

FIRST DEFINE YOUR OBJECTIVES

Before writing out the questions, define the objectives of the question set you are compiling. The chances are that there will be slightly a different set of questions for each of the groups set out in Figure 12.7 (see Chapter 12), which is fair enough because each group is going to shed light of a different aspect on the target's market and competitive position. The importance of well-defined objectives for each question set cannot be over emphasized. A set of questions that is banged out without a clear goal is bound to overlook important issues and annoy respondents by asking pointless questions, or meander aimlessly, causing them to lose interest. You must avoid the general. An objective 'to gauge the level of satisfaction with the performance of the target's software' may sound clear, but in that form it is not a clear question at all. What do we mean by 'satisfaction' and what do we mean by 'performance'? To understand either, we must first understand what customers expect from the software and then determine the extent to which the software measures up against their expectations. The rating is likely to be across a host of functions and features from installation, to ease of upgrade, to customer support, to reliability, to ease of use. You must also understand what you are talking about. For example not having a clear understanding of CSFs and KPCs (see Chapters 7 and 8) leads to all sorts of confusions. When KPCs and CSFs get confused during market interviews, customers and others end up commenting on CSFs as well as KPCs – but CSFs are internal and customers have no idea what internal things like 'time to market' mean, so they interpret them in their own way according to their own understanding. To them 'time to market' means whether or not products arrive on time, which is not quite what the term means in its strategic context when it is about the target's speed in getting new products to market.

Once the objectives are clear, write out the topics that need to be covered and then stand back and think again about the objectives. This will help to prioritize the topics, which you must do in case you run out of time. Know what is important and what can be missed out.

THINK ABOUT QUESTIONNAIRE LENGTH

Most researchers make the mistake of asking too many questions. This often arises from a poor understanding of how to meet the research objectives. A good rule of thumb in CDD is to aim for a telephone discussion of about 20–30 minutes. In practice, conversations are frequently longer. Discussions of 90 minutes are not uncommon, which bears out studies that have shown that the length of a questionnaire does not necessarily affect response. More important than length is content. An interviewee is more likely to respond if they are involved and interested in the topic – so make the questions meaningful and interesting.

GET THE QUESTION ORDER RIGHT

The first questions should be simple, objective and interesting. If the respondent cannot answer the opening questions easily or finds them uninteresting, that could spell the end of the interview. Similarly, if the questions cause suspicion, if for example they come over as a sales call in disguise, responses may be guarded and answers distorted. It is essential that the first few questions relax and reassure the respondent. Background questions are usually put first because they are easier to answer and therefore ease the respondent into the discussion.

Transitions between questions should be smooth. Each question should follow comfortably from the previous question with all questions on one topic being completed before moving onto the next. Grouping questions that are similar will make it easier for the questioner to get through them and at the same time make the respondent more comfortable. Questions that ask for controversial or sensitive information should be placed near the end of the question set for three reasons:

- By this time the interviewer will have had ample time to establish a rapport with the respondent.
- The respondent, having got this far, will feel committed to getting to the end.
- If the end questions do prove sensitive, at least any suspicion or resentment will not influence the answers to preceding questions.

Try to start each group of topics with general questions and move on to the specific. Putting the general questions first reduces the likelihood that answers to the later questions will be biased.

CONSIDER QUESTION CONTENT

Think first about the general nature of the question and the information it is designed to produce. The specific wording can come later. There are five areas to think about:

- The need for the data
- The ability of the question to produce the data
- The ability of the respondent to answer accurately
- The willingness of the respondent to answer accurately
- The potential for external events to bias the answer.

The need for the data

Make every question count towards the final answer. Do not ask questions for the sake of it or because the data may 'come in'. Each question should have a specific purpose. The goal of the questions is to obtain the required information. This is not to say that all questions must directly ask for the desired data. In some cases, questions can be used to establish rapport with the respondent, especially when you are seeking sensitive information. Other non-relevant questions that are permitted are those designed to maintain the integrity of the answers. As mentioned above, asking customers about the target's performance is almost guaranteed to elicit a positive response. People tend to exaggerate their positive feelings towards a company if they think it is sponsoring a customer survey. Therefore it is sometimes worth adding a few questions that are designed to disguise the exact information you are after.

Do not under do it either. Make sure there is a question to generate every piece of data needed from the particular group of respondents for which the question set is being designed. The best way to check is with a dummy run.

The ability of the question to produce the data

Sometimes one question will generate the data needed; sometimes it will need a series. For example, rating purchase criteria requires at least two passes. First, what are the key criteria? Second, how important is each? As far as possible, each question should provide data that are subject to only one interpretation, therefore if two answers are needed, two questions are also needed.

If possible and only where relevant, try to quantify questions. Quantitative questions are by definition more exact than qualitative questions. For example, what do the terms 'flexible' or 'value for money' mean? Qualitative questions must be carefully constructed to avoid ambiguity and to avoid putting too big a demand on the respondent, who has to think more than with quantitative questions.

The ability of the respondent to answer accurately

Inability to answer a question arises for one of three reasons:

- the respondent does not know;
- the respondent has forgotten;
- the respondent knows but is unable to articulate an answer.

THE RESPONDENT DOES NOT KNOW

One of the most common mistakes is to assume that the respondent knows the correct answer to a question; yet often in CDD we want quite specific answers. For example, very few people would be able to answer the question, 'What percentage of your marketing budget is taken up with exhibitions?' with any precision and few will take the time and trouble to go and look it up. If you ask questions like this, it is important to understand that the responses are rough estimates and that there is a strong likelihood of error.

With other types of question, people are reluctant to admit lack of knowledge on a topic and the way the question is worded can exaggerate this. Compare, for example, 'Do you know who the biggest competitor to Target Co. is?' with 'Who is the biggest competitor to Target Co.?' The second question implies that the respondent should know the answer and will encourage guessing. The first question, on the other hand, implies that there are some people who might not know, which makes it easier for the respondent to admit lack of knowledge.

Look at each question and decide if all respondents will be able to answer it. Do not assume anything. For example, the question, 'What effect will government proposals on attachment of earnings for magistrates court fines have on the number of successful bailiff recoveries?' assumes that the respondent knows all about forthcoming legislation, which may not be the case.

THE RESPONDENT HAS FORGOTTEN

Memory decays with time. The greater the impression that a particular situation makes, the greater the probability of us remembering it. Unfortunately, many of the things that interest us in CDD mean nothing to the people we interview. We put the target under the microscope and in so doing erroneously assume that the weight and importance we give to the target's products and the way it does business is given equal importance by the people we talk to. They are not and, worse, studies indicate that questions that rely on unaided recall result in the understatement of minor events and overstatement of well-rehearsed events.

The solution is to provide cues or aids to recall. For example, you might first ask a respondent to name the target's biggest competitors, wait for the unprompted response, then read out a list of names and ask which of these the respondent considers to be direct competitors (you may even ask a third question asking them to rate the 'directness' with which each competes and a fourth that asks for an explanation of the rating given).

THE RESPONDENT KNOWS BUT IS UNABLE TO ARTICULATE AN ANSWER

How many times have you bought something without understanding why or for a reason other than the one you admitted at the time? Now think back to one of those purchases and consider what you would say now to someone who is interested in your purchasing behaviour. The reasons you would give would be conventional and logical, not the actual ones.

One method for overcoming a respondent's inability to verbalize answers involves projective techniques. Projective techniques use a vague question or stimulus and attempt to project a person's attitudes from the response. Techniques might include word association and fill-in-the-blank sentences. Projective methods are difficult to analyse and are better suited for exploratory research than for descriptive or casual research.

The willingness of the respondent to answer accurately

Respondents may refuse to answer one particular question; they may get to a point in the discussion and refuse to go on or they may deliberately provide an incorrect answer – which is the worst because it is hard to detect. Respondents refuse to answer questions accurately for one of four reasons. They may be perceive the question as:

- none of the interviewer's business;
- embarrassing;
- one which has a bearing on prestige or encourages answers which correspond with socially desirable choices;
- hypothetical.

NONE OF THE INTERVIEWER'S BUSINESS

Most people will answer questions they think are legitimate; that is, they are reasonable given the situation and the person asking them is seen as having a right to ask. If you go to see the doctor, you will answer any deeply personal question the doctor asks but you would think twice about answering if the receptionist asks the same questions. The quality of the introduction plays a big part here and is one of the reasons why it is best to be able to position the research as being carried out on behalf of the target. A brief introduction and the mention of a consultancy that the person on the other end of the telephone has not heard of does not, sadly, make any question the consultant wishes to ask legitimate in the eyes of the respondent. What does work, though, is an explanation of why a particular piece of information is required, as shown in Case Study 37.

CASE STUDY 37

MAKING IT THE INTERVIEWER'S BUSINESS

In one assignment, the target company's plan assumed a 10 per cent volume increase from one of its biggest distributors who, it was claimed, was going to drop another supplier. Just coming out and asking the distributor if what the target claimed was true was not a good idea because it would put the distributor on the spot. Fortunately,

CASE STUDY 37 – *continued*

the CDD consultant was able to tell the distributor that the target was refinancing and that a team were conducting CDD on behalf of the banks. It was unlikely that it would have been able to get an answer without telling the distributor what was really going on and thus letting him in on the big secret, at the same time more or less obliging the distributor to trade secrets. The next move was to make sure that the questions were posed in such a way that they did not create any obligation on the distributor's part. CDD needed an honest assessment of the chances of that 10 per cent extra volume coming through without any feeling that a 'yes' would commit the distributor to placing extra orders later in the year. First, the consultant told him what the target had said and asked him for the background. Next she said that nothing he said would get back to the target. Finally, after saying that a lot could happen between now and the other supplier being dropped, she asked if he had budgeted for the switch of supply. The answer was 'no' followed by a long explanation, which amounted to a view that there was a 60 per cent chance of the target gaining the 10 per cent extra sales.

Techniques that increase the likelihood of a response to sensitive questions and facilitate a more honest response include:

- placing the question in a series of less personal questions;
- phrasing the question in terms of other people, not the respondent;
- providing choices that specify ranges, not exact numbers.

EMBARRASSING

Embarrassing questions dealing with personal or private matters should be avoided. Data is only as good as the trust the respondents have in you and if you make them feel uncomfortable, you will lose their trust.

In addition, some topics are difficult. The best way of removing the embarrassment factor is with the use of counter biasing statements. These involve beginning the question with a statement that will make the potentially embarrassing response hard to deny, such as: 'Recent studies have shown that ...'

QUESTIONS THAT HAVE A BEARING ON PRESTIGE OR ENCOURAGE ANSWERS THAT CORRESPOND WITH SOCIALLY DESIRABLE CHOICES

It is best to avoid questions that involve prestige or social norms. Ask someone about their educational achievements or readership of highbrow magazines and there will be an upward bias. Respondents will always talk up their prestige, but will at the same time bias answers to the socially acceptable. For example, survey evidence suggests there is strong support for educational TV, but few people watch it. Similarly, respondents will say price is an important purchase criterion, but just as many will buy as if price was not that important.

There is little that can be done to prevent prestige bias other than make the questionnaire as private as possible. Telephone interviews are better than face-to-face interviews for doing this because the further the respondent is away from the critical eye of the researcher, the more honest the answers.

HYPOTHETICAL

Hypothetical questions force the respondent to consider something that they may never have had to think about before, as this is not conducive to the production of clear and consistent data representing real opinion. Hypothetical questions should therefore be avoided.

The potential for external events to bias the answer

Finally, one should also bear in mind that bias can be introduced to responses because of factors outside the questionnaire itself. Customer interviews, for example, can be unduly negative, but only because you have given customers the opportunity to complain. Similarly, ex-employees' responses always need truth filters applying.

THINK CAREFULLY ABOUT THE PHRASING OF QUESTIONS

There is not much point asking a question if the respondent thinks you are asking another. The issues to be considered are:

- Are the words understandable?
- Are the words 'biased' or 'loaded'?
- Are all the alternatives involved in the questions clearly stated?
- Are any assumptions implied by the question clearly stated?
- What frame of reference is the respondent being asked to assume?

Case Study 38 illustrates how much difference the correct phrasing can make.

CASE STUDY 38

THINKING CAREFULLY ABOUT THE PHRASING OF QUESTIONS

As discussed in Chapter 1, in the absence of special measures, the Internet is the least secure means of communication there is. Anyone could be looking at your messages and anyone could change those messages without either sender or recipient knowing. In most cases this does not matter, but imagine you are a bank sending out mortgage agreements over the Internet. Would you be happy without some guarantee that the phrase, 'the borrower undertakes to pay the lender £XX per month' cannot be changed without your knowledge to 'the lender undertakes to pay the borrower £XX per month'? Of course not. And it gets worse, because even if you encode messages so that they cannot be read and changed, there is no way of knowing who is on the computer at the other end. You definitely do not want to make an agreement with the wrong person. The only guarantee you have is that the computer is the one it says it is, but anyone could be operating it. Building societies, banks and other organizations, such as research departments in large drug companies, that rely on secure high-value one-to-one Internet traffic need a system which prevents the interception and modification of messages and at the same time guarantees that sender and recipient are who they say they are. The target company sold a system called Public Key Infrastructure (PKI). PKI is a security system that does exactly what our bank needs. Not only does it encode Internet messages, but it also guarantees that both sender and recipient are who they say they are, but it is by no means the only way of securing Internet comm-

CASE STUDY 38 – *continued*

unications. To size the market, CDD first had to understand the benefits sought from Internet security solutions by organizations with high-value one-to-one transactions. There were tears after the first dozen attempted interviews because nobody would talk. Looking at the question it was immediately obvious why. The first question went something like: 'Tell me all about your Internet security.' Is this the sort of information your average unsuspecting bank security officer is going to tell a complete stranger on the telephone? Definitely not. The question guide has to work up to a topic as sensitive as that. What needed to happen here was for the interviewer to throw themselves on the mercy of the respondent. Changing the opening to the following did the trick:

> We are carrying out a piece of strategic analysis for an investor in a PKI company. This is obviously a very complex area and quite frankly one that I am struggling to understand. On the other hand, I suspect you have spent a lot of time thinking about PKI and its application and that you are one of the world's greatest experts on the topic, could you please help me?

Are the words understandable?

The use of technical language with non-specialists is a major issue here. For example, it is no good leaping in with a load of consultant speak about 'business models' and 'paradigm shifts' to a maintenance engineer in a Swedish paper mill. Another concern is the precise meaning of even common words. What does 'usually' mean? Every day? Once a week? On a regular basis? Do not take words at their face value. You should ask the following four questions of each one:

- Does it mean what is intended?
- Does it have any other meanings?
- If so, does the context make the intended meaning clear?
- Can we use a simpler word or phrase?

Also consider the who, what, when, where, why and how dimensions of the question. Seemingly straightforward questions such as 'Which brand of shoe polish do you use?' are not always as unambiguous as they seem. Who for example does the 'you' refer to? and when and where is this shoe polish used? At home? While travelling? Both? The question might be better phrased as, 'Which brand of shoe polish has your family used at home during the past six months?'

You should avoid the use of colloquial or ethnic expressions that might not be equally used by all respondents and technical terms that assume a certain level of background should also be avoided. Abbreviations are only OK if you are certain that every single respondent will understand their meanings. Similarly, try to avoid emotionally loaded or vaguely defined words. Quantifying adjectives (most, least, majority) mean different things to different people.

Are the words 'biased' or 'loaded'?

Biased or loaded words and phrases are emotionally coloured and suggest an automatic feeling of approval or disapproval.[1] Leading questions suggest what the answer should be. A good example is the annual survey that comes from my local council. The degree of bias built into questions such as, 'Would you favour permission being given for additional housing without investment in the facilities needed to accommodate the extra residents?' is breathtaking. Put like that, of course, nobody would, but most would be in favour of additional housing simply because houses hereabouts are too expensive and no one is naïve enough to believe the extra facilities needed will be built before the new houses are. Leading questions are easily spotted because they use negative phraseology: 'Wouldn't you prefer the council to withhold planning permission until the necessary infrastructure is in place?'; 'Don't you think additional housing will add an unacceptably large burden to the local infrastructure?'

Similarly the question, 'Is this the best HR software package you have ever used?' is fairly typical of the kind of superlative question that is common in poorly thought out questionnaires. The signal sent by the use of the word 'best' is that the questioner thinks it is the best interface and so should everyone else.

A more tricky example is where verbs come at a question from different perspectives. Consider, for example:

- Do you agree with the user group's plan to oppose the ending of support for version 9.1?
- Do you agree with the user group's plan to petition for continuing support for version 9.1?

One asks the question in a negative way and the other in a positive way. Both will produce different data. It is impossible to predict how the outcomes will vary. One way around this is to be aware of different ways to word questions and provide a mix throughout your question set. You might also consider several versions of the same questionnaire so that the effects are cancelled out (this is known as a split ballot).

Are all the alternatives involved in the questions clearly stated?

Here is another example.[2] What appears to be the same question was put to groups of non-working housewives:

1 Would you like to have a job, if this were possible?
2 Would you prefer to have a job, or do you prefer to do just your housework?

The second version merely makes explicit the implied alternative in the first so it is hardly likely to make any difference is it? Well, yes, actually. When these two questions were read to two random samples of nonworking housewives, number 1 produced 19 per cent who said they would not like to have a job. Number 2 produced 68 per cent who would prefer not to have a job. The moral is that relevant alternatives should be stated unless there is a good reason for not doing so, but vary their order because the evidence shows that if respondents do not have a strong preference and/or the alternatives are long or complex, they will choose the last one presented.

A corollary of the above is that questions should ask for an answer on only one dimension. For example, consider the following question about a piece of software: 'Do you like the sequencing of the screens and the look of each one?' That is two questions. If the answers is 'yes', which question is being answered? A good question only asks for one piece of information.

Are any assumptions implied by the question clearly stated?

Try not to ask questions in such a way that respondents have to make assumptions about the world about them. For example, 'Are you in favour of permission being given for additional housing?' will elicit different answers depending on the respondent's assumptions about the quantity, quality and location of such housing. A better way of asking is, 'Are you in favour of permission being given for additional housing if this is built on green belt land on the outskirts of town?'

What frame of reference is the respondent being asked to assume?

We interview in CDD to elicit opinions. What we want to know is what the respondent thinks about the target, its products, the way the market is going and the competition. Questions, therefore, should be aimed at getting an answer that tells us about the respondent's personal frame of reference. Consider the following:

1 Do Target Co.'s products perform adequately?
2 Do you believe Target Co.'s products perform adequately?
3 Are you satisfied with the performance of Target Co.'s products?

Question 3 is the one that asks what we really want. Question 1 wants the person on the end of the telephone to benchmark Target Co.'s products against other people's standards and question 2 gets an answer to a question that is somewhere between 1 and 3.

THINK CAREFULLY ABOUT THE RESPONSE REQUIRED

Because CDD is concerned with exploratory research, we want detail, not 'yes' and 'no' answers so we normally ask open-ended questions. These are questions where the respondent is free to choose any response deemed appropriate. An example would be, 'Who do you see as the tier 1 competitors in this market?'. Alternative formats are:

- Multiple-choice: 'Which of the following do you see as tier 1 competitors in this market . . . ?'
- Dichotomous: 'Do you see XYZ as a tier 1 competitor?'

Each format has its strengths and weaknesses and the decision on which form to use should be based on the objective for each question.

Open-ended questions

Open-ended questions are those that ask for unprompted responses. They have a number of advantages and disadvantages as set out in Table 13.1.

Multiple-choice questions

The essential feature of a multiple-choice question is that it presents the respondent with a list of possible answers from which to choose. Multiple-choice questions have a number of advantages and disadvantages as set out in Table 13.2.

Table 13.1 The advantages and disadvantages of open-ended questions

Advantages of open-ended questions	*Disadvantages of open-ended questions*
Good for soliciting subjective data because the respondent is not influenced by a pre-stated set of response categories.	Each response must be considered individually. Tabulation or statistical analysis is difficult and becomes a sizeable proportion of the total cost of the research.
Good when the range of responses is not tightly defined.	Each researcher will bias the answers by interpreting the questions in a slightly different way, by varying their response and their probing to the answers given and recording answers differently. Even the length of time the interviewer waits after a respondent stops speaking before asking the next question can introduce bias that is hard to detect.
Elicits a wide variety of responses that truly reflect the opinions of the respondents, often leading to unexpected and insightful comments that could not have been predicted.	Require more thought and time on the part of the respondent. The more that is asked of them, the greater the chances of tiring or boring them.
Excellent for warming up respondents.	Can end up being a measure of respondent articulateness because some respondents will answer clearly in depth and others with equal knowledge will find it hard to present themselves.
Allows us to convey a feel for the quality of the information in the final report by using quotes.	

Table 13.2 The advantages and disadvantages of multiple-choice questions

Advantages of multiple-choice questions	*Disadvantages of multiple-choice questions*
Generally easier for both questioner and respondent.	Requires more effort in putting the questions together.
Reduces interviewer bias.	If some possible alternatives are not included, no information will be gathered on them. Even if an 'other' category is included respondents tend to pick from the listed alternatives.
Reduces bias introduced by different levels of interviewee articulateness.	Giving respondents a list of answers may introduce bias. Alternatives that they had not thought about before may be selected over an alternative that they would have thought of on their own.
Makes analysis much simpler. It is easy to calculate percentages and other hard statistical data over the whole group or any sub-group.	
Useless or extreme answers can be filtered out.	

DESIGNING QUESTIONS

All of the points listed above apply to the design of multiple-choice questions. Themes deserving special mention are:

- deciding how many alternatives to list;
- all possible answers accommodated;
- quantifying alternatives;
- balanced and unbalanced alternatives.

How many alternatives? A critical decision with multiple-choice questions is how many alternatives to have. The ritualists will mutter 'MECE' (Mutually Exclusive and Collectively Exhaustive, see Chapter 12), however, it is not always practical to list all possible alternatives. In practical terms you are never interested in alternatives only a few people will select. These can go in the 'other' category with only the popular alternatives being listed. There needs to be sufficient choices to fully cover the range of answers but not so many that the distinction between them becomes blurred. Usually this translates into five to ten possible answers per question. For questions that measure a single variable or opinion, such as ease of use, or measure degree within a range, for example from easy to use to difficult to use, conventional wisdom says there should be an odd number of alternatives. This allows for a neutral response in the middle.

There will also be occasions when strong alternatives have to be considered to stop them overwhelming everything else so for example you might ask a multiple-choice question which goes, 'Apart from competitive prices and acceptable quality, what must a supplier of own brand chocolate offer?'

All possible answers accommodated On the other hand, asking a question that does not accommodate all possible responses can confuse and frustrate a respondent. For example consider the question, 'Which HR software packages have you evaluated?' What if the respondent has not evaluated any? What if they have evaluated a number, but the question only seems to ask for one answer? Suppose they have evaluated packages that are not on the list? The answer is to use dichotomous questions to 'qualify' the respondent (in this case to confirm that they have evaluated some HR packages), allow multiple responses and have an 'other, please specify' slot.

Quantifying alternatives As already mentioned, questions must be clear, succinct and unambiguous. Eliminating the chance that a question will mean different things to different people is the biggest challenge in, and the area that causes the greatest source of mistakes in, questionnaires. If possible, it is best to phrase questions empirically and avoid the use of adjectives. Table 13.3 shows how this is done in practice.

Balanced and unbalanced alternatives We met positively and negatively worded questions above. Consider the alternatives for the same question listed in Table 13.4.

Table 13.3 Quantifying alternatives in multiple-choice questions

	Choices open to interpretation	*Choices quantified*
1	Very often	Every day or more
2	Often	2–6 times a week
3	Sometimes	About once a week
4	Rarely	About once a month
5	Never	Never

Table 13.4 Alternative lists for the same question

Question: Is the service you receive form Target Co.:	
Positively worded alternatives	*Negatively worded alternatives*
Extremely good?	Extremely poor?
Very good?	Very poor?
Good?	Poor?
OK?	Indifferent?
Indifferent?	OK?
Poor?	Good?

Just like the question above about continued support for version 9.1, the results obtained from the two sets of answers will be very different. This is an extreme example, but the point remains. Think about the list, try to balance it and be on guard for heavily unbalanced design that leads the respondent.

When my performance as a conference speaker is rated by delegates, they are given a form and asked to rate each speaker's performance on a scale of 1 to 5 where 1 is awful and 5 is superb. No one ever gives me a 5 no matter how brilliant I was. Mercifully no one ever gives me a 1 either. Beware: when using numbers to get a rating or an estimate, there is a tendency for respondents to play safe and go for the middle. This can lead to hypotheses being confirmed even though they may be incorrect. The solution is a split ballot, where different questionnaires are used on parts of the sample with the expected answer placed in different places along the list of numbers and the result averaged between the two.

Avoid asking respondents to order or rank more than five items. As the number of items increases, the answers become less reliable. This becomes especially problematic when asking respondents to assign a percentage to a series of items. To do it successfully, the respondent must continually adjust their answers to make sure they add up to 100 per cent. Limiting the number of alternatives to five or less makes this much easier.

Finally, if three or four relatively long or complex alternatives are read to the respondents, there will be a bias in favour of the last alternative. Try to avoid long complex alternatives and if they cannot be avoided think about using a split ballot.

The construction and application of multiple-choice questions is not easy, but it is the best technique for collecting certain types of data, such as multiple answers and where you are trying to measure the degree of something, and it really comes into its own with large surveys.

Dichotomous questions

Dichotomous questions allow only two responses such as 'yes/no', 'agree/disagree'. The two categories are supplemented by a third neutral category such as 'don't know', 'no opinion', 'both' or 'neither'. The dichotomous question is well suited to determining points of fact and to clear-cut issues on which the respondents are likely to hold well-crystallized views. The decision on whether or not to use this form of questioning depends on whether or not the respondents approach the issue in 'yes/no' terms. Although the answer may be 'yes' or 'no', getting there may involve a whole series of 'ifs' maybes' and 'probablys'. Take the simple question, 'Do you intend to renew your fabric maintenance contract with Target Co. when the present one ends in two years' time?' It may elicit a 'yes' from one respondent and

Table 13.5 The advantages and disadvantages of dichotomous questions

Advantages of dichotomous questions	*Disadvantages of dichotomous questions*
Questions are quick and easy to ask.	Susceptible to error caused by implied alternatives rather than stated alternatives (see below).
Questions are quick and easy to answer.	Starting the question in a positive or negative manner can have a big effect on responses.

'no' from another when both are thinking along the lines of, 'Probably, if the finance director does not outsource all our facilities management to a managing agent.' The optimist replies 'yes' and the pessimist 'no'.

As set out in Table 13.5, the advantages of dichotomous questions are similar to those of multiple-choice questions.

A yes/no question that asks, 'is this the best HR software package you have ever used?' is highly leading because even if the respondent loves the package but has a favourite that it is not this one, they would be forced to reply 'no'. A better way to ask the same question would be to use multiple-choice to avoid subtly leading questions and supply a range of choices, as follows:

To what extent do you agree with the statement, 'this is the best HR software package I have ever used?'

- Totally agree
- Somewhat agree
- Neither agree nor disagree
- Somewhat disagree
- Totally disagree

There is always a debate about whether or not to include a neutral category. If a neutral category is allowed, it may increase accuracy if a number of people are truly neutral. Unfortunately, many who are not completely neutral will select the neutral category rather than expend the mental effort required to choose one alternative or the other.

Tips for successful interviewing

Successful interviewing depends on keeping a few simple rules in mind. Most respondents are quite happy to talk. The issue for the interviewer is keeping them to the point while listening intently for anything unexpected. This means:

- not being imprisoned by the script;
- sometimes taking the indirect approach;
- letting the interviewee talk;
- stopping when you have the answer;
- paraphrasing;
- being professional;
- trading information;
- avoiding mindless interviewing;

- seeking opinions;
- paying attention to the end of the interview.

DON'T BE IMPRISONED BY THE SCRIPT

First of all do not read the platform script verbatim – you will sound like a call centre operator trying to sign up new customers. You believe the platform, so improvise. You will sound clear and credible and it will work. Next the question set: you do not have to grind through every single question with every respondent, especially if they are in a hurry (see below). Also, do not forget that the issues will change as the project goes on. If you use the same script on the last interview as you did on the first, you have not improved your understanding of the issues at all.

TAKE THE INDIRECT APPROACH

The question you may want to ask is, 'Why do you buy from the target company and not someone else', but if you do, you run the risk that the customer will get back to the target and ask why that outfit doing the customer care survey are suggesting that they buy from someone else. So only be that direct if you are the masochistic type that likes a good kicking and a bent ear. Much better are the indirect questions, such as: 'How would you characterize Target Co. in one sentence?' Similarly, you should not ask about the target relative to the competition. You should also ask how both the target and the competition could improve. Probing users for dissatisfaction with the performance of all suppliers is a way of probing for the target's relative performance where it matters.

LET THE INTERVIEWEE TALK

As obvious as it may sound, the objective of interviewing is to pick the brains of the person on the other end of the line. Ask the question and then let them talk. Do not interrupt except to keep the interview on track, but do let the other person know that you are there and interested with the odd 'yes' or 'I see' now and again.

Even experienced interviewers have an irritating habit of snatching defeat from the jaws of victory by asking a brilliant question then answering it themselves as the respondent draws breath. Either that or they will pick up on some point and ask a question about that while the respondent is in full flight. This is not the fifth degree or a cross examination or a televised political interview; it is you, the humble researcher, trying to elicit the opinions of articulate people who know what they are talking about. For goodness sake, ask the question then shut up. If the answer throws up sub-issues or something you do not understand, be patient. Wait until you have an answer to the original question before asking another one.

STOP WHEN YOU HAVE THE ANSWER

At the other end of the spectrum is the interviewer who keeps the respondent on the telephone for the sake of it. Some people love to show off their knowledge, others would love to help but are short of time, others feel positively threatened. You are not going to get everything out of everybody and indeed you do not need to. There will only be a couple of important topics that absolutely must be covered. There is no need to question an unwilling respondent aggressively. Do not feel the need to squeeze everyone dry. Even without the benefit of body language it is possible to tell if the person on the other end is in a hurry. As pressed for time as they may be, you have them on the telephone. If they are in a hurry, ask the most important questions and let them get off. You can always finish by asking permission to call back another time to cover you against having missed something. Similarly, if someone gives a short but complete answer, one that is perfectly reasonable and understandable, there is nothing to be gained by going round and round in circles. A clear and complete answer is a clear and complete answer. It is not going to get any better by picking away at it and all you will succeed in doing is irritating the other person.

PARAPHRASE

If you ever read the transcript of an interview, you will realize how rambling and unstructured even the most articulate of us can be. People will set off down one road, unexpectedly veer off into an irrelevanancy, swerve into an anecdote, bob along through a number of minor details and, with your help, may arrive at the answer. Repeating back to them the main points of what you think you have heard gives you the chance to get them to confirm that you have heard correctly. It also gives them the opportunity to add points or amplify the ones they see as the most important.

BE PROFESSIONAL

Sound important. What you have to say is important because you have a lot of information and experience. What you do is important because you work for investors and/or important industry players and therefore a respondent will miss out if they do not talk to you. But you are also humble. You may be an expert, but you will never know as much as the person on the other end of the telephone. However, you love this subject and this comes through in your enthusiasm. You are interested in what the other person has to say and grateful that they have found the time in a busy schedule to share knowledge with you.

TRADE INFORMATION

As we have already noted, a CDD interview gives the interviewee an opportunity to stop and reflect and to find out about what their peers are doing and thinking. Do not deny them this opportunity. Summarizing what you have found out so far also gives the interviewee something to agree with or modify. This is far more interesting for all parties than running through a question set.

AVOID MINDLESS INTERVIEWING

Beware of the tendency towards mindless interviewing. Just because 50 interviews is the 'going rate', it is not compulsory. If you have the answer after 20, there really is no point going on. A good antidote to mindless interviewing is to take stock at the end of each day. Encourage team members to pull out the proposal and under each of the things you said you were going to cover, get them to jot down what they have learnt today and how it is going to help answer the question. They may be answering the questions on the interview sheets, but if they are not edging closer to an answer every day, there is not much progress being made. The only way they will edge closer is to avoid getting trapped in the detail and that is precisely the point of this daily ritual. Keep these pages and come back to them when you start report writing. As early as is feasible, produce an interim report (see Chapter 12) to force yourself take stock of where you are.

SEEK OPINIONS

The point of interviewing market participants is to get opinions, not verifiable figures to three decimal places. If you ask someone for an opinion and the answer is 'I don't know', the chances are they are just being evasive. Persist.

PAY ATTENTION TO THE END OF THE INTERVIEW

When the interview comes to an end you should thank the respondent for their time and not forget to ask:

- whether it would be OK to call back should any further questions arise – always leave the door open for further discussions;
- who else you should talk to, either internally or externally.

Never forget that the best information often comes at the very end when the respondent is at their most relaxed. This is the time to ask the really tricky question. Remember the TV detective Colombo? Just as he was leaving he would ask, 'Just one more thing ...', and inevitably that would be the question that nailed the miscreant. This is the moment to slip in the $64 million question, almost *en passant*, as you are ending: 'So I can take it you will be renewing your contract with target co when it runs out in a couple of years time?' Getting answers to the meaty questions at the end of the interview is even more relevant with face-to-face interviews. At the end, physically put down your pen, close your note pad and chat.

Competitor interviewing

Interviewing competitors is a necessary feature of CDD. Relying on customer interviews alone is not good enough; as mentioned above, they have a particular angle. They will not be over-critical of the target because that makes them look dumb for being customers, but they will always say they are being charged too much. Competitors have an altogether different perspective, usually with the opposite bias, that is, where the target is going wrong. In addition:

- Competitors experience the same market forces as the target company and therefore are vital in testing the story put forward in the information memorandum.
- Competitors just might reveal that they are about to do something dramatic.
- They are often the home of ex-employees, as we have already seen, one of the most valuable sources of inside information.

Some of the best and most satisfying interviews you will ever do will be with competitors. They will also give you some of the best information. The more you do, the more you will enjoy them. But this is the extreme of pretext interviewing and therefore needs meticulous preparation.

Competitor interviewing comes towards the end of an assignment. Identifying competitors is relatively easy from interviews with the target company and from early customer/market interviews. You should have a few of these under your belt before turning to competitors because you need to pick up the telephone in a position of knowledge. You also need to gather as much market data as you can, partly to trade, but partly also to avoid wasting their time and yours asking for publicly available information. Do some background research into their history and activities. Think about your platform, does it motivate them to co-operate? Does it:

- Stimulate the two basic human instincts, greed and fear?
- Address the topics likely to attract their attention, that is, opportunities and threats to their business?
- Purport to come from someone with whom they would like to talk, such as a potential customer, partner, investor or expert?

Rehearse your platform. The most important thing is that you are comfortable with it. For this reason, the closer to the truth it is, the better. Platforms that work include saying that you are:

- Conducting a market review for the target. Telling a competitor that you are working on behalf of the target leads to one of two extreme reactions. Either the telephone goes down immediately or you are treated to an hour-long conversation with an invitation to lunch. The more senior the person you approach, the more likely this platform is to work, but as you only get one chance to speak to a competitor, you have to be reasonably certain that it will work or have plenty of others to fall back on. If your platform is 'market review for the target', avoid the words 'market research' at all costs.
- Conducting a market review for a potential supplier.
- Conducting a market review for a regulator or government body. Examples could be the European Commission reviewing the industry to assess the Far Eastern threat to jobs or the World Bank reviewing the market on behalf of an Indian supplier.
- Working for a potential customer. Here, the platform is something like 'I am reviewing potential suppliers for a client', or 'I am drawing up a list of potential suppliers for an overseas company'. There is nothing more guaranteed to get a competitor into full flow than the prospect of business.
- Working for a potential investor. Your client could be a venture capitalist looking to invest in:
  - a distributor in the competitor's industry (could it be one of theirs?);
  - one of the competition (where the slant could be, 'please help us kill this mad idea of investing in your industry');
  - a corollary supplier.
- Working for an existing investor. Here you are working for minority investors uncertain about industry prospects. This has the added advantage that the review is not for operational management, but for a group distant from the day-to day business. There may also be something in it for the respondent. If the stake comes free, it may have the opportunity to buy a competitor.

- Working for a potential partner. This could be a major US/Far Eastern/European player considering entering the market through a partnership. It has some unique technology but no infrastructure, so it makes sense to talk to potential partners (like you) who do.
- Working for a stockbroker or other financial institution, trying to keep in touch with a fast-changing industry.
- An MBA student.
- A Headhunter. Do you know anyone who has refused to take a call from a headhunter?

Whichever platform you choose to use, make sure you are comfortable with it. When you do find one that works for you, stick to it throughout the assignment, otherwise you will get confused. Also run through the checklist a number of times to give yourself the confidence needed and to satisfy yourself that it covers all the issues and is pitched at the right level.

Preparation is very important, but you must avoid getting lost in diversionary activity. At some point, you have to pick up that telephone and dial the number, so you cannot prepare forever. Sooner is better than later. Set aside a morning, get the contact list ready and just blitz your way through it.

Dialling the number is often the scariest bit. You never quite know what reception you are going to get. In fact, most people want to talk. This is what they do for a living and, even better, you are giving them the chance to rattle on about their pet theories, something their partners and friends gave up doing long ago. Nonetheless, a warm introduction is a huge help in removing their anxiety about who you are. To get a warm introduction, try to get referred from a third party, for example from an important industry figure or the trade press. Introductions help because they help lower the interviewee's guard. If you know Mr Industry Expert you must be an insider worth talking to. Besides, if Mr Industry Expert has given you my name, he must expect me to talk to you and if he has already done so then why shouldn't I? Which brings us back to preparation. Before you get to the competitor interviews, ask everyone you contact if they know someone that works for the competitor – even the ad salesmen on the industry newspapers. As a courtesy, always ask if you can mention the introducer's name.

When interviewing competitors, start with the smallest, least important or least direct competitor. This allows the platform to be tested and the question set to develop before you get to the important ones. It also builds interviewer confidence and gives insights to be tested later. And don't forget to ask for referrals. The respondent may know (or have even worked for) one of the other competitors: 'I have to talk to ABC Ltd., who would you suggest? Who really knows their way around this market with your level of experience and insight?'

As with all interviewing, put the soft, easy questions first. They want to talk to you. The rapport you develop with those easy questions in the first couple of minutes will determine for how long. Start with a soft introduction, for example:

We have lots of information, we want to talk to experts in the market who can confirm our findings ...
We have lots of information, can we share ...?
We are finishing off our report and want to show it to you ...

Then a soft question: 'Just for my information, can you tell me a little bit about your company?' Giving out publicly available information about themselves is no threat to anyone. Stay soft, while feeding in as much non-confidential information as you have in the form of statements to be challenged ('I am confused, company A told me this and company B told me that. They don't seem consistent to me. Who is right?'). Keep the respect level as high as possible throughout with the use of phrases such as, 'Really, I didn't know that ...', 'That's interesting ...', 'Is that right ...?' You are charming and you will use flattery, but above all you are sincere.

Hide the hard questions:

- In soft language, for example: 'Would you say you make more profit from baked beans or bananas?' 'Wouldn't it make sense for you to enter the parsnip market given its high growth rate?'
- Behind somebody else, for example: 'Somebody I spoke to earlier said bananas are really unprofitable, which seems odd me. Is he right?' Or: 'Lots of people have been saying parsnips are fraught with danger. What do you think?'
- In a range: some people are reluctant to give out numbers for sales, employees or whatever. Make it easy for them by giving them a range to slot them into.

But sometimes as a last resort it may be necessary to provoke: 'Someone at (the fiercest competitor) said your company is facing a few problems at the moment.' With luck, this will make them spring to the defence.

Keep to the logical flow of the question set, but do not be imprisoned by it by interrupting the respondent's flow or by preventing them from developing an interesting angle that you had not thought of. Try not to overrun. If you have said the discussion will last 20 minutes, make sure it does, or at least give the respondent to option to duck out after 20 minutes. They will respect you for this and will be happy to talk again if necessary. If they sound pressed, offer to call back at another time, make an appointment and keep it. At the end of the conversation, do not forget to ask who else you should talk to, either internally or externally and so leave the door open to call back.

During the course of a competitor interviewing programme, you are bound to come across a few objections. Table 13.6 sets out the main objections and how to deal with them.

Above all, stay cool. They are only looking reassurance. Their worry is that you are someone they should not be talking to. They do want to talk to you, they do want to be an expert; all you have to do is to give them the excuse. They will find the conversation useful and your role as a sounding board is invaluable. They are used to talking about their companies, on this occasion they happen to be doing it with you.

However good your story and no matter how well you have sold yourself, there will always be a few people who are too busy or self-important to help. It's them not you; just move on – but try the mobile first. You never know, alone in the car on a Friday afternoon, no interruptions and no secretaries ...

Other forms of interviewing

Telephone interviews are the norm in CDD, but in some assignments they can be usefully supplemented by focus groups and mystery shopping.

Table 13.6 Objections in interviews and how to deal with them

Objection	*Response*
'Why can't you tell me who you are working for?'	'I am very sorry but I cannot breach confidentiality' ('I am serious, this is a serious business'). 'I really wish I could tell you. I know this is crazy but our client has insisted. What I can say is that it is a big bank whose name begins with W'.
'How did you get my name'	'You are well known in the industry'
'How do I know you are not working for the competition'	'You can take my word for it. I can assure you that I am not trying to collect sensitive information and if I inadvertently touch on sensitive areas, please tell me.'
'Why does the World Bank want to know my margins?'	Get the platform right!
'Who are you?'	'A consultancy, please feel free to visit our website.' (A bit tricky this one if you are not a consultancy.)
'He is very busy. He has not time to talk to you.'	'Could we schedule just 10 minutes on say Friday morning?'
'Please leave your message after the tone ...'	Do not be frightened of answering machines. Succinct messages can work and, having left a message, you have credibility when you call back. They may even call you back.

FOCUS GROUPS

Focus groups are especially useful in testing new ideas, evaluating services or understanding consumer behaviour and really should be used more often in CDD. Focus groups are particularly relevant when visual material, brand strength or the effectiveness of advertising is being tested. The time taken to organize a focus group is what counts against them, but it is important to establish the required profile of respondents and to recruit as close to the profile as possible. Recruitment in all cases is best left to a recruitment specialist.

As focus groups are nothing more than a means of interviewing between six and ten people at a time, all of the guidelines above on interviewing apply. Groups last around an hour and a half. Depending of the size of the group, this should give time for five or six key questions, certainly no more. As with interviews, what is covered in the time must be carefully worked out so that it contributes most to whatever it is you are trying to understand. With only five questions you really must make everyone count. Remember, this is a one-off event, so you must stay focused, keep the momentum going and, above all, get an answer to your question before moving on. Do not try to take notes. Either have someone there to do it for you or, better still, tape the session.

Focus groups are often held in purpose-built facilities so that the client can witness proceedings from behind a two-way mirror. This is by no means always necessary and it is just as acceptable to hold sessions in a conference room. Whatever facilities are used, make sure they are comfortable, with adequate airflow and lighting, and do not forget to provide refreshments. It is important that all members participate as much as possible, so give them name badges so that they can address each other and configure chairs in the round so they can see each other. Before getting started, it is best to welcome the participants, introduce them, tell them the agenda and tell them the goal of the session. When facilitating the session, be sure that participation is even; if one or two people are dominating, it can intimidate other, more reticent, members.

Focus groups have a number of drawbacks, which you have to try to guard against. The main ones are:

- one dominant member of the group influencing others;
- 'professional' focus group attendees – make sure participants are carefully chosen;
- members saying what they think you want to hear rather than giving opinions.

MYSTERY SHOPPING

Mystery shopping is a way of measuring service quality using covert observation. It is widely used in both private sector and government market research. Researchers act as customers to assess the quality of the processes and procedures used in the delivery of a service. They do this through personal visits or, if appropriate, by telephone.

As a research technique it is subject to many of the potential biases of any sampling method. Mystery shopping research has to be statistically designed to allow general conclusions to be drawn about the market, which means having a suitable sample and a common set of measurements. Here lies one of the big problems. Because mystery shopping relies on the judgement of those carrying it out, it cannot be wholly objective and is therefore only indicative.

Mystery shoppers are usually recruited to match the profile of the target's customer base. They are given a list of assessment criteria drawn up by whoever is leading the research and trained to act out a scenario designed to replicate a common scenario. Once the researcher leaves the premises or puts down the telephone, they have to complete a structured questionnaire. The easier this is to complete, the better. Some answers are purely factual, such as how many staff were available, how long the queue was, how many rings it took before someone answered the telephone. Other measures are more subjective and open to bias. Perception of the politeness or knowledge of a staff member is just that, a perception, and their individual performance on the day can be hugely influenced by factors that have nothing to do with the service under consideration. Subjectivity is controlled by the use of rating scales. Staff must justify why they have chosen the ratings they have used, but we are still left with a picture of events in one shop, cinema or health club on one day. When a large number of samples are collected, either from one location over time or from a number of different locations, one can be more confident both about overall conclusions and about comparing locations.

Why not just ask real shoppers for their views? The reason for this is that real shoppers are generally described as naïve about evaluating service quality, which is another way of saying they do not really know what is or is not important or how to measure it. They therefore apply their own subjective frame of reference. Service times in restaurants always seem slow if you are hungry or alone and you may simply not notice the dirty fingernails or dropped fork. Mystery shoppers, on the other hand, can be trained to be systematic observers and to be on the look out for important aspects of service quality that regular customers do not notice.

Conclusion

Much of the expenditure on market research is to help clients satisfy and impress their bosses and investors rather than to understand what is going on. The core of CDD is using market interviews to find out what is going on. Other people's experiences are the best teacher. Why reinvent the wheel when others have already been there and done it? Being prepared for the interviews is a pre-requisite for successful interviewing.

Preparation begins with paying special attention to the content of the discussion guide and the wording of the questions within it. Questionnaire design demands careful attention. Care is needed to make sure the data collected by the questions meet the objectives of the investigation. You cannot begin to formulate questions and worry about wording unless you know what you want to accomplish. Questionnaires allow the collection of both subjective and objective data. However, they are only as good as the questions. Questions must be carefully thought through to avoid bias and make them understandable by all concerned. Like anything else, they need rigorous quality testing. The respondent defines the type of questions you can ask, the words you can use and the areas you can explore. To find out what respondents think, you should ask them questions they can truthfully answer. Let them tell you. Do not impose your values perceptions, language or anything else on them.

Make sure the team is as thoroughly briefed as is possible from desk research and management briefings. The more knowledgeable they sound, the more credibility they will have and the more they will have available when they come to trade information.

Good interviewing is a question of practice, but there are a number of basics to bear in mind always. Do not be imprisoned by the script. This is not market research. You should see the questionnaire as a guide and be ready to follow interesting lines of discussion should they open up. Interviews should be designed to probe for insights on current buying criteria, how these are expected to evolve, how the target performs against what customers expect and versus the competition and what it must do better to win share. Be prepared to take the indirect route if this helps the discussions along. Let your interviewees talk. You want their thoughts and opinions. Do not be tempted to interrupt with your own answers. Paraphrase what they have said to check your understanding. Next, remember all you need from them is the answer. There is no point going on once you have what you need. And because all you need is the answer, the number of interviews to be conducted is a function of the concentration of buyers within the target's markets and the diversity of the responses received. The more concentrated the customer base and the less variable the responses, the fewer the number of interviews that are needed and vice-versa. Be professional at all times and be prepared to trade non-confidential information. Finally, pay attention to the end of the interview. The end of the interview is a not a time for winding down, as it is often at this juncture that the most revealing facts and opinions come out. Competitor interviews require extra special care. Set aside a time to do them, but practice the platform first. Pay extra special attention to the order of the questions and try to make sure that the hard questions are disguised. Finally, when planning your CDD do not overlook the possibility of supplementing telephone interviews with other forms of interviewing, notably focus groups and mystery shopping.

Notes

1. Oppenheim, A.N. (1966) *Questionnaire Design and Attitude Measurement.* London: Heinemann Educational.
2. Tull, Donald S. and Hawkins, Del I. (1976) *Marketing Research.* New York: Macmillan.

CHAPTER

14 *Writing the Report*

Inspired research, brilliant analysis and inspired conclusions are in vain if the reader for whom the work is intended either does not read the report, cannot understand it without undue effort or does not accept the facts, findings, conclusions and recommendations. Report writing is much more than presenting facts. It is about communicating in a way that is both acceptable and intelligible to the intended readers. If readers do not understand, they will reject what a writer has to say. This chapter deals with report writing. Using and presenting numbers needs special care. This topic is dealt with in Appendix B.2.

Start by putting the report in context

The beginning of the report needs to set the rest in context by saying what you have done, how you have done it and where the information has come from. Therefore always start with a page that lists the following:

- the objective, for example, 'to verify Target Co.'s 3-year sales and gross margin forecasts';
- the issues examined, for example, 'market size and growth, drivers of growth and their longevity and Target Co.'s relative performance';
- method, for example, 'desk research and interviews with 50 experienced managers active in Target Co.'s market';
- scope, for example, 'scope was limited to the UK and German markets, which make up 80 per cent of target Co's sales'.

Keep the structure logical

In the 1950s, a McKinsey consultant wrote what is still seen as the classic work on structuring reports.[1] For a book that is supposed to be about good communication, it is a very disappointing read and I suspect experienced report writers do most of what she says by instinct. Nonetheless, it is worth distilling the essence of what the author, Barbara Minto, says – be logical and stick to the answering the question – because one reads so many reports that flop around all over the place.

Minto's governing points are that all reports should:

- give the answer via a logical hierarchy of issues;
- deal with one issue at a time;
- group similar issues to make understanding easier.

As a practical example of how these three points translate into practice. The right-hand side of Figure 12.5 (see Chapter 12) applies Minto's 'pyramid principle' to a CDD report.

Give the answer via a logical hierarchy of issues

The basic rule of the pyramid is that ideas at any level must be summaries of the ideas grouped below them, because they were derived from them.

When a grouping of ideas conveys a deductive argument, the idea above is easy to derive because it is a simple summary that leans heavily on the final conclusion. But when the grouping is an inductive one made up of a set of statements that you see as closely related in some way, the idea above must state what the relationship implies.'[2] Only if you have these types of groupings can you put a simple unifying headline at the top of the page. If not, you have to resort to bland assertions such as 'there are five threats to the business'.

Cover one issue at a time

The mind cannot hold more than seven items in its short-term memory. Five is better, three good and the easiest, one. Minto's central theme is that reports should deal with issues one at a time and feed them up to a single overriding thought – hence the notion of a pyramid. This also fits exactly with the time-honoured approach of one message per page, which says that the general rule should be to present one point per page. Each page should have a succinct headline, which summarizes the information on the page below. It sounds easy, but it is amazing how many times in draft reports you see page content that says something different from the headline that is supposed to summarize them, or a headline that is so cryptic that it is impossible to understand the point being made. If the page contains charts, remember they are a means of communicating complex thoughts and information in a readily understandable manner. The simpler they are, the easier they are to understand. Just because Microsoft PowerPoint® lets you create complicated charts does not mean you have to overcomplicate. If a chart contains a number of messages, copy it onto a second page and put the second message at the top.

Also think of your grandmother when mapping out the story you want to tell. Would you try to explain any subject to her without keeping it logical and simple? It is a mistake to think that because you are dealing with intelligent, high-powered business executives and bankers who can handle difficult ideas that you do not have to organize your material in any way that is easy for them to follow and makes the main points stand out. These people's heads are full of a million other things. If they cannot see the point immediately, they have neither the time nor the inclination to work it out.

Minto advocates a S–C–Q approach, which stands for:

- Situation: for example, ABC has the opportunity to invest in XYZ.
- Complication: ABC will only invest if XYZ can meet its forecasts.
- Question: How do we know it will meet its forecasts?

It is far from clear how this widely quoted requirement of good structuring actually helps. For the writer, S–C–Q is meant to remind rather than inform, but so what? Once you get to the central question, 'How do we know it will meet its forecasts?', you are off. For example, we know the target will meet its forecasts because:

- The market is booming.
  - We know the market is booming because:
    - everyone says it is;
    - market statistics confirm this;
    - the product is in short supply;
- The US market is 5 years ahead and went through a similar growth pattern:
  - these were the drivers of growth in the USA;
  - the same structural factors are in place here;
  - and here is what has happened in the USA.
- The target's products meet a core need.
  - We know the targets products meet a core need because we have done research amongst consumers and this is what they say.

And:

- The competition are a shambles
  - We know the competition are a shambles because:
    - customers say so;
    - mystery shopping confirms the poverty of their product offerings;
    - the target is gaining share.

The point is to be absolutely ruthless about answers feeding upwards so that the whole argument rests on firm foundations.

Group similar issues to make understanding easier

The mind groups things in order to simplify. Your job is to see the groupings and get the people to whom you are reporting to see the same groupings. To do this, you need to summarize a main idea and then the individual ideas being summarized. Link points together in this way – summarizing idea linked to individual ideas – and you will be automatically presenting the groupings as you see them. The logic of this is also that only ideas with a common link to the summarizing idea can be grouped together. If you do not present things in this way, the person on the receiving end will be struggling to create their own groupings and once this starts to happen you have not only lost control of the report/presentation, but you will also probably have baffled your audience because they might not see the connections. Worse still, they will be sitting there only half listening trying to work out where the groupings are.

GROUP BY LOGICAL FLOW

The obvious way of forming groups is to use logic to develop themes. In any reasoning process, you always deal with three distinct elements:

Table 14.1 Different types of logic

Deduction		
Rule:	If the prospects for target are good you should buy it.	If A then B
Case:	The target's prospects are good.	A
Result:	Therefore you should buy it.	Necessarily B
Induction		
Case:	The target's prospects are good.	A
Result:	You should buy it.	B
Rule:	The reason you should buy it is that its prospects are good.	If A then probably B
Abduction		
Result:	You should buy the target company.	B
Rule:	The reason you should buy it is that its prospects are good.	If A then B
Case:	The target's prospects are good.	A

- A rule (a belief about the way the world is structured)
- A case (an observed fact that exists in the world)
- A result (an expected occurrence, given the application of the rule in this case).

As is shown in Table 14.1, there are three types of logic.

The application of logic to CDD means a logical flow like the one shown in Figure 14.1.

The logic here is inductive because it groups like things – the market, competitive position and management's implementation skills (measured by its ability to achieve plan) – and says these three conditions are right, therefore we can conclude that the prospects are good, therefore invest. This structure is as good as any. The problem it often creates is that people then try to shoehorn issues into the wrong categories to preserve the logic structure. It can also create a structure that the reader finds hard to follow. As CDD is always about three things – attractiveness of the market, ability to compete, ability to capitalize – it can

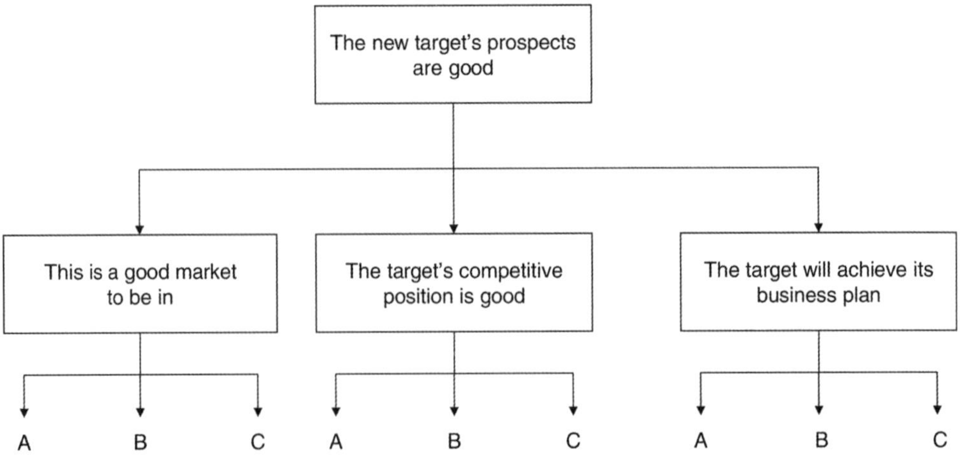

Figure 14.1 A logical CDD report structure

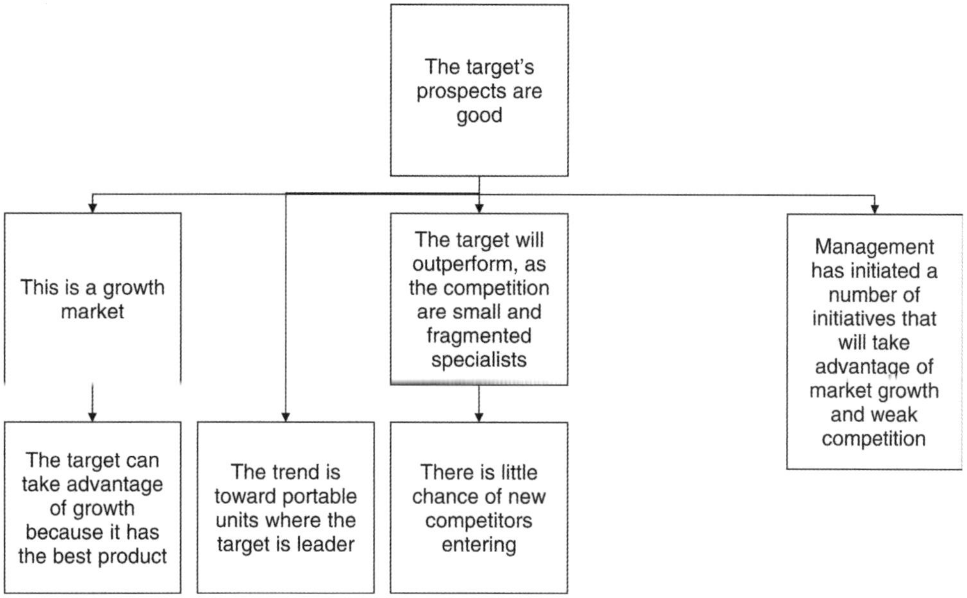

Figure 14.2 Deductive reasoning applied to CDD

make sense to employ a semi-deductive structure as in Figure 14.2, which resolves the issues one at a time rather than the reader having to remember all the market issues and mentally match them up with the competitive and implementation issues.

CLASSIFY LIKE THINGS TOGETHER

As you go down the pyramid, groups are harder to form using logic. Nonetheless the reader will still expect similar ideas to be grouped. For example, Figure 14.3 gives three groups of reasons why the fitted kitchen market will shrink. Group 1 is to do with the housing market, Group 2 is about market saturation and Group 3 is about shortages of skilled labour.

Always ask yourself of any group: Why have I brought together these particular ideas and no others? The answer will be either that:

- they all fall into the same narrowly defined category and they are the only ideas that fall into that category, in which case the summary will be a statement about their sameness (Group 3); or
- they are all the actions that must be taken together to achieve a desired effect, in which case the summary point states what the effect is (Groups 1 and 2).

Ideas in any grouping should be placed in a logical order. The question is, what order? There should be no problem with deductive reasoning because there is the logical flow, but it is a bit more tricky with inductive reasoning. However groupings usually:

- determine causes of an effect – reasons why the kitchen market will slow down, as in Figure 14.3;
- divide a whole into its parts – for example, Market 1, Market 2 ...

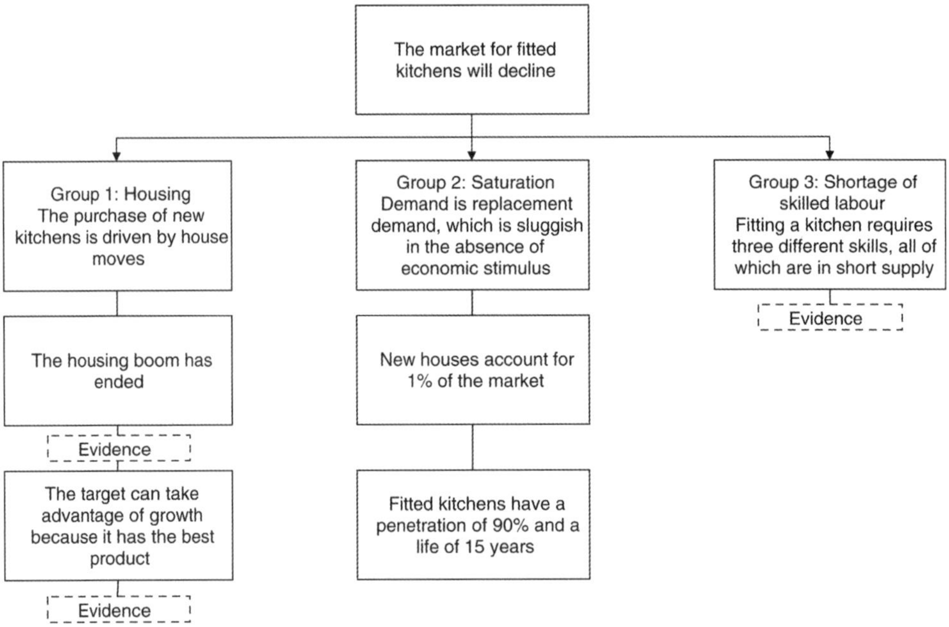

Figure 14.3 Classifying findings into groups

It is also recommended to order logically the points that are grouped. Three is a good number to have. As members of a group should share the same characteristic but contain it to a different degree, they can be ranked by the degree to which they possess the shared characteristic. If using bullet points, because all points should be the same kind of idea, their sameness can be emphasized by using the same grammatical form for each. For example, if the first idea in a group begins with a verb, all the rest must as well. If it begins with an indirect object, so should the other bullets in the list.

USE SIGN-POSTS

One idea per page is a lot of pages in the average CDD investigation. Sometimes these ideas will be supporting the point being made and at other times they will be a new point altogether. Make life easy for readers by putting in transitions so that they know when one section is finished and the next is about to begin. A simple way to do this is to map out the structure of the report at the beginning, then include a signpost on the top of each subsequent page to show which section each page belongs to.

MECE

Clearly in order to follow such tight logical structures, not only must everything be in the correct group, but also nothing must be left out and there must be no overlaps between the groups – which brings us back to MECE (mutually exclusive, collectively exhaustive), which we first met in Chapter 12.

Writing style

KEEP TO THE POINT

It is very easy in CDD to stray off the point into something interesting but not relevant. For example, if you are talking about what CDD does rather than the outcomes of CDD, talk only about what CDD does. Keep to the flow. Do not pitch things in because they seem to belong. A description of the CDD process must contain only issues relevant to a description of the process. Other issues to do with CDD, such as the outcomes of CDD, belong elsewhere under a different heading. They do not belong in a description of the process, which would be as follows:

- CDD assesses a target company's ability to meet the forecasts in its business plan. Assessing the ability to meet the business plan numbers involves three strands of enquiry:
  - The market
  - The target's competitive position
  - The management's ability to implement the plan.

The outcomes of CDD will be contained in another set of groupings. The outcomes of CDD show and evaluate factors that may affect the future sales of the target company. Here, as an example, are the outcomes or results of CDD on Target Co.:

- Market
  - The market dynamics will change as new capacity comes on stream to balance supply and demand.
  - The price of substitute products is falling.
- Competitive position
  - As supply and demand balance, competing successfully will mean a switch from a features-based approach to a price-based approach.
- Management
  - Management are marketeers and salesmen without the experience or collective focus to drive cost out of the business.

Keeping to the point also means also means answering the question and avoiding the merely interesting. You will collect an awful lot of interesting data, but never forget that you set out with an objective in mind. Think very hard about which are the important points and which are the details and examples that illustrate them.

BE DIRECT

Keeping to the principle of one idea per page with ideas organized in logical groupings means avoiding wishy-washy headlines like, 'the target is well placed for the future' or 'the target is vulnerable to changes at the retail level over which it has little influence'. The latter may well be a summary of the following findings:

- The sales force cannot reach retailers on a regular basis.

- Keeping salesmen on the road is expensive.
- The company sells through distributors.
- Retailers have an enormous influence over what the consumer buys.
- The product range is adequate, but is no different from that of the competition even though the company takes great care to add features where it can.
- The price of alternative materials is falling.
- Final customer spending has shifted from fittings to appliances.
- The final customers are not that price sensitive.
- Distributors stock and deliver what is asked for, they do not proactively sell.
- The company is slightly more expensive than the competition.

Apart from bullets not sharing the same grammatical form, it is all over the place. The groupings need to be sorted out. The above contains information about four groups:

- The sales force
- The product
- Prices
- The market.

The bullets can therefore be organized into a series of separate points as follows. Normally the format would be one point per page.

Point 1: The sales force

Headline: A tele-marketing operation aimed at retailers is a logical first step to creating pull through demand from retailers.

- The company sells through distributors.
- Distributors stock and deliver what retailers ask for, they do not proactively sell.
- Retailers have an enormous influence over what the consumer buys.
- Keeping salesmen on the road is expensive.
- The sales force cannot visit retailers on a regular basis.

Point 2: The product

Headline: Directly influencing retailers will help differentiate the product and stem the threat from alternative materials.

- The product range is adequate but is no different from that of the competition, even though the company takes great care to add features where it can.
- The price of alternative materials is falling.

Point 3: Prices

Headline: Directly influencing retailers may also allow the target to continue to command a premium price ...

- The target is slightly more expensive than the competition.
- The final customers are not that price sensitive.

- The price of alternative materials is falling, which, in the absence of proactive selling by retailers, could make them attractive to the target's traditional customer base.

Point 4: The market

Headline: ... and win a greater share of end customer spend.

- Final customer spending has shifted from fittings to appliances.

BE CLEAR AND KEEP IT SIMPLE

'To compose clear sentences begin by seeing what you are talking about. The reader, in turn, will re-create this image from your words'.[3] Keep the reader in mind. Keep a mental picture of your readers in mind at all times. Make sure you are writing the report for them and not for you and write to express, not impress. You should keep the acronym KISS (keep it simple, stupid)[4] in mind at all times. Keeping it simple is simplicity itself if you can keep to a few simple basics:

- Use plain English, which means writing words you would use in everyday speech. Good ideas ought not to be dressed up in bad prose. Remember, 'overloading with jargon and employing a tortuous and cramped style is largely a matter of fashion, not necessity'.[5] When it comes to word choice, longer is not always better. Try to avoid words and phrases that make the prose sound pompous (Appendix B).
- Avoid language that creates distance between you and the reader. Would you ever try to invite someone to dinner with the immortal chat-up line: 'Following our telephone conversation yesterday, I deem it necessary that we meet at Aroma this evening.'
- Make sure you understand. If you understand it the chances are that you will be explain a topic to someone else.
- Think of your grandmother once more. How would you explain the workings of the market for electricity transmission monitoring equipment to her? You would not expect her to follow a story full of highly technical language, riddled with jargon and with no logical flow. Nor should you expect it of anyone else.
- Keep sentences short – less than 20 words is a good target – but do make sure you vary the length and constructions of sentences, otherwise your prose will have a staccato rhythm.
- Produce a good executive summary and use plenty of pointers and summaries as you go along. The average intelligent reader has a reading speed of about 225 words per minute and understands roughly 75 per cent of what is read. Most investors have the attention span of a goldfish and deliberately misunderstand everything. Both sets of readers will process information much more easily if they know in advance what it is about and what it says.
- One message per page. Put the message in a headline at the top of the page in much the same way as you would begin a paragraph with a topic sentence. This is a conclusion you have drawn from the evidence collected. For example: 'Target Co. is not differentiated from other providers with high carer to child ratios.' The page then fills out the headline with examples of why you have drawn the conclusion you have. You should be able to write the executive summary by simply listing all the page headlines.
- Charts and figures should be self-explanatory and even if you think they are perfect, never assume that readers will draw the right conclusions. Always say what they mean.

- Avoid cross-referencing. Try to exhaust a topic the first time it comes up. If you must cross-reference, refer to the first discussion the second time it comes up. Referring forward makes the reader question why they should bother to read the first part.

Say it as it is

Euphemisms and over-writing are features of modern life. You are supposed to be producing a report that tells a potential acquirer whether or not to buy a business. Tell them in as direct a manner as possible by avoiding all of the following:

- Overwriting and padding: write, 'the target only caters to the high end of the market', not 'the target does not set out to serve any segment of the market with the exclusive exception of the upper echelons'.
- Using a noun if there is a verb: you do not 'make revisions', you 'revise'. Never 'conduct a study' of the problem, but 'study the problem'.
- Using an adjective if there is a verb: compare, 'the decrease in sales during March is indicative that sales are heavily dependent on the level of advertising', with, 'the decrease in sales during March indicates that sales depend on the level of advertising'.
- Using a negative to express a positive: 'These peas are not uninteresting' is much better as 'These peas are interesting'. Why would anyone use the word 'not', a negative word, to express the positive? It is not remotely logical – illogical even.
- Negative words and phrases: use the positive wherever possible. Write, 'We believe the sales force is inadequate', not, 'We do not believe the sales force is adequate.'
- Stalinisms: Stalin was a past master at writing phrases like 'it is axiomatic that' (when it was nothing of the sort) or 'it is widely held' (usually when the exact opposite was held). In a CDD report you will go onto prove the statements you make, so you can avoid needless attribution.

USE QUOTES TO SUPPORT ASSERTIONS

Using quotes from credible sources (any of those listed in Figure 12.7 (see Chapter 12) would be credible) brings life to statements and conclusions.

MAKE EVERY WORD COUNT

Use words sparingly 'as if you were planting a garden one seed at a time – not throwing out handfuls of seed willy-nilly, hoping a few kernels might land in the right spot and take hold'.[6] Eliminate redundant words. Think of Julius Caesar: 'Veni, vidi, vici' – 'I came, I saw, I conquered' – he did not need to say anything more about his visit to Britain. Using words sparingly means avoiding:

- Wordy phrases: replace wordy expressions such as 'in the final analysis' with a single word like 'finally', and 'due to the fact that' with 'because'. If a word adds nothing to understanding, delete it. As Mark Twain put it, 'as a matter of fact precedes many a statement that isn't'.
- Repetition: very powerful in speech but not in writing. In most cases, it will deaden not enliven.

Trust a word to do its work. In everyday business writing, nouns do not need adjectives or any other word to help them. Therefore avoid:

- Redundant modifiers such as 'almost unique' (itself an oxymoron) or 'past histories' (see Appendix B).
- Inessential categories such as 'heavy in weight' – it would not be heavy in colour or diameter would it?
- Hackneyed word pairs such as 'each and every', 'first and foremost'. Law and accountancy have their own word pairs – 'suffer or permit', 'true and fair', but that does not make them right in everyday writing.
- Redundant pairings such as 'basic fundamentals', 'end result', 'final outcome', 'important essentials'.
- Hedges – do you really need words like 'probably' or 'often' 'usually', 'sometimes', 'apparently', 'seem', 'appear'?
- Hollow hedges – do you really need meaningless words like 'rather', 'somewhat', 'sometimes', 'virtually' and 'actually'? As in 'Customers are rather concerned by the sales director's somewhat unconventional approach'.
- Intensifiers – do you really need words like 'indeed', 'clearly', 'absolutely', 'unquestionably', 'invariably', 'always', 'every', 'any' and 'all'?
- Hollow intensifiers – do you really need meaningless words like 'effectively', 'certainly', 'altogether' and 'literally'? What does the word 'literally' add to 'Customers are literally delighted with the level of service'?
- Over qualification – CDD is about giving firm advice based on detailed market knowledge, so it goes against the grain to see prose that conveys timidity and uncertainty. Compare, 'it appears fairly likely that an increased level of advertising expenditure might lead to higher sales', with, 'There is a strong link between sales and advertising expenditure.'
- Tautologies: just as a woman cannot be a 'little bit' pregnant, nor can anything be 'totally unanimous' or 'nearly unique'.

Finally, use place-holding words like 'it', 'there' and 'what' very carefully. Compare, for example, 'it takes 3 weeks of interviewing and analysis to produce a good piece of CDD', with, 'a good piece of CDD takes 3 weeks of interviewing and analysis'. Holding words do a good job in placing new, unexpected or dramatic information at the end of a sentence, which is where they rightly belong because this is where the stress in a sentence naturally falls.

GET THE SENTENCE STRUCTURE RIGHT

A sentence is a complete expression of thought. It has a subject, a verb and an object, normally in that order. Remember what the subject is. 'Customer surveys revealed a number of service difficulties and have not improved' means that customer surveys have not improved. Much better is, 'Customer surveys revealed a number of service difficulties that have not improved', or, 'Customer surveys revealed a number of service difficulties. The situation has not improved.'

Avoid twisted sequences, Why write 'A new customer service system will be implemented by the target in April'? when you could write, 'The target is going to implement a new customer service system in April?'

Get the sentence beginnings and the endings right

The first and last words of a sentence get more attention than those in the middle. Learn to trim sentences so that the most important words go to the end. In other words:

- know when to stop;
- know the words or phrases on which to end;
- avoid qualifying introductions.

Always end sentences with the words or phrases that need to be emphasized. This means first of all not going on longer than you should and losing sight of what it is that needs to be emphasized. It also means thinking about where the emphasis should lie. For example, in the sentence, 'A good piece of CDD identifies and analyses the three key ingredients of the target's business, which explain why it makes money', 'the three key ingredients of the target's business' is the important phrase, so get it to the end by getting rid of the subordinate clause, 'which explain why it makes money'. This would be better as a separate sentence as follows: 'A good piece of CDD identifies and analyses the three key ingredients of the target's business. There are always three key ingredients that explain why a target business makes money.'

Ending on an up beat also avoids flat 'so what' sentences, such as, 'The target needs to reorganize its sales force, which is not an easy thing to do.' Why not write instead, 'The target needs to reorganize its sales force, which will take a lot of time and resource'? Now you are telling the client what it is letting itself in for.

Sometimes achieving the effect may call for some reorganization. For example, 'ABC plc switched to a new supplier because the target's deliveries were unreliable' is perfect if the aim is to stress the target's poor delivery record. However, if the point is to explain which contracts have been lost, the sentence order should be reversed to: 'Because the target's deliveries were unreliable, ABC plc switched to a new supplier.'

Readers have to keep qualifying introductions in mind until they are resolved. This is irritating because it stops them getting stuck into what is being said. Do not write: 'While the sales force has been strengthened, it is still not sufficiently professional to take advantage of market opportunities.' Write instead: 'The sales force is still not sufficiently professional to take advantage of market opportunities, even though it has been strengthened.'

Avoid the passive

Use the active voice ('the target provides excellent customer service') to the passive voice ('excellent customer service is provided by the target'), unless you can't possibly avoid it, which you might not be able to in the following cases:

- When you want to say something is being done and who is doing it is not important ('A new sales director will be appointed next week').
- When the result is more important than the action ('A new computer system has been installed to remedy customer service problems').

- Where there is nothing to be gained by mentioning the subject of the sentence ('The IT department has developed an improved customer relationship management system', versus, 'An improved customer relationship management system has been developed').
- Where the performer of the action is unknown ('Customers are all experienced users of the product' versus 'The product is well understood'), or where you want to avoid saying who did perform the action ('The sales director handled the biggest customer badly' versus 'The biggest customer was badly handled').

Instead of using the passive, make sentences tell stories. To do this, give them characters and action. Not, 'There was an incident that resulted in an employee being charged', but, 'An employee faces charges following an incident.' The first is a mere fact. The second is a story, it has a character and action.

BE OBJECTIVE

CDD always relies on an interpretation of the evidence as well as the hard facts, but this does not mean a CDD report is a platform for personal opinions and feelings. The aim is to present a coherent argument properly supported. As mentioned in the Chapter 13, the pattern is always the same – assert, then support. As the assertion comes from the evidence, arguments should always be properly supported. When they are not, it is because you are too close to the evidence. Be on the look out for:

- Irrelevant examples.
- Drawing broader conclusions than the evidence warrants.
- Sweeping statements or conclusions that you may believe to be true, but nonetheless cannot be proved. If, for example, you have only interviewed three prospective subscribers to a business information service out of an estimated population of 100, you cannot possibly say that there is little prospect of growth coming from new subscribers even if all three said they would not subscribe. All you can say is that you have asked three and they said 'no'.

Supporting evidence needs to be:

- accurate – check everything you write for accuracy;
- specific and detailed;
- sufficient and complete;
- relevant and connected to the argument;
- meaningful and appropriate to the audience.

BE SPECIFIC

There is nothing more annoying than a page summary that says: 'Most people said ABC ... but some said the opposite.' In any interview programme, there will always be some who said the opposite. CDD is about drawing conclusions from unfinished, incomplete and contradictory data, so draw the conclusion! Market research is about reporting the output of 50 interviews: 'In tests, nine out of ten dog owners said they preferred Rover's Tasty Chunks.' In addition to drawing a firm conclusion, words like 'mostly', largely', and 'substantially' merely raise the question, 'So how much is that then?' It is much better to use something more concrete like 'about a third'.

SPELL CHECK

There is no excuse in this age of electronic spell checkers not to check spellings. Incorrect spelling indicates carelessness and lack of attention to detail. And for goodness sake check that everyone knows how to spell the target's name and those of its main competitors. What credibility would you give to a market report that cannot even get the names of the main protagonists right?

Make sure individual contributions are consistent

Getting a group of disparate people to work together to a tight deadline is asking for trouble unless there is a shared understanding of the report's direction. It is best to agree on a theme beforehand, which then acts like a backbone from which everything hangs. You also need:

- Consistent application of a common set of rules: it is a waste of precious time to have to make abbreviations consistent. Say from the outset whether millions of pounds is going to be abbreviated to £m, £M, £ million or £ mio. Are you going to spell numbers or write them as numbers? The main points to think about are set out in Appendix B.3, but beware there will always be at least one team member who will not read them or will forget to apply them! As well a short list of rules, have a guide such as *The Economist Style Guide*[7] to hand.
- The same goes for formatting: you need a style guide. For example, is it full stop, space, capital letter or full stop, space, space, capital letter?
- Consistent application of a common set of names and descriptions: there will always be names and terms that are specific to the project. If, for example, the target's name is going to be abbreviated, make sure the abbreviation is consistent throughout.

Produce an interim report

The best way to ensure clarity in a report is to write it, wait a day or two and then revise it. In most CDD assignments there will be no time for this at the end. The next best thing is to produce an interim report after a couple of weeks. An interim is a great aid to clarity in the final report.

Vendor CDD reports

Vendor CDD (VCDD) is the name for any due diligence reports that are commissioned by the current owners of the business in preparation for their sale. Acquirers are presented with a CDD report that has been commissioned (and paid for) by the sellers. Sellers do this to:

- speed up the process;
- present as much information as possible to prospective acquirers;

- get all the bad news out up front, so its discovery later is not used as an excuse to chisel the price;
- minimize follow-up and renegotiation.

It hardly needs saying that if you are commissioned to produce VCDD there is a conflict inherent in being paid by one side that wants to maximize the sale price, while providing a fair and balanced view that the other side can rely on. In fact, sellers do themselves no good whatsoever by trying to hide weaknesses. Not surprisingly, acquirers are doubly sceptical about the contents of VCDD reports (see below) and will probe the contents mercilessly. Anything that does not look right or does not make sense they will investigate independently and as soon as they start to do that, the seller has thrown away one of the advantages for producing VCDD in the first place. VCDD reports should, therefore, be balanced and appear independent, otherwise they will not be credible. This means that the VCDD team should not be afraid to disagree with management's assessments of competitive position or their forecasts – or indeed anything else.

VCDD reports should be produced as independent reports that can be read in isolation. This means starting from first principles. They must explain what the business does, what market is served, how that market segments, who the target company's customers are and why they buy from the target rather than another supplier, who the competition are, what they offer and how their offering compares with the target's. In other words, VCDD is just like a piece of CDD! The process is very similar to CDD too. There should be close interaction with management, but VCDD should not take up too much of their time because there will be many other advisors also vying for their attention. The trick is to make the process as easy as possible for all concerned.

Also, just like CDD, you need to remember that life, and the business, continues after the deal, so the report should provide value to management by, for example, examining growth opportunities or looking at post-deal market positioning.

ASSESSING VENDOR DUE DILIGENCE

Acquirers confronted with a pre-packaged report presented by the seller should be wary. Even if the independent organization that conducted the work has the highest reputation, it will have been briefed by the seller and, despite appearances to the contrary, it may have been encouraged not to expose potential weaknesses to their full.

Table 14.2 sets out some guidelines on how to assess a VCDD report.

In extreme cases, sceptical purchasers should commission their own independent commercial investigations. This has inevitable difficulties, as the seller will see little need to co-operate, arguing that the ground has already been covered.

Conclusion

Report writing is a case of keeping things simple. You have been asked a question; answer it. You will have gathered an awful lot of data and have a great many ideas, but nothing should make the final report unless it contributes to the answer. Write the report for the layman. You know what it's about, you are familiar with the data and you know the answer. Do not assume that your readers do. Start by putting the report in context, so that anyone

Table 14.2 Assessing the validity of a VCDD report

Issue	*Implication*
Who did the work?	
Strategy firm	Quality and neutrality of output should both be good.
Accounting firm	Quality will be restricted by financial culture and lack of depth in the commercial terms of reference. Fear of litigation will make the report neutral, to the point of being bland.
CDD specialist	Quality and neutrality of the output will probably be good.
Other firm	Uncertain quality due to lack of CDD culture, possible lack of focus on competitive position and management. In addition, some small firms may be influenced by the seller.
Will the seller allow you to contact the firm?	
No	Be very cautious and sceptical of the report contents.
Yes	Speak to the writers of the VCDD report and ask them: • Was your bill paid in full? • When did the bulk of your work finish (a delay between the VCDD work finishing and the report being issued may indicate substantial redrafting). • What had to be reworded/redrafted. • What was deleted? • How many draft reports were there? The more drafts, the less you should believe the report. • What are the greatest challenges facing the business? • Have you been paid yet? If so, have you been paid in full? A consultancy should not accept its report being directed or rewritten by its client. This can lead to conflict, to the point of not being paid in full. • What were the issues that the client saw as positive, but the consultancy saw as negative? How does that compare to what is written in the report? • Are there 'real' issues not in the report? • And finally, the Colombo question: Would you buy the company? (Emphasize that the question is 'off the record', particularly when dealing with the major accounting firms.)
Further work	
Would a limited 'top-up' exercise be possible?	A limited amount of further work provides the opportunity to address any unresolved concerns.

unfamiliar with the background can understand what it is all about. Create a logical structure, using a pyramid if possible. This means giving the answer through a logical hierarchy of issues. Issues on one level address the issue on the level above and so on upwards until the overriding question is answered. Issues are grouped together and dealt with one at a time, preferably one issue to a page in the final report, keeping strictly to the point being made at all times.

Having created a clear and logical structure, do not spoil it. You are writing a story, not a stodgy expert report. Think about your readers. Keep it simple and bring it to life by creating images that they can relate to. Do not turn you readers off with pompous, jargon-ridden prose. Say what you mean in a way that anyone, not just specialists, can understand. The same applies to charts. A picture is only worth a thousand words if it conveys a striking message without the need for explanation. Let the words you chose do their job. If you have chosen them properly in the first place, you do not have to dress them up. Think about sentences and how best to structure them to get the point across. The beginnings and endings should be the high points. Use the active voice. Come to conclusions because your job is to weigh the evidence and come up with an answer, it is not to report. Finally do not forget that Microsoft Word® comes with a spellchecker, that at least one team member will manage to spell the client's name wrong and that four team members will use four different styles unless told otherwise. Devise a report writing style guide and make sure everyone reads, understands and uses it.

Vendor CDD is CDD commissioned and paid for by the seller and given to potential acquirers. The main difference as a producer of CDD reports is the need to manage the inherent conflict of pleasing to sides with opposite interests. If you receive a piece of VCDD, do not take it at face value, but do your own CDD on the report.

Notes

1. Minto, B. (1987) *The Pyramid Principle*. London: Financial Times.
2. Minto, *The Pyramid Principle* (see note 1), p. 147.
3. Minto, *The Pyramid Principle* (see note 1), p. 172.
4. And not as one intern interpreted it, 'Keep It Simple *AND* Stupid'.
5. Minto, *The Pyramid Principle* (see note 1), p. 171.
6. Wilbers, S. (2000) *Keys to Great Writing*. Cincinnati, OH: Writer's Digest Books.
7. The Economist Newspaper (2001) *The Economist Style Guide*. London: Profile Books.

APPENDIX

A Checklists

The following checklists are intended to cover each stage of CDD, from the initial brief, to giving a quantification of threats and opportunities, to providing a framework with which to assess the management team.

Checklist 1: CDD briefing

These are the questions that should be asked of the acquirer before starting CDD:

- Are there code words for the transaction and parties involved?
- What are the companies/assets being acquired?
- What is the type of transaction; that is, assets deal, share deal or mixture?
- What companies are to be investigated?
- Give a description/history of the target company?
- Please provide information about the target's:
  - product and company literature
  - group structure.
- Please provide a copy of the sale memorandum (if there is one).
- Please provide a copy of the target's business plan (if there is one).
- What is the timetable?
- Please provide copies of any confidentiality agreements.
- Please provide an outline of the buyer's business strategy.
- Please provide a description of how acquisitions fit into your business strategy.
- How does the target fit the strategy?
  - What is the strategic rationale
  - What other perceived benefits are there?
- Have you prepared sufficiently for the due diligence exercise?
  - Are you giving enough attention to the 'soft' areas like culture and management?
  - Is there enough time to complete the process? If not, what are you going to do about it?
  - Have you explained the process to the seller?
  - Have you agreed access to people and documents with the seller?
  - Please provide an outline of which advisers are doing what.
  - Please provide a contacts list.
- Where are the synergies going to come from? Have you tried to quantify them in detail? What further information is needed?
- To what extent will the target be integrated? Over what timescale? What is the implementation plan with regard to the following:
  - Asset sales?

  - Business closures?
  - Development plans (when, where and timescales/priorities)?
- Have you considered any organizational re-design opportunities the acquisition creates, for example, outsourcing as an alternative to in-house resources?
- Have you explored all the consequences of the deal, for example, the effects on current operations, existing personnel, the industry and competitors?
- Have you set materially limits for the due diligence investigation?
- What is your attitude to risk? Is this the same for all types of risk?
- Please provide copies of any internal papers justifying the deal.
- What do you already know?
- What are your concerns?
- What is the audience for the CDD report (board, bankers, and so on)?

Checklist 2: A full CDD exercise

EXECUTIVE SUMMARY

Summarize the main findings, including an assessment of the trends in the target's market, its competitive position and an overall assessment of prospects for sales (and gross margin), both for the target and for the combined entity (if applicable). The target's stand-alone prospects should be summarized in such a way that findings can be fed into the valuation model.

PRODUCTS/SERVICES

Definition

- What are the products/services?
- Is the bulk of the company's profits based on one product?
- What are the distinguishing advantages of the products/services?
- Do the products require special knowledge?
- How important is after sales-service?
- Are there products which do not fit the post-acquisition strategy?
  - Could these be sold?
  - Should these be sold?
- Are there gaps in the product range?
- Could more products be added? (What are the implications of doing this?)
- Could the products be better targeted?

Analyse the market for each product/service

- Define the market in terms of customer benefits/the role of the target's products in the value chain.
- What are the substitute products/services?
- What are the geographical boundaries of the market?
- What is the size of this market?
- What is the historical market growth rate?
- What drives the market?
- Quantify likely future growth (if possible in terms of volume and price).
- Identify complementary products and services and any alternative applications for products and services.
- Assess market cyclicality and the impact of economic variables, for example, recession, interest rates, exchange rates.
- Describe market structure (market shares, routes to market, and so on), how the structure has changed over time and determine the drivers of change, for example, technology, legislation/regulation, consolidation, globalization, impact of e-commerce and their likely impact over the next 3–5 years.
- Segment the market, describe the differences in market trends between segments. Where does the target sit?
- Assess market attractiveness.

CUSTOMERS (BY SEGMENT)

- Who are the customers of the target company?
- What are their motives for purchasing?
- Can the target company influence these motives?
- How do these motives influence the market?

Purchase decision process

- How important is the product to its buyers?
- How much evaluation goes into the product purchase?/ Do customers buy this product as a commodity or as something more special requiring significant input from the target?
- How good is the target company in the evaluation process?

KPCs

Relative importance of (and target and competitor ratings against):

- Quality/performance
- Price
- Technical support
- Service
- Delivery
- Availability of stock
- Availability of spare parts
- Purchase decision process
- Single-supplier vs. multiple-sourcing
- Future?

Alignment of the target's sales and distribution alignment to customer purchase process

- What distribution strategy has the company chosen (exclusive, selective, and so on)?
- Does the product require highly skilled salespeople?
- If so, are the sales staff of sufficient quality?
- Is a specialist distribution network needed?
- Who are the influencers on this market?
- How do these influencers influence the market?
- Does the target company influence the influencers?

R&D

- How important is the innovation to the customer base?
- How innovative are the target's products?
- How high are R&D costs?
- Does the target company create new needs?

COMPETITORS

Who are the competitors? Profile competitors in terms of the following:

- Ownership
- Size
- Summary financial information
- Main activities
- Customers and segments served
- Commitment to each market area
- Sources of competitive advantage
- What are their main strengths and weaknesses?
- Performance relative to KPCs
- Do they meet the needs of customers better?
- Distinguishing advantages of the competitors
- Relative strengths and weaknesses by product/segment served
- Do they control access to distribution channels?
- Are there new entrants in the pipeline?

THE TARGET COMPANY

- Describe and evaluate the target's market positioning vs. competitors.
- Has the company succeeded in differentiating itself from the competition?

Competitive position

- What is the supply/demand balance in the relevant market?
- How well does the company perform relative to the competition?
- Are there indirect competitors?
- Do the distinguishing advantages of the products correspond with the KPCs?
- How well does the company perform relative to the KPCs? Rate the target's performance against customers' KPCs.

ASSESS THE TARGET'S RELATIVE PRODUCT/SERVICE PERFORMANCE:

- What is the target's product/service quality relative to the competition?
- Could quality be improved?
- Does the company fully exploit product/service advantages?
- Does the target company influence the way clients consume?
- Does the target company create new needs/is the company adding new options especially in complementary products and services?
- If not, why not? Is there scope for this?

CARRY OUT CUSTOMER REFERENCING

ASSESS THE TARGET'S MARKET STRATEGY (SEE CHECKLIST A3)

COMMENT ON THE RELATIVE STRENGTHS AND WEAKNESSES OF THE TARGET'S KEY PRODUCTS AND SERVICES

Branding

Is there any brand loyalty? If so, what are its origins? How enduring is it?
Is the brand name fully exploited?

Pricing

- Analyse pricing vs. the competition.
- What is the price policy (maximization of profits, of market share, and so on)?
- Does the price cover all the costs?
- Is the price consistent with the quality offered?
- Is pricing consistent with products?
- Is pricing consistent with the competition?
- Describe and assess the relevance for the target of each of the competitive forces based on Porter's Five Forces analysis (barriers to entry, demand/supply balance, relative bargaining power, impact of buyer consolidation etc.). Give an opinion on the outlook for prices.

Suppliers

- Who are they?
- Is the target dependent on a small number of critical products?
- Is the target dependent on a small number of suppliers?
- Does the target have a good relationship with its suppliers?
- What is the supply/demand balance in the supply industry? How is this likely to change?

Seek external views on management

Checklist 3: Marketing

MARKET STRATEGY

- Does the target have the mechanisms and processes for management to focus on strategy?
- Are they looking to the future, confronting industry changes?

Market choices

- Do management have a view of market definition based on customer needs and customer differences?
- Do they have a model of market segmentation based on customer benefits?
- Does their market segmentation link strategy to operations?
- Do they know what we are looking for in markets (marketing attractiveness) and in marketing position?
- Are they avoiding the trap of being stuck in unrewarding businesses (see Figure 11.3, Chapter 11).
- Can they list their priority markets and segments on a single sheet of paper and justify those choices?

The value proposition

- Are the target's core competencies the basis of their differentiating capabilities?
- Does the target have a basis for competitive differentiation that is both effective and sustainable?
- Can management write down the target's value proposition on half a sheet of paper? Does it look convincing?
- What does the target do to help its customers achieve the following:
  - Increase revenues?
  - Decrease costs?
  - Increase profitability?
  - Better respond to the needs of their customers, to new threats or opportunities that might be presented to them?
  - Improve productivity?
  - Improve their cycle time?
  - Improve the satisfaction, retention and growth of their customers?
  - Improve quality?
  - Improve the satisfaction of their employees?

Distributors

- What value do distribution partners contribute to the value delivered by the target?
- What is the target's value proposition to its distribution partners?

HOW GOOD IS THE TARGET AT TRACKING AND MEETING CUSTOMER NEEDS?

Question: What are the main benefits you deliver for your most important customers?

These are generic category benefits. If management cannot name a small number without hesitation it does not understand its customers.

Question: Do you deliver these for all your customers?

All benefits should be delivered to all customers because all are looking for the same generic benefits.

Question: Do your competitors offer these benefits?

If not, alarm bells should ring. Either these are not generic benefits after all or management does not understand the competition.

Question: How regularly do you monitor your performance on these benefits?

Daily or hourly would be a good answers. Minute by minute would be even better!

Question: Which of these statements most describes your company?

1 We are better than the competition.
2 We are different from the competition.

Being better is a more important driver of profitability than being unique.

Question: What is your USP?

If a convincing USP does not pop out immediately, do not be concerned. Customers are buying benefits, not a USP.

Question: How 'front of mind' do you think you are when potential buyers are contemplating their next purchase of this type of product?

If the target is not in the top few, start to worry because the top few win a disproportionate amount of business.

Question: Do management have a shared vision of how and why customers buy your type of product, generate their list of potential providers and narrow that list down to their final selection?

If not, how do they know where to focus their energies on what really matters?

Question: What do your competitors do really well and what are they trying to do better?

Alarm bells should ring if the target does not know.

Question: What would the market beg you and your competitors to do better?

How hard is the target thinking about innovation or out performing the competition if it does not know?

Question: How responsive are you to customer needs? (Complete the following table.)

Table A.1 How customer-focused is the target?

	Marks out of 10	
	Management's view	*Customer research results*
What is the state of current relationships with customers?		
Do you measure customer satisfaction?		
(Do you know) what matters to customers?		
How good are you at doing what matters to the customers?		
Is service delivery and value creation tuned to what the customer wants rather than what is most convenient for the target?		
How innovative and ready to change are you? To what extent are you trying to develop new ways of meeting customer needs?		
Do customer satisfaction measurements influence marketing policies?		
Do all staff understand the customer service and quality strategy?		
Do you use customer satisfaction measurements to evaluate and reward staff?		
How regularly do you evaluate your competitors' service and quality provision?		
Total (out of 100)		

Table A.2 Evaluating strong and weak marketing strategies

Question	*Strong marketing strategy*	*Weak marketing strategy*
Which segments do you target?	'Targets are distinct and homogenous groups of customers with similar needs, for example companies with less than 1000 employees with complex payroll requirements.'	'Targets are groups that come under the same classification heading, but do not necessarily have the same needs, for example medium sized companies.'
What are your value propositions?	'It depends on which segment you are talking about because the offer is driven by segment requirements.'	'Similar value propositions based on what the target has to offer with perhaps some minor tweaking.'
Give me five reasons why customers would buy from you rather than your competitors	'It depends on the customer. For customer type A it is XYZ, for customer type B it is ABC; and so on.	'Price'.
Give me five weaknesses your business has in comparison to your competitors.	'They are ... (and this is what we are doing to address them).'	'We have no competitors'.
What are your strengths and weaknesses?	'Our strengths (relative to the competition) are X,Y and Z, our relative weaknesses are A,B and C and (this is the important bit) our strategy makes the most of X,Y and Z and minimizes our exposure to A,B and C.'	'Our strengths are X,Y and Z and we don't really have any weaknesses.'
What about the future?	'We have worked out the way this market is going and our approach reflects our thinking.'	'Our approach has not let us down yet. If it ain't broke, don't fix it.'
What about the competition?	'We don't have any head-on competitors because we target different segments and serve them in different ways.'	'We are all much of a muchness.'

Checklist 4: Five Forces

Table A.3 below is designed to be a structured means of assessing each of Porter's Five Forces. It is to be completed from the target's point of view. It is important to get the scoring the right way round. The higher the score, the more the influence of the Five Forces and therefore the less benign the industry structure. For example, no economies of scale would rate a 5 because this would increase the chances of entry, whereas if the target's product or service is important to the customer in terms of quality, the score would be a 1 because that would make customer switching much more difficult. Think carefully before entering a score.

Table A.3 Assessing the Five Forces

The threat of new entrants: barriers to entry

Factor	*Extent to which the factor applies: Tick appropriate box (5 = low/easy, 1 = high/very difficult)*				
Score	1	2	3	4	5
What is the extent of economies of scale if any?					
Is the experience curve important?					
What size of investment is required to reach cost parity with existing players?					
To what degree do consumers perceive products or services to be clearly differentiated? (5 = not at all, 1 = very much so)					
How big are customers' switching costs?					
To what degree is the industry regulated?					
Total					

The threat of new entrants: Access to cost advantages that are independent of scale

Factor	*Ease of access: Tick appropriate box (5 = low/easy, 1 = high/very difficult)*				
Score	1	2	3	4	5
Access to distribution channels					
Access to essential technology					
Access to raw materials					
Access to favourable locations					
Access to other cost advantages which are independent of scale					
Total					

The threat of new entrants: Summary

Score	1	2	3	4	5
Grand Total					

The bargaining power of suppliers

Factor	*Extent to which the factor applies: Tick appropriate box (1 = low, 5 = high)*				
Score	1	2	3	4	5
The degree of concentration among suppliers					
The size of suppliers relative to buyers					
The degree of substitutability between products of the various suppliers					
The amount of, and potential for, vertical integration					
The extent to which the target is important to the supplier (5 = low, 1 = high)					
How easily can the target company switch suppliers?					
Total					

Customer bargaining power

Factor	*Extent to which the factor applies: Tick appropriate box (1 = low, 5 = high)*				
Score	1	2	3	4	5
The degree of concentration amongst customers					
The size of customers relative to the target					
How easy is it for customers to substitute between products of their suppliers and potential suppliers?					
The ease with which customers can switch suppliers (5 = easy, 1 = difficult))					
The amount of, and potential for, vertical integration by customers					
The costs/practicability of customers switching suppliers					
Sub-total					
Factor	*Extent to which the factor applies: Tick appropriate box (1 = low, 5 = high)*				
Score	1	2	3	4	5
The importance to the customer of the target's product or service in terms of its cost base					
The importance to the customer target's product or service in terms of quality (1 = high, 5 = low)					
Total					

The threat of substitutes

Factor	*Extent to which the factor applies: Tick appropriate box (1 = low, 5 = high)*				
Score	1	2	3	4	5
How big is the threat of substitute products?					

Internal industry rivalry

Factor	*Extent to which the factor applies: Tick appropriate box (1 = low, 5 = high)*				
Score	1	2	3	4	5
Relative market share (There is usually a 'U'-shaped relationship between industry concentration and industry rivalry; a high concentration will not necessarily mean a high level of competition)					
Importance of the product to the main competitors					
Extent to which the objectives of the main competitors are driven by turnover and market share					
'Normal year' supply/demand balance					
Number of competitors					
Industry growth (5 = low because low growth makes pursuit of market share more likely)					
Degree of industry differentiation (5 = low because low differentiation means a higher propensity to price wars)					
Fixed costs relative to variable costs (the higher the relative fixed costs the higher is industry sensitivity to volume around breakeven)					
Stage of industry cycle (1 = peak, 5 = trough)					
Height of industry exit barriers					
Total					

Summary

Force	Extent to which the force applies (enter scores)				
Score	1	2	3	4	5
The threat of new entrants					
The bargaining power of suppliers					
Customer bargaining power					
The threat of substitutes					
Internal industry rivalry					
Total					

Checklist 5: Identifying resources and capabilities

- Is the target as profitable as its competitors?
- What does it take to be successful in this industry?
- Why are some firms are more successful than others?
- What resources and capabilities is their success is based on? (See below.)
- What are the stages of the value chain?
- What capabilities are needed at each stage?
- What resources are these capabilities based on?

RESOURCES AND CAPABILITIES CHECKLIST

Technology related

- Research expertise
- Product innovation capability
- Expertise in a given technology
- Use of IT/Internet
- Patent protection.

Manufacturing related

- Low-cost production
- Quality of manufacture
- High use of fixed assets
- Low-cost plant locations
- High labour productivity
- Low-cost product design
- Manufacturing flexibility.

Distribution related

- Strong network of wholesalers/dealers
- Getting shelf-space
- Fast delivery.

Marketing related

- Fast, accurate technical assistance
- Courteous customer service
- Accuracy of order fulfilment
- Completeness of order fulfilment
- Timeliness of order fulfilment
- Breadth of product line
- Merchandizing skills
- Product styling
- Guarantees
- Advertising.

Skills related

- Superior workforce
- Better quality control
- Design expertise
- Development expertise
- Expertise in vital technologies
- Speed in bringing new products to market.

Organizational capability

- Superior information systems
- Flexibility to change with market conditions
- Management
- Workforce.

Checklist 6: Threats and opportunities

Table A.4 lists common threats and opportunities.

Table A.4 Threats and opportunities

Area	*Threats/opportunities*
The economy	Will demand be affected by changes to drivers of aggregate demand? Strength of the economy Level of consumer borrowing Direction of interest rates Stock market levels Exchange rates
Labour market	Availability of appropriately skilled labour
Technology	Is there a threat to demand from changing technology?
Sociocultural	Demographic changes Will pressure groups influence demand or affect industry location
Government	Government spending Tax rates Regional aid policy Industry incentives Industry regulation Competition law
Suppliers	The availability of critical raw materials
Customers	Changes in preferences and purchasing power Changes in distribution M&A activity
Competitors	Changes in competitive strategies Innovation
The media	Good and bad publicity

Checklist 7: Determining KPCs

STEP1: MANAGEMENT MEETING

Ask management:

- to list the top five KPCs used by customers in each of their target segments or business unit (it is important to get a comprehensive list early on);
- whether the relative importance of each KPC is likely to change in the future (useful for assessing future competitive position);
- to articulate their strategy (value proposition) for each of their target segments;
- to explain which measures (KPIs) they use to monitor performance.

STEP 2: CUSTOMER INTERVIEWS

Ask interviewees:

- in the first few interviews, to validate the list of KPCs offered by management (they may not be the same!) and amend as necessary;
- to give an importance weighting for each of the KPCs on the template and get them to rate those competitors with which they are familiar (including the target).

Enter the results into a template.

Checklist 8: Commonly sought management competencies

The five main subject headings below form a framework of competencies against which to assess management in either interviews or tests (or both).

INDIVIDUAL COMPETENCIES

Flexibility: The ability to change direction or modify the way in which the individual does things. Flexibility would include a willingness to try, adaptability and a positive outlook.

Decisiveness: This is the readiness to take decisions and to act, that is, coming to conclusions and taking appropriate action.

Tenacity: The ability to stick with a problem until it is solved (and to recognize when there is no solution).

Independence: The willingness to question the accepted way of doing things.

Risk Taking: The extent to which a manager is prepared to take calculated risks.

Integrity: The recognition and maintenance of high personal standards and the implementation of appropriate moral and ethical norms.

INTERPERSONAL COMPETENCIES

Communication: The ability to convey information clearly, both orally and in writing. The ability to listen.

Impact: The ability to create a favourable first impression.

Persuasiveness: The ability to persuade and influence others.

Personal awareness: The awareness of other people and the need to take into account their thoughts and feelings before acting.

Teamwork: Contributing in an active and co-operative way with the rest of the team. Supporting others. Making decisions by consensus.

Openness: The ability to take constructive criticism. The ability to build on the contributions of other people.

ANALYTICAL COMPETENCIES

Innovation: The ability to come up with imaginative and practical solutions to problems.

Analytical skills: The ability to break problems down and work on them sequentially.

Numerical problem solving: The ability to understand and analyse numerical information.

Problem solving: The ability to evaluate a situation and come to with solutions which meet customers' needs.

Practical learning: Being able to absorb, learn and apply new methods.

Detail consciousness: The ability to process large amounts of complex information.

MANAGERIAL COMPETENCIES

Leadership: The ability to guide the actions of, and achieve results through, other people.

Empowerment: The concern for developing other people and allowing them freedom of manoeuvre.

Strategic planning: The ability to hover above the day-to-day detail and see the bigger picture.

Corporate sensitivity: An understanding of where the business is going.

Project management: The ability to define the requirements of a project and lead a group towards its satisfactory completion.

Management control: The appreciation of how a business needs to be controlled and subordinates organized.

MOTIVATIONAL COMPETENCIES

Resilience: The ability to 'bounce back' when things are not going to plan.

Energy: Otherwise known as stamina and drive.

Motivation: The ability to motivate self and others.

Achievement orientation: The drive to set challenging targets and the drive to meet them.

Initiative: The ability to spot and solve problems before they arise and to act on opportunities when they present themselves.

Quality focus: The commitment to getting a job done well.

Checklist 9: Competency-based interviewing

Competency-based interviewing seeks to use past performance as a guide to the future. The interviewer must therefore gather evidence from specific examples from the interviewee's career. The structure for each example should be as follows:

SITUATION

- What was the situation or task?
- Describe the circumstances.
- What was your responsibility?
- Who else was involved?

ACTIONS

- What happened?
- What do you specifically do/say?
- What problems were there?
- How did you handle these problems?

EFFECT

- What was the effect/outcome?
- What impact did that have?
- How did you measure your success?
- What lessons have you learnt?

Checklist 10: Sample questions for competency-based interviews

SAMPLE QUESTIONS FOR CHAIRS

Strategic

- What would you say was your biggest strategic development? What did you do to achieve it?
- How did you influence strategic development? How did you communicate it? What was the outcome?
- How much influence did you have over the strategic direction of the company (for example, M&A strategy, new product development (NPD), and so on)?
- What were your long-term goals for the company? What did you do to position it towards these goals? And with what results?

Commercial

- Give me an example of where you have influenced improvement in the performance of the business. How did you do this?
- When have you maximized value for shareholders? What did you do to achieve this? Against what criteria?
- Give me an example of where you have identified operational shortcomings. How did you work with management to overcome them?
- Give me an example of where the commercial aspirations of management and the shareholders have differed. What did you do to ensure the right commercial decision was made?

Leadership

- Give me an example of where you think your approach to leadership has had greatest impact. What did it involve?
- Describe how you have mentored management teams. How did you influence the development of the team?
- How did you go about recruiting non-executive directors (NXDs)? What did you look for? What impact did they have on the business?
- What has been your toughest people-related decision? How did you handle it?
- Give me an example of where you have needed to resolve boardroom conflict. How did you go about it? What was the end result?

Persuasiveness

- What has been your most difficult negotiation? Why? What did you do to influence the outcome?
- Give me an example of where you have won a venture capitalist over to your way of thinking.
- In your last chairmanship, in what areas did you have the greatest impact? How did you bring influence to bear? With what results?
- Tell me how you balanced the diverse views of a board. What were the issues? How did you resolve the differences? What was the eventual outcome?

SAMPLE QUESTIONS FOR BOARD MEMBERS AND SENIOR MANAGEMENT

Leadership

- Give me an example of where you think your approach to leadership has had greatest impact
- What has been your toughest people-related decision? How did you handle it?
- Describe a time you had to bring people with you during a time of major change.
- How did you go about building your management team?
- Tell me about a time you were able to motivate/inspire others to achieve a challenging goal.

Strategic

- What were your long-term goals for the company? How did you set about positioning it to achieve these goals? With what results?
- What would you say was your biggest strategic impact? How did you go about developing that strategy? What was the outcome?
- What kind of vision did you have for the organization? How did you develop it and communicate it?
- How much influence did you personally have over the strategic direction of the company (for example, M&A strategy, NPD, and so on)?
- How did you keep up to date with a fast changing market?

Commercial

- What was the profit performance of your company? How did you influence this?
- Where do you think you added most value to your company? How would you quantify this? What did you do?
- Was cost control an issue? How did you go about improving this?
- What did you have to do to improve the commercial operations of the business?
- Where were your greatest successes in growing the top line? What personal role did you play in this?

Problem solving

- What was your biggest challenge and how did you resolve it?
- What have been the main issues facing the business? How did you prioritize and address them? What research/analysis did you do?
- How successful were you in dealing with these issues?
- What do you think was your most innovative/radical step? How did you manage this through?

Checklist 11: Things that can go wrong on CDD projects

Team members:

- fail to communicate with each other and the project manager;
- reinvent the wheel;
- do not flag problems early enough;
- get distracted by irrelevant details;
- cannot spot/are not guided as to what an answer is;
- do their own private thing;
- ignore the timetable;
- ignore agreed methods and objectives;
- slow down due to distant deadlines.

Project managers:

- do not understand the client's question and its context;
- do not work out what needs to be found out to answer the client's question;
- do not have a project management/progress monitoring system;
- do have a system, but do not use it;
- fail to take control of the project;
- react to problems as opposed to pro-actively spotting them and heading them off;
- get the balance between technical (have we done 50 calls?) and strategic (what is the answer?) wrong;
- get too busy to do the project justice;
- do not get advice ideas from colleagues;
- fail to set an internal interim 'answer' deadline;
- finish the report too late (just before presenting);
- allow the urgent to crowd out the important.

APPENDIX

B Report Writing

Words and phrases to be avoided in report writing

Table B.1 lists redundant modifiers that you should avoid.

Table B.1 Redundant modifiers

active consideration	free gift	refer back
basic essentials	future plan	repeat twice
climb up	important essentials	sudden crisis
completely finish	new initiatives	terrible tragedy
consensus of opinion	past history	true fact
descend down	past memories	various different
each individual	personal beliefs	
end result	personal opinions	
final outcome	present status	

Table B.2 lists redundant categories that you should avoid.

Table B.2 Redundant categories

area of mathematics	in a confused state	period of time
at an early time	odd in appearance	pink in colour
extreme in degree	of a strange type	round in shape
heavy in weight	of a cheap quality	shiny in appearance
honest in character	period in time	unusual in nature

You should also avoid rhythmic pairings. The most common are listed in Table B.3.

Table B.3 Rhythmic pairings

any and all	full and complete	precious and few
basic and fundamental	hope and desire	true and accurate
each and every	one and only	various and sundry
few and far between	over and done with	and so on and so forth
first and foremost	peace and quiet	

Wordy expressions that add nothing to meaning are listed in Table B.4.

Table B.4 Wordy expressions

Replace ...	*With ...*	*Replace ...*	*With ...*
on the grounds that	because	both of these are	both are, they are
for the reason that	because	relative to	regarding, about
inasmuch as	because	as regards	regarding, concerning, about
insofar as	because	pertaining to	about
due to the fact that	because	in regard to	regarding, on, about
based on the fact that	because	in respect to	on, about
in view of the fact that	because	in connection with	about, concerning
owing to the fact that	because	in spite of	despite
in spite of the fact that	although, despite	in support of	to, for
in the amount of	for	in the event that	if
a majority of	most	in a situation in which	if, when, where
a number of	some, many	in instances in which	if, when, where
as of this date	today/a date	in the region of	near, close to
until such time as	until	in the vicinity	near, close to
in due course	after	in (close) proximity to	near, close to
prior to	before	in the area of	in
in advance of	before	in the field of	in
subsequent to	after	in terms of	by, through
at the conclusion of	after	together with	with
on a regular basis	regularly	the question as to whether	whether
on a daily (etc.) basis	daily (etc.)	he is a man who	he [does]
in this day and age	now, today	she is a woman who	she [does]
at this point in time	now	is indicative of	indicates
at the present time	now	make reference to	refer to
at the present point in time	now	have the capability to	can
time period	time, period	make a contribution to	contribute
at an early date	soon	take into consideration	consider
during the course of	during	make a connection with	connect
during the time that	during	with reference to	of, on, for, about
in order to	to	with regard to	of, on, for, about
so as to	to	with respect to	on, for, about
so as to be able to	to	with the possible exception of	except
with a view to	to	we are ...	we ...
for the purpose of	for, to	... of the understanding that	... understand that
by means of	by	... of the opinion that	... think that
by virtue of	by	... of the belief that	... believe that
through the use of	by, with		
both of them are	both are, they are		

Avoid pointless words. Pointless words add little to the report and can be removed without changing meaning, emphasis or tone. Favourite pointless words include those in Table B.5.

In addition to pointless words, there are also pointless phrases. These are listed in Table B.6.

Table B.5 Pointless words

Absolutely	Basically	Existing	Quite
Abundantly	Current	Extremely	Really
Actually	Currently	Obviously	Very

Table B.6 Pointless phrases

All things being equal
As a matter of fact
As far as I am concerned
A total of
At the end of the day
At this moment in time
During the period from
Each and every one
I am of the opinion that
In other words
In the end
In the final analysis
In this connection
In total
In view of the fact that
It should be understood
Last but not least
Of course
Other things being equal
Really quite
Regarding XYZ
he fact of the matter is
The month(s) of
To all intents and purposes

Presenting numbers

ROUNDING

You should aim for consistency when rounding. Most calculators achieve this by adopting the 4/5 principle. Values ending in 4 or less are rounded down (1.24 becomes 1.2), amounts ending in 5 or more are rounded up (1.25 becomes 1.3). This can cause problems if carried too far:

- The difference between 3.4 and 4.4 is around 30 per cent yet both will round to 3.0
- Two times two can be anywhere between 2 and 6 depending on when and how the rounding is done:
  - $2 \times 2 = 4$
  - 1.5×1.5 (which could be rounded to 2×2) $= 2.25$, which rounds to 2.0
  - 2.4×2.4 (which could be rounded to 2×2) $= 5.76$, which rounds to 6.0

Therefore:

- only round after multiplying or dividing, never before;
- when starting with rounded numbers, never quote the answer to more significant figures than the most rounded (that is, least precise) number.

NUMERICAL CONSISTENCY

There is nothing more annoying than a table of inconsistently rounded numbers, as shown in Table B.7.

SIGNIFICANT FIGURES

Table B.7 Inconsistently rounded numbers

	2001	*2002*	*2003*	*2004*	*2005*
	Inconsistently rounded numbers				
Target sales	2.32	2	2.467	3.05	2.9
	Consistently rounded numbers				
Target sales	2.3	2.0	2.5	3.1	2.9

Let us say a competitor has sales of £2 403 275 in its latest accounts. For accounting purposes, it is important to know that exact number, but for CDD, £2.4 million, or even £2 million, conveys the message with enough precision and a good deal more clarity. The important thing is that sales are £2 million not £20 million or even £200 million. Although significant figures convey precision, sometimes more is conveyed by leaving figures out.

SPURIOUS ACCURACY

Under 'significant figures' above, it was argued that simplified numbers can get the message across more effectively than the 'real' numbers. A trap to avoid is the opposite – seemingly precise numbers constructed on less than perfect data. Let us say we are trying to calculate a competitor's sales from knowledge gleaned from an equipment supplier. Indeed, had the first amount been estimated, say, from market share and sales price, the first figure, effectively a seven-figure approximation, would be ridiculous. This type of 'spurious accuracy' is something that writers of information memoranda and providers of vendor due diligence are frequently guilty, so do not fall into the sales trap.

INDEX NUMBERS

Index numbers are a fantastic means of comparing changes over a period that start from different bases. They can also be used to combine on one chart two or more series of numbers with different units (see Case Study 39).

CASE STUDY 39

CALCULATING SUSTAINABLE GROWTH

In 1994, the system for writing parking tickets and collecting the subsequent fines in England and Wales was decriminalized. This meant that instead of tickets being issued by the police, they would be issued by local authorities who could keep the revenue thus generated. The system was first introduced in the London area. A renewed focus on enforcement by local authorities, no doubt spurred on by the extra cash and without the distraction of criminals to catch, led to a more than doubling of the number of parking enforcement notices almost overnight. In and around London, a high proportion of these go unpaid (London collection rates are only around 20 per cent). Local authorities use certificated bailiffs to collect unpaid fines. Certificated bailiffs earn their money by charging the debtor for the recovery of the debt – that is, the service is free to local authorities and bailiffs' revenues are dependent on success.

In 2004, the partners in one of the big four certificated bailiff firms decided to retire and sell out to management. This side of the business had been founded in 1995. Sales had grown from £2.1 million in 2001 to £7.3 million in 2004.

One of the obvious questions for CDD was whether this sales increase had been 'bought' and whether it was sustainable. Indexing the target's sales against those of the biggest bailiff companies (Figure B.1) showed that they had all grown impressively on the back of decriminalization, but that the target had grown more.

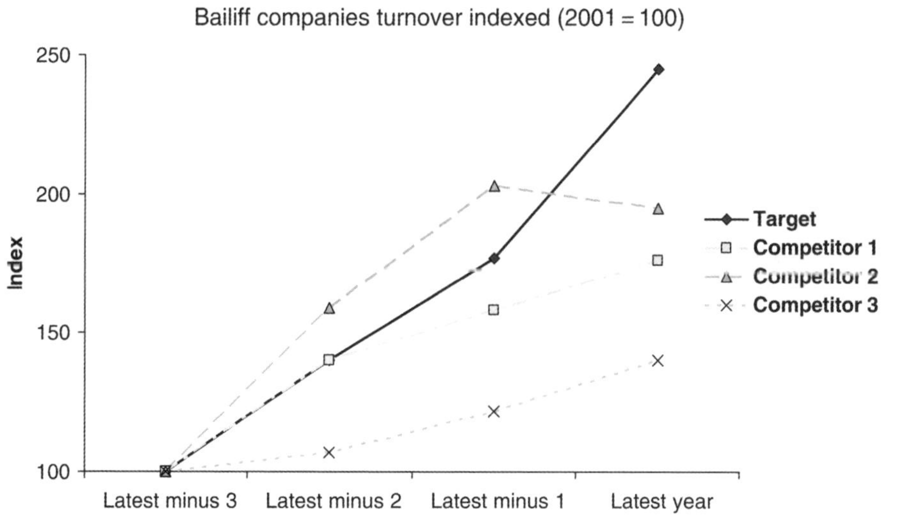

Figure B.1 Sales growth of certificated bailiff companies

This is how index numbers are calculated. Make the base value 100 by dividing it by itself and multiplying by 100. Then calculate subsequent index values based on the percentage change from the initial amount. This is most easily done by dividing each number in the series by the base number and then multiplying by 100. Table B.8 shows how this is done in practice.

Table B.8 Calculating index numbers

Year	*Target Co.'s sales (£ million)*	*For 2006 = 100*		*For 2001 = 100*	
		Divide sales for the year by 2006 sales	*Multiply by 100*	*Divide sales for the year by 2001 sales*	*Multiply by 100*
2001	162	1.670	167.0	1.000	100.0
2002	141	1.454	145.4	0.870	87.0
2003	138	1.423	142.3	0.852	85.2
2004	122	1.258	125.8	0.753	75.3
2005	111	1.144	114.4	0.685	68.5
2006	97	1.000	100.0	0.599	59.9

To rebase an index so that some new period equals 100, simply divide every number by the value of the new base.

Averages

The average is the most commonly used summary measure. It identifies the mid-point of a distribution. The purpose of the average is to represent a group of individual values in a simple and concise manner so that the mind can get a quick understanding of the general size of the individuals in the group. This being so, any average must be representative of the group. Always ask, before calculating an average: What conclusions will be drawn from the number I am about to calculate? Will it create a false impression?

Mean

The most familiar average is obtained by adding all the numbers together and dividing by the number of observations. This gives a single figure, which is a sort of balancing point or centre of gravity for a distribution. The mean is the most versatile average. It is widely understood, easy to calculate and it uses every value in a series. However, there are drawbacks and it is vital to appreciate that.

Harmonic mean

The harmonic mean is the average to use when dealing with rates and prices (that is, a measure that is expressed as per something – miles per hour, pounds per kilo, and so on). Consider an aeroplane that flies round a square whose side is 100 miles long. It flies the first side at 100 miles per hour, the second at 200, the third at 300 and the fourth at 400. The time taken is:

- first side 100 miles at 100 m.p.h. = 1 hour;
- second side 100 miles at 200 m.p.h. = 30 minutes;
- third side 100 miles at 300 m.p.h. = 20 minutes;
- fourth side 100 miles at 400 m.p.h. = 15 minutes.

This makes a total of 2 hours and 5 minutes in all. Four hundred miles in 2 hours and 5 minutes is an average speed of 400/2.08 hours = 192 m.p.h, not (100 + 200 + 300 + 400)/

4 = 250 m.p.h. To get the right answer, you have to take the reciprocal, that is:

$$\begin{aligned}\text{Time taken} &= 4/(1/100 + 1/200 + 1/300 + 1/400) \\ &= 4/(25/1200) \\ &= 4 \times 1200/25 \\ &= 192\end{aligned}$$

Compound annual growth rate

Compound annual growth rate (CAGR) is the year-on-year average growth rate over a specified period of time. It is calculated by taking the nth root of the total percentage growth rate, where n is the number of years in the period being considered. This can be written as:

$$(\text{End value}/\text{Beginning value})\,\hat{}\,(1/\text{number of years}) - 1$$

So if a market has grown from 120 to 145 over 3 years, the compound annual growth rate is:

$$\begin{aligned}&= (145/120)\,\hat{}\,(1/3) - 1 \\ &= 6.5\%\end{aligned}$$

Care has to be taken to get the number of years right. It is the number of spaces between years that matters, so 2003–06 is three years. CAGR does not represent reality; like all averages it is indicative, it is an imaginary number that describes the rate at which an investment grew as though it had grown at a steady rate.

Again, in common with all averages, care also has to be taken with the start and finishing point so that obvious outlyers do not get in the way of true representation (see Case Study 40).

CASE STUDY 40

Figure B.2 shows the growth of penalty charge notices (PCNs) in England and Wales since parking was first decriminalized.

As already noted in Case Study 39, decriminalization means that local authorities have taken over the issuing of parking tickets from the police and, as described earlier, partly because of other police priorities and partly because of the incentive local authorities have to issue parking tickets (because they bring in extra revenue), the number of PCNs has risen dramatically, as can be seen from the graph. At first, London boroughs were the only authorities to issue their own tickets. They were followed by a selection of local authorities in the South of England with the remaining councils more or less being forced to decriminalize before 2011. As a result, the number of PCNs will continue to rise, but if one were to calculate growth rates to illustrate what a healthy market this would make for suppliers, which periods would it be best to choose? Table B.9 gives the possibilities. There are two ways of approaching this. The growth rates could tell the PCN story. How many PCNs were issued

CASE STUDY 40 – *continued*

when it was just London Boroughs issuing parking tickets? How many were added by non-London Boroughs? How many more will be issued before the market settles down?

However, surely the above approach is getting carried away with the market story rather than relating it to the business under examination. Relating growth rates to the business plan gives the only story of any interest in CDD. The decriminalization market has grown by 18.8 per cent compound since it began, but by 21.8 per cent during the period covered by historic financials in the plan. If the market has grown by 21.8 per cent a year, but the business by 15 per cent, that is a relevant discovery as it would be if the business has grown by 30 per cent per annum. Similarly, one would be technically correct to say that the market will grow by an average of 12 per cent in each of the next few years. However, the number of PCNs are forecast to increase by 23.6 per cent on average over the forecast period and that is the relevant benchmark for CDD

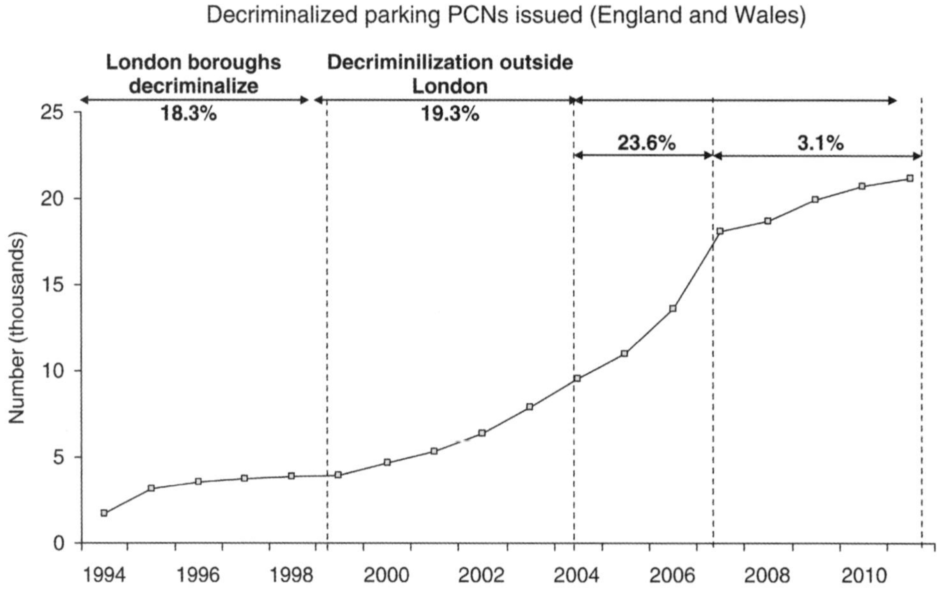

Figure B.2 The growth of parking penalty charge notices in England and Wales

Table B.9 Parking decriminalization in England and Wales

Period	*Event*	*CAGR (%)*
1994–99	Parking decriminalization in London	18.3
1994–04	Decriminalization to date	18.8
1999–04	Decriminalization outside London to date	19.3
2001–04	Business plan actual numbers	21.8
2004–07	Business plan forecast period	23.6
2004–11	Forecast of PCNs from remaining decriminalization	12.0
2007–11	Final period of decriminalization	3.1

The median

An average that is not affected by extreme values (outliers) is a useful alternative to the mean. One such measure is the median; this is simply the value occupying the middle position in a ranked series. Put the observations in order and read off the central amount.

The mode

The third main average is the mode. It is simply the value that is most common in a series. This is the average that the factory manager is thinking of when they tell you the target sells more 3-metre black worktops than any other colour/size combination. Be aware that some series do not have a single mode.

CHOOSING AND USING THE AVERAGE

As a general rule, prefer the mean unless there is good reason for selecting another average. Use the median or mode only if they highlight the point you want to make, or if the data cannot have a mean.

Avoid averaging two averages. For example, the mean of (2,4,6) is 4 and the mean of (3,5,7,9) is 6. The mean of 4 and 6 is 5. But the mean of the two sets combined (2,4,6,3,5,7,9) is 5.14. With real-life situations, the discrepancies are frequently much larger. Either go back to the raw data or apply a little cunning. If you know that three numbers have a mean of 4, they must sum to 12 ($12/3=4$). Similarly, four numbers with a mean of 6 must total 24 ($24/4=6$). The two totals, 12 and 24, add together to reveal the sum of the combined data. Since there are seven numbers in total, the mean of the combined series is $(12+24)/7=5.14$. This was deduced without knowledge of the actual numbers in the two averages.

Lastly, if presented with average, always ask on what basis was it calculated.

TABLES AND CHARTS

While measures such as averages and totals summarize data within one or two figures, tables and charts bring order while still presenting all the original information. Tables and charts are powerful aids to interpretation. Tables are generally capable of conveying information with a greater degree of precision than charts, but charts can capture far more information in one go. Charts are exceptionally good at getting a message across, especially in weighty reports and presentations.

Tables

There are four rules for constructing tables:

- Be concise. Eliminate non-essential information, round to two or three significant figures (including, preferably, no more than one decimal place) and convert original numbers to index form if they are clumsy.
- Be informative. Include summary measures (for example row and column totals or averages, and/or percentage changes), clear and complete labels and a two-line written summary.
- Order tables in columns (it is easier to follow a sequence of numbers down a column, rather than across a row); by importance (do not bury the important columns/rows in the middle of the table; and by size (arrange figures according to orders of magnitude in the key rows/columns).

- Be compact. Omit grid lines and avoid too much white space (which makes it hard to compare related data).

Charts

A chart is an immensely powerful way of presenting numerical data. All the information is summarized in one go, in a way that the eye can readily absorb. Trends, proportions and other relationships are revealed at a glance. Although there is always some loss of accuracy, this seldom outweighs the impact of visual presentation. Where underlying values are to be communicated, they can be written on the graph or listed in an accompanying table. Remember, though, that too much information on one chart can be confusing.

All charts have a source, and a sub-heading to say what they are about. The x-axis (along the bottom) and y-axis (up the side) should be labelled, unless it is crystal clear what they represent. If, for example, the x-axis goes 2001, 2002, 2003, 2004, 2005 it is pretty obvious that it represents years. Even so, it may still require a label such as 'Financial year ending June'. The y-axis will nearly always need a label. If you do not write £ billions or $000 how is anyone to know what the units are?

Different charts for different purposes

The best charts communicate the key points, very clearly. They are there to inject clarity and a possible 'Aha!' into the audience's understanding. Charts should always have a message (which tells part of the story in a sentence), a title and a source and have clearly labelled axes.

Notes should be used liberally to help clarify, illuminate and to disclaim! Charts should be clear, simple and concise. It is best to avoid 3D charts as they tend to redraw the data.

As shown in Figure B.3, which summarizes which chart to use when,[1] charts really are self-selecting.

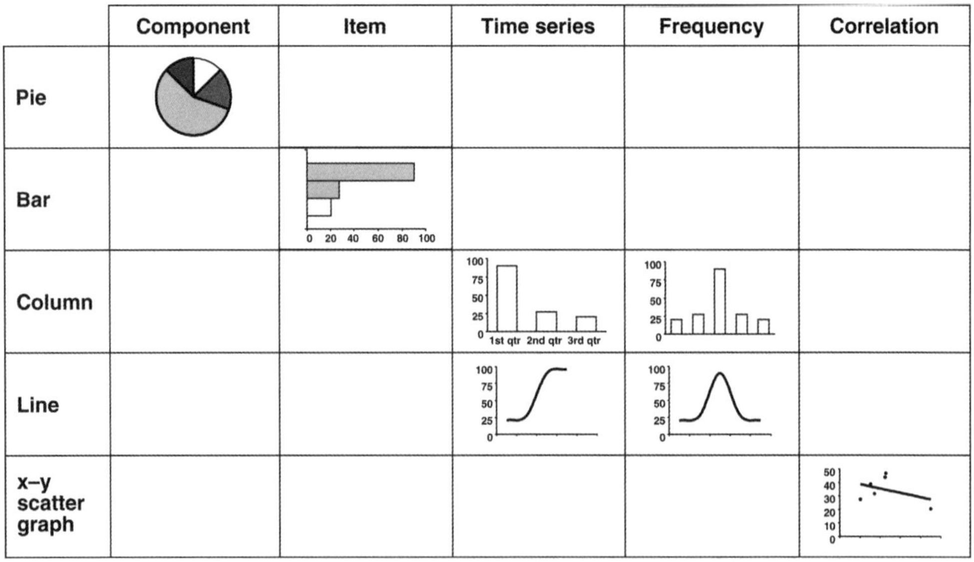

Figure B.3 Charts are self-selecting

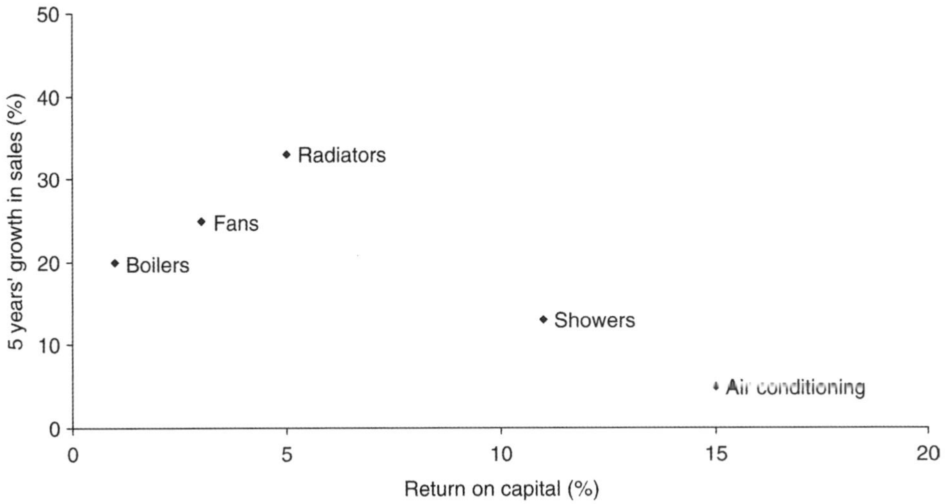

Figure B.4 A scatter chart showing relative sales growth and return on capital of subsidiary companies

The graphs in Figure B.3 are used as follows:

- Pie chart: used to show the breakdown of a single variable into its component parts, particularly to emphasize that together the parts add to 100 per cent. Pie charts should never be used side by side to make comparisons.
- Bar chart: used to present discrete data to compare the behaviour of a small number of different variables or movements over a short period pf time, when a line graph may appear awkward. Stacked bar charts are used to show how the breakdown of a variable into its component parts fluctuates. They are best avoided because unless the number of parts is limited, they are difficult to follow.
- Column charts: used to show time series or frequency. A line chart is normally better for long runs of time.
- Line charts: used to present continuous data, especially movements over a large number of time periods. They are also best for comparing the behaviour of a large number of variables, especially when they are close together and would be difficult to distinguish in a bar chart. Line charts are sometimes used for frequency, although column charts are better.
- x–y or scatter graph: used to understand the relationship between two variables. Scatter graphs can be very useful in the early stages to help set the scene. Figure B.4 shows the relationship between sales growth and return on capital for a portfolio of heating, ventilation and air conditioning (HVAC) products.

Other charts which are commonly used to show relationships include:

- Relatives
- Perceptual maps.

RELATIVES

One way to compare two items is to draw two lines. As lines present a lot of values at one stroke, they are invaluable in revealing relationships between two sets of data (see Figure B.5).

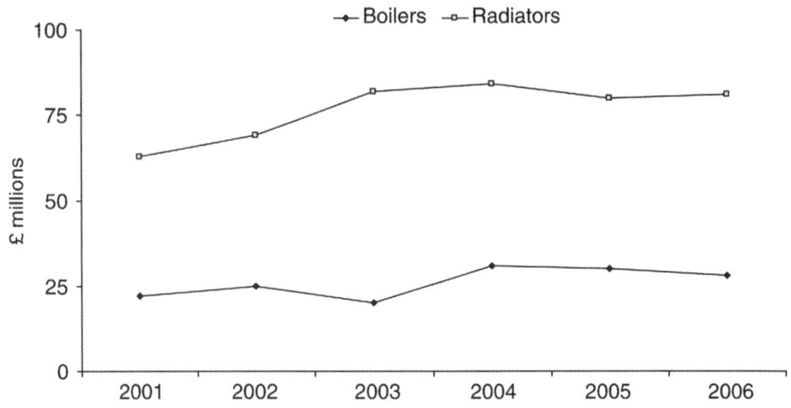

Figure B.5 Target Co.'s sales (2001–06)

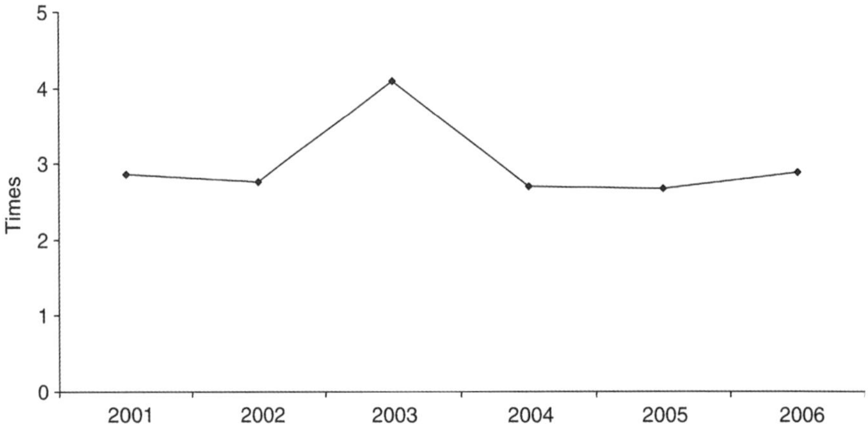

Figure B.6 Radiator sales relative to boiler sales (2001–06)

Another way is to straighten out one of them and see how the other moves in relation. You do this by dividing the second series (radiators) by the one for the series to be straightened (boilers). As can be seen from Figure B.6, there appears to have been a reasonably consistent relationship between boilers and radiators in all years except 2003 when something out of the ordinary happened.

PERCEPTUAL MAPS

Perceptual maps are (usually) two-dimensional plots of relative position. Some perceptual maps use different sized circles to indicate the sales or market share of the various competing firms or products. Figure B.7, which plots relative price and quality of four very different suppliers, shows a typical perceptual map.

Plotting market perceptions of existing products is only half the story. Providing the right dimensions have been chosen, plotting consumers' ideal combinations of the two dimensions will show market segments (where there are clusters of ideal points) and demand voids (areas without ideal points, useful for testing the target's new product aspirations. Perceptual maps need not come from detailed study. Intuitive maps, created

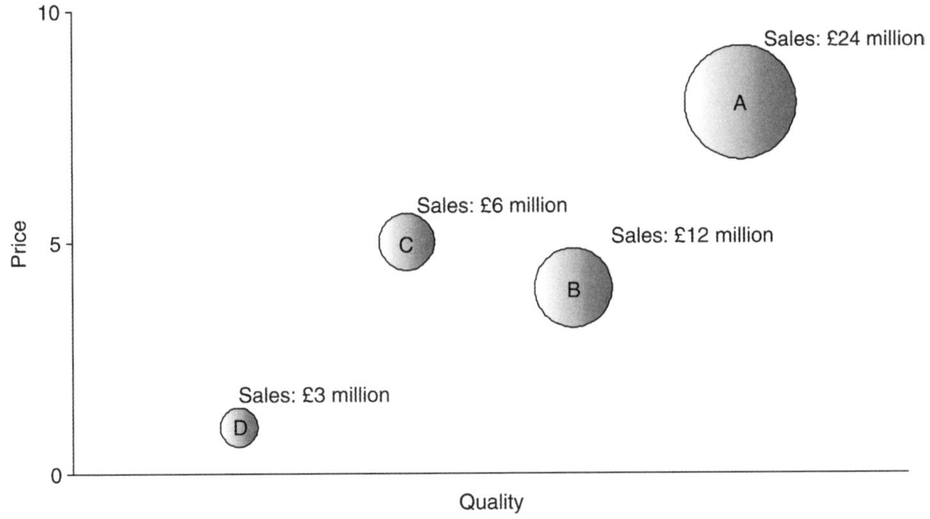

Figure B.7 A perceptual map
Note: Circle area is proportionate to sales

from understanding or judgement, are a little too common but they can play a role in explaining how a market works.

Points to watch (or how not to do it)

As illuminating as charts can be, they can also be constructed to deliberately mislead. It does not happen often, but all the same it is not unknown for an information memorandum to present charts in a way that, while not dishonest, presents the target in the most favourable light possible. CDD is all about getting the message over in as direct a way as possible while not misleading. The following is a list of tricks to watch out for when receiving and when giving information in chart form:

- Charts that do not start at zero
- A compressed vertical or horizontal axis
- Inverted vertical scales
- Joining the points on a graph
- The size of pie charts and circles on perceptual maps
- The convergence of index numbers
- Hiding controversial items in 'other'
- Small samples
- Straightforward misinterpretation
- Presenting unrelated occurrences as cause and effect
- Has the right question been asked?
- Are comparisons fair?

CHARTS THAT DO NOT START AT ZERO

Always make the scales on a chart start at zero and, if you cannot do that, make it plain that the vertical axis covers only the range of values plotted, rather than starting at zero. Usually

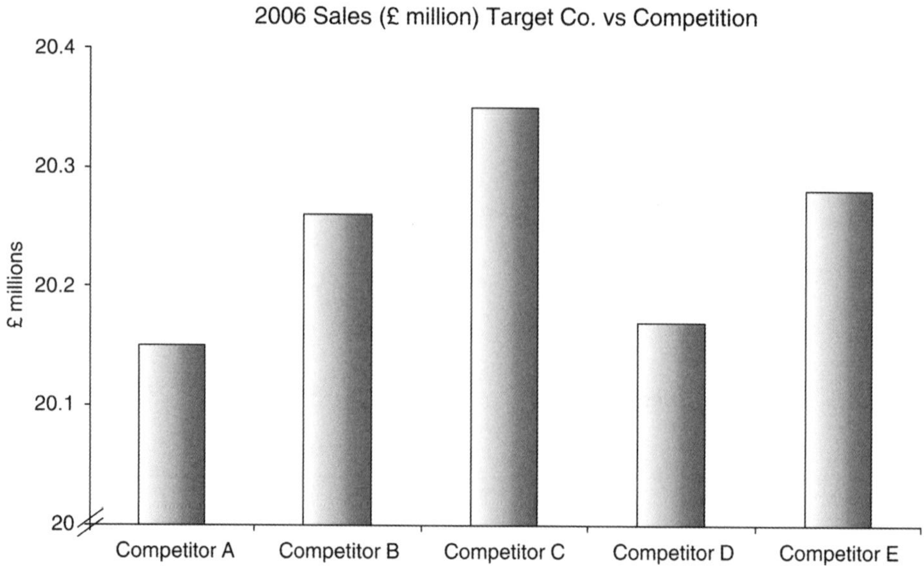

Figure B.8 Restricting the y-axis magnifies the differences between bar values

the only excuse is that the bar values are so close together that any chart starting at zero would be fairly meaningless. Figures B.8 and B.9 illustrate these two points.

In Figure B.8, there is exactly 1 per cent difference between the two competitors with the highest and lowest sales, although the chart does not give the impression that there is such a small difference. However, Figure B.9 shows that the effect of doing the job properly, by starting at zero, does very little to get the point across.

Where a trend is being shown, there is no excuse for not starting the y-axis at zero. If you ever saw a trend chart that does not start at zero, you would be forgiven for drawing the

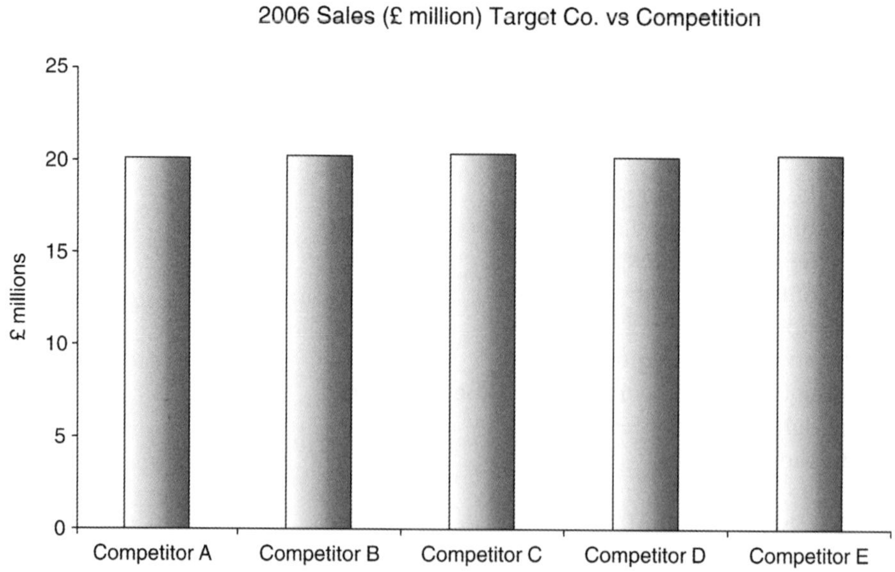

Figure B.9 Starting the y-axis at zero illustrates little when there is only a small variation

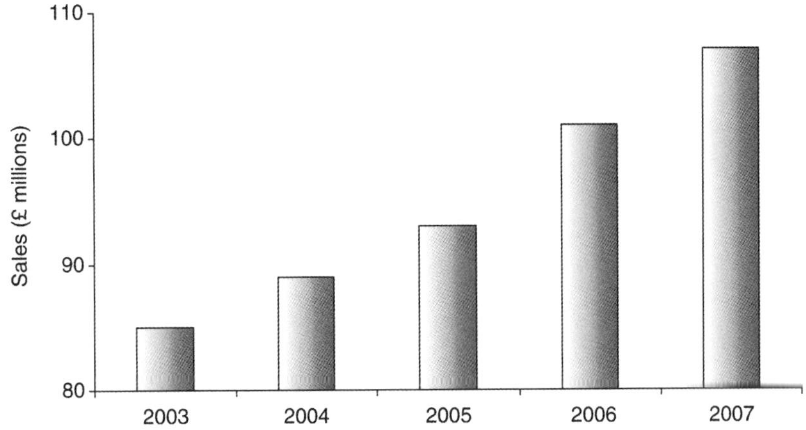

Figure B.10 Target Co.'s 5-year sales history

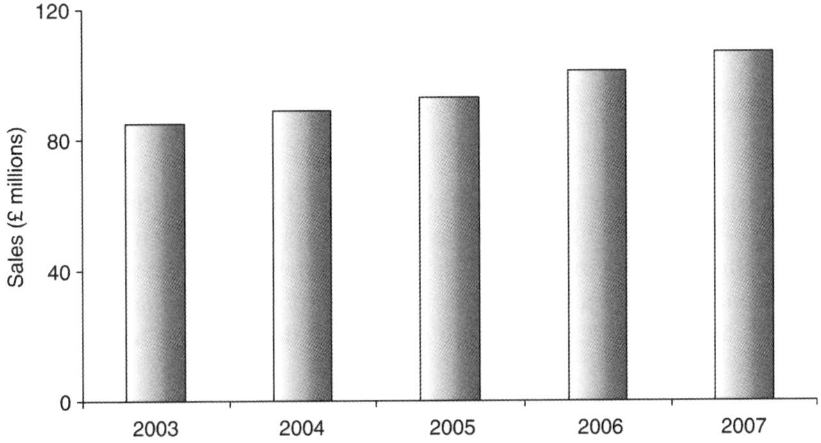

Figure B.11 Target Co.'s 5-year sales history revisited (1)

obvious conclusion, that the writer has set out to deceive. Figure B.10 shows how the writer of an Information Memorandum has exaggerated sales growth over the last 5 years by choosing to start the scale on a bar chart at 80, rather than choosing the more conventional, and less misleading, zero (Figure B.11).

A COMPRESSED VERTICAL OR HORIZONTAL AXIS

As Figure B.12 shows, compressing or stretching the y-axis can have a dramatic effect on the same set of numbers.

INVERTED VERTICAL SCALES

Charts that decrease in value towards the top (that is, the axis is upside down) are the easy way to make declining profits look presentable. This is a legitimate presentation technique when it conveys the right impression. Its most widespread use is with currencies. Currencies are usually expressed relative to other currencies and especially relative to the US dollar. Since its inception, the euro has progressed steadily against the dollar. At one time a dollar would buy two euros, it has, however, weakened considerably and will now buy about three-

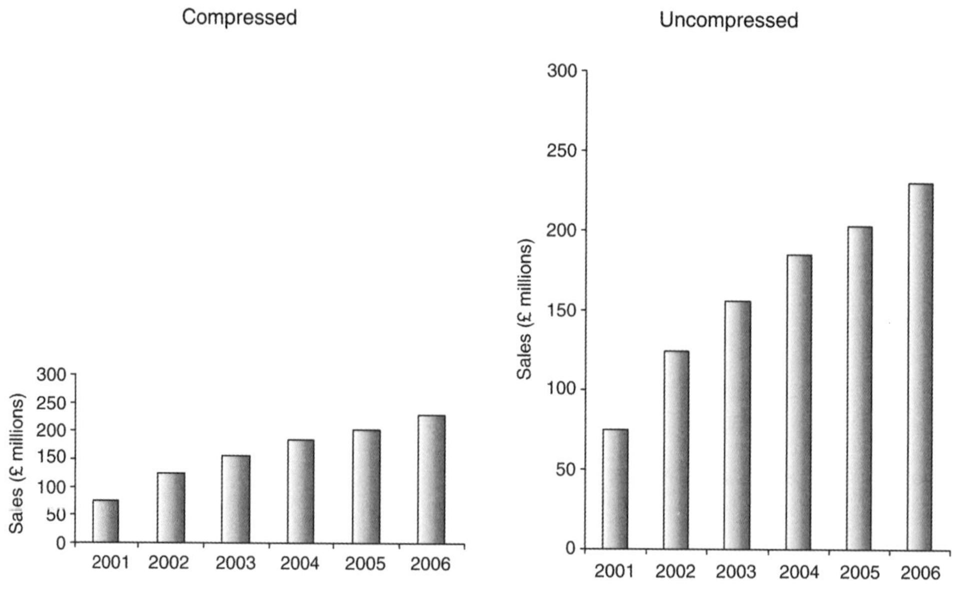

Figure B.12 Target Co.'s 5-year sales history revisited (2)

quarters of a euro. This is what is shown by Figure B.13, which is fine for an American audience because the chart shows what has actually happened to their currency.

To present the same data in the same way for a European audience would be misleading because for them their currency now buys a lot more dollars. It would be much better to invert the scale as in Figure B.14 to illustrate the point that the euro has strengthened.

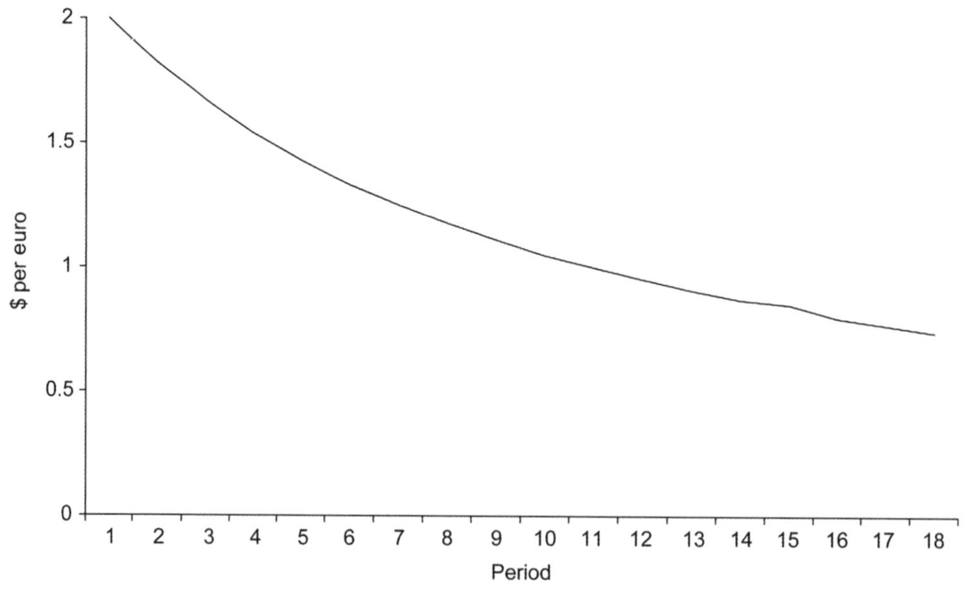

Figure B.13 US dollar/euro exchange rate

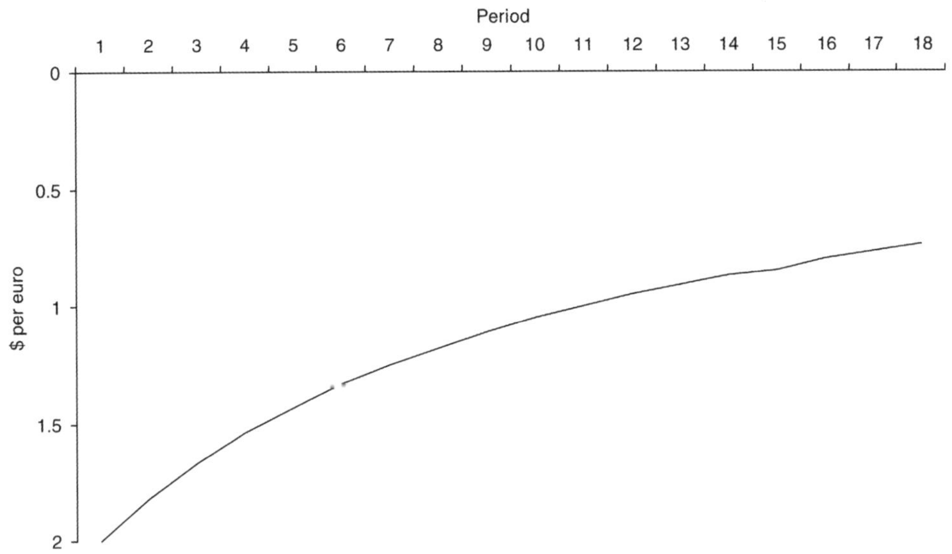

Figure B.14 US dollar/euro exchange rate with inverted y-axis

JOINING THE POINTS ON A GRAPH

Theoretically, only continuous data should be linked by a line. Usually, though, it is meaningful to link the points in some way. This may be justifiable as it reveals trends at a stroke. A straight line between two points may conceal, for example a line between two points showing healthy year-end financial balances may cover up a plunge into the red in the intervening period.

THE SIZE OF PIE CHARTS AND CIRCLES ON PERCEPTUAL MAPS

Doubling the diameter of a circle increases its area by a factor of four. Take care, then, with drawing and interpreting multiple pies. The area of a circle is found from $\pi \times r^2$, where r is the radius (half the diameter) and π (the Greek letter pi) is the constant 3.14159. For example, a circle with a radius of 5 cm has an area of $3.14159 \times 5^2 = 3.14159 \times 5 \times 5 = 78.5\,cm^2$.

The same is true when a chart plots competitors in a market as in Figure B.7. The sales of the four companies and the diameters of the circles needed to keep turnovers in proportion are shown in Table B.10 below.

So although company D has a turnover that is six times that of company A, the diameter of circle D is less than three times the size of circle A.

Table B.10 Keeping circle diameters proportionate to turnover

Company	Sales (£m)	Circle diameter to make circle area equal to sales
A	3	1.38
B	6	1.95
C	12	2.76
D	24	3.90

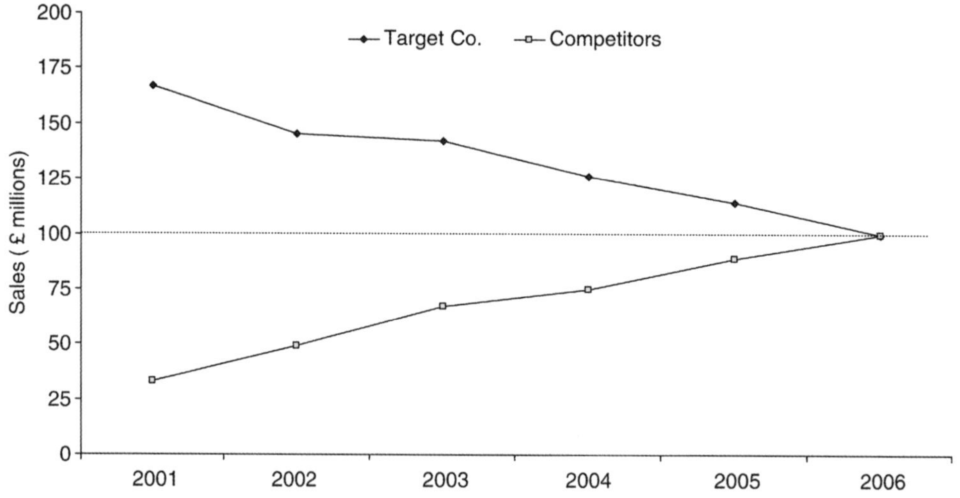

Figure B.15 The convergence of index numbers (2006 = 100)

THE CONVERGENCE OF INDEX NUMBERS

When dealing with index numbers, watch for illusory convergence on the base. Two or more series will always meet at the base period because that is where they both equal 100 (see Figures B.15 and B.16). This can be highly misleading.

Look at the two charts. Both are constructed from exactly the same sales figures for the target and its main competitors between 2001 and 2006. In the first graph, the target is on top, albeit declining. In the second, the positions are reversed and the competition is now on top. Whenever you come across indices on a graph, the first thing you should do is check where the base is located.

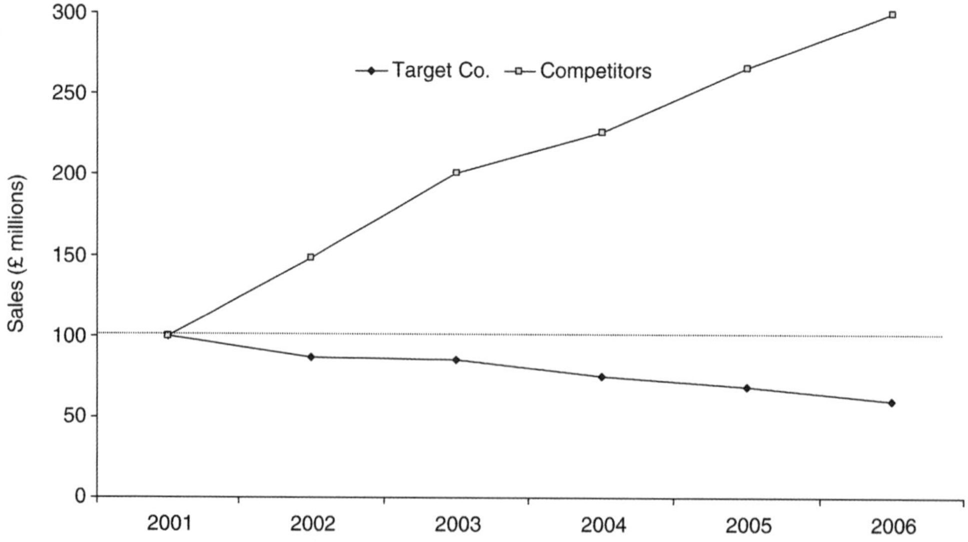

Figure B.16 The convergence of index numbers (2001 = 100)

HIDING CONTROVERSIAL ITEMS IN 'OTHER'

Pie charts are less open to graphically chicanery than bar charts are (see above). As the proportion of the pie is what it is, data cannot be under- or overplayed as it can with a bar chart. But pie charts can be used just as easily to lead to the unsuspecting reader to the intended conclusion. The 'other' portion is a favourite. It pays always to ask what is in 'other', especially if it is large in relation to the other portions of the pie. Many years ago, a young accountant was hauled into the office of his ultimate boss, the finance director of a blue chip company, to proof the shareholder presentation scheduled for the next day. 'Just one question,' he said, 'what is in "other"?' His finance director blanched and uttered something about another meeting. 'Other' came to about £2 million – a relative drop in the ocean for a company with a turnover in billions and he had only asked for the sake of something to say. What he found out later that the £2 million was the net of £158 million negative and £160 million positive.

SMALL SAMPLES

All statistical presentations should clearly state the sample size. How many customers were asked? Was it 15 or was it 90? Above a certain number it does not matter that much – but below about 30 it does and the lower it is, the more it matters.

STRAIGHTFORWARD MISINTERPRETATION

Charts should always come with an interpretation of what they say to prevent the busy reader from drawing the right conclusions. If you are that busy, always have a look for yourself. Authors can be cavalier with their interpretation of data as illustrated in Figure B.17. The message, illustrated by the pie chart, was that the client was first or second choice for the majority of acquirers. Hmm.

While we are on the subject, it always pays with a pie chart to check that the percentages add up to what they are supposed to and question if all the pies do not come to 100 per cent without good reason.

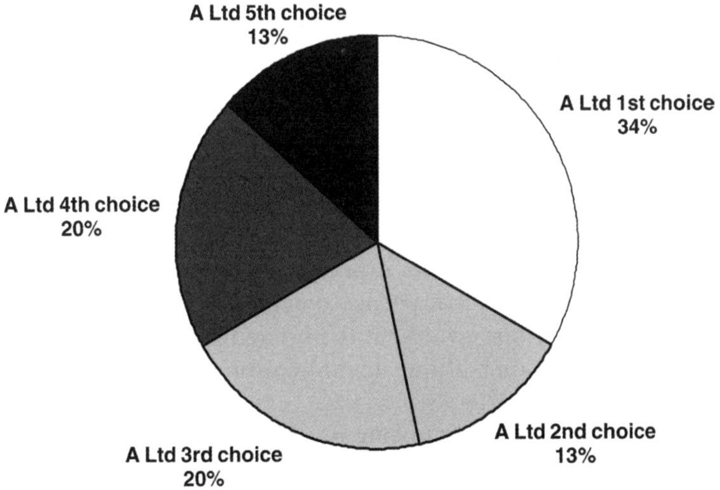

Figure B.17 'The majority of acquirers rate A Ltd as either No.1 or No.2 choice' – or do they?

PRESENTING UNRELATED OCCURRENCES AS CAUSE AND EFFECT

Another old favourite is to claim that because two things happen at the same time, there is cause and effect. An increase in the number of births may well coincide with an increase in the stork population, but until you actually see a new born babe being carried in a stork's beak, I would not rush to the conclusion that the two are related. An increase in sales may well be due to the new total quality initiative introduced six months ago and therefore be sustainable. It could also be the case that the biggest competitor's factory has just burnt down.

HAS THE RIGHT QUESTION BEEN ASKED?

The two points above raise a general principle – do not take what you are told as some sort of fundamental truth without thinking it through. Sadly, those on the receiving end of statistics frequently take the numbers at face value and do not try to look behind them. They should, because often the question being asked has a huge impact on the result. If someone does not ask the right question in the first place, we should hardly be surprised if we get the wrong answer. The BBC gives a good example. Apparently, after tin hats were introduced in World War I, the number of head injuries went up dramatically. This ought to be surprising since common sense says that tin hats would afford better protection than the cloth hats they replaced. They did – it is just that the statistics only totted up head injuries. When fatalities were factored in, it turned out that head injuries were up precisely because the new tin hats were saving soldier's lives. There were head injuries but fewer deaths – therefore more head injuries to be counted. The question should not have been 'Have head injuries gone down?' but 'Has the survival rate gone up?'

ARE COMPARISONS FAIR?

Finally, there is the basis of comparison. A business may have grown sales over a 10-year period by a compound average of 10 per cent, but if the starting point in year 1 was a very small number compared with other numbers in the series, is this really telling us much? Similarly, is the average really representative of the series as a whole? Because of the way in which compounding works, 10 per cent over 10 years could quite easily be 22 per cent over the first 8 and 2 per cent over the last 2.

The main problem with statistics is not so much that they are 'damn lies', it is that people will choose the numbers that favour their case. It pays to recognize this and ask some fairly basic questions before believing them.

FORECASTING

If I could forecast how exchange rates or house prices were going to move over the next 3 years with absolute certainty, I would not be sitting here in the London gloom typing this. However, about once every 3 weeks, I am expected to pronounce on the future with some authority. Even more surprising is that people sometimes seem to believe me. Why, when the only cast iron certainty I can give about the future is that my forecast will be wrong? Why, when 'economic forecasting, like weather forecasting in England, is only valid for the next 6 hours or so'?[2]

The answer is that CDD is all about being roughly right. Indeed, business in general is about being roughly right, which means plenty of judgement as well as plenty of numbers. There are three types of forecasting, as shown in Figure B.18.

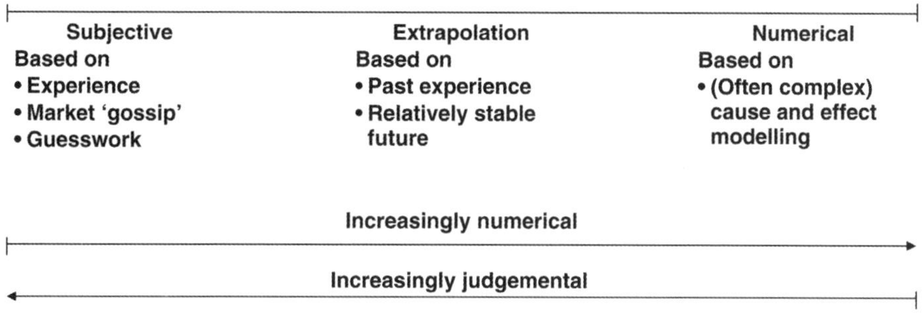

Figure B.18 The forecasting 'spectrum'

No one method is intrinsically better than any other, it depends on the circumstances. Certainly quantitative is not necessarily right. The problem with numbers, especially in a numbers-driven business like M&A, is that they sometimes assume an authority they do not deserve – a bit like saying 'I saw it in the paper so it must be true.' Even numerical, model-based forecasting should always have a good deal of qualitative assessment applied to them, if only in the form of a sanity check.

Time series

Time series are great for decomposing a set of numbers into their constituent parts as an aid both to understanding and to forecasting. Where time series become dangerous is to somehow pretend that they can be used to tell the future.[3] Where time series become pointless is where the trends are not particularly marked – so do not be mesmerized by supposed seasonality because it might not exist.

Take a look at Figure B.19, a target's sales figures plotted monthly over a 3-year period. Any series is the sum of up to four component which can be identified separately:

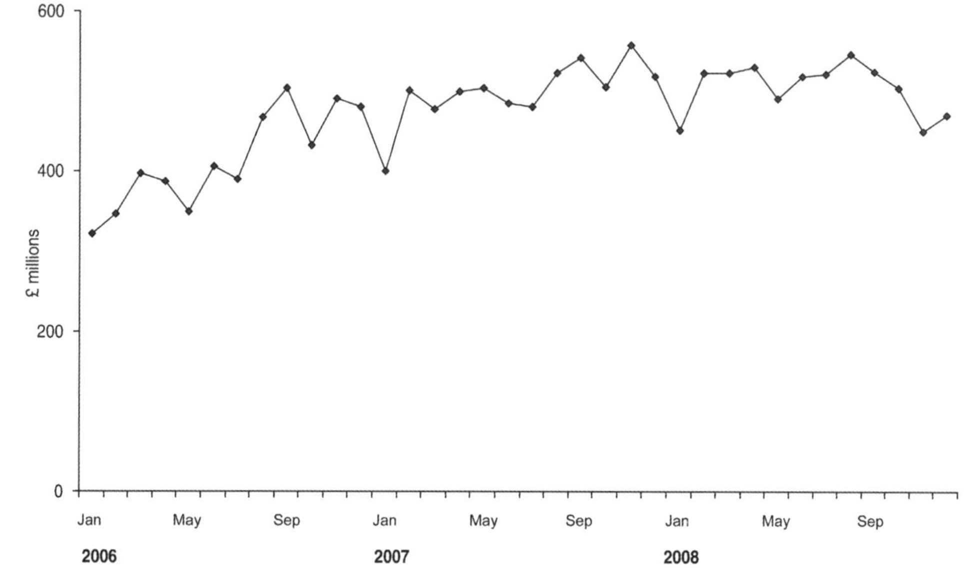

Figure B.19 Target Co.'s sales (2004–06)

- A trend
- A cycle
- Seasonality
- A residual 'random walk'.

The general starting point is to consider which influences (trend, seasonality, cycles or inflation) are relevant for the forecast. Not all will be relevant in every case. The component parts may be thought of as adding or multiplying together to form the overall series (X). In shorthand, either $X = T + C + S + R$ or $X = T \times C \times S \times R$.

The second, multiplicative, model is more appropriate for most business situations.

THE TREND

This is the general, long-run path of the data, probably identified using regression analysis or moving averages (see below). In Figure B.20 this is the bottom line (which is the graph in Figure B.19 with cyclical and seasonal effects removed). There is a slight but steady rise in the trend, perhaps due to growing demand.

THE CYCLE

Sales trends and other business data frequently contain one or more cyclical components. These reflect factors such as the industry or product life cycles or the general business cycle. Most economies exhibit a recession–depression–recovery–boom pattern, which typically lasts for 4 or 5 years with underlying longer-term cycles.[4] Figure B.21 shows an exaggerated cycle of about 3 years' duration.

SEASONALITY

Seasonality is a very short-term pattern that repeats every 12 months (for example, increased demand for ice cream in the summer). To identify seasonality, look out for repeating

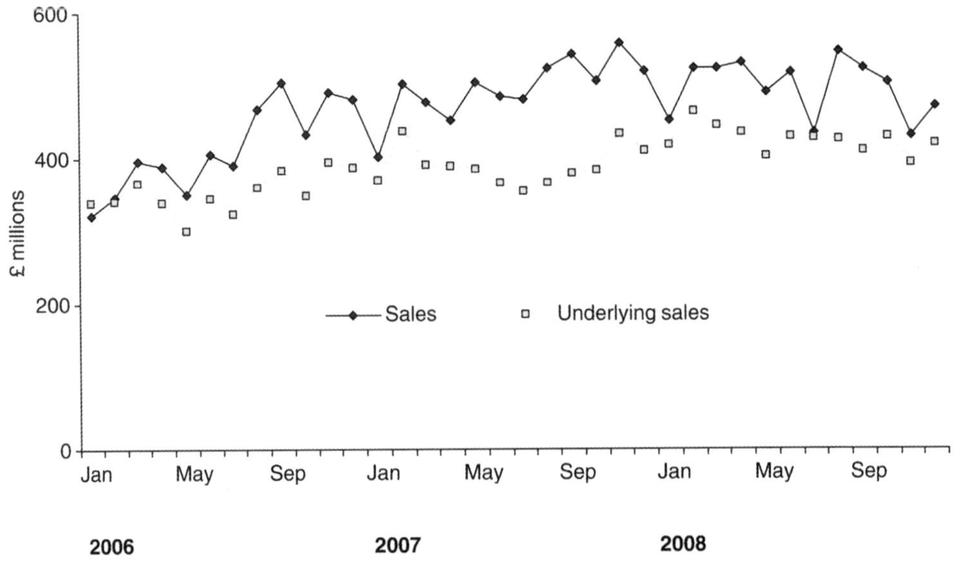

Figure B.20 Target Co.'s sales (2004–06) with cyclical and seasonal effects extracted

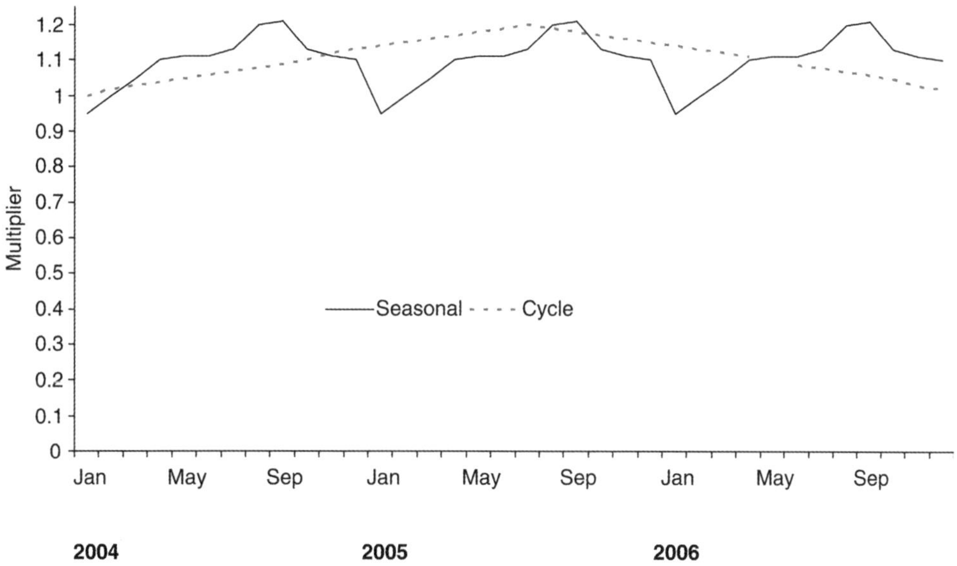

Figure B.21 The seasonal and cyclical effects

patterns once the trend has been plotted. Seasonality is one of the most important elements to identify when analysing and forecasting short-term developments. It is best to think of the seasonal effect as a percentage of the trend, as it is not likely to be a constant, but a number that is dependent on the general level of business at the time. For example, a retailer sells £1000 worth of greeting cards every month except December, when seasonal influences push card sales to £1100. Is this seasonal variation additive (base amount + £100) or multiplicative (base amount × 110%)? The answer is probably the latter, since if regular monthly sales suddenly doubled, perhaps due to higher demand or inflation, it would be more realistic to expect December's sales to be £2000 × 110% = £2200, rather than £2000 + £100 = £2100.

Seasonality is not relevant if data are annual totals that by definition contain a complete seasonal pattern.

THE RESIDUAL

It is rarely possible to explain every factor that affects a time series. When the trends, seasonality and cycles have been identified, the remaining (that is, the residual) unexplained random influence is all that is left.

TRENDS

Before decomposition, Figure B.19 looks like a random collection of numbers organized around a steadily rising trend. CDD will often want to take a set of sales figures like these and get a quick overview of what has been going on to give some idea of what the near term may hold. Moving averages is a good way of pulling the trends out of a jagged graph like Figure B.19.

Moving averages

Moving averages is easy with a spreadsheet. A 3-month moving average is calculated by adding the first 3 months' data and dividing by 3. Next, move down a row by copying the @sum formula, which will drop the first value and add the 1 after the last. On you go until you run out of sets of three numbers. With monthly sales data, the fist point would be (Jan + Feb + Mar) /3, the second is (Feb + Mar + Apr) /3 and so on. For 6-month averages, add six consecutive points and divide by 6, for 12-month averages, add 12 consecutive points and divide by 12. Figure B.22 comprises moving averages for the data used in Figure B.19.

Purists say that moving averages should be centred (that is, the Jan to March 3-month average should go in the Feb slot). I would not bother myself, especially if you are using the moving average for forecasting because you will get a gap at the end of the trend. If you are using moving averages for forecasting, make sure you remove any seasonal patterns from the raw data (and add them back when you have finished the base forecast). Also, when forecasting, you might wish to give the most recent numbers more weight. Do this by using percentages. So in a 3-month moving sales average, last month's figure might get a 60 per cent weighting, the month before, 30 per cent and the remaining month, 10 per cent. It saves extra maths if the weights do add up to 100 per cent.

Regression analysis

Regression identifies the equation of the line of best fit that links two sets of data and reveals the strength of the relationship. The general approach is:

- line up the two series to be regressed;
- find the equation that describes the relationship; and
- test the strength of the relationship (the correlation) between the two series.

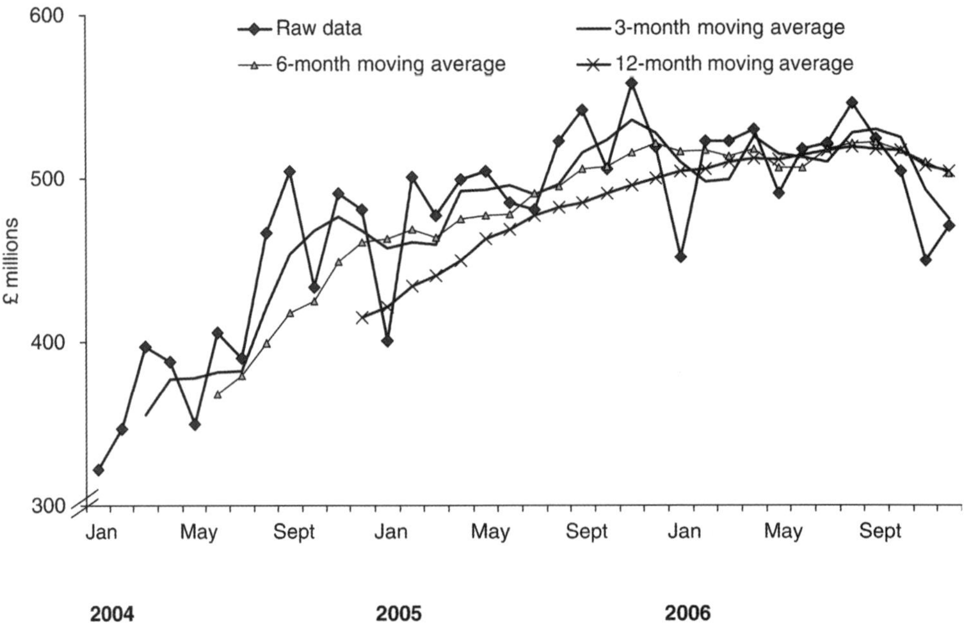

Figure B.22 Moving averages

Essentially, regression analysis fits a line that minimizes the average vertical distance between the line of best fit and each scattered point. The Excel Analysis ToolPak (an add-in for Microsoft Excel) contains a regression analysis tool.

MEASURING THE STRENGTH OF THE RELATIONSHIP

Regression analysis provides some important indicators of how well the identified relationship works.

The coefficient of correlation Better known as r, the coefficient of correlation identifies the correlation (the strength of the relationship) between the two sets of data represented by x and y. This coefficient will always be between -1 and $+1$. If $r=0$, there is no linear correlation between the two series. If $r-1$ or $r-$ 1 there is perfect linear correlation. The sign indicates the slope of the line of best fit.

The coefficient of determination Better known as r^2 ($=r \times r$), the coefficient of determination indicates how much of the change in y is explained by x; r^2 will always be between 0 and 1.

Style and report writing

When writing reports, note the following:

- The best messages are 'joined up' to others in the story and do not depend on supporting data.
- Supporting evidence must reflect the message; it must also make sense all on its own.
- Make sure you know the correct spelling of the company/product names and the names of competitors. If you are not sure, find out; do not guess.

SOME STANDARD APPROACHES TO ANALYSIS

For each market segment:

- compare the target's forecast growth versus CDD estimate;
- state assumptions clearly;
- show how much growth is accounted for by the market and how much of the target's growth is accounted for by taking market share;
- show market size by historical trends and forecasts;
- show the share of each segment by competitor;
- show revenues by customer groups;
- show what drives demand;
- show trends in key industry drivers.

Always:

- spell check;
- spell out numbers up to ten;

- use 'and' *not* '&' (except in a company name when it is its legal public name, for example, Saatchi & Saatchi);
- use dashes to start a parenthetical phrase; use them like brackets, not like commas;
- define complex words or phrases the first time they are used in the document, then use the acronym, for example, Deoxyribonucleic Acid (DNA) (a glossary may also be helpful);
- company names should be defined first too, for example Procter and Gamble Inc (P&G), British Petroleum plc (BP).

Never:

- contract words; it is 'cannot', 'will not' and 'they are', not 'can't', 'won't', and 'they're'; it is always 'do not', never 'don't';
- use the vernacular (except in a direct quote), for example, 'those guys'.

Notes

1. Zelazny, G. (1996) *Say It with Charts*. New York: McGraw-Hill.
2. Moroney, M.J. (1978) *Facts from Figures*. Harmondsworth: Penguin.
3. Readers are referred to Moroney's unflinching denunciation of time series as a means of predicting the future. He likens it to astrology: 'There are many who believe in the efficacy of these things who have written about them at great length. You may read their books ... Read them for fun and I promise you a jolly time. Read them for practical profit and I promise you a loss' (Moroney, *Facts from Figures* (see note 2), p. 323).
4. Russian economist, founder of the Moscow Institute for Business Conditions, Kondratieff identified the half-century 'long wave' in his famous 1922 tract and 1926 article ('The World Economy and its Condition During and After the War', 1922, Moscow and 'The Long Waves in Economic Life', 1926, Moscow). One of the architects of the first Soviet Five Year Plan, he was rewarded by Stalin with imprisonment in one of his Siberian camps, in which he died sometime in the 1930s.

Index